SMALL-SCALE URBAN GREENING

Small-scale urban greening projects are changing the urban landscape, shifting our experience and understanding of greenspaces in our cities. This book argues that including power dynamics, symbolism, and aesthetics in our understanding of the human relationship to urban nature can help us create places that nurture ecological and human health and promote successful and equitable urban communities. Using an interdisciplinary approach to current research debates and new comparative case studies on community perceptions of these urban greening projects and policies, this book explores how small-scale urban greening projects can impact our sense of place, health, creativity, and concentration while also being part of a successful urban greening program. Arguing that wildness, emotion, and sense of place are key components of our human–nature relationship, this book will be of interest to designers, academics, and policy makers.

Angela Loder is Vice President, Research, for the International WELL Building Institute. In this role she is responsible for identifying, directing, and managing evidenced-based research that supports the WELL Building Standard. She has been a core member of the Health in Buildings Roundtable (HiBR) with the National Institutes of Health since 2009. She is a Canada-U.S. Fulbright Scholar, a board member of the Institute for the Built Environment at Colorado State University, Adjunct Faculty at the University of Denver, and part of the first cohort of WELL Faculty and a WELL AP. She holds a collaborative PhD in Health and Urban Geography and Environmental Studies from the University of Toronto.

SMALL-SCALE URBAN GREENING

Creating Places of Health, Creativity, and Ecological Sustainability

Angela Loder

Routledge
Taylor & Francis Group
LONDON AND NEW YORK

First published 2020
by Routledge
2 Park Square, Milton Park, Abingdon, Oxon OX14 4RN

and by Routledge
52 Vanderbilt Avenue, New York, NY 10017

Routledge is an imprint of the Taylor & Francis Group, an informa business

British Library Cataloguing-in-Publication Data
A catalogue record for this book is available from the British Library

Library of Congress Cataloging-in-Publication Data
Names: Loder, Angela, author.
Title: Small-scale urban greening : creating places of health, creativity, and ecological sustainability / Angela Loder.
Description: Abingdon, Oxon ; New York, NY : Routledge, 2020. | Includes bibliographical references and index.
Identifiers: LCCN 2019049317 (print) | LCCN 2019049318 (ebook) | ISBN 9780367900830 (hbk) | ISBN 9781138187870 (pbk) | ISBN 9781315642857 (ebk)
Subjects: LCSH: City planning–Environmental aspects. | Environmental sustainability.
Classification: LCC HT166 .L6164 2020 (print) | LCC HT166 (ebook) | DDC 307.1/216–dc23
LC record available at https://lccn.loc.gov/2019049317
LC ebook record available at https://lccn.loc.gov/2019049318

ISBN: 978-0-367-90083-0 (hbk)
ISBN: 978-1-138-18787-0 (pbk)
ISBN: 978-1-315-64285-7 (ebk)

Typeset in Caslon Pro
by Wearset Ltd, Boldon, Tyne and Wear

Contents

Illustrations

Figures

Tables

Plates

Acknowledgements

Though in the end a solitary endeavour, writing a book requires the help and patience of many, without whom this book would never have materialized. First and foremost, I'd like to thank Dr. Bob Mugerauer at the University of Washington, without whose prompting after my dissertation I would never have considered turning my doctoral research into a book. Though the format of this book has veered in a much different direction than the original dissertation, some of the core arguments remain the same, if expanded with new case studies and research. These core arguments focus around what is the human relationship to nature in cities, how our cultural values, expectations, and experiences shape this relationship, and their implications for our health, well-being, and sense of place. These ideas were nurtured and supported by my doctoral supervisors, Professor Ted Relph and Professor Sarah Wakefield at the University of Toronto, and encouraged by Professor Ingrid Stefanovic, who served on my doctoral committee. They were also helped by our cultural nature reading group at the time, particularly Nik Luka, Valentine Cadieux, and Laura Taylor, who opened up my eyes to the research world of the social construction of nature and saved me months of literature searching as a new graduate student (and who also shared my love of cheese, good wine, and cottage retreats, which makes graduate work much more palatable). Lastly, Dr. Judi Heerwagen with the General Services Administration wisely suggested narrowing the scope of the book at its conception, and thus I owe her a debt of gratitude for making this a more manageable project.

Crucially, the research and writing of this book could not have happened without the input from over 25 key stakeholder interviews drawn from those working in municipalities, non-profits, universities and citizen activist groups. These key stakeholders were involved in the design, implementation, and maintenance of these small-scale urban greening projects that form the core of the book. Their insight and dedication to the urban greening projects that they helped to develop and manage shone through in their willingness to share what was working, what were challenges, and their visions for the future of urban greening for this book. For overall vision and inspiration around urban greening, I'd like to thank Ryan Gravel, Founder at Sixpitch and a key driver behind the Atlanta Beltline project; for insight into one of America's original green infrastructure projects and policies; Pam Emerson, Green Infrastructure Planner, Office of Sustainability and Environment, City of Seattle.

For the City of Philadelphia, I'd like to thank Anna Shipp, Executive Director, The Sustainable Business Network of Greater Philadelphia; Jessica Brooks, Director, Green Stormwater Infrastructure Unit, Philadelphia Water Department; Nancy Goldenberg, President and CEO, West Laurel Cemetery and Funeral Home (formerly Vice President Planning, Development and Research, Executive Director, City Center District Foundation, City Center District, Philadelphia); Jessica Noon, Strategic Partnerships Supervisor, Green Stormwater Infrastructure Unit, Philadelphia Water Department; Aparna Palantino, Deputy Commissioner, Philadelphia Parks and Recreation; Julianne Schrader Ortega, Vice President, Chief of Programs, Pennsylvania Horticultural Society; Stefania Chiorean, Green Stormwater Infrastructure Planning, Office of Watersheds, Philadelphia Water Department; Kira Strong, Design and Construction, Rebuild, City of Philadelphia; David Gould, Community Engagement and Communications, Rebuild, City of Philadelphia; and Nicole Westerman, Executive Director, Rebuild, City of Philadelphia. All of them gave their time and insight into helping me understand the policy and urban greening landscape in Philadelphia.

For the City of Toronto, I'd like to thank Sheila Boudreau, Senior Landscape Architect and Planner, EOR Inc (Formerly Senior Landscape Architect, Special Projects and Design Services, Project Management Office, Toronto and Region Conservation Authority, and Urban Designer, City of Toronto); Angela Murphy, Manager, Research and Partnerships, Ryerson Urban Water, Faculty of Science, Ryerson University; Carolyn Johns, Associate Professor, Department of Politics and Public Administration, Ryerson University; Jane Welsh, Project Manager, Strategic Initiatives, Policy, and Analysis, Toronto City Planning; Shayna Stott, Environmental Planner, City of Toronto; Chandra Sharma, Director, Watershed Strategies, Toronto and Region Conservation Authority; Helen Mills, Program Development Consultant at Toronto Green Community; and Marc Yamaguchi, Project Manager, Raingardens United. Their insight was instrumental in understanding the policy and trajectory of urban greening development in Toronto.

For the City of Chicago, I'd like to thank Michael Berkshire, Green Projects Administrator, Department of Planning and Development, City of Chicago for his tireless patience and insight into Chicago's urban greening leadership; Paul Gobster, Research Landscape Architect, U.S. Department of Agriculture, U.S. Forest Service, for his ongoing insight and leadership around the human relationship to urban nature; Jeanne Chandler, Formerly Project Coordinator, Department of Planning and Development, City of Chicago; Kathy Dickhut, Deputy Commissioner, Department of Planning and Development, City of Chicago; Ben Helphand, Executive Director, Neighbor-Space.org, and Jamie Simone, Associate, Sam Schwartz, (Formerly Program Director, Urban Parks Program, John W. Baird Fellow for Urban Conservation, Trust for Public Land), all of whom helped immensely with understanding Chicago's greening initiatives.

This book would also not have happened without the patience, moral support, and editing and comments of multiple drafts of chapters and outlines of this book from our writing group at the University of Boulder, in particular Professors Georgia Lindsay (now at the University of Tasmania), Shawhin Roudbari, Danielle Rivera, and Stacey Schulte. Georgia Lindsay in particular helped provide support and practical advice on publishing and book formatting, in addition to being a willing partner in crime for taking breaks at museums and being a great friend.

Behind every book is a research assistant to help manage all the details that can get in the way of actual writing, a big thanks goes to research assistants Katherine Vega, Donna Merten, and in particular Sara Long, who tirelessly formatted, chased down and edited references, followed up on interview and photo permissions and policy map changes, and other administrative details without which I could not have finalized the book. A big thanks to Sophanut Jamonnak for creating the mental map in Figure 1.1 from my napkin scribbles. Linda Hughes transcribed the interviews, saving me from hours of work. I would also like to thank the editors at Routledge who have been supportive over the years with the vision and timeline of the book, particularly with childbearing delays, and in particular Sade Lee, Aiofe McGrath, and Sophie Robertson. A big thanks also goes to my content editor Amy Thompson, who reviewed the book in its entirety for cohesiveness and clarity, a task which by that point was beyond me as I was, to use a waitressing term, 'in the weeds' with writing.

I would be remiss to not mention the importance of friendship and support during this long process, particularly from friends who have been through the doctoral journey with me, and with whom I could count on both intelligent and hilarious support and feedback; Drs Jennifer Forkes, Kate Parizeau, Carrie Mitchell, Asya El Meehy, and Whitney Austin Gray. You ladies are wicked smart *and* a boatload of fun.

Lastly, it would be an impossible challenge to write without the support of family. A big thanks to my parents, and in particular my mum, Linda Loder, who has always been my biggest supporter around education and career, my sister, who provides endless moral support and hilarity, and last, but definitely not least, my boys. This book spanned a preschooler, two babies, and a significant shift in job positions, and it required enormous amounts of patience, babysitting, and taking care of business while I wrote in the evenings and weekends. A big thanks to my husband Mark, who bore the brunt of my seemingly endless workdays and who would definitely have preferred to be camping, as well as my young sons Marcus and Luca, who watched as I finished what I started even through the most tempting sunny weekend days. You may not have always understood what mama was doing, but hopefully it teaches you perseverance and trying, in your own way, to understand how to make the world a little better than you found it.

INTRODUCTION

Urbanites, nature, and re-thinking urban greenspace

Nature has been in the news a lot recently, and the overarching storyline is depressing, if not overwhelming: long-standing environmental protection laws worldwide are being threatened or scrapped due to politics, evidence is mounting of the toxicity of many of the chemicals and materials in our everyday environment, and ecological collapse from climate change, pollution, and habitat destruction is impending. The depressing facts driving this narrative grow out of assumptions that nature's only role is to provide resources for exploitation, and perhaps even that the problems are insurmountable for either the public or the private sector. But there is another narrative that has been steadily, if less dramatically, growing – one that is smaller-scaled and hopeful, and that shows a creative, resilient response to problems we face in cities: disparity in access to amenities and employment between neighbourhoods; stress, burnout, and long working hours; rising levels of obesity and inactivity; and infrastructure that is often inadequate when faced with population growth and increasingly severe weather from climate change. This second narrative focuses on the intersection of nature and cities and points to opportunities for positive action and creating mutual environmental and human benefits. Rather than viewing nature only in terms of resource use and environmental destruction, this narrative reframes nature and urbanites' relationship with it.

Specifically, this new narrative, which is explored in this book, provides innovative examples of how creatively bringing nature into cities can provide multiple benefits that can help to mitigate many of the urban problems we face. If this sounds somewhat familiar, that is because we have been here before: the City Beautiful movement over a century ago gave us numerous city parks, including New York's famous Central Park (Rosenzweig and Blackmar 1992) and Chicago's vast waterfront parkland on the shores of Lake Michigan (Chicago Park District 2019). One of the key arguments for these urban greenspaces was that these spaces encouraged civic pride while reducing stress for the working poor, thus reducing potential unrest (Perdue, Stone et al. 2003). Galen Cranz, in her well-known

The Politics of Park Design (Cranz 1982), which surveys the rise of the park system from 1850 to the present day, outlines four stages of park design, each with their own goals: pleasure ground, reform park, recreation facility, and, more recently, open space systems that had explicit environmental goals such as preservation and linking urbanites to natural areas (Cranz 1982). These types of parks remain, for the most part, as part of our urban fabric, and in many ways are mimicked or recreated in green-field park developments of commuter communities in city outskirts.

But the types of urban greening being offered alongside the tales of environmental destruction are getting attention not because they are recreating these familiar park types. These tales of daylighted rivers turning into riverside parks, expressways becoming playgrounds and markets, parking spaces turned into planter-filled café spaces, and abandoned rail lines turned into ecologically minded elevated parks are capturing the imagination of communities, researchers, and planners. These projects are doing this not only for their innovation and hope in the face of endless bad news (Gibson 2017), but because they are shifting the conversation: they are popularizing and legitimizing urban greening through easily digestible research on the health benefits of urban nature; they are addressing urban socio-economic issues by recognizing that current urban parks are not meeting the needs of urbanites equitably; they address current environmental dilemmas by explicitly calling for ecological and biodiversity goals to be incorporated into urban greening; and they are re-imagining what the city can and should be by creatively using previously neglected interstitial and post-industrial land to do so.

The new nature narrative: a story in four parts

Nature and health: making it popular

Unlike some previous urban greening initiatives, these urban greening projects are supported by current media attention to research on the human benefits of nature in ways that are clearly understood, and thus reinforce commonly held beliefs about the benefits of nature for both private and public projects. Headlines on the benefits of nature being so well-established that doctors are prescribing Nature Rx (Melamed 2017; Radcliffe 2018; McGroarty 2019) to address a 'nature deficit disorder' (Louv 2006) for kids and stressed adults use established ways of talking about health – here medical prescriptions and attention deficit disorder – as a vehicle to legitimize and popularize over 30 years of research showing the health and well-being benefits of contact with nature (Kaplan and Kaplan 1989; Ulrich, Simons et al. 1991). This research is even influencing building design decisions. Studies such as that of Lee, Williams et al. (2015), that show that people have better concentration after viewing a picture of a green roof after only 40 seconds, offer the promise of increased productivity for workers, supporting the popular – but sometimes deemed 'frivolous' – addition of greenspace and plants in and around the workplace and in many building certification standards (International Living Future Institute 2016; International WELL Building Institute 2018; U.S. Green Building Council 2018). This framing is helping to justify added expenditure on better buildings, park maintenance and improvement, and the protection of open space for municipalities and individual building owners that has been traditionally cut when budgets are tight.

Urban nature: a health equity approach

The second way in which this new 'nature narrative' differs from previous discussions around urban nature is the recognition that traditional park space, even when adequate and available, is not always meeting the needs of all urbanites (PennPraxis 2010; Rupprecht and Byrne 2014). These parks may be too far away, lack connectivity, not be welcoming to different groups, or just not very high quality (City of Philadelphia 2019; Denveright. 2019). Building on similar work in urban planning around walkability and livability in cities (Smart Growth America and The National Complete Streets Coalition 2018), this new narrative focuses specifically on the needs of a city's more vulnerable populations (Benfield 2012; Speck 2012) and ways that urban greenspace can be used and enjoyed by all (City and County of Denver and Historic Denver 2018). For example, Colorado's GoCo (Great Outdoors Colorado) program has recently used some of its funding – traditionally allocated for mountain open space – for playground updates in parks around the greater Denver area, partly in response to criticism that open space was used mainly by wealthier, white residents (GOCO 2019). This focus on use, access, and equity frames urban greenspace in what urban planners and public health practitioners term a *socio-ecological* approach, acknowledging all the factors that interact to influence desired health outcomes (Sallis, Owen et al. 2008; Salihu, Wilson et al. 2015). As the benefits of urban nature become more publicized, this second nature narrative is taking it further by framing urban greening as a tool for public health, and in particular, health equity outcomes (Jennings, Larson et al. 2016).

However, many researchers and policy makers realize that it is not enough to focus on existing parks; they need to re-imagine what cities might look like if they were designed with these specific populations in mind, and these creative approaches are capturing media attention. For example, Barcelona's recent 'Urban Forest' initiative (Davies 2018), organized by Tata Inti, a local non-profit that provides education to children under six, is creating pop-up play areas with many nature-inspired toys across Barcelona. The initiative supports the city's €20.7 million program to make Barcelona a more child-friendly city with the creation of

89 new play spaces and the renovation of 150 existing ones, and complements UNICEF's Child Friendly Cities Initiative (UNICEF 2019). Barcelona's Urban Forest initiative is a great example of the key role that urban nature plays in these re-imagined more accessible cities; their Urban Forest initiative complements their Green Infrastructure and biodiversity plan (Ajuntament de Barcelona 2013) and aligns well with the call for small-scale urban nature interspersed throughout the city in a recent report on children and cities (Arup 2017).

Putting the 'green' into urban greening

The call for ecology and biodiversity to play a central role in urban greening initiatives is the third way that this nature narrative differs from previous 're-greening' of cities. While the creation of open space and areas of preservation near cities in the last 30 years has addressed the interdependency of cities with larger ecological systems (Rees and Wackernagel 2008; Environmental Protection Agency 2019), cities are recognizing that most *urban* greenspace is not addressing increasingly urgent urban ecological problems from climate change, such as hotter, drier, temperatures, flooding, and waterway pollution from stormwater overflow. And while the call for nature to be recognized as a potentially important part of urban infrastructure has been around for at least 20 years, particularly in Europe (Sukopp and Weiler 1988; Koehler and Keeley 2003; Zerbe, Maurer et al. 2003), the urgency of urban environmental issues, and the exorbitant (and only moderately effective) cost of business-as-usual, or 'big pipe' solutions (Knight 2017), has renewed interest in alternatives in North America. Thus many cities, sometimes supported by large foundations such as Bloomberg and the Rockefeller Foundation, have created and committed to climate adaptation and mitigation plans (City of Chicago 2008; Teale 2018; 100 Resilient Cities 2019; Durkin 2019) which almost always recognize the importance of urban nature, even calling them their local version of a 'green new deal' (Durkin 2019). This is reflected in a 2016 analysis of U.S. cities by the U.S. Green Building Council (USGBC) which found that 21 of the 28 cities with climate change action plans reviewed mentioned green infrastructure (Brown 2016). Green infrastructure in these plans ranges from more familiar urban forests to newer and novel forms such as green roofs. Given their relative novelty in North America, the popularity of newer types of urban nature is particularly noticeable: as of late 2018 there were at least 5.4 million square feet (500,000 square metres) of green roofing in North America and multiple cities enacting green roof legislation (Living Architecture Monitor 2018; Pyzyk 2018), while numerous cities have enacted or are considering integrating green infrastructure into their policy and infrastructure plans (Partnership for Water Sustainability in BC 2011).

Creatively re-thinking city space

The popularity of adding greenspace to non-traditional urban spaces may be partly explained by a simple lack of space: many city officials, community organizers, and researchers interviewed for this book admitted that new large traditional greenspaces are less likely to happen and are not always viable in densely built-up areas (Sinha 2014), and that "people are looking all over the city with new eyes" (Helphand 2019) and seeing opportunity in previously ignored spaces. However, incorporating 'nature' into cities in non-traditional ways is notoriously difficult, as it requires interdepartmental collaboration and a rare type of accounting that values public space and public benefits that cross multiple sectors (Matthews, Lo et al. 2015). It is perhaps this combination of slow-moving bureaucracy with increased ecological urgency and health equity that has created the last – and perhaps most captivating – theme of the new nature narrative, which focuses on small-scale, sometimes temporary, and interstitial urban greening. This type of urban greening has a few distinctive characteristics, specifically around how and where it occurs. Called variously urban acupuncture (Lydon and Garcia 2015), tactical urbanism (Lydon, Bartman et al. 2012; Steuteville 2017), or sometimes biophilic acupuncture (Walker 2015; Bannon-Godfrey and Macies 2017), this type of intervention started with traffic-calming initiatives that took over space for people from cars in the centre of many European cities (Ben-Joseph 1995). The most famous example in North America was under the direction of Jeanette Sadik-Khan as part of a larger walkability initiative for New York City. This used cheap lawn chairs, potted plants, and arts programming as an inexpensive, temporary way for people to re-vision what Times Square could be, eventually turning the square into a permanent car-free popular public space (Goldwyn 2014; Lydon and Garcia 2015). So-called pocket parks, which take a variety of formats but more recently involve a few parking spaces taken over for a summer for public seating, are also an increasingly common example of this approach, and almost always include added temporary greenspace such as plants in pots (Faraci 1967; City and County of San Francisco 2015; Denver Office of Economic Development 2017).

While these examples include some form of nature, the most arresting examples integrate ecological goals, and a matching aesthetic, into existing infrastructure or spaces. The most famous example in North America is New York City's High Line (Gravel 2016; Friends of the High Line 2019), but similar projects are popping up all over North America whether at grade or above ground: Atlanta's Belt Line project, Chicago's 606 trail, Philadelphia's Rail Park, Los Angeles' river project, and the proposed burial of Toronto's Gardiner Expressway (Bozikovic 2018). While these projects vary in scale and scope, they are all re-imagining these post-industrial and marginal land spaces into something more beneficial for residents that are interactive, responsive, and community-empowered. Ryan Gravel, who spearheaded the Atlanta Belt Line initiative and who reviews many of these types of projects in his recent book *Where We Want to Live*, puts it this way:

> I think that all these sorts of urban innovations are early indicators of a pretty significant shift culturally in the way that we build cities and the way we think about how we live. … People are reclaiming old forgotten spaces, the spaces in-between things or for new kinds of purposes … because they are interested in seeing other people and finding new ways to move around and connecting in ways that are unexpected or interesting.
>
> (Gravel 2016)

These projects are also being integrated into the fabric of the city in unusual ways; corridors, rooftops, and right of ways. Thus while the eventual scale of these projects can end up being fairly large – whether collectively as in vacant lot re-greening, or in terms of length, such as elevated rail turned into linear parks – these urban greening projects are in fact small-scale due their interstitial characteristic, this 'fitting into the cracks' of the city. Combined with their often community-driven implementation format, this makes these 'small-scale urban greening' (SSUG) projects different from previous urban greening initiatives that gave us large waterfront parkways or whole city blocks, both in terms of who is spearheading them and the potential impact they have on people's daily lived experience of the city.

However, while these initiatives are a positive example of the second nature narrative, they are not without conflict. Though well intentioned, many examples of SSUG that have been implemented have garnered controversy and criticism, even from the communities they are intended to help (Rodkin 2018a, 2018b). Public policy assumptions about the popularity of urban nature have failed to explain why similar urban greening projects have been fraught with disagreements: are naturalized lawns ecological models or weedy eyesores? Who are these projects intended to benefit, and who actually does? Part of the issue is that despite increasing interest in the benefits of urban nature, given their relative novelty there is little research on what people think about these new small-scale urban greening projects (Gravel 2016), if they influence their health or sense of place, or how they may link to climate change adaptation and mitigation strategies. Thus we have both an inspiring alternative nature narrative and groundswell of initiatives, and conflict and tension in what should be universally liked, according to popular research used in policy. It is this tension that forms the core of this book.

Using new research and case studies on perceptions of small-scale urban greening projects that fit into the trends outlined above, and comparative case studies of urban greening policies, this book explores how SSUG projects can positively impact our sense of place, health, and creativity while also addressing current gaps and tensions around equity, sustainability, and public perception. Examination of these case studies not only demonstrates that assumptions about the human relationship to nature can create conflict or missed opportunities for SSUGs, but also highlights some alternative research lenses that can help to develop new methods, interpretations, and design options from this more holistic viewpoint.

The book can thus be read on two different levels: as a critical examination of the research – and the role of the underlying values that inform this research – on the human relationship to nature and its relationship to these urban greening trends; and as an evaluation of the policy, implementation, and activism tools used to create and implement these case studies. Chapters 2, 3, and 4 each contain this dual lens, and seek to answer the following questions: (1) how (and if) research is being used to justify and implement the case studies, and by whom; (2) how factors around implementation (such as funding sources and larger policy goals) impact the design of the projects; (3) how the projects fit into or contrast with larger debates around urban greening, nature, and health; (4) key insights and results from these projects; and (5) gaps and current issues. Each of the four chapters also covers one of the key trends in the new nature narrative: Chapter 1 reviews current research on the human relationship to nature; Chapter 2 looks at ecological goals and green infrastructure; Chapter 3 examines elevated greenspace (here green roofs); and Chapter 4 considers vacant lots and post-industrial elevated parks. The book concludes with insights into our valuation and experience of nature, as well as education and design implications to help us create SSUG projects and programs that benefit all urbanites' sense of place, health, and well-being while also supporting larger socio-economic and environmental goals.

While there are many inspiring examples of these kinds of urban greening projects all over the world, this book focuses on case studies in the U.S. and Canada. Though there have been great historical examples of good-quality urban greenspaces in these countries, there has also been a long history of anti-urbanism and uneven investment that makes the renewed interest in cities as a place of creative and environmental action particularly interesting.

Chapter 1 – 'Nature, health, well-being and sense of place: what do we know? What don't we agree on?' – provides an overview of and discusses what we currently know about the relationship between nature, health, and well-being, some of the key debates and conflicts in research in these fields, and some new areas of inquiry that are promising for SSUG. Key questions include: "What do we know already?" "What don't we agree on?" and "Why does it matter how we measure and understand the human relationship to nature, health, and sense of place?" The central argument of this chapter is that, despite some convergence between methods and the integration of different paradigms, continued differences and lack of clarity on the normative assumptions underlying each approach leads to confusion in the specification of 'nature' in health, well-being, and place research. This chapter also discusses how these tensions, while seemingly academic, influence conflicts on the ground in the implementation of SSUG projects such as green roofs. In pointing out some of the tensions between psychometric and social constructionist approaches to nature, health, and well-being, this chapter helps to bridge the gap between different theoretical and epistemological research methods that can complicate research and practice. It establishes the theoretical context and foundation from which to interpret and understand the insights and results from specific case studies. This chapter will be of interest to research disciplines that look at nature, health, and well-being, as well as a more general readership interested in deeper questions about our human relationship to nature.

Chapter 2 – 'Ecology in the margins: green infrastructure and stormwater management' – examines case studies that exemplify one of the two key reasons green infrastructure is implemented in North America – stormwater management. Green infrastructure (GI), and in particular, GI implemented in right-of-ways, also encapsulates two of the trends in *why* SSUG is happening: increased attention to the ecological benefits that urban nature can have, and the use of in-between, or interstitial spaces. Using recent GI initiatives of two cities – Toronto and Philadelphia – this chapter examines the policies, programs, and research supporting the integration of GI in each city. Drawing from interviews with key stakeholders involved with the projects and analysis of media coverage and policy goals, the chapter looks at: the policy and local community context that preceded the GI initiatives; key stakeholders or drivers that helped move the initiative forward; policy or research precedent and support; the goals, implementation, and outcomes of implemented projects; and key successes, challenges, and lessons learned for each project. While each case study covers policy and implementation (which will be taken up again in the conclusion), as well as some key insights from both, the larger focus of the chapter is on the intersection of research and implementation. Key insights for implementation include: the role of leadership and policy integration and alignment; current tensions between bureaucratic frameworks, ecology frameworks, and community planning and outreach; and potential options for creatively moving forward as highlighted by some academic researchers and champions. The chapter concludes with a discussion of tensions and current limitations in measuring and understanding human health and well-being from an ecology and policy framework and suggests some options from research that may bridge these gaps. It also discusses the way that interstitial GI that has explicit ecological goals may begin to change the lived experience of place for urbanites, and the role that aesthetics, biodiversity, and emotion may play in this experience. This chapter will be of interest to policy makers and GI champions as well as researchers interested in a more nuanced discussion of the current gaps and opportunities around GI and stormwater in North America.

Chapter 3 – 'Meadows in the sky: a green roof case study' – considers the second trend in SSUG – green roofs – as an example of green infrastructure implemented to address issues of air quality and the urban heat island effect exacerbated by climate change. It builds on the theoretical perspectives discussed in Chapter 1 on the human relationship to nature and compares them to one of the few examples we do have of urbanites' perceptions of these SSUGs. Using an in-depth case study on office workers' perceptions of green roofs, place, and aesthetics in Toronto and Chicago as a pivot point, the chapter examines: (a) what we can learn about the human relationship to urban nature from this case study; (b) how this research links to nature, health, and sense of place research discussed in Chapter 1; and (c) how Toronto and Chicago approached policy and implementation. Using this central case study as an organizing theme, this chapter explores how a phenomenological methodology influences our understanding of participant responses. It then compares these qualitative responses with survey responses from the same population. The chapter examines the values, expectations, and assumptions underlying preferences and contradictory viewpoints expressed by participants about green roofs and 'nature' in the city. This perspective is particularly important given that traditional studies on nature-building relationships have argued that nature is less valued when experienced in conjunction with built form; results from this case study seem to imply that buildings, when combined with a 'wild' ecological aesthetic, may in fact increase acceptance of 'wilder' urban greening projects by providing cues to care, references to regional habitat, and childhood memories. As there is little qualitative data using real world green roofs (rather than visualizations or proxies), this chapter contributes to our understanding how we value and think about urban nature and green roofs, and can be used by policy makers to inform green roof policies, designers, and academics.

Chapter 4 – 'Reclaiming the city: vacant lots and post-industrial corridors' – examines the third type of urban greening happening in cities in North America: vacant lots and interstitial or marginal spaces, and post-industrial and elevated spaces. Urban greening happening in marginal and post-industrial spaces also reflects two of the trends suggesting *why* SSUG is happening: urban greening that is small-scale, tactical, and sometimes temporary due to a lack of space, and the explicit linking of urban greenspace with public health. Using the initiatives of two cities that have recently created policy and programs to support the revitalization of marginal and post-industrial land – Chicago and Philadelphia – this chapter examines the policies, programs, and research around marginal and post-industrial land revitalization in each city. Specifically, the chapter looks at policies to invest in disadvantaged communities through the revitalization of vacant land in both cities, and two projects that have re-imagined post-industrial disused railway corridors as new public greenspace – The 606 in Chicago and the Rail Park in Philadelphia. Drawing from interviews with key stakeholders involved with the projects and analysis of media coverage and policy goals, the chapter looks at: the policy and local community context that preceded these initiatives; key stakeholders or drivers that helped move the initiative forward; policy or research precedent and support; the goals, implementation, and outcomes of implemented projects; and key successes, challenges, and lessons learned for each project. While each case study covers policy and implementation (which will be taken up again in the conclusion), as well as some key insights from both, the larger focus of the chapter is on the intersection of research and implementation. Key insights include the distinct reasons why the projects were implemented, the recognition of these projects as both social *and* ecological, and the role that research plays in both supporting these projects and policies, and challenging them. Of particular note is the conflict around many of these projects and the criticism of SSUG as an agent of gentrification and displacement, and the response of researchers, policy makers, and community groups. The chapter concludes with a discussion of the potential positive role of marginal land, particularly as a place for free play and non-consumerist spaces, biodiversity, and learning. This chapter will be of interest to policy makers, community advocates, and researchers interested in how cities are creatively addressing these pockets and corridors of vacant and post-industrial land, the arguments used to justify these initiatives, and some alternative ways to address current areas of conflict.

The conclusion continues the dual lens approach and is split into two main sections: the first gives an overview of key policy and implementation lessons learned from the case studies, and the second looks at research, education, and design insights and implications for moving forward. The first, policy, section examines the key insights and lessons learned that can help us to more effectively design, implement, and maintain SSUG projects and programs. It does this by reviewing insights and lessons learned for each of the types of SSUG based on the criteria evaluated in each chapter: drivers and goals of the policies and programs, precedent and key actors and stakeholders, successes, challenges, and lessons learned for moving forward. Key insights from the typologies of SSUG projects examined in this book include: the need to move beyond ecological-only drivers for green infrastructure; the need for departmental alignment and the recognition of the symbolism of green roofs; the role of policy gaps and activism for elevated post-industrial parks and trails; and the role of community activism and a socio-ecological understanding of urban greenspace for vacant lots. Key lessons learned include the need for alignment, framing the issue, appropriate governance structure, and the role that tactical urbanism can play.

The second half of the conclusion looks at what we can learn about the human relationship to nature from our experience with SSUG, and how we can use SSUG to have a more effective, intimate, and inspiring relationship with nature in cities. First, it considers how we value urban nature now versus previous urban greening iterations through the case studies of SSUG: as woven into the fabric of the city, in the cracks and the spaces in-between, with the explicit goals of health, community, and equity benefits alongside the more traditional ecological goals. Second, it looks at SSUG projects as key ways that we experience, and will continue to experience, urban nature through the lens of research. How can the tensions between key areas of research that examine and explain how we experience urban nature be used to teach us about our daily lived experience? How can we use this tension to find new research methods and approaches to help us move forward and better understand how everyone, regardless of class, ethnicity, or gender, can benefit from urban nature? Lastly, the conclusion discusses how SSUG can be a tool for education and a more active relationship with nature, as well as key design implications for ways to create SSUG projects that work for everyone, align with existing urban initiatives, and can adapt to the needs of present and future urban conditions.

At the core of the new nature narrative and these initiatives are the questions of what kind of public space we want, what kind we need, and for whom. What constitutes good space, and how does urban greenspace, or nature, fit into this? The research and case studies discussed in this book explore what these projects can tell us about our values, our beliefs, and our shifting vision for what this might look like, while providing inspiration for how this might be done in ways that are equitable, joyful, and creative responses to the ecological and economic urgency facing us.

References

100 Resilient Cities (2019). "100 Resilient Cities." Retrieved May 10, 2019, from https://100resilientcities.org.

Ajuntament de Barcelona (2013). *Barcelona Green Infrastructure and Biodiversity Plan 2020.* Barcelona: Ajuntament de Barcelona.

Arup (2017). *Cities Alive: Designing for Urban Childhoods.* London.

Bannon-Godfrey, R. and R. Macies (2017). How implementing biophilic architecture can soothe transit riders. *Metro*, Metro Magazine.

Ben-Joseph, E. (1995). "Changing the residential street scene: Adapting the shared street (Woonerf) concept to the suburban environment." *Journal of the American Planning Association* **61**(4): 504–515. https://doi.org/10.1080/01944369508975661.

Benfield, K. (2012). "10 techniques for making cities more walkable." Retrieved July 14, 2019, from www.citylab.com/solutions/2012/12/10-techniques-making-cities-more-walkable/4047.

Bozikovic, A. (2018). Tear down the Gardiner? It's a billion-dollar question. *The Globe and Mail*. Toronto.

Brown, H. J. (2016). "Green infrastructure: City climate action planning." U.S. Green Building Council. Retrieved September 2, 2016, from www.usgbc.org/articles/green-infrastructure-city-climate-action-planning.

Chicago Park District (2019). "Lake Shore Park." *Parks and Facilities*. Retrieved July 14, 2019, from www.chicagoparkdistrict.com/parks-facilities/lake-shore-park.

City and County of Denver, Parks and Recreation Department and Historic Denver Inc. (2018). *City Park Master Plan Update*. Denver.

City and County of San Francisco (2015). "Street and sidewalk pocket parks." Retrieved July 23, 2019, from www.sfbetterstreets.org/why-better-streets.

City of Chicago (2008). *Chicago Climate Action Plan*. Chicago Climate Task Force. Chicago.

City of Philadelphia (2019). "Rebuild." Retrieved May 2, 2019, from www.phila.gov/programs/rebuild.

Cranz, G. (1982). *The Politics of Park Design: A History of Urban Parks in America*. Cambridge, MA: MIT Press.

Davies, S. (2018). "Cities go wild with child-friendly design." *Thomson Reuters Foundation News*.

Denver Office of Economic Development (2017). "New pocket park opens in Westwood." *Newsroom*. Retrieved July 23, 2019, from www.denvergov.org/content/denvergov/en/denver-office-of-economic-development/newsroom/2017/new-pocket-park-opens-in-westwood.html.

Denveright (2019). *Game Plan for a Healthy City*. City and County of Denver.

Durkin, E. (2019). "New York City unveils ambitious plan for local steps to tackle climate change." *The Guardian*, April 18.

Environmental Protection Agency (2019, May 30). "Smart growth and open space conservation." *Smart Growth*. Retrieved July 15, 2019, from www.epa.gov/smartgrowth/smart-growth-and-open-space-conservation.

Faraci, P. (1967). *Vest Pocket Parks*. Chicago: American Society of Planning Officials.

Friends of the High Line (2019). "High Line." Retrieved July 15, 2019, from www.thehighline.org.

Gibson, E. (2017). "18 'rail-to-trail' projects following in the High Line's footstep." *Dezeen*, June 27.

GOCO (2019). "GOCO awards $5.4 million to Colorado parks, outdoor recreation facilities, and school playground projects." *Blog*. Retrieved July 14, 2019, from www.goco.org/news/goco-awards-54-million-colorado-parks-outdoor-recreation-facilities-and-school-playground.

Goldwyn, E. (2014). "How 'People-Centered' Design Made Times Square the Place to Be on New Years Eve." *Next City*, December 30.

Gravel, R. (2016). *Where We Want to Live: Reclaiming Infrastructure for a New Generation of Cities*. New York: St. Martin's Press.

Helphand, B. (Executive Director, Neighbor-Space.org). Interview with A. Loder. 2019.

International Living Future Institute (2016). *Living Building Challenge 3.1: A Visionary Path to a Regenerative Future*. Seattle: International Living Future Institute.

International WELL Building Institute (2018). *The WELL Building Standard version 2 pilot (WELL v2)*. New York.

Jennings, V., L. Larson and J. Yun (2016). "Advancing sustainability through urban green space: Cultural ecosystem services, equity, and social determinants of health." *International Journal of Environmental Research and Public Health* **13**(196): 1–15. doi:10.3390/ijerph13020196.

Kaplan, R. and S. Kaplan (1989). *The Experience of Nature: A Psychological Perspective*. New York: Cambridge University Press.

Knight, S. (2017). "What would an entirely flood-proof city look like?" *The Guardian*, September 25.

Koehler, M. and M. Keeley (2003). "The Green Roof Tradition in Germany: The Example of Berlin." *Earthpledges Handbook: Green Roofs*. New York: Earthpledge.

Lee, K. E., K. J. H. Williams, L. D. Sargent, N. S. G. Williams and K. A. Johnson (2015). "40-second green roof views sustain attention: The role of micro-breaks in attention restoration." *Journal of Environmental Psychology* **42**(0): 182–189. http://dx.doi.org/10.1016/j.jenvp.2015.04.003.

Living Architecture Monitor (2018). 2017 "Green Roof Industry Survey Shows Washington DC in Top Spot for Most Green Roofs Installed." Toronto.

Louv, R. (2006). *Last Child in the Woods: Saving our Children from Nature-Deficit Disorder*. Chapel Hill, NC: Algonquin Books of Chapel Hill.

Lydon, M., D. Bartman, T. Garcia, R. Preston and R. Woudstra. (2012). *Tactical Urbanism: Short Term Action, Long-Term Change.* Miami; New York: NextGen and T. S. P. Collaborative.

Lydon, M. and A. Garcia (2015). *Tactical Urbanism: Short-term Action for Long-term Change.* Washington, DC: Island Press.

Matthews, T., A. Y. Lo and J. A. Byrne (2015). "Reconceptualizing green infrastructure for climate change adaptation: Barriers to adoption and drivers for uptake by spatial planners." *Landscape and Urban Planning* **138**(0): 155–163. http://dx.doi.org/10.1016/j.landurbplan.2015.02.010.

McGroarty, B. (2019). Global Wellness Summit releases in-depth report, "Eight wellness trends for 2019." *Cision PRWeb.* New York: Volcus PRW Holdings.

Melamed, S. (2017). "Philly doctors are now prescribing park visits to city kids." *The Philadelphia Inquirer*, July 6.

Partnership for Water Sustainability in BC (2011). "Green infrastructure is spreading to all corners of the North American Continent." *Rainwater Management.* Retrieved July 14, 2019, from https://waterbucket.ca/rm/2011/11/20/green-infrastructure-is-spreading-to-all-corners-of-the-north-american-continent.

PennPraxis (2010). *Green2015: An Action Plan for the First 500 Acres.* Philadelphia Parks and Recreation. City of Philadelphia.

Perdue, W. C., L. A. Stone and L. O. Gostin (2003). "The built environment and its relationship to the public's health: The legal framework." *American Journal of Public Health* **93**(9): 1390–1394. doi:10.2105/ajph.93.9.1390.

Pyzyk, K. (2018). "DC is home to the most green roofs in North America." *Smart Cities Dive*, Industry Dive.

Radcliffe, S. (2018). "'Park prescriptions' can help lower stress levels." *Health News.* Retrieved July 14, 2019, from www.healthline.com/health-news/park-prescriptions-can-lower-stress#6.

Rees, W. and M. Wackernagel (2008). "Urban Ecological Footprints: Why Cities Cannot be Sustainable – and Why They are a Key to Sustainability." *Urban Ecology: An International Perspective on the Interaction Between Humans and Nature.* J. M. Marzluff, E. Shulenberger, W. Endlicher, M. Alberti, G. Bradley, C. Ryan, U. Simon and C. ZumBrunnen. Boston, MA, Springer. **16:** 537–555.

Rodkin, D. (2018a). "Home-repair grants aim to slow gentrification near 606." *Crain's Chicago Business.*

Rodkin, D. (2018b). "Was gentrification around the 606 inevitable?" *Crain's Chicago Business.*

Rosenzweig, R. and E. Blackmar (1992). *The Park and the People: A History of Central Park.* Ithaca, NY: Cornell University.

Rupprecht, C. D. D. and J. A. Byrne (2014). "Informal urban greenspace: A typology and trilingual systematic review of its role for urban residents and trends in the literature." *Urban Forestry and Urban Greening* **13**(4): 597–611. http://dx.doi.org/10.1016/j.ufug.2014.09.002.

Salihu, H. M., R. E. Wilson, L. M. King, P. J. Marty and V. E. Whiteman (2015). "Socio-ecological model as a framework for overcoming barriers and challenges in randomized control trials in minority and underserved communities." *International Journal of Maternal and Child Health and AIDS* **3**(1): 85–95.

Sallis, J. F., N. Owen and E. B. Fisher (2008). "Ecological models of health behavior." *Health Behavior and Health Education: Theory, Research, and Practice.* K. Glanz, B. K. Rimer and K. Viswanath. San Francisco, CA: Jossey-Bass: 465–485.

Sinha, A. (2014). "Slow landscapes of elevated linear parks: Bloomingdale Trail in Chicago." *Studies in the History of Gardens and Designed Landscapes* **34**(2): 113–122. doi:10.1080/14601176.2013.830428.

Smart Growth America and The National Complete Streets Coalition (2018). "The Best Complete Streets Initiatives of 2017." Washington, DC.

Speck, J. (2012). *Walkable City: How Downtown Can Save America, One Step at a Time.* New York, Farrrar, Straus and Giroux.

Steuteville, R. (2017). "Great idea: Tactical urbanism." *Public Square: A CNU Journal*, February 16.

Sukopp, H. and S. Weiler (1988). "Biotope mapping and nature conservation strategies in urban areas of the Federal Republic of Germany." *Landscape and Urban Planning* **15**: 39–58. https://doi.org/10.1016/0169-2046(88)90015-1.

Teale, C. (2018). "Seattle, Atlanta first winners in American Cities Climate Challenge." *Smart Cities Dive*, Industry Dive.

U.S. Green Building Council (2018). LEED v4.1, U.S. Green Building Council.

Ulrich, R. S., R. F. Simons, B. D. Losito, E. Fiorito, M. A. Miles and M. Zelson (1991). "Stress recovery during exposure to natural and urban environments." *Journal of Environmental Psychology* **11**: 201–230. https://doi.org/10.1016/S0272-4944(05)80184-7.

UNICEF (United Nations Children's Fund) (2019). "Child friendly cities intiative." Retrieved July 22, 2019, from https://childfriendlycities.org.

Walker, J. (2015). "Biophilic urban acupuncture: The importance of biophilia in urban places." Terrapin Bright Green Blog.

Zerbe, S., U. Maurer, S. Schmitz and H. Sukopp (2003). "Biodiversity in Berlin and its potential for nature conservation." *Landscape and Urban Planning* **62**(3): 139–148. https://doi.org/10.1016/S0169-2046(02)00145-7.

1

Nature, health, well-being, and sense of place

What do we know? What don't we agree on?

While popular consensus has generally viewed urban nature (especially in the form of parks and gardens) as beneficial, up until fairly recently it remained relegated to the mainly ornamental category, and thus subject to budget cuts when competing with other priorities. Recently, however, research on the benefits of nature has been spilling out of academic journals and into popular media and governmental policies, thus giving urban nature an unprecedented popularity and legitimacy. The research of interest ranges from discussions on the nature deficit disorder in children (Louv 2006, 2011), to trends giving 'nature prescriptions' to improve health (Hunter, Reuben et al. 2012; Jiang, Chang et al. 2014), to the need for ecosystem services – traditionally focused on how nature can help city infrastructure and now inclusive of how it can help human health and well-being (Millennial Ecosystem Assessment 2003; Young 2010; Gómez-Baggethun and Barton 2013; Wu 2013). This shift in perspective on urban nature from an ornamental extra (nice to have but not essential) to a key component in urban planning and public health is largely due to the influence over the last 30 years of select research programs on public policy.

These research programs have provided vast amounts of empirical data to support the now well-established observation that access to nature has benefits for human health and well-being (van den Berg, Jorgensen et al. 2014; Lee, Williams et al. 2015; Honold, Lakes et al. 2016; Wyles, White et al. 2019). However, while this research has played a central role in the development of policy, it represents only part of the vast and diverse field of inquiry on the human relationship to nature. Furthermore, these research programs – most often, but not exclusively, from environmental psychology – have been unable to explain conflicts surrounding some urban nature initiatives (Gobster 2000; Palardy, Boley et al. 2018a), apathy from certain populations on actual use of urban greenspace (Hitchings

2013; Boyd, White et al. 2018), or conflicting aesthetic preferences (Schirpke, Altzinger et al. 2019). This means that not only are urban greening projects potentially missing key insights that may make them more successful, but also that it is difficult to see where gaps, conflicts, or potential synergies exist in order to create more successful urban greening projects.

To begin to address these gaps and tensions, as well as suggest where we may find these synergies, this chapter provides an overview and discussion of what we currently know about the relationship between nature, health, and well-being; key debates and conflicts in current research; and new areas of inquiry that hold promise for small-scale urban greening and public health. Some of the key questions I ask include: "What do we know already?", "What don't we agree on?", and "Why does it matter how we measure and understand the human relationship to nature, health, and well-being?" Throughout this review I argue that the gaps and conflicts between research programs stem from key differences in the *paradigms* that underlie them, and that these paradigms are not only of academic interest; rather, they can have real-world influence on how small-scale urban greening projects are conceived, created, and received. Specifically, the biggest tension centres on whether or not research programs use a *biological* or *utilitarian* (Williams and Patterson 2008) versus a *relational* and *socially constructed* approach or paradigm (Flint, Kunze et al. 2013; Kolinjivadi, Van Hecken et al. 2019) to two key questions: 'What is nature?' and 'What is the human relationship to nature?' Furthermore, the terminology used to describe perceptions, images, or valuations of *nature* itself often overlap with research on the human *relationship* to nature, making distinctions somewhat arbitrary (Flint, Kunze et al. 2013). This semantic imprecision makes it difficult to understand where the gaps and conflicts exist. Nevertheless, insights from sense-of-place research – which, like that on nature, is also informed by multiple research traditions (Williams and Patterson 2008) – is helpful in understanding how different underlying paradigms in human–nature research traditions impact their methods, research questions, and even their understanding of nature itself. Though there are significant differences between biological and utility paradigms, and between relational and social constructionist paradigms, they are informed by similar underlying worldviews, and thus are grouped together (see Figure 1.1).

In reviewing current research and debates that try to answer these questions, I show that research paradigms based on a biological or utilitarian definition of nature – while more easily adapted into ecological services models and planning policy – tend to miss the cultural, social, political, and economic influences that shape access to, values around, and perceptions of urban greening projects, health and well-being, and sense of place. These socio-cultural factors in the human

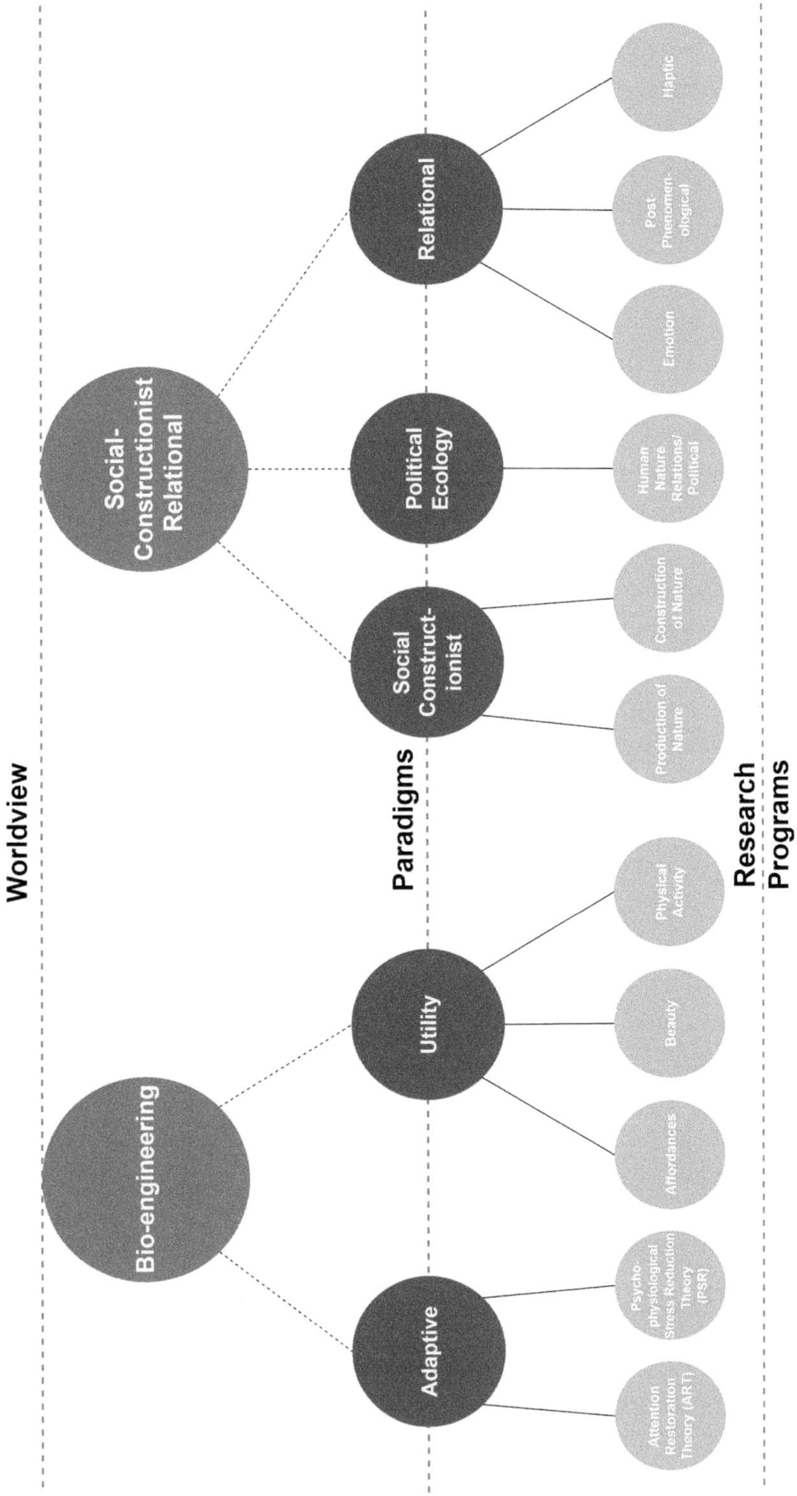

Figure 1.1 Paradigms in nature-human relationship research programs.

relationship to nature, as will be seen in the following chapters, may in fact be key to creating small-scale urban greening (SSUG) projects that promote health, creativity, and ecological sustainability. Understanding these differences and gaps thus provides a foundation from which to examine the case studies and new research on small-scale urban greening examined in the rest of the book. The chapter finishes with an examination of new areas of inquiry that offer promising insights that can also be applied to the case studies in subsequent chapters.

Examining different research programs that look at the human relationship to nature is further complicated by the wide range and scale of research (Flint, Kunze et al. 2013). For example, influential research ranges from discourse analysis of historical, economic, and cultural valuations of nature (Nash 1982; Cronon 1995; Smith 1996; Huber 2018; Schirpke, Altzinger et al. 2019), to more empirically oriented social science investigations that focus on individual perspectives and reactions (Ulrich 1986; Kaplan and Kaplan 2005; Korpela, Ylen et al. 2009; Hazer, Formica et al. 2018), to investigations of values, attitudes, and behaviours (Gagnon Thompson and Barton 1994; Schultz and Zelezny 1999; Dunlap, Van Liere et al. 2000; Schultz, Shriver et al. 2004; Colléony, White et al. 2019). Some research examines how nature influences human health and well-being (Ward Thompson, Roe et al. 2013; Houlden, Weich et al. 2018; Kim and Jin 2018), while some ignores this aspect entirely (Dunlap, Van Liere et al. 2000; Ekers and Loftus 2013; Lorimer, Hodgetts et al. 2019).

Biological paradigm: adaptive and utility

What is nature?

Both the adaptive and utility paradigms have been immensely influential in public policy and in shaping discussions about what nature is and how we relate to it. Nature is seen as a relatively constant, stable entity that does not need explaining or deconstructing: it just is. This is closely aligned with the popular perception of nature as a given (Williams 1976; Nelson 1996) and echoes classic Anglo-American representations of nature. This idea of nature mostly follows the popular assumption of wilderness as "pure" or "strong" nature (Kaplan and Kaplan 1989; Kuo 2001; Kowarik 2013; Corliss 2019) against which all other forms of nature can be seen as a weaker imitation, and the goal of much of this research has been to show that urban (or 'weaker' nature) also has value and benefits. For instance, Kuo – one of the original researchers on this topic – writes:

> Moreover, the empirical literature suggests that the rejuvenating effect of nature extends to far less "pure" forms of nature than wilderness and that it results in systematically greater effectiveness on a wide variety of tasks. Thus

> … the availability of even relatively weak forms of nature could enhance residents' effectiveness in the tasks they face.
>
> (Kuo 2001)

For the most part, as nature is a stable construct, researchers following a biological or adaptive paradigm use a wide variety of what counts as the nature variable in their studies: viewing nature from a window (Kaplan 1993; Tennessen and Cimprich 1995; Kaplan 2001; Olszewska-Guizzo, Escoffier et al. 2018; Wang, Kuo et al. 2019), plants in the workplace (Lohr, Pearson-Mims et al. 1996; Larsen, Adams et al. 1998; Shibata and Suzuki 2002; Lee, Williams et al. 2015; Adamson and Thatcher 2019), partaking in active "nature" experiences, such as gardening (Cimprich 1993; Armstrong 2000; Ossola, Locke et al. 2019), walks through urban parks (Hull and Michael 1995; Herzog, Chen et al. 2002; Li, Deal et al. 2018; Ayala-Azcárraga, Diaz et al. 2019), and even wilderness excursions (Kaplan 1984; Hartig, Mang et al. 1991; Meyer, Rathmann et al. 2019). This wide variety of what counts as "nature" in the studies has been seen as positive proof of the strength of the human-nature relationship and shaped over 30 years of research: "The diversity of methodologies employed in these studies (on nature) makes the persistence of positive findings particularly compelling … (e.g., naturalness of setting, frequency of contact with nature, total time spent in nature)" (Kuo 2001). Positing that even popularly viewed "weak" forms of nature give health benefits supports the urban greening activism of many of the researchers in this paradigm to portray urban or nearby nature as valuable (Kaplan 1983; Kuo, Bacaicoa et al. 1998; Kaplan 2001; Sugiyama, Carver et al. 2018) and to understand which types of nature give which type of benefit.

The adaptive paradigm: nature as opportunity for survival

One of the dominant paradigms in the study of the human experience of the environment is what Williams and Patterson (2008) refer to as the adaptive paradigm, which is grounded in the assumptions that biological survival motivates psychological and physiological responses to the environment, and that certain environments are better suited to human health and well-being than others (Williams 2008). The most common research programs originating from this paradigm revolve around questions of (1) human adaptive responses to certain environments or features that are restorative to human cognitive fatigue and overall well-being, or (2) recovery from stressful environments and improved positive mood. The bulk of research over the last 30 years has focused on so-called restorative environments, testing either Stephen and Rachel Kaplan's Attention Restoration Theory (ART) (Kaplan 1995; Kaplan and Kaplan 2005; Wyles, White et al.

2019) or Roger Ulrich's Psychophysiological Stress Reduction Theory (PSR) (Ulrich 1993; Tyrväinen, Ojala et al. 2014). Both theories are explicit in their drawing on an adaptive paradigm, though they differ in their explanation. ART draws on William James' (1892) theory of directed attention, which argues for the importance of sustained attention for adequate human functioning. The Kaplans argue that nature (which follows popular perceptions of nature described above) possesses the attributes necessary to hold our attention involuntarily (or without effort) and to be experienced as relaxing. This aspect, they argue, reduces attentional or cognitive fatigue (Kaplan 1995). Specifically, according to the ART model, nature possesses four attributes that make it particularly restorative: fascination, mystery, coherence, and the feeling of 'being away' from our everyday lives (Hartig, Mang et al. 1991; Hauru, Lehvävirta et al. 2012).

Though qualitative methods are used in this restorative environments approach (Korpela, Ylen et al. 2008; Brown, Rhodes et al. 2018), and the initial research included qualitative methods (Kaplan and Kaplan 1989), the vast majority of research programs testing the ART use a dose–response model, looking for linkages between specific environmental features or stimuli and psychological functioning or well-being (Williams and Patterson 2008; Hazer, Formica et al. 2018). Most often, this involves using standardized psychological tests and scales and measures of cognitive fatigue or potential restoration in response to various images of natural scenes, or after walks in parks, etc. The PSR model also draws on an evolutionary biology theory, which argues that because humans evolved (and have spent most of their time) in natural settings, they are uniquely adapted to respond to natural stimuli, either through biophilia (love of nature), or biophobia (innate fear of nature, such as snakes) (Ulrich 1993; von Lindern, Bauer et al. 2013). Most of the research testing the PSR theory has used a combination of physiological (such as monitoring of heart rate and cortisol levels (Tsunetsugu, Lee et al. 2013; Beute and de Kort 2014; Lee, Hur et al. 2018; Grassini, Revonsuo et al. 2019) and psychological tests to measure stress responses and recovery in a controlled experimental setting, such as a lab showing images of nature (van den Berg, Jorgensen et al. 2014; Reynolds, Rodiek et al. 2018). Unlike ART which focuses on cognition, the PSR theory argues that human responses occur in specific parts of the brain involved with fight-or-flight responses, and focus on recovery from stress and improved affect or mood when exposed to nature (Parsons 1991; Hazer, Formica et al. 2018). Most recently, researchers such as William Sullivan and colleagues have collaborated with neuroscientists to show that reactions to nature (both representations, such as pictures, and in-situ, such as walks in a park) are an affective response involving the amygdala and hippocampus, both of which are also involved in fight-or-flight, immediate responses (Ulrich 1986; Parsons 1991; Li, Deal et al.

2018). These are argued to be innate and thus support the evolutionary biology theory they are based on (Martinez-Soto, Santos et al. 2015). Though these research programs initially focused on separate aspects of restoration, many researchers now refer to the restorative aspects or qualities of nature for *both* stress reduction and cognitive fatigue (Flint, Kunze et al. 2013; Jung, Woo et al. 2015).

These theories have resulted in empirical studies that have shown a clear connection between contact with nature – broadly defined – and enhanced human health and well-being. For example, studies have been conducted at a population health level comparing satellite imagery of available greenspace in urban areas with birth weight, a key factor in neonatal and infant mortality. They found that neighbourhood greenness – such as parks and trees – within a 100-metre buffer for expectant mothers was weakly, but positively, associated with higher birth weight; in other words, babies born to mothers who had more access to greenspace had a higher birth weight, which is associated with better infant health outcomes (Dzhambov, Dimitrova et al. 2014). Meta-analysis studies have also been conducted that compare the presence of street trees in London with rates of prescription for anti-depressant medication, and it was found that there was a decrease of 1.8 prescriptions per thousand population per unit increase in trees per kilometer of street (Taylor, Wheeler et al. 2015).

Most studies following the adaptive paradigm, however, and the ART and PSR theories in particular, have been done on a small scale and have focused on participant reactions to and perceptions of nature, where "nature" is represented as everything from views of natural scenes from a window, to walks in natural areas such as parks (Bratman, Daily et al. 2015) and, most commonly, images of nature on a screen (Wilkie and Clouston 2015; Grassini, Revonsuo et al. 2019). Most of these studies have focused on the restorative aspects of nature, measuring some combination of improved cognition (Bratman, Daily et al. 2015; Pilotti, Klein et al. 2015), improved affect (emotions and mood) (Kinnafick and Thøgersen-Ntoumani 2014; Pilotti, Klein et al. 2015) and faster recovery from stress (Ward Thompson, Roe et al. 2012; Tyrväinen, Ojala et al. 2014; Razani, Niknam et al. 2019). For example, one recent study that randomly assigned 60 participants to a 50-minute walk in either a natural or an urban environment around Stanford, California found that those who walked in natural areas had improved affect (decreased anxiety, rumination, and negative affect), as well as improved cognition, here measured by working memory performance (Bratman, Daily et al. 2015). Many studies on cognition have focused on increased self-control, or higher executive functioning, and overall improved coping skills as a result of contact with nature (Beute and de Kort 2014; Hystad, Payette et al. 2019). For example, a study with youth aged 11 with a range of behavioural problems found that those who attended a forest school had improved mood, stress, and reflection on personal goals over students in a conventional indoor school (Roe and Aspinall 2011). This supports earlier findings in public housing projects in Chicago that showed that those living in apartments with more nature have better attention spans (Wells 2000; Taylor, Kuo et al. 2001), reduced aggression and violence (Kuo, Bacaicoa et al. 1998; Kuo and Sullivan 2001) and better overall coping skills (Kuo 2001). More recent studies have confirmed the link between contact with nature and increased social cohesion, sense of community (Sullivan, Kuo et al. 2004; Arnberger and Eder 2012; Petrovic, Simpson et al. 2019), and feelings of safety (Maas, van Winsum-Westra et al. 2009) all of which are theorized to come from creating vital neighbourhood spaces for social interaction and increasing 'eyes on the street' to reduce crime (Korpela, Borodulin et al. 2014; Branas, South et al. 2018). While the links between social cohesion and nature are not as well studied as links between restoration from stress or cognitive fatigue and nature, these studies are gaining traction in ecosystem and human health and well-being models (Millennial Ecosystem Assessment 2003), public health discussions (Denver Regional Council of Governments 2011), and studies on park use and benefits (Brown, Rhodes et al. 2018).

Studies following the adaptive paradigm have also examined how contact with nature reduces stress, often using both psychological (self-reported) and physiological measures of stress (Mennis, Mason et al. 2018). For example, a recent study found that contact with nature (here a three-minute exposure to slides of nature) had beneficial effects on mood and heart rate variability, a physiological measure related to exertion of self-control and stress levels (Beute and de Kort 2014). Other studies have found that stressed individuals tend to prefer rest, walking, and the chance to see animals in nature (Stigsdotter and Grahn 2011), that visits to forests can be both psychologically and physiologically restorative to patients suffering from exhaustion disorder (Sonntag-Öström, Nordin et al. 2014), and that stressed workers tend to use or seek out nature more (Colley, Brown et al. 2017). Forests have been found to be particularly restorative, especially in countries that have a cultural tradition of visiting forests for restorative experiences. This can be seen in the Japanese tradition of 'forest bathing' (Park, Tsunetsugu et al. 2010; Hansen, Jones et al. 2017). A study of 48 young urban males in Japan found significantly lower blood pressure, higher parasympathetic nervous activity and lower sympathetic nervous (fight-or-flight) activity, and a lower heart rate (also associated with less stress) from contact with forests (Tsunetsugu, Lee et al. 2013). Similarly, many Finnish studies have looked at forest perceptions and health: a recent study found that while both an urban park and woodland have restorative effects and can reduce cortisol levels (an indicator of stress), the urban woodland was found to have a slightly higher positive influence on stress relief (Tyrväinen, Ojala et al. 2014). Many of these studies build on Roger Ulrich's famous 1984 gallbladder study, in which patients facing a brick wall versus a park needed more pain medication, were more difficult to deal with, and took longer to recover (Ulrich 1984). Further research has supported Ulrich's findings that contact with nature has been associated with faster recovery from illness (Sherman, Varni et al. 2005; Bengtsson and Grahn 2014).

The last main area of research focus in the adaptive paradigm has looked at environmental and aesthetic preferences for different types of nature, and urban versus 'nature' scenes in particular. These studies also have their origin in an evolutionary perspective foregrounding the link between nature preferences and survival and argue that, because early humans evolved in certain types of landscapes (usually the savannah), they developed aesthetic preferences for landscapes that would enhance their chances of survival. This evolutionary explanation has been used to justify the outcomes of many early studies on aesthetic preferences which found that participants tended to like calm open bodies of water, tall mature trees, and grassland (Kaplan and Kaplan 1989; Ulrich 1993). Many of these studies also got participants to rate their preference for urban versus more natural scenes (Kaplan and Talbot 1988; Hartig 1993), and usually found that participants tended to prefer more natural scenes versus ones with evidence of human activity (Ulrich 1981). Early research also found that preferences for savannah-type landscapes tended to be common across cultures (Kaplan and Herbert 1987; Kaplan and Talbot 1988; Yu 1995), thereby supporting the adaptive paradigm argument that these responses are innate. More recent studies have examined the validity of psychological preference assessment tools, focusing on qualities such as the coherence, complexity, and familiarity of the 'nature' being assessed (van der Jagt, Craig et al. 2014). Others have developed studies that linked landscape preferences with perceived restoration (Herzog, Chen et al. 2002; Scopelliti, Carrus et al. 2019), arguing that participants prefer landscapes they perceive to have a higher restoration potential and that this possibly explains their preference (Wilkie and Clouston 2015). Lastly, recent studies have examined the relationship between aesthetic landscape preferences and various activities, such as recreation potential (Zhang, Chen et al. 2013) or scenery importance (Palmer and English 2019), as well as individual moderating factors that influence aesthetic preferences, such as landscape expertise (Dupont, Antrop et al. 2015; Coldwell and Evans 2018), information provision (van der Wal, Miller et al. 2014), or, more recently, non-Western preferences for urban nature (Gwedla and Shackleton 2019; Pham, Labbé et al. 2019).

These studies have provided to urban planners and public health officials an enormous amount of empirical data demonstrating the link between access to nature and improved human health and well-being. In particular, the recent trend in this research paradigm to further quantify or rigorously test the causality between greenspace and health (Sullivan, Kuo et al. 2004; Brown and Cummins 2013; Lee, Hur et al. 2018; Becker, Browning et al. 2019), as well as examine specific mediators and moderators influencing the nature–human health and well-being relationship (Lachowycz and Jones 2013; Wilkie and Clements 2018), has given public policy makers and planners the kind of replicable, quantifiable evidence that is easily translated to policy. This kind of research has been instrumental in bringing urban nature into public policy and planning discussions, such as urban resiliency plans (Denver Environmental Health 2014) and the biophilic cities movement (Biophilic Cities Network 2016; School of Architecture 2018). It has also started to show up in discussions on biophilic design for workplaces and urban revitalization (International WELL Building Institute 2018; 100 Resilient Cities 2019), which often includes small-scale urban greening (SSUG) projects. Recent initiatives like these have increased the value of urban nature in public policy and design discussions – whereas before the value was mainly aesthetic (and therefore dispensable), it is now evident in multiple environmental, social, and health and well-being benefits.

The utility paradigm: nature as offering opportunities for action or benefits

The utility paradigm also examines the role that nature, or the environment, plays in human health and well-being, but it starts with the assumption that enhanced well-being comes from opportunities in the environment to satisfy specific social or intrapersonal needs (Williams and Patterson 2008; Hadavi, Kaplan et al. 2015; Hadavi 2017; Araújo, Brymer et al. 2019). Research following this paradigm often views the environment as a setting for action, and the individual as a rational decision-maker evaluating the opportunities, or affordances (Heft 2010; Laaksoharju, Rappe et al. 2012; Hooper, Boruff et al. 2018) offered by the setting for their individual needs. This focus on the environment as a site of *action* is a key difference from much of the research in the adaptive paradigm, which often relies on the visual aspects of nature – usually through images – to elicit and then test psychological and physiological responses. Three of the most common mechanisms that researchers use to explain positive individual health outcomes and access to nature in this paradigm are (1) physical activity, (2) restorative and stress-alleviating experiences, and (3) social interaction, cohesion, and/or safety (Korpela, Borodulin et al. 2014; Villeneuve, Jerrett et al. 2018; Dadvand, Hariri et al. 2019). While there is overlap between the restorative and stress-alleviating experiences research area and the adaptive paradigm – as well as acknowledgement that they are interrelated (Lachowycz and Jones 2013) – the focus in the utility paradigm tends to view psychosocial and physiological benefits as part of an *action* taken on the part of the individual, often physical activity in nature versus more urban settings. Partly this emphasis on action is in response to perceived gaps in research in the adaptive paradigm, including in the explanation of individual, social, or built environment characteristics that influence or moderate the relationship between greenspace and health outcomes (Lachowycz and Jones 2013) and in the focus on visual aspects of nature at the expense of lived experience in nature (Heft 2010). It is also due to the overlap of researchers working on nature and health in the utility paradigm and those in public health, urban planning, and park management (Williams and Patterson 2008; Hooper, Boruff et al. 2018). The utilitarian paradigm attempts to 'fill in' some of the gap in our understanding of the link between the environment as greenspace and health.

For example, while the importance of physical activity for positive health outcomes is well established (Brown, Schebella et al. 2014; Sugiyama, Carver et al. 2018), research from public health using the socio-ecological model (Colorado Department of Public Health and the Environment 2015) has helped planners and public health officials better understand human behaviour around physical activity, particularly around mediating factors such as individual characteristics and physical, social, and economic barriers to physical activity (Koppen, Sang et al. 2014; Reyes, Páez et al. 2014; Douglas, Briones et al. 2018). Researchers in the utility paradigm have addressed these factors by examining: (a) barriers to access to parks, as this is associated with increased physical activity; (b) the role of greenspace as a potential mediator between physical activity and improved health and well-being; and (c) attitudes and perceptions of greenspace that may influence physical activity. Researchers have found for example that perceived urban park accessibility includes both physical factors (i.e. distance, number of parks, and walkability) and social aspects (such as cultural activities and fit, shared activities, amount of leisure time available, and perceived safety) (Wang, Brown et al. 2015; Mak and Jim 2018; Denveright. 2019). Other research has focused on the type and quality of the greenspace, finding positive associations with increased levels of physical activity and the amount of residential greenery (Villeneuve, Jerrett et al. 2018), the distance to the nearest urban greenspace (Kaczynski, Potwarka et al. 2009; Ayala-Azcárraga, Diaz et al. 2019), the size of the greenspace (Paquet, Orschulok et al. 2013), and presence of specific features, often linked to play or activity (Kaczynski, Potwarka et al. 2009; van Dijk-Wesselius, Maas et al. 2018). Recently, specific characteristics of greenspace that encourage or discourage physical activity for specific groups has been a popular focus, particularly around environments that encourage children's play (Louv 2006; Laaksoharju, Rappe et al. 2012; Mårtensson, Jansson et al. 2014) or non-white groups (Pham, Labbé et al. 2019).

Lastly, following public health models that include social support as a determinant of health, some studies have looked at the role that greenspace plays in providing opportunities for social cohesion and interaction (Adinolfi, Suárez-Cáceres et al. 2014), particularly for urban parks. This last stream of research also often overlaps with work in the adaptive paradigm, but again focuses on the evaluation of greenspace for *action*, defined here as opportunities for socialization (Brown, Rhodes et al. 2018; Larrea, Muela et al. 2019). Research in this area has been very helpful in advocating for urban greenspace as a means to improve population health. It has also been quick to adopt innovative community engagement methods to try to increase physical activity levels among vulnerable populations (Morris and O'Brien 2011; Brown, Schebella et al. 2014), particularly when combined with approaches from ecological design (Hadavi, Kaplan et al. 2015). Recently this area has also embraced different, more interactive methods of assessment and community engagement, particularly around social media, with the hopes of engaging non-traditional user groups (Brown, Rhodes et al. 2018; Bubalo, van Zanten et al. 2019; Plunz, Zhou et al. 2019). However, some meta-studies have found an ambiguous or no correlation between different health measures and available greenspace (Maas, van Winsum-Westra et al. 2009; Paquet, Orschulok et al. 2013), and this has led many researchers to focus on identifying and testing *which* mediators and moderators influence physical activity levels (Lachowycz and Jones 2013; Schipperijn, Bentsen et al. 2013; Vich, Marquet et al. 2019), or to develop models that can help explain all of the potential mediators and moderators in this relationship (Lachowycz and Jones 2013). Most of these models focus on quantitative measurement of the amount of greenspace or characteristics of greenspace that provide opportunities for action, which has meant that 'nature' is often interchangeable with 'environment' or 'greenspace.' Because features of the environment are valuable for their utility, versus their symbolic or inherent meaning and values, they have been argued to be interchangeable or reproducible, a useful quality for urban planners and park management. This can be seen in current park management initiatives in the Denver, Colorado region that are evaluating park amenities and potential rates of physical activity based on a checklist of amenities for each park (City of Golden Parks and Recreation 2016; Denveright, 2019). It also fits well with economic resource valuation approaches (Williams and Patterson 2008) that can be useful for policy makers to justify the expense of creation or maintenance for urban greenspace. Though research in the utility paradigm has not been as extensive as research in the adaptive paradigm, given its crossover with public health and park management goals, it has been fairly influential in public policy and design discussions (Curl, Ward Thompson et al. 2015).

The types of research conducted under these models reflect the dominance of an underlying psychometric paradigm commonly used by researchers who use adaptive and utilitarian paradigms, particularly, though not exclusively, environmental psychologists (Patterson and Williams 2005). This is not surprising given the biological origins of much of this work, and the types of research that are considered valid and 'good science' (see Figure 1.1). Key aspects of the psychometric paradigm include: (1) a telic ontology (or belief about reality) that aims to understand and generalize human relationships with nature and find common foundational aspects; (2) an axiology (or the goals of science) in which theoretical concepts and definitions are precise enough to be quantified and replicated; and (3) the use of categories, psychological tests, and statistical controls to simplify the world into a closed system for study, develop testable theories, and use a priori categories of nature (Herzog, Chen et al. 2002). This focus on measurement as a way to know the world reflects an epistemological model of behaviour that is mostly linear, individualistic, and reductionist, and focuses on understanding the *mechanism* between the phenomena (here, nature) and the response in the individual. Nature in the psychometric, adaptive, and utilitarian paradigms is seen as a relatively constant entity that does not need explaining: it just is (Uzzell and Rathzel 2009). This closely aligns with the popular cultural conception of nature as a given (Williams 1976; Nelson 1996), and with the tradition of Anglo-American nature writing – in the vein of Thoreau, Muir and Leopold (Leopold 1971; Muir 1997; Thoreau 2004) – as well as with the bio-engineering model of nature in reports such as the Millennium Ecosystem Health assessment (Millennial Ecosystem Assessment 2003).

Understanding the underlying paradigm(s) beneath these research programs thus clarifies their choice of methods and current research questions. This foundation has a profound influence on what kinds of things get studied, and what explanations are given to the results that are generated. As indicated by Williams and Patterson in discussing place, a similarly complex phenomenon as nature, "methods are not passive instruments for rendering place meanings, but in fact (they) impose structures on observations that shape what counts as meaning" (Williams and Patterson 2007). For example, as seen above, there are differences between research programs looking at restorative environments in terms of stress reduction or reduced attentional fatigue, or the role of greenspace in providing opportunities for behaviour changes to improve health and well-being. Despite these differences, there is a general consensus that exposure to nature – ranging from viewing images of nature to being physically active in 'wilderness' – improves well-being, and that the key research questions that remain are to further define the mechanisms by which this happens (Carrus, Scopelliti et al. 2015; Li, Deal et al. 2018; van den Berg, van Poppel et al. 2019). Following the general psychometric paradigm that forms the bulk of this research, this is usually achieved by further dividing, isolating, and reducing the component parts of nature and individual experience in order to establish causality between nature and health and well-being, as well as better understand design and health implications. Because it shows causality and is quantifiable, this approach is well suited to policy and design decisions and finds easy dissemination in both popular media and academic journals (Ashford 2015; Clemens 2015; Lee, Williams et al. 2015).

While this empiricism and emphasis on quantitative data are necessary for much of the research to be considered rigorous and valid in their host discipline (and for environmental psychology in particular), these modes have been criticized by many social scientists as missing key components of the human relationship to nature. These critiques centre on different interpretations and beliefs around the understanding of (a) what nature is, and (b) what our relationship to it is, which are the questions explored in this chapter. First, critics have argued that using a biomedical or bio-engineering definition of nature reduces it to something that works mechanistically through exposure on human health, well-being, and behaviour rather than something that is perceived and related to (Carpenter 2013). Second,

> by conceptualizing the environment as a natural (as opposed to socially defined) phenomenon, studies following the adaptive paradigm tend not to address the larger context of place including economic, social, and political forces that structure environmental conditions and distributions of power to access and regulate these conditions within society.
>
> (Williams and Patterson 2008)

Similarly, the utilitarian paradigm has been criticized for its limited understanding of the socio-economic and socio-cultural factors influencing access to nature, reduction of environmental values to utility, and general disregard for the symbolic meaning of nature for humans (Williams and Patterson 2008; Carpenter 2013).

While these limitations are partially rooted in a preference for statistical analysis and the visual experience of nature (Brown and Cummins 2013; Hitchings 2013), it also reflects the linear exposure–reaction/action paradigm underlying much of the adaptive and utilitarian research programs, versus the relational approach favoured by many social scientists discussed in the next section. Specifically, this means that these research programs can, due to their paradigms and methods, ignore or reduce to simple categories the full experiential quality of the human relationship to nature, viewing it as exposure–reaction, instead of humans and nature influencing and acting upon one another in a reciprocal relationship. Furthermore, these research programs have tended to view values, perceptions, and understandings of nature as fixed and immutable instead of shifting and subject to multiple influences. This can happen even when researchers working under the adaptive or utilitarian paradigm try to incorporate more qualitative measures into their understanding of the human relationship to nature. For example, while incorporating sense of place into models of how people feel about nature is promising (Korpela, Ylen et al. 2009; Wilkie and Clements 2018), studies that reduce the role of sense of place to cognitive constructs like place attachment and satisfaction (Stedman 2003) have been criticized for misunderstanding the original nuance in sense-of-place studies that were a backlash against psychometric paradigms to begin with (Williams 2014). Similarly, the paucity of studies looking at why people do *not* go into nature, even when they know it is good for them, demonstrate a lack of evaluation of the whole lived experience of the individual or group, not just at a particular moment in time and place (Hitchings 2013; Boyd, White et al. 2018). While this more relational understanding of nature is starting to be recognized by researchers who have traditionally been working under the adaptive or utilitarian paradigms (Brown and Cummins 2013; von Lindern, Bauer et al. 2013; Home, Lewis et al. 2019), and in particular those who also work in public health (Ward Thompson, Roe et al. 2012) or urban park work (Palardy, Boley et al. 2018b), the ease of translation of statistical results and quantification to policy have made it difficult for relational approaches to be incorporated into most urban planning and design policy.

Nevertheless, there are key exceptions. As mentioned above, though psychometrics is the *dominant* paradigm that often coincides with and supports the adaptive and utilitarian paradigms underlying most of this research, there is a multitude of research practices within the adaptive and utilitarian paradigms. In particular, there has been some movement to incorporate more qualitative and nuanced understandings of place and the human relationship to and understanding of nature and health. For example, a few studies have incorporated more qualitative, exploratory research on nature and health (Sullivan, Frumkin et al. 2014) and blended different paradigms and assumptions (Ozguner and Kendle 2006; Hitchings 2013), particularly around the role of emotion and a connection to nature (Pearce, Davison et al. 2015; Knez, Sang et al. 2018; Wyles, White et al. 2019). There has also been promising work that has used qualitative methodology and exploratory methods to explore larger themes such as fear of nature and children's sense of place (Milligan and Bingley 2007; Bagot, Allen et al. 2015), motivations for visiting nature (Pasanen, Neuvonen et al. 2018), and some promising projects that recognize that urban greening needs to also incorporate socio-ecological values and cultural preferences (Kowarik 2019). Other research has begun to examine individual or group experiences, particularly for non-Western populations (Pham, Labbé et al. 2019), job type (van den Berg, Vlek et al. 1998; Flint, Kunze et al. 2013; Colley, Brown et al. 2017), rural versus urban residency (Yu 1995), and the role of time and memory in place identity and nature perceptions (Ratcliffe and Korpela 2018) for the role they play in preferences for different types of landscapes, finding that these preferences can be mediated by numerous factors that may interrelate and change over time. Other studies (Korpela and Ylen 2007; Ratcliffe, Gatersleben et al. 2013) have used more qualitative research methods, such as participant observation, interviews, or open-ended responses, and have called for even more qualitative research and interdisciplinary collaboration (Kaplan and Kaplan 2009; Hitchings 2013), particularly to explain the role that attachment and special places have in restoration or preferences (Korpela, Ylen et al. 2008; Korpela, Ylen et al. 2009; Wilkie and Stavridou 2013) or more interactive ways of measuring life experience (Norwood, Lakhani et al. 2019). There has even been some exploration of virtual reality (Birenboim, Dijst et al. 2019) and criticism of value- and context-neutral use of neuroscience for human–nature studies (Roberts and Christopoulos 2018), which is a promising avenue to avoid some of the pitfalls of the psychometric model. Lastly, some American researchers have begun to collaborate heavily with Chinese researchers to understand cultural differences and values that influence the human relationship to nature (Sullivan, Frumkin et al. 2014; Jiang, Zhang et al. 2015), and there have been numerous calls for longitudinal studies (Brown and Cummins 2013; Lachowycz and Jones 2013) and a better understanding of the role of movement, access to nature, and real-world outcomes to understand long-term population impacts (Li, Deal et al. 2018; Norwood, Lakhani et al. 2019). While these strands of place-based or more qualitative research, or innovative use of mobile methods are not dominant, their attempt to blend qualitative and quantitative research has proved useful for urban policy makers interested in urbanites' use and valuation of urban nature, particularly in walkability and place-making design policies. Still, differences in these key research programs that are based in different paradigms mean that the insights and knowledge of a relational and socially constructed approach, discussed below, are rarely incorporated into small-scale urban greening projects or urban policy.

The social construction paradigm: constructed, political, and relational

Examining how nature is studied by social scientists using a social constructionist or relational approach is complicated by the fact that unlike the adaptive and utilitarian work, the focus has not generally been on how nature influences health through empirical studies. Instead, the focus in socially constructed and relational work has been on how larger discourses in popular culture have influenced how we think and feel about nature, or on other ways we experience and understand nature, such as through the body or through animals. This can make it difficult to compare the research programs, since they are at different scales and with a different focus. Nevertheless, insights from the social constructionist and relational approaches on the human relationship to nature have been very useful in explaining the *why* behind likes and dislikes, conflicts over urban greening projects, and apathy towards nature from even 'green' urbanites.

Though research programs in the social sciences vary considerably in how they study nature, most use, or react against, a social constructionist paradigm that was popularized by the so-called cultural turn in geography in the 1980s. This social constructionist paradigm generally (1) questions or challenges nature as a stable category, or (2) is interested in how economic, cultural, gendered, and historical interactions with nature helped to create our representation or understanding of it, sometimes referring to the resultant culture–nature hybrid as 'socio-nature' (Loftus 2007). Current research programs on nature vary, but generally they respond to the cultural turn by either continuing their line of inquiry or reacting against it (the so-called relational turn, described below). Much has been written on the shift from the cultural to the relational turn on our understanding of nature (Neumann 2011; Simonsen 2013), and the research programs described below are still very much in flux. While these research programs have been far less influential in urban greening policy, their insights have the potential to address some of the conflicts and ambiguity around perceptions of small-scale urban greening (SSUG) projects. Below is an overview of key research programs that have been or are currently the most influential in discussions on nature, as well as their views on nature and health, if any.

Social constructionists and 'the cultural turn'

Though less commonly known outside of academia – with the occasional upset in popular media (Cronon 1995) – and rarely referenced in environmental psychology, the cultural turn in geography in the 1980s was very influential on how nature was perceived in the social sciences, to the point where the term 'nature' is rarely used by geographers, due to the complexity of meanings associated with it (Braun 2005). The types of research conducted on nature in the cultural turn reflect an underlying social constructionist paradigm that has a general ontology that there is no essential, stable reality to be discovered through systematic observation, but rather that knowledge and identity are plural, partial, contested, and shifting, depending on who is in power and who is positioned as the subject, or knower. This means that while for social constructionists a real empirical world *is* held to exist independently of our categorizations (i.e. the biophysical 'nature'), it is filtered through a subjective perspective, influencing the decisions and beliefs about scientific methods or theoretical concepts and models used to study it (Robbins 2004; Cockayne, Ruez et al. 2017). Because of this focus, discourse – or the way debates are framed and discussed – is seen as not only representing the world, but also creating it (Braun 2008), so discourse analysis, whether through language, signs, or concepts, is privileged in this paradigm as a means of deconstructing hidden power structures and dynamics that shape the world. Following this privileging of discourse and deconstruction, the methods predominantly employed by social constructionists seek to explore the symbols, politics, and personal narratives of a particular situation, theme, or event through in-depth interviews, textual analysis, and/or case studies (Willems-Braun 1997; Katz 1998; Kuus 2019). Though there is considerable variation among the types of approaches taken by social constructionists, their common aim is the destabilization of 'nature' as a self-evident concept and thing that is not influenced by cultural, economic, and gendered factors. They thus reject the premise of the adaptive and utilitarian paradigms that reactions to nature are innate and biophysical.

The production and construction of nature

The most influential research programs on nature from the cultural turn are (a) the *production* of nature, and (b) the *construction* of nature. The production of nature was popularized by Neil Smith's *Uneven Development* (Smith 1984), which takes a structuralist Marxist view (which views all relationships through the lens of capitalism) to examine how nature is transformed and turned into a commodity under the processes of capitalist production (Smith 1984), leading to a false sense of separation for workers, consumers, and urban dwellers (Talbot 1998). This reification of our relationship to nature (Williams 1973; Smith 1996) gives consumers the false impression that they are linked to a universal, unifying nature yet simultaneously separated from it. This domination of nature and our perception of it as filtered through capitalist modes of production form the basis of many aspects of this research program (Smith 1996; Willems-Braun 1997; Keil and Graham 1998; Huber 2018) and has been used recently to critique the construction of space for and values around urban greening (Wachsmuth and Angelo 2018). At its most extreme, this version of the social constructionist paradigm has been used by researchers to promote a 'hard' constructivist approach, arguing that nature is actually something physically produced, as, for example, in the biotechnology industries (Katz 1998; Castree 2000).

Similarly, research programs that looked at the *construction* of nature tend to arise from a historical materialist perspective, which assume our understanding of 'nature' is not innate but has been created by shifting historical relationships (Loftus 2007). Key contributions from these research programs have challenged the concept of 'nature' itself, deconstructing our perceptions of what we understand by 'nature' by asking *which* 'nature' we are discussing and unveiling the complexities surrounding the use of the term (Williams 1976). This is particularly important as our understanding of nature is hindered by its long association with the unmediated and given (Olwig 1995: 380), and by the fact that 'nature' refers simultaneously to both the physical world around us and our cultural and historically mediated understanding of it (Williams 1976: 184). More specifically, researchers using the social constructionist paradigm have stressed distinctions between wilderness and nature (Cronon 1995; Merchant 1995), deconstructing nature's changing historical valuation (Nash 1982; Tuan 1990; Schirpke, Altzinger et al. 2019). For example, the way early European settlers perceived wilderness, which was often as a fearful 'other' to be battled (Nash 1982), contrasts sharply with current Anglo-American ideals of wilderness that equates it with leisure (White 1995; Duncan and Duncan 2001; Martin 2004) and spiritual purity (Proctor 1995; Cooper, Brady et al. 2016). More recently, this strand of research has begun to look at non-Western perspectives of nature and challenged the Anglo-American-centricity of previous research (Loftus 2019).

Social constructionism, nature, and health: which nature, and for whom?

Research programs following the cultural turn to understand nature have tended to deconstruct the popular assumption that nature improves well-being. Part of the classic Anglo-American narrative associates nature and, in particular, wilderness, with the spiritual and mental rejuvenation that directly benefits well-being and was extolled by Thoreau and others. Social constructionists have counteracted this view by emphasizing that nature can also be threatening, a dangerous wasteland, or a place of exclusion (Nash 1982; Tuan 1990; Merchant 1995; Duncan and Duncan 2001). The idea that the preservation of wilderness is beneficial to all has been questioned in studies that note the exclusion of marginalized, and often non-Anglo-American, peoples from discussions about the use and rights to nature, particularly wilderness reserves (Guha 1989; Willems-Braun 1997; Katz 1998; Duncan and Duncan 2001; Fairhead, Leach et al. 2012; Rode 2017). If there *is* a benefit to contact with nature, social constructionists following the cultural turn have historically tended to view this critically – as nostalgic at best and colonialist at worst (Relph 1985; Merchant 1995; Olwig 1995). This has led social constructionists to view claims about the innate benefits to people's well-being from contact with nature with caution, even though many of the authors are self-proclaimed environmentalists (Cronon 1995; White 1995). More recently, social constructionists have argued that studies of well-being have ignored context, culture, and the influence of the so-called 'more than human' (see below), focusing on individual experiences instead of embodied, relational experiences of place and culture (Smith and Reid 2018). Lastly, the social constructionist tendency to privilege rational, intellectual experiences of nature over more relational, emotional, and affective responses has meant that affective responses to nature are also generally viewed with suspicion. This means that though there is strong evidence emerging from the adaptive and utilitarian paradigm research programs on the role of affective responses to nature as key to understanding the nature–health relationship, social constructionist research programs following the cultural turn have generally ignored this aspect of the human relationship to nature.

Insights from the cultural turn are particularly relevant when public policy discussions are made about what counts as 'nature' and which parts of it should be saved, an increasingly pressing issue given the rate of urban expansion and discussions about how to 'bring nature back' into cities. It has also been instrumental in the critique, at least in academic circles, of the devaluation of urban nature versus sacred, untouched wilderness (Cronon 1995; Davison 2008). The complexity of our understanding of what counts as 'nature' can be seen in ecological restoration debates that raised the issue of *which* 'nature' to restore – the pre-European or pre-*human* forest (Elliot 2000; Gobster 2000; Hobbs, Higgs et al. 2009), and for *whom* (Hertog and Turnhout 2018). This debate has also highlighted how certain types of nature are viewed as appropriate only in certain places. For example, 'wild' nature, valued as a refuge *far from* the city, has often been seen as dirty, unsanitary, and a symbol of neglect when it occurs *in* a city (Hough 2004; Kaika 2006; Marvin and Medd 2006; Rega-Brodsky, Nilon et al. 2018), a problematic valuation given the trend towards ecologically beneficial urban greening projects that often have a 'wild' aesthetic (Church 2015). Though these insights have not often seeped into public policy or design discourse, they have the potential to bring insight and knowledge to create better small-scale urban greening projects.

Post-cultural turn: political ecology and the relational turn

Though useful, research programs following the social constructionist paradigm have been criticized on multiple fronts, in part because of this basic question: if there is no one nature, and nature can be reduced to our cultural interpretation, which 'nature' (if any) do we bother to save? The social constructionist position that there is no stable, common world to be understood has also made it difficult to make policy recommendations. As a consequence, social constructionist research programs on nature have been criticized for not helping to resolve current dilemmas such as the value and role of urban nature for health and well-being (Gobster 2000; Egan, Hjerpe et al. 2011); others have argued that this paradigm undermines wilderness preservation as well (Waller 1998; Katz 2000; Martin 2017). Second, the social constructionist perspective has been criticized for giving no agency or power of influence to nature itself (Castree 2000; Simonsen 2013; Lorimer, Hodgetts et al. 2019), leaving it solely an empty canvas upon which humans project our economic, social, and cultural desires.

The critiques of the cultural turn have led to numerous post-cultural research programs in the last ten years. Much of the recent work on nature in the post-cultural turn has been focused on trying to fill in and explore the qualities, power, and attributes of nature that challenge human practices (Braun 2008; Kuus 2019). This work has generally focused either on (a) the properties of nature that resist, or have power against, human actions, or (b) challenging the prioritization of representation as a way of knowing and exploring other ways of understanding nature, focusing in particular on local, embodied, emotional, and performative experiences of nature. Though these research programs have not had nearly the same impact on policy as environmental psychology research programs, they offer some promise for negotiating conflicts and equity around urban greening.

Political ecology and nature: politics, identity, labour and land-rights

Research programs in political ecology have both built on and critiqued social constructionist research programs following the cultural turn (Neumann 2011). While research programs in political ecology can be generally characterized by a focus on the interplay of political, social, and environmental factors (Curtis and Oven 2012), current research programs can be roughly divided into two foci. First, they are recognizing the physical presence of nature that resists economic production and influences social and economic activities (Castree 1995; Prudham 2005; Jackson and Neely 2015). Some of this research has focused on the hybrid 'nature,' or 'socio-nature,' created by the interaction between capitalism, nature, and human labour in cities (Heynen, Kaika et al. 2006; Newell and Cousins 2014; Wachsmuth and Angelo 2018). More recently, some work has even looked at how physical nature can impact human physical health, for example through altering the microbiome (Pearson, Rzotkiewicz et al. 2019). Second, research programs in political ecology have argued for the need to focus on indigenous, local, and rooted-in-place knowledge and the embodied experience (Neumann 2011; Ekers and Loftus 2013; Loftus 2019). Political ecology thus bridges the so-called representational (or a focus on visual representation and discourse) and structuralist focus of the cultural turn, and the place-based, experiential, relational, and post-structuralist focus of the relational turn discussed below. Though the relationship between them is complex and currently debated, one of the main differences is that political ecology views these nature–human relationships as inherently political – asking for example *why* these bodies are in this space in the first place – whereas non-representational approaches have been criticized for eschewing a political lens (Neumann 2011; Mountz 2018). In this way research programs in political ecology are still found within the social constructionist paradigm, but with modifications against its so-called extremes. Lastly, the relationship between nature and health has not traditionally been a focus of political ecology, though there have been recent calls to expand research programs from a mainly disease ecology focus to a broader health–nature realm of inquiry (Jackson and Neely 2015; Neely and Nading 2017).

Key contributions from political ecology include the argument that struggles over nature and meaning are also struggles for social identity, belonging, exclusion and land-rights, particularly in rural production landscapes (Neumann 2011; Clement 2019), or conflicts around urban greening efforts (Simpson and Bagelman 2018). Political ecology has been useful for understanding the politics around our experience of nature. For example, work on the production and consumption of the American lawn have shown that rather than being an 'innate' aesthetic preference, it is part of a dominant discourse that divides urban 'nature' into 'good' and 'bad' nature in very specific places, and with specific practices and economies, in cities and suburbs (Robbins and Sharp 2003).

The relational turn: the experience of nature as sensuous, emotional, daily lived experience of place

The last influential area of research that looks at nature falls under what is broadly termed the 'relational turn.' The relational turn is the most recent reaction against and rejection of the cultural turn. Contrary to the adaptive, utilitarian, and social constructionist paradigms, research programs falling under the relational turn deploy a variety of paradigms – from performance theory, to post-phenomenology, to social network theory (Dowling, Lloyd et al. 2018; Radil and Walther 2018) to Marxism (Simonsen 2013) – and a multiplicity of methods. While significant differences in paradigmatic or ontological approaches underlie these research programs' examination of nature, they share the rejection of representationalism (or focus on the visual) and structuralism (i.e. using a single lens to frame relationships, such as capitalism) that characterizes social constructionism under the cultural turn. Instead, research programs in the relational turn focus on sensuous, local, daily lived experiences of place, often using personal, in-depth, ethnographic-style methods. Central to the relational turn's approach to nature is the recognition of the vigour and inventiveness of the natural world (Kearns 2003; Newell and Cousins 2014; Lorimer, Hodgetts et al. 2019) and its resistance to description or mastery due to its complexity (Thrift 2005). Of importance for understanding the human relationship to nature in cities are research programs that examine the re-enchantment with geography and landscape (Woodyer and Geoghegan 2013;

Bonnett 2017), the study of emotion and affect in human–nature relations (Wright 2010; Curtis and Oven 2012; Uhlmann, Lin et al. 2018), and haptic (or body-centred) knowledge (Paterson 2009; Evans 2017; Whaley 2018).

Work in the relational paradigm has attempted to fill in some perceived gaps in the social constructionist paradigm regarding our understanding of the human relationship to nature, particularly the privileging of the visual, intellectual, and economic aspects of nature. Political ecology's inclusion of politics, labour, place and identity in their work offers insight into some of the sources of conflict and apathy that influence urbanites' relationships with and reactions to urban nature. Work from the relational turn, in contrast, has focused on the local lived embodied experience, the role of place, and the role of affect (or emotion) in understanding the human relationship with nature. As potentially useful as this is, little of this work has found much traction in either public policy or the design fields, with some exceptions that look at public perceptions of public land (Gilchrist, Brown et al. 2015), parks (Baur, Tynon et al. 2013; Roberts, Sadler et al. 2019), or the role of emotion in urbanites' reactions to climate change (Curtis and Oven 2012; Derkzen, van Teeffelen et al. 2017; Wang, Geng et al. 2019). This is likely due to the privileging of quantitative work in public policy and the difficulty of translating critical theory, which tends to take things apart, into policy and design decisions, which needs to put things back together. With the exceptions indicated above, particularly around some qualitative work on favourite places and identity, this work has also not had much traction with most of the dominant research in the adaptive and utilitarian paradigms. This is despite the attempt to include all possible mediators and moderators in many current models that explain human nature–health relationships and outcomes, particularly around health, ecosystem services, and climate change (Millennial Ecosystem Assessment 2003; Lachowycz and Jones 2013).

New directions in nature, health, and well-being research

Though the above research paradigms constitute the majority of past and current work on the human relationship to nature and how it impacts our health, well-being, and sense of place, there are a few other strands of research which are important to our examination of small-scale urban greening (SSUG) projects and which may point to promising new directions for collaboration, insight, and synergies. These strands of research tend to fall in-between the dominant research paradigms, or even outside them, and include new work that is exploring the role biodiversity plays in restoration and well-being, finding both that perceived biodiversity increases well-being (Carrus, Scopelliti et al. 2015; Southon, Jorgensen et al. 2018; Schebella, Weber et al. 2019), and that beauty was a higher predictor of well-being than perceived biodiversity (Muratet, Pellegrini et al. 2015). Other work has looked at how being connected to or experiencing beauty in nature directly impacts well-being (Zhang, Howell et al. 2014; Berto, Barbiero et al. 2018), or the role an emotional connection to nature plays in understanding positive health outcomes (Perrin and Benassi 2009; Pearce, Davison et al. 2015; Dean, Shanahan et al. 2018). Some work from the relational turn has critiqued the lack of political context for haptic, or body-centred work (Mountz 2018; Kuus 2019), while others have called for different methods to more fully address the paradigm-shifting work around nature as thriving, active, more-than-human, and relational (Dowling, Lloyd et al. 2017; Millington and Wainwright 2017; Dowling, Lloyd et al. 2018). Other promising work examines the role of access to nature in creativity (Pasanen, Neuvonen et al. 2018); for example, a study in Denmark among creative professionals found that time in nature made them more curious, able to get new ideas, and flexible in their thinking. It found that the restoration of directed attention (a key component of the restoration theory under the adaptive paradigm) also helped with the analysis and further development of ideas, as well as the preparation and incubation phase of creative thinking (Plambech and Konijnendijk van den Bosch 2015). Further studies have found that self-identified nature lovers are more likely to score higher on cognitive styles associated with creativity, such as an adaption-innovation and analytic-holistic thinking style (Leong, Fischer et al. 2014). There is also promise in studies that are using a phenomenological, place-based approach to understand how people's relationship with and understanding of nature is dynamic, socially mediated, and changeable, for example finding that everyday experiences and conditions can both limit and encourage time in a neighbourhood forest – in other words, that these relationships are not constant (Skår 2010), thus challenging some of the universal findings of the psychometric approach.

This builds on work that has explored sense of place not only as key to understanding the mediators and moderators in our relationship to nature, but also as a foundation of being human; experience, life, and action begin *in place* (Relph 2008). The phenomenological approach in particular, as will be discussed in Chapter 3, can be useful for understanding values and attitudes about complex, daily lived experiences that may not yet be articulated, allowing researchers to get at the *why* and *how* and go beyond likes and dislikes. Lastly, in a completely different research paradigm, research programs that look at biomedicine have traditionally examined the molecularization of life and the relation between socio-natures and the body. Until recently the environment, or nature, has been largely a black box – in other words, an explanatory factor if all others failed to explain health outcomes. Recent work in environmental epigenetics, however, has shown that exposure to chemicals and on-going environmental stressors are actually changing the expression of phenotypes and having multi-generational, long-term health impacts (Guthman and Mansfield 2013; Jackson and Neely 2015; Nilsson, Sadler-Riggleman et al. 2018; Prior, Manley et al. 2019). This transdisciplinary work is showing that the environment, or 'nature,' is co-producing not just psychological health, but biophysical health as well (Pearson, Rzotkiewicz et al. 2019), and challenging the separation between the bio-engineering and socially constructed/relational paradigms that have looked at nature and health, with significant implications for urban greening projects, as we will see in Chapter 4.

Moving forward: research, policy, and practice on nature and health in cities

This chapter has given an overview of what we currently know about our understanding of the human relationship with nature and its influence on our health and well-being, what we don't agree on, and why our approach to these questions matters. It examined two key groups of research based on their underlying paradigms around the questions: "What is nature?" and "What is the human relationship to nature?" Research programs using a bio-engineering model of nature and health – in particular those using adaptive and utilitarian paradigms – tend to leave the concept of nature as a given, an attitude that parallels nineteenth-century American writing on nature, such as that of Thoreau and Muir. They also tend to view human psychological and physiological reactions to nature as innate, biological responses honed over our evolution, a theory commonly referred to as the biophilia hypothesis (Wilson 1984; Kellert 2014). Barring some key exceptions, they also tend to view the relationship between nature and human health, well-being, and behaviour as a linear exposure–reaction model that can be reduced to individual parts and quantified in order to develop with universal explanations and theories. While they have provided a substantial body of empirical evidence on the benefits of access to nature for human health and well-being, and they have been instrumental in bringing urban nature to the forefront of public policy and design discussions, these research programs have been unable to explain conflicts over urban greening projects, the *why* behind urbanities' likes and dislikes, or apathy on the part of even 'greenie' urbanites over greenspaces. They have also tended to discount or not include in their models the role that social, cultural, political, and economic factors play in our perceptions and valuation of, and even access to, urban nature in the first place.

Researchers following a social constructionist paradigm, on the other hand, reject both the self-evident characteristics of the word 'nature' and the idea that our reactions to it are innate. They argue instead that nature is influenced by dominant cultural and economic discourses, changing from a threatening wilderness for pioneers to a sacred, universal, and distant concept far from daily life and production for most urbanites. This viewpoint has been criticized, however, for reducing nature to culture, privileging intellectual and representational understandings of nature, and harming conservation and restoration efforts. Researchers using a political ecology paradigm have argued that all relationships with nature are inherently political, asking *why* our bodies are in nature in the first place (i.e. labour or leisure) (Mountz 2018), and how those relationships are expressions and fights for identity, labour, and place. Lastly, researchers falling under a broadly defined relational paradigm have rejected the representational, structural, and intellectual focus of most of the other research on nature and argued for an emotional, individual, place- and body-based narrative understanding of nature. With some notable exceptions, most of the research using a social constructionist or relational paradigm has not been very influential in popular media, public policy decisions, or design discourses as they do not fit easily into policy. This is despite their potential to help provide insight into conflicts, aesthetic preferences, and apathy around urban greening projects.

Understanding how underlying paradigms influence current research and debates about nature and health in our cities helps us to understand where current gaps in our knowledge may exist. For example, due to the dominance of adaptive and utilitarian research in public policy that can reduce the human–nature relationship to its smallest parts, there is a risk that urban greening projects, and SSUG projects in particular, will be designed with little understanding of how to maximize potential health, sense of place, and other benefits that speak to the whole person and a lived experience of place, relying instead on the minimum required for a design or municipal building credit. As will be seen in Chapter 3, these 'minimum urban greening projects' provide little in the way of health and well-being benefits for urbanites and in fact can give rise to negative perceptions and disappointment. Relying heavily on *imagined* restorative benefits (often from college students) of a visual depiction of nature in experimental settings, versus *actual* restoration when part of one's daily lived experience, also raises questions about the ability of one method or approach to fully capture something as complex as the human relationship to nature in cities, a sentiment which is increasingly finding traction and acceptance among some nature–health researchers (Brown and Cummins 2013; Wartmann and Purves 2018), but not necessarily in public policy or design.

The heavy reliance on the bio-engineering model of nature and health in public policy and design also impedes a fuller exploration and understanding of which aesthetic preferences are malleable through, say, education, and which are unlikely to change. This limitation is problematic given that many new urban greening projects have specific ecological objectives that encourage a 'wilder' aesthetic that traditionally has not been viewed positively by North American urbanites. As we will see in Chapter 3, better understanding how urbanites feel and why they do about small-scale urban nature can help policy makers and designers go beyond likes and dislikes and begin to create more equitable and sustainable places that support, and even encourage, health and well-being. Incorporating some of the insights from the social constructionist and relational paradigm research can help to unpack the conflicts, apathy, and aesthetic preferences that must be understood for small-scale urban greening projects to be successful. Given policy makers' wish to create vibrant, equitable, sustainable, and healthy places to live in cities, understanding these psychosocial factors can be an important component of designing urban greening projects that benefit everyone.

References

100 Resilient Cities. (2019). "100 Resilient Cities." Retrieved May 10, 2019, from https://100resilientcities.org.

Adamson, K. and A. Thatcher (2019). *Do Indoor Plants Improve Performance Outcomes? Using the Attention Restoration Theory*. Cham: Springer International Publishing.

Adinolfi, C., G. P. Suárez-Cáceres and P. Cariñanos (2014). "Relation between visitors' behaviour and characteristics of green spaces in the city of Granada, south-eastern Spain." *Urban Forestry and Urban Greening* **13**(3): 534–542. http://dx.doi.org/10.1016/j.ufug.2014.03.007.

Araújo, D., E. Brymer, H. Brito, R. Withagen and K. Davids (2019). "The empowering variability of affordances of nature: Why do exercisers feel better after performing the same exercise in natural environments than in indoor environments?" *Psychology of Sport and Exercise* **42**: 138–145. https://doi.org/10.1016/j.psychsport.2018.12.020.

Armstrong, D. (2000). "A survey of community gardens in upstate New York: Implications for health promotion and community development." *Health and Place* **6**: 319–327. doi:10.1016/S1353-8292(00)00013-7.

Arnberger, A. and R. Eder (2012). "The influence of green space on community attachment of urban and suburban residents." *Urban Forestry and Urban Greening* **11**(1): 41–49. http://dx.doi.org/10.1016/j.ufug.2011.11.003.

Ashford, K. (2015). "Looking at green roofs may boost your productivity." *Forbes*, May 29.

Ayala-Azcárraga, C., D. Diaz and L. Zambrano (2019). "Characteristics of urban parks and their relation to user well-being." *Landscape and Urban Planning* **189**: 27–35. https://doi.org/10.1016/j.landurbplan.2019.04.005.

Bagot, K. L., F. C. L. Allen and S. Toukhsati (2015). "Perceived restorativeness of children's school playground environments: Nature, playground features and play period experiences." *Journal of Environmental Psychology* **41**(0): 1–9. http://dx.doi.org/10.1016/j.jenvp.2014.11.005.

Baur, J. W. R., J. F. Tynon and E. Gómez (2013). "Attitudes about urban nature parks: A case study of users and nonusers in Portland, Oregon." *Landscape and Urban Planning* **117**(0): 100–111. http://dx.doi.org/10.1016/j.landurbplan.2013.04.015.

Becker, D. A., M. H. E. M. Browning, M. Kuo and S. K. van den Eeden (2019). "Is green land cover associated with less health care spending? Promising findings from county-level Medicare spending in the continental United States." *Urban Forestry and Urban Greening* **41**: 39–47. https://doi.org/10.1016/j.ufug.2019.02.012.

Bengtsson, A. and P. Grahn (2014). "Outdoor environments in healthcare settings: A quality evaluation tool for use in designing healthcare gardens." *Urban Forestry and Urban Greening* **13**(4): 878–891. http://dx.doi.org/10.1016/j.ufug.2014.09.007.

Berto, R., G. Barbiero, P. Barbiero and G. Senes (2018). "An individual's connection to nature can affect perceived restorativeness of natural environments: Some observations about biophilia." *Behavioral Sciences* **8**(3): 34. doi:10.3390/bs8030034.

Beute, F. and Y. A. W. de Kort (2014). "Natural resistance: Exposure to nature and self-regulation, mood, and physiology after ego-depletion." *Journal of Environmental Psychology* **40**(0): 167–178. http://dx.doi.org/10.1016/j.jenvp.2014.06.004.

Biophilic Cities Network (2016). *Washington, DC joins Biophilic Cities Network*. Biophilic Cities.

Birenboim, A., M. Dijst, D. Ettema, J. de Kruijf, G. de Leeuw and N. Dogterom (2019). "The utilization of immersive virtual environments for the investigation of environmental preferences." *Landscape and Urban Planning* **189**: 129–138. https://doi.org/10.1016/j.landurbplan.2019.04.011.

Bonnett, A. (2017). "The enchanted path: Magic and modernism in psychogeographical walking." *Transactions of the Institute of British Geographers* **42**(3): 472–484. doi:10.1111/tran.12177.

Boyd, F., M. P. White, S. L. Bell and J. Burt (2018). "Who doesn't visit natural environments for recreation and why: A population representative analysis of spatial, individual and temporal factors among adults in England." *Landscape and Urban Planning* **175**: 102–113. https://doi.org/10.1016/j.landurbplan.2018.03.016.

Branas, C. C., E. South, M. C. Kondo, B. C. Hohl, P. Bourgois, D. J. Wiebe and J. M. MacDonald (2018). "Citywide cluster randomized trial to restore blighted vacant land and its effects on violence, crime, and fear." *Proceedings of the National Academy of Sciences* **115**(12): 2946–2951. doi:10.1073/pnas.1718503115.

Bratman, G. N., G. C. Daily, B. J. Levy and J. J. Gross (2015). "The benefits of nature experience: Improved affect and cognition." *Landscape and Urban Planning* **138**(0): 41–50. http://dx.doi.org/10.1016/j.landurbplan.2015.02.005.

Braun, B. (2005). "Environmental issues: Writing a more-than-human urban geography." *Progress in Human Geography* **29**(5): 635–650. https://doi.org/10.1191%2F0309132505ph574pr.

Braun, B. (2008). "Environmental issues: Inventive life." *Progress in Human Geography* **32**(5): 667–679. https://doi.org/10.1177/0309132507088030.

Brown, G., J. Rhodes and M. Dade (2018). "An evaluation of participatory mapping methods to assess urban park benefits." *Landscape and Urban Planning* **178**: 18–31. https://doi.org/10.1016/j.landurbplan.2018.05.018.

Brown, G., M. F. Schebella and D. Weber (2014). "Using participatory GIS to measure physical activity and urban park benefits." *Landscape and Urban Planning* **121**(0): 34–44. http://dx.doi.org/10.1016/j.landurbplan.2013.09.006.

Brown, T. and S. Cummins (2013). "Intervening in health: The place of urban green space." *Landscape and Urban Planning* **118**(0): 59–61. http://dx.doi.org/10.1016/j.landurbplan.2013.06.003.

Bubalo, M., B. T. van Zanten and P. H. Verburg (2019). "Crowdsourcing geo-information on landscape perceptions and preferences: A review." *Landscape and Urban Planning* **184**: 101–111. https://doi.org/10.1016/j.landurbplan.2019.01.001.

Carpenter, M. (2013). "From 'healthful exercise' to 'nature on prescription': The politics of urban green spaces and walking for health." *Landscape and Urban Planning* **118**(0): 120–127. http://dx.doi.org/10.1016/j.landurbplan.2013.02.009.

Carrus, G., M. Scopelliti, R. Lafortezza, G. Colangelo, F. Ferrini, F. Salbitano, M. Agrimi, L. Portoghesi, P. Semenzato and G. Sanesi (2015). "Go greener, feel better? The positive effects of biodiversity on the well-being of individuals visiting urban and peri-urban green areas." *Landscape and Urban Planning* **134**(0): 221–228. http://dx.doi.org/10.1016/j.landurbplan.2014.10.022.

Castree, N. (1995). "The nature of produced nature: Materiality and knowledge construction in Marxism." *Antipode* **27**(1): 12–48. https://doi.org/10.1111/j.1467-8330.1995.tb00260.x.

Castree, N. (2000). The Production of Nature. *A Companion to Economic Geography*. E. Sheppard and T. J. Barnes. Oxford: Blackwell: 275–289.

Church, S. P. (2015). "Exploring Green Streets and rain gardens as instances of small scale nature and environmental learning tools." *Landscape and Urban Planning* **134**(0): 229–240. http://dx.doi.org/10.1016/j.landurbplan.2014.10.021.

Cimprich, B. (1993). "Development of an intervention to restore attention in cancer patients." *Cancer Nursing* **16**: 83–92.

Clemens, D. (2015). "Study: Trees in your neighborhood make you feel richer, younger." *Discovery.com*.

Clement, V. (2019). "Beyond the sham of the emancipatory Enlightenment: Rethinking the relationship of Indigenous epistemologies, knowledges, and geography through decolonizing paths." *Progress in Human Geography* **43**(2): 276–294. doi:10.1177/0309132517747315.

Cockayne, D. G., D. Ruez and A. Secor (2017). "Between ontology and representation: Locating Gilles Deleuze's 'difference-in-itself' in and for geographical thought." *Progress in Human Geography* **41**(5): 580–599. doi:10.1177/0309132516650028.

Coldwell, D. F. and K. L. Evans (2018). "Visits to urban green-space and the countryside associate with different components of mental well-being and are better predictors than perceived or actual local urbanisation intensity." *Landscape and Urban Planning* **175**: 114–122. https://doi.org/10.1016/j.landurbplan.2018.02.007.

Colléony, A., R. White and A. Shwartz (2019). "The influence of spending time outside on experience of nature and environmental attitudes." *Landscape and Urban Planning* **187**: 96–104. https://doi.org/10.1016/j.landurbplan.2019.03.010.

Colley, K., C. Brown and A. Montarzino (2017). "Understanding knowledge workers' interactions with workplace greenspace: Open space use and restoration experiences at urban-fringe business sites." *Environment and Behavior* **49**(3): 314–338. doi:10.1177/0013916516629194.

Colorado Department of Public Health and the Environment (2015). Cancer, Cardiovascular Disease and Pulmonary Disease Grant Program RFA #1244: Appendix A: Strategy Specifications and Metrics. Colorado, Colorado Department of Health and Environment.

Cooper, N., E. Brady, H. Steen and R. Bryce (2016). "Aesthetic and spiritual values of ecosystems: Recognising the ontological and axiological plurality of cultural ecosystem 'services'." *Ecosystem Services* **21**: 218–229. doi:10.1016/j.ecoser.2016.07.014.

Corliss, J. (2019). *White Wilderness: Race, Capitalism, and Alternative Knowledges of Natural Space*. Chicago, IL: DePaul University.

Cronon, W. (1995). The Trouble with Wilderness: or, Getting back to the Wrong Nature. *Uncommon Ground*. W. Cronon. New York: W. W. Norton & Co.: 69–90.

Curl, A., C. Ward Thompson and P. Aspinall (2015). "The effectiveness of 'shared space' residential street interventions on self-reported activity levels and quality of life for older people." *Landscape and Urban Planning* **139**(0): 117–125. http://dx.doi.org/10.1016/j.landurbplan.2015.02.019.

Curtis, S. E. and K. J. Oven (2012). "Geographies of health and climate change." *Progress in Human Geography* **36**(5): 654–666. doi:10.1177/0309132511423350.

Dadvand, P., S. Hariri, B. Abbasi, R. Heshmat, M. Qorbani, M. E. Motlagh, X. Basagaña and R. Kelishadi (2019). "Use of green spaces, self-satisfaction and social contacts in adolescents: A population-based CASPIAN-V study." *Environmental Research* **168**: 171–177. doi:10.1016/j.envres.2018.09.033.

Davison, A. (2008). "The trouble with nature: Ambivalence in the lives of urban Australian environmentalists." *Geoforum* **39**(3): 1284–1295. https://doi.org/10.1016/j.geoforum.2007.06.011.

Dean, J. H., D. F. Shanahan, R. Bush, K. J. Gaston, B. B. Lin, E. Barber, L. Franco and R. A. Fuller (2018). "Is nature relatedness associated with better mental and physical health?" *International Journal of Environmental Research and Public Health* **15**(7): 1371. doi:10.3390/ijerph15071371.

Denver Environmental Health (2014). *City and County of Denver: Climate Change Adaptation Plan*. Denver, CO.: 93.

Denver Regional Council of Governments (2011). *Metro Vision 2035 Plan*. Denver, CO.

Denveright (2019). *Game Plan for a Healthy City*. Denver, CO: City and County of Denver.

Derkzen, M., A. J. A. van Teeffelen, P. H. Verburg (2017). "Green infrastructure for urban climate adaptation: How do residents' views on climate impacts and green infrastructure shape adaptation preferences?" *Landscape and Urban Planning* **157**: 106–130. doi:10.1016/j.landurbplan.2016.05.027.

Douglas, J. A., M. D. Briones, E. Z. Bauer, M. Trujillo, M. Lopez and A. M. Subica (2018). "Social and environmental determinants of physical activity in urban parks: Testing a neighborhood disorder model." *Preventive Medicine* **109**: 119–124. https://doi.org/10.1016/j.ypmed.2018.01.013.

Dowling, R., K. Lloyd and S. Suchet-Pearson (2017). "Qualitative methods II: 'More-than-human' methodologies and/in praxis." *Progress in Human Geography* **41**(6): 823–831. doi:10.1177/0309132516664439.

Dowling, R., K. Lloyd and S. Suchet-Pearson (2018). "Qualitative methods III: Experimenting, picturing, sensing." *Progress in Human Geography* **42**(5): 779–788. doi:10.1177/0309132517730941.

Duncan, J. S. and N. G. Duncan (2001). "The aestheticization of the politics of landscape preservation." *Annals of the Association of American Geographers* **91**(2): 387–409. https://doi.org/10.1111/0004-5608.00250.

Dunlap, R., K. Van Liere, A. G. Mertig and R. E. Jones (2000). "Measuring endorsement of the new ecological paradigm: A revised NEP scale." *Journal of Social Issues* **56**: 425–442.

Dupont, L., M. Antrop and V. Van Eetvelde (2015). "Does landscape related expertise influence the visual perception of landscape photographs? Implications for participatory landscape planning and management." *Landscape and Urban Planning* **141**(0): 68–77. http://dx.doi.org/10.1016/j.landurbplan.2015.05.003.

Dzhambov, A. M., D. D. Dimitrova and E. D. Dimitrakova (2014). “Association between residential greenness and birth weight: Systematic review and meta-analysis.” *Urban Forestry and Urban Greening* **13**(4): 621–629. http://dx.doi.org/10.1016/j.ufug.2014.09.004.

Egan, D., E. E. Hjerpe and J. Abrams (2011). *Human Dimensions of Ecological Restoration: Integrating Science, Nature, and Culture*. Washington, DC: Island Press/Center for Resource Economics.

Ekers, M. and A. Loftus (2013). “Revitalizing the production of nature thesis: A Gramscian turn?” *Progress in Human Geography* **37**(2): 234–252. doi:10.1177/0309132512448831.

Elliot, R. (2000). Faking Nature. *Environmental Restoration*. W. Throop. Amherst, New York: Humanity Books: 71–82.

Evans, B. (2017). Nature and Corporeality. *International Encyclopedia of Geography*. Hoboken, NJ: John Wiley & Sons.

Fairhead, J., M. Leach and I. Scoones (2012). “Green grabbing: A new appropriation of nature?” *The Journal of Peasant Studies* **39**(2): 237–261. doi:10.1080/03066150.2012.671770.

Flint, C. G., I. Kunze, A. Muhar, Y. Yoshida and M. Penker (2013). “Exploring empirical typologies of human–nature relationships and linkages to the ecosystem services concept.” *Landscape and Urban Planning* **120**(0): 208–217. http://dx.doi.org/10.1016/j.landurbplan.2013.09.002.

Gagnon Thompson, S. C. and M. A. Barton (1994). “Ecocentric and anthropocentric attitudes toward the environment.” *Journal of Environmental Psychology* **14**(2): 149–157. https://doi.org/10.1016/S0272-4944(05)80168-9.

Gilchrist, K., C. Brown and A. Montarzino (2015). “Workplace settings and wellbeing: Greenspace use and views contribute to employee wellbeing at peri-urban business sites.” *Landscape and Urban Planning* **138**(0): 32–40. http://dx.doi.org/10.1016/j.landurbplan.2015.02.004.

Gobster, P. H. (2000). “Introduction: Restoring Nature: Human Actions, Interactions, and Reactions.” *Restoring Nature: Perspectives from the Social Sciences and Humanities*. P. Gobster and Bruce Hull. Washington, DC: Island Press: 1–19.

Gómez-Baggethun, E. and D. N. Barton (2013). “Classifying and valuing ecosystem services for urban planning.” *Ecological Economics* **86**: 235–245. http://dx.doi.org/10.1016/j.ecolecon.2012.08.019.

Grassini, S., A. Revonsuo, S. Castellotti, I. Petrizzo, V. Benedetti and M. Koivisto (2019). “Processing of natural scenery is associated with lower attentional and cognitive load compared with urban ones.” *Journal of Environmental Psychology* **62**: 1–11. https://doi.org/10.1016/j.jenvp.2019.01.007.

Guha, R. (1989). “Radical American environmentalism and wilderness preservation: A Third World critique.” *Environmental Ethics* **11**(1): 71–85. doi:10.5840/enviroethics198911123.

Guthman, J. and B. Mansfield (2013). “The implications of environmental epigenetics: A new direction for geographic inquiry on health, space, and nature-society relations.” *Progress in Human Geography* **37**(4): 486–504. doi:10.1177/0309132512463258.

Gwedla, N. and C. M. Shackleton (2019). “Perceptions and preferences for urban trees across multiple socio-economic contexts in the Eastern Cape, South Africa.” *Landscape and Urban Planning* **189**: 225–234. https://doi.org/10.1016/j.landurbplan.2019.05.001.

Hadavi, S. (2017). “Direct and indirect effects of the physical aspects of the environment on mental well-being.” *Environment and Behavior* **49**(10): 1071–1104. doi:10.1177/0013916516679876.

Hadavi, S., R. Kaplan and M. C. R. Hunter (2015). “Environmental affordances: A practical approach for design of nearby outdoor settings in urban residential areas.” *Landscape and Urban Planning* **134**(0): 19–32. http://dx.doi.org/10.1016/j.landurbplan.2014.10.001.

Hansen, M. M., R. Jones and K. Tocchini (2017). “Shinrin-yoku (forest bathing) and nature therapy: A state-of-the-art review.” *International Journal of Environmental Research and Public Health* **14**(8). doi:10.3390/ijerph14080851.

Hartig, T. (1993). “Nature experience in transactional perspective.” *Landscape and Urban Planning* **25**: 17–36.

Hartig, T., M. Mang and G. Evans (1991). “Restorative effects of natural environments experiences.” *Environment and Behaviour* **23**: 3–26. https://doi.org/10.1177/0013916591231001.

Hauru, K., S. Lehvävirta, K. M. Korpela and D. J. Kotze (2012). “Closure of view to the urban matrix has positive effects on perceived restorativeness in urban forests in Helsinki, Finland.” *Landscape and Urban Planning* **107**(4): 361–369. http://dx.doi.org/10.1016/j.landurbplan.2012.07.002.

Hazer, M., M. K. Formica, S. Dieterlen and C. P. Morley (2018). “The relationship between self-reported exposure to greenspace and human stress in Baltimore, MD.” *Landscape and Urban Planning* **169**: 47–56. https://doi.org/10.1016/j.landurbplan.2017.08.006.

Heft, H. (2010). Affordances and the Perception of Landscape: An Inquiry into Environmental Perception and Aesthetics. *Innovative Approaches to Researching Landscape and Health: Open Spaces: People Space 2.* C. Ward Thompson, P. Aspinall and S. Bell. Abingdon, UK: Routledge.

Hertog, I. M. and E. Turnhout (2018). "Ideals and pragmatism in the justification of ecological restoration." *Restoration Ecology* **26**(6): 1221–1229. doi:10.1111/rec.12680.

Herzog, T. R., H. C. Chen and J. S. Primeau (2002). "Perception of the restorative potential of natural and other settings." *Journal of Environmental Psychology* **22**: 295–306.

Heynen, N., M. Kaika and E. Syngedouw (2006). *In the Nature of Cities: Urban Political Ecology and the Politics of Urban Metabolism.* New York: Routledge.

Hitchings, R. (2013). "Studying the preoccupations that prevent people from going into green space." *Landscape and Urban Planning* **118**(0): 98–102. http://dx.doi.org/10.1016/j.landurbplan.2012.09.006.

Hobbs, R. J., E. Higgs and J. A. Harris (2009). "Novel ecosystems: Implications for conservation and restoration." *Trends in Ecology and Evolution* **24**(11): 599–605. https://doi.org/10.1016/j.tree.2009.05.012.

Home, R., O. Lewis, N. Bauer, A. Fliessbach, D. Frey, S. Lichtsteiner, M. Moretti, S. Tresch, C. Young, A. Zanetta and M. Stolze (2019). "Effects of garden management practices, by different types of gardeners, on human wellbeing and ecological and soil sustainability in Swiss cities." *Urban Ecosystems* **22**(1): 189–199. doi:10.1007/s11252-018-0806-2.

Honold, J., T. Lakes, R. Beyer and E. van der Meer (2016). "Restoration in urban spaces: Nature views from home, greenways, and public parks." *Environment and Behavior* **48**(6): 796–825. doi:10.1177/0013916514568556.

Hooper, P., B. Boruff, B. Beesley, H. Badland and B. Giles-Corti (2018). "Testing spatial measures of public open space planning standards with walking and physical activity health outcomes: Findings from the Australian national liveability study." *Landscape and Urban Planning* **171**: 57–67. https://doi.org/10.1016/j.landurbplan.2017.12.001.

Hough, M. (2004). *Cities and Natural Processes: A Basis for Sustainability.* London and New York: Routledge.

Houlden, V., S. Weich, J. Porto de Albuquerque, S. Jarvis and K. Rees (2018). "The relationship between greenspace and the mental wellbeing of adults: A systematic review." *PLOS ONE* **13**(9): e0203000. doi:10.1371/journal.pone.0203000.

Huber, M. (2018). "Resource geographies I: Valuing nature (or not)." *Progress in Human Geography* **42**(1): 148–159. doi:10.1177/0309132516670773.

Hull, R. B. and S. E. Michael (1995). "Nature-based recreation, mood change, and stress reduction." *Leisure Sciences* **17**(1): 1–14. https://doi.org/10.1080/01490409509513239.

Hunter, M. C. R. and D. G. Brown (2012). "Spatial contagion: Gardening along the street in residential neighborhoods." *Landscape and Urban Planning* **105**(4): 407–416. http://dx.doi.org/10.1016/j.landurbplan.2012.01.013.

Hystad, P., Y. Payette, N. Noisel and C. Boileau (2019). "Green space associations with mental health and cognitive function: Results from the Quebec CARTaGENE cohort." *Environmental Epidemiology* **3**(1): e040. doi:10.1097/ee9.0000000000000040.

International WELL Building Institute (2018). *The WELL Building Standard version 2 pilot (WELL v2).* New York.

Jackson, P. and A. H. Neely (2015). "Triangulating health: Toward a practice of a political ecology of health." *Progress in Human Geography* **39**(1): 47–64. doi:10.1177/0309132513518832.

James, W. (1892). *Psychology: The Briefer Course.* New York: Holt.

Jiang, B., C.-Y. Chang and W. C. Sullivan (2014). "A dose of nature: Tree cover, stress reduction, and gender differences." *Landscape and Urban Planning* **132**(0): 26–36. http://dx.doi.org/10.1016/j.landurbplan.2014.08.005.

Jiang, B., T. Zhang and W. C. Sullivan (2015). "Healthy cities: Mechanisms and research questions regarding impacts of urban green landscapes on public health and well-being." *Landscape Architecture Frontiers* **3**(1): 24–35.

Jung, W. H., J.-M. Woo and J. S. Ryu (2015). "Effect of a forest therapy program and the forest environment on female workers' stress." *Urban Forestry and Urban Greening* **14**(2): 274–281. http://dx.doi.org/10.1016/j.ufug.2015.02.004.

Kaczynski, A. T., L. R. Potwarka, B. J. A. Smale and M. E. Havitz (2009). "Association of parkland proximity with neighbourhood and park based physical activity: Variations by gender and age." *Leisure Sciences* **31**: 174–191. https://doi.org/10.1080/01490400802686045.

Kaika, M. (2006). The Political Ecology of Water Scarcity: The 1989–1991 Athenian Drought. *In the Nature of Cities: Urban Political Ecology and the Politics of Urban Metabolism*. N. Heynen, M. Kaika and E. Syngedouw. New York: Routledge: 157–172.

Kaplan, R. (1983). "The role of nature in the urban context." *Human Behaviour and Environment: Advances in Theory and Research* **6**: 127–161.

Kaplan, R. (1984). "Wilderness perception and psychological benefits: An analysis of a continuing program." *Leisure Sciences* **6**(3): 271–290. https://doi.org/10.1080/01490408409513036.

Kaplan, R. (1993). "The role of nature in the context of the workplace." *Landscape and Urban Planning* **26**: 193–201. https://doi.org/10.1016/0169-2046(93)90016-7.

Kaplan, R. (2001). "The nature of the view from home: Psychological benefits." *Environment and Behavior* **33**(4): 507–542. https://doi.org/10.1177/00139160121973115.

Kaplan, R. and E. Herbert (1987). Cultural and sub-cultural comparisons in preferences for natural settings. *Landscape and Urban Planning* **14:** 281.

Kaplan, R. and S. Kaplan (1989). *The Experience of Nature: A Psychological Perspective*. New York: Cambridge University Press.

Kaplan, R. and S. Kaplan (2005). Preference, Restoration, and Meaningful Action in the Context of Nearby Nature. *Urban Place: Reconnecting with the Natural World*. P. Barlett. Cambridge: MIT Press: 330.

Kaplan, R. and J. F. Talbot (1988). "Ethnicity and preference for natural settings: A review and recent findings." *Landscape and urban planning* **15**(1–2): 107–117. https://doi.org/10.1016/0169-2046(88)90019-9.

Kaplan, S. (1995). "The restorative benefits of nature: Toward an integrative framework." *Journal of Environmental Psychology* **15**(3): 169–182. https://doi.org/10.1016/0272-4944(95)90001-2.

Kaplan, S. and R. Kaplan (2009). "Creating a larger role for environmental psychology: The Reasonable Person Model as an integrative framework." *Journal of Environmental Psychology* **29**(3): 329–339. https://doi.org/10.1016/j.jenvp.2008.10.005.

Katz, C. (1998). Whose Nature, Whose Culture? *Remaking Reality: Nature at the Millennium*. B. Brown and N. Castree. London: Routledge: 46–63.

Katz, E. (2000). The Big Lie. *Environmental Restoration*. W. Throop. Amherst, New York: Humanity Books: 83–93.

Kearns, M. (2003). "Chaos and control: Nanotechnology and the politics of emergence." *Paragraph* **29**(2): 57–80.

Keil, R. and J. Graham (1998). Reasserting Nature: Constructing Urban Environments after Fordism. *Remaking Reality: Nature at the Millenium*. B. Braun and N. Castree. London: Routledge: 100–125.

Kellert, S. (2014). "Biophilia and biomimicry: Evolutionary adaptation of human versus nonhuman nature." *Intelligent Buildings International* **8**(2): 51–56. 10.1080/17508975.2014.902802.

Kim, D. and J. Jin (2018). "Does happiness data say urban parks are worth it?" *Landscape and Urban Planning* **178**: 1–11. https://doi.org/10.1016/j.landurbplan.2018.05.010.

Kinnafick, F.-E. and C. Thøgersen-Ntoumani (2014). "The effect of the physical environment and levels of activity on affective states." *Journal of Environmental Psychology* **38**: 241–251. http://dx.doi.org/10.1016/j.jenvp.2014.02.007.

Knez, I., Å. O. Sang, B. Gunnersson and M. Hedblom (2018). "Wellbeing in Urban Greenery: The role of naturalness and place identity." *Frontiers in Psychology* **9**: 491. doi:10.3389/fpsyg.2018.00491.

Kolinjivadi, V., G. Van Hecken, D. V. Almeida, J. Dupras and N. Kosoy (2019). "Neoliberal performatives and the 'making' of Payments for Ecosystem Services (PES)." *Progress in Human Geography* **43**(1): 3–25. doi:10.1177/0309132517735707.

Koppen, G., Å. O. Sang and M. S. Tveit (2014). "Managing the potential for outdoor recreation: Adequate mapping and measuring of accessibility to urban recreational landscapes." *Urban Forestry and Urban Greening* **13**(1): 71–83. http://dx.doi.org/10.1016/j.ufug.2013.11.005.

Korpela, K. M. and M. Ylen (2007). "Perceived health is associated with visiting natural favourite places in the vicinity." *Health and Place* **13**: 138–151. https://doi.org/10.1016/j.healthplace.2005.11.002.

Korpela, K. M., K. Borodulin, M. Neuvonen, O. Paronen and L. Tyrväinen (2014). "Analyzing the mediators between nature-based outdoor recreation and emotional well-being." *Journal of Environmental Psychology* **37**: 1–7. http://dx.doi.org/10.1016/j.jenvp.2013.11.003.

Korpela, K. M., M. Ylen, L. Tyrvainen and H. Silvennoinen (2008). "Determinants of restorative experiences in everyday favorite places." *Health and Place* **14**: 636–652. doi:10.1016/j.healthplace.2007.10.008.

Korpela, K. M., M. Ylen, L. Tyrvainen and H. Silvennoinen (2009). "Stability of self-reported favourite places and place attachment over a 10-month period." *Journal of Environmental Psychology* **29**(1): 95–100. https://doi.org/10.1016/j.jenvp.2008.05.008.

Kowarik, I. (2013). "Cities and wilderness: A new perspective." *International Journal of Wilderness* **19**(3): 32–36.

Kowarik, I. (2019). "The "Green Belt Berlin": Establishing a greenway where the Berlin Wall once stood by integrating ecological, social and cultural approaches." *Landscape and Urban Planning* **184**: 12–22. https://doi.org/10.1016/j.landurbplan.2018.12.008.

Kuo, F. E. (2001). "Coping with poverty: Impacts of environment and attention in the inner city." *Environment and Behaviour* **33**(1): 5–34. https://doi.org/10.1177/00139160121972846.

Kuo, F. E. and W. C. Sullivan (2001). "Aggression and violence in the inner city: Effects of environment via mental fatigue." *Environment and Behaviour* **33**(4): 543–573. https://doi.org/10.1177/00139160121973124.

Kuo, F. E., M. Bacaicoa and W. C. Sullivan (1998). "Transforming inner-city landscapes: Trees, sense of safety, and preference." *Environment and Behaviour* **30**(1): 28–59. https://doi.org/10.1177/0013916598301002.

Kuus, M. (2019). "Political geography I: Agency." *Progress in Human Geography* **43**(1): 163–171. doi:10.1177/0309132517734337.

Laaksoharju, T., E. Rappe and T. Kaivola (2012). "Garden affordances for social learning, play, and for building nature–child relationship." *Urban Forestry and Urban Greening* **11**(2): 195–203. http://dx.doi.org/10.1016/j.ufug.2012.01.003.

Lachowycz, K. and A. P. Jones (2013). "Towards a better understanding of the relationship between greenspace and health: Development of a theoretical framework." *Landscape and Urban Planning* **118**(0): 62–69. http://dx.doi.org/10.1016/j.landurbplan.2012.10.012.

Larrea, I., A. Muela, N. Miranda and A. Barandiaran (2019). "Children's social play and affordance availability in preschool outdoor environments." *European Early Childhood Education Research Journal* **27**(2): 185–194. doi:10.1080/1350293X.2019.1579546.

Larsen, J. C., J. Adams, B. Deal, B.-S. Kweon and E. Tyler (1998). "Plants in the workplace: The effects of plant density on productivity, attitudes, and perceptions." *Environment and Behaviour* **30**(3): 261–281. http://dx.doi.org/10.1177/001391659803000301.

Lee, K. E., K. J. H. Williams, L. D. Sargent, N. S. G. Williams and K. A. Johnson (2015). "40-second green roof views sustain attention: The role of micro-breaks in attention restoration." *Journal of Environmental Psychology* **42**(0): 182–189. http://dx.doi.org/10.1016/j.jenvp.2015.04.003.

Lee, K. J., J. Hur, K.-S. Yang, M.-K. Lee and S.-J. Lee (2018). "Acute biophysical responses and psychological effects of different types of forests in patients with metabolic syndrome." *Environment and Behavior* **50**(3): 298–323. doi:10.1177/0013916517700957.

Leong, L. Y. C., R. Fischer and J. McClure (2014). "Are nature lovers more innovative? The relationship between connectedness with nature and cognitive styles." *Journal of Environmental Psychology* **40**(0): 57–63. http://dx.doi.org/10.1016/j.jenvp.2014.03.007.

Leopold, A. (1971). *A Sand County Almanac with other essays on conservation from Round River.* New York: Oxford University Press.

Li, D., B. Deal, X. Zhou, M. Slavenas and W. C. Sullivan (2018). "Moving beyond the neighborhood: Daily exposure to nature and adolescents' mood." *Landscape and Urban Planning* **173**: 33–43. https://doi.org/10.1016/j.landurbplan.2018.01.009.

Loftus, A. (2007). "Working on the socio-natural relations of the urban waterscape in South Africa." *International Journal of Urban and Regional Research* **31**(1): 41–59. https://doi.org/10.1111/j.1468-2427.2007.00708.x.

Loftus, A. (2019). "Political ecology I: Where is political ecology?" *Progress in Human Geography* **43**(1): 172–182. doi:10.1177/0309132517734338.

Lohr, V. I., C. H. Pearson-Mims and G. K. Goodwin (1996). "Interior plants may improve worker productivity and reduce stress in a windowless environment." *Journal of Environmental Horticulture* **14**(2): 97–100.

Lorimer, J., T. Hodgetts and M. Barua (2019). "Animals' atmospheres." *Progress in Human Geography* **43**(1): 26–45. doi:10.1177/0309132517731254.

Louv, R. (2006). *Last Child in the Woods: Saving Our Children from Nature-Deficit Disorder.* Chapel Hill, NC: Algonquin Books of Chapel Hill.

Louv, R. (2011). *The Nature Principle: Human Restoration and the End of Nature-Deficit Disorder.* Chapel Hill, NC: Algonquin Books of Chapel Hill.

Maas, J., M. van Winsum-Westra, R. A. Verheij, P. Spreeuwenberg and P. P. Groenewegen (2009). "Does green space in the living environment influence people's feelings of social safety?" *Environment and Planning, A* **41**: 1763–1777. https://doi.org/10.1068/a4196.

Mak, B. K. L. and C. Y. Jim (2018). "Examining fear-evoking factors in urban parks in Hong Kong." *Landscape and Urban Planning* **171**: 42–56. https://doi.org/10.1016/j.landurbplan.2017.11.012.

Mårtensson, F., M. Jansson, M. Johansson, A. Raustorp, M. Kylin and C. Boldemann (2014). "The role of greenery for physical activity play at school grounds." *Urban Forestry and Urban Greening* **13**(1): 103–113. http://dx.doi.org/10.1016/j.ufug.2013.10.003.

Martin, D. (2004). "Apartheid in the great outdoors: American advertising and the reproduction of a racialized outdoor leisure identity." *Journal of Leisure Research* **36**(4): 513–535. doi:10.1080/00222216.2004.11950034.

Martin, D. M. (2017). "Ecological restoration should be redefined for the twenty-first century." *Restoration Ecology* **25**(5): 668–673. doi:10.1111/rec.12554.

Martinez-Soto, J., L. G. Santos and F. Barrios (2015). *The Influence of Exposure to Restorative Environments in the Brain Resting State Networks.* Los Angeles: Environmental Design and Research Association.

Marvin, S. and W. Medd (2006). Flows of Fat through Bodies, Cities, and Sewers. *In the Nature of Cities: Urban Political Ecology and the Politics of Urban Metabolism.* N. Heynen, M. Kaika and E. Syngedouw. New York: Routledge: 143–156.

Mennis, J., M. Mason and A. Ambrus (2018). "Urban greenspace is associated with reduced psychological stress among adolescents: A Geographic Ecological Momentary Assessment (GEMA) analysis of activity space." *Landscape and Urban Planning* **174**: 1–9. https://doi.org/10.1016/j.landurbplan.2018.02.008.

Merchant, C. (1995). Reinventing Nature: Western Culture as a Recovery Narrative. *Uncommon Ground.* W. Cronon. New York: W. W. Norton & Company: 132–159.

Meyer, M. A., J. Rathmann and C. Schulz (2019). "Spatially-explicit mapping of forest benefits and analysis of motivations for everyday-life's visitors on forest pathways in urban and rural contexts." *Landscape and Urban Planning* **185**: 83–95. https://doi.org/10.1016/j.landurbplan.2019.01.007.

Millennial Ecosystem Assessment (2003). Washington, DC: Island Press.

Milligan, C. and A. Bingley (2007). "Restorative places or scary spaces? The impact of woodland on the mental well-being of young adults." *Health and Place* **13**: 799–811. doi:10.1016/j.healthplace.2007.01.005.

Millington, J. D. A. and J. Wainwright (2017). "Mixed qualitative-simulation methods: Understanding geography through thick and thin." *Progress in Human Geography* **41**(1): 68–88. doi:10.1177/0309132515627021.

Morris, J. and E. O'Brien (2011). "Encouraging healthy outdoor activity amongst under-represented groups: An evaluation of the Active England woodland projects." *Urban Forestry and Urban Greening* **10**(4): 323–333. http://dx.doi.org/10.1016/j.ufug.2011.05.006.

Mountz, A. (2018). "Political geography III: Bodies." *Progress in Human Geography* **42**(5): 759–769. doi:10.1177/0309132517718642.

Muir, J. (1997). *Nature Writings 1838–1914.* New York: Library of America.

Muratet, A., P. Pellegrini, A.-B. Dufour, T. Arrif and F. Chiron (2015). "Perception and knowledge of plant diversity among urban park users." *Landscape and Urban Planning* **137**(0): 95–106. http://dx.doi.org/10.1016/j.landurbplan.2015.01.003.

Nash, R. (1982). *Wilderness and the American Mind.* Binghamton, NY: Yale University Press.

Neely, A. H. and A. M. Nading (2017). "Global health from the outside: The promise of place-based research." *Health and Place* **45**: 55–63. https://doi.org/10.1016/j.healthplace.2017.03.001.

Nelson, M. P. (1996). "Rethinking wilderness: The need for a new idea of wilderness." *Philosophy in the Contemporary World* **3**(2): 6–9. doi:10.5840/pcw1996328.

Neumann, R. P. (2011). "Political ecology III: Theorizing landscape." *Progress in Human Geography* **35**(6): 843–850. doi:10.1177/0309132510390870.

Newell, J. P. and J. J. Cousins (2014). "The boundaries of urban metabolism: Towards a political–industrial ecology." *Progress in Human Geography* **39**(6): 702–728. doi:10.1177/0309132514558442.

Nilsson, E. E., I. Sadler-Riggleman and M. K. Skinner (2018). "Environmentally induced epigenetic transgenerational inheritance of disease." *Environmental Epigenetics* **4**(2). doi:10.1093/eep/dvy016.

Norwood, M. F., A. Lakhani, S. Fullagar, A. Maujean, M. Downes, J. Byrne, A. Stewart, B. Barber and E. Kendall (2019). "A narrative and systematic review of the behavioural, cognitive and emotional effects of passive nature exposure on young people: Evidence for prescribing change." *Landscape and Urban Planning* **189**: 71–79. https://doi.org/10.1016/j.landurbplan.2019.04.007.

Olszewska-Guizzo, A., N. Escoffier, J. Chan and T. Puay Yok (2018). "Window view and the brain: Effects of floor level and green cover on the alpha and beta rhythms in a passive exposure EEG experiment." *International Journal of Environmental Research and Public Health* **15**(11): 2358. doi:10.3390/ijerph15112358.

Olwig, K. (1995). Reinventing Common Nature: Yosemite and Mount Rushmore – A Meandering Tale of Double Nature. *Uncommon Ground*. W. Cronon. New York: W. W. Norton & Co.**:** 279–407.

Ossola, A., D. Locke, B. Lin and E. Minor (2019). "Greening in style: Urban form, architecture and the structure of front and backyard vegetation." *Landscape and Urban Planning* **185**: 141–157. https://doi.org/10.1016/j.landurbplan.2019.02.014.

Ozguner, H. and A. D. Kendle (2006). "Public attitudes towards naturalistic versus designed landscapes in the city of Sheffield (UK)." *Landscape and Urban Planning* **74**(2): 139–157. https://doi.org/10.1016/j.landurbplan.2004.10.003.

Palardy, N. P., B. B. Boley and C. J. Gaither (2018a). "Resident support for urban greenways across diverse neighborhoods: Comparing two Atlanta BeltLine segments." *Landscape and Urban Planning* **180**: 223–233. https://doi.org/10.1016/j.landurbplan.2018.08.021.

Palardy, N. P., B. B. Boley and C. J. Gaither (2018b). "Residents and urban greenways: Modeling support for the Atlanta BeltLine." *Landscape and Urban Planning* **169**: 250–259. https://doi.org/10.1016/j.landurbplan.2017.09.006.

Palmer, J. F. and D. B. K. English (2019). "An index of viewer sensitivity to scenery while engaged in recreation activities on U.S. National Forests." *Landscape and Urban Planning* **189**: 91–98. https://doi.org/10.1016/j.landurbplan.2019.03.006.

Paquet, C., T. P. Orschulok, N. T. Coffee, N. J. Howard, G. Hugo, A. W. Taylor, R. J. Adams and M. Daniel (2013). "Are accessibility and characteristics of public open spaces associated with a better cardiometabolic health?" *Landscape and Urban Planning* **118**(0): 70–78. http://dx.doi.org/10.1016/j.landurbplan.2012.11.011.

Park, B.-J., Y. Tsunetsugu, T. Kasetani, T. Kagawa and Y. Miyazaki (2010). "The physiological effects of *Shinrin-yoku* (taking in the forest atmosphere or forest bathing): Evidence from field experiments in 24 forests across Japan." *Environmental Health and Preventive Medicine* **15**: 18–26. doi:10.1007/s12199-009-0086-9.

Parsons, R. (1991). "The potential influences of environmental perception on human health." *Journal of Environmental Psychology* **11**: 1–23. https://doi.org/10.1016/S0272-4944(05)80002-7.

Pasanen, T. P., M. Neuvonen and K. M. Korpela (2018). "The psychology of recent nature visits: (How) are motives and attentional focus related to post-visit restorative experiences, creativity, and emotional well-being?" *Environment and Behavior* **50**(8): 913–944. doi:10.1177/0013916517720261.

Paterson, M. (2009). "Haptic geographies: Ethnography, haptic knowledges and sensuous dispositions." *Progress in Human Geography* **33**(6): 766–788. doi:10.1177/0309132509103155.

Patterson, M. E. and D. R. Williams (2005). "Maintaining research traditions on place: Diversity of thought and scientific progress." *Journal of Environmental Psychology* **25**(4): 361–380. doi:10.1016/j.jenvp. 2005.10.001.

Pearce, L. M., A. Davison and J. B. Kirkpatrick (2015). "Personal encounters with trees: The lived significance of the private urban forest." *Urban Forestry and Urban Greening* **14**(1): 1–7. http://dx.doi.org/10.1016/j.ufug.2014.11.003.

Pearson, A. L., A. Rzotkiewicz, J. L. Pechal, C. J. Schmidt, H. R. Jordan, A. Zwickle and M. E. Benbow (2019). "Initial evidence of the relationships between the human postmortem microbiome and neighborhood blight and greening efforts." *Annals of the American Association of Geographers* **109**(3): 958–978. 10.1080/24694452.2018.1519407.

Perrin, J. L. and V. A. Benassi (2009). "The connectedness to nature scale: A measure of emotional connection to nature?" *Journal of Environmental Psychology* **29**(4): 434–440. https://doi.org/10.1016/j.jenvp. 2009.03.003.

Petrovic, N., T. Simpson, B. Orlove and B. Dowd-Uribe (2019). "Environmental and social dimensions of community gardens in East Harlem." *Landscape and Urban Planning* **183**: 36–49. doi:10.1016/j.landurbplan.2018.10.009.

Pham, T.-T.-H., D. Labbé, U. Lachapelle and É. Pelletier (2019). "Perception of park access and park use amongst youth in Hanoi: How cultural and local context matters." *Landscape and Urban Planning* **189**: 156–165. https://doi.org/10.1016/j.landurbplan.2019.04.021.

Pilotti, M., E. Klein, D. Golem, E. Piepenbrink and K. Kaplan (2015). "Is viewing a nature video after work restorative? Effects on blood pressure, task performance, and long-term memory." *Environment and Behavior* **47**(9): 947–969. doi:10.1177/0013916514533187.

Plambech, T. and C. C. Konijnendijk van den Bosch (2015). "The impact of nature on creativity: A study among Danish creative professionals." *Urban Forestry and Urban Greening* **14**(2): 255–263. http://dx.doi.org/10.1016/j.ufug.2015.02.006.

Plunz, R. A., Y. Zhou, M. I. Carrasco Vintimilla, K. McKeown, T. Yu, L. Uguccioni and M. P. Sutto (2019). "Twitter sentiment in New York City parks as measure of well-being." *Landscape and Urban Planning* **189**: 235–246. https://doi.org/10.1016/j.landurbplan.2019.04.024.

Prior, L., D. Manley and C. E. Sabel (2019). "Biosocial health geography: New 'exposomic' geographies of health and place." *Progress in Human Geography* **43**(3): 531–552. doi:10.1177/0309132518772644.

Proctor, J. D. (1995). Whose Nature? The Contested Moral Terrain of Ancient Forests. *Uncommon Ground.* W. Cronon. New York: W. W. Norton & Co.: 269–297.

Prudham, S. (2005). *Knock on Wood: Nature as Commodity in Douglas-Fir Country*. London: Routledge.

Radil, S. M. and O. J. Walther (2018) "Social networks and geography: A review of the literature and its implications." *arXiv e-prints*.

Ratcliffe, E. and K. M. Korpela (2018). "Time- and self-related memories predict restorative perceptions of favorite places via place identity." *Environment and Behavior* **50**(6): 690–720. doi:10.1177/0013916517712002.

Ratcliffe, E., B. Gatersleben and P. T. Sowden (2013). "Bird sounds and their contributions to perceived attention restoration and stress recovery." *Journal of Environmental Psychology* **36**: 221–228. http://dx.doi.org/10.1016/j.jenvp.2013.08.004.

Razani, N., K. Niknam, N. M. Wells, D. Thompson, N. K. Hills, G. Kennedy, R. Gilgoff and G. W. Rutherford (2019). "Clinic and park partnerships for childhood resilience: A prospective study of park prescriptions." *Health and Place* **57**: 179–185. https://doi.org/10.1016/j.healthplace.2019.04.008.

Rega-Brodsky, C., C. Nilon and P. Warren (2018). "Balancing urban biodiversity needs and resident preferences for vacant lot management." *Sustainability* 10(5). doi:10.3390/su10051679.

Relph, E. (1985). "Geographical Experiences and Being-in-the-World: The Phenomenological Origins of Geography." *Dwelling, Place, Environment.* D. Seamon and R. Mugerauer. Oxford, New York: Columbia University Press: 15–31.

Relph, E. (2008). "Senses of Place and Emerging Social and Environmental Challenges." *Sense of Place, Health and Quality of Life*. J. Eyles and A. Williams. Aldershot, Hampshire: Ashgate.

Reuben, A. (2019) "Science's newest miracle drug is free." *Outside*, May 1.

Reyes, M., A. Páez and C. Morency (2014). "Walking accessibility to urban parks by children: A case study of Montreal." *Landscape and Urban Planning* **125**(0): 38–47. http://dx.doi.org/10.1016/j.landurbplan.2014.02.002.

Reynolds, L., S. Rodiek, M. Lininger and M. A. McCulley (2018). "Can a virtual nature experience reduce anxiety and agitation in people with dementia?" *Journal of Housing for the Elderly* **32**(2): 176–193. doi:10.1080/02763893.2018.1431583.

Robbins, P. (2004). *Political Ecology: A Critical Introduction*. Malden, MA: Blackwell Publishing.

Robbins, P. and J. Sharp (2003). "Producing and consuming chemicals: The moral economy of the American lawn." *Economic Geography* **79**: 425–451.

Roberts, A. C. and G. I. Christopoulos (2018). "Comment on 'Using functional Magnetic Resonance Imaging (fMRI) to analyze brain region activity when viewing landscapes'." *Landscape and Urban Planning* **172**: 25–28. https://doi.org/10.1016/j.landurbplan.2017.12.006.

Roberts, H., J. Sadler and L. Chapman (2019). "The value of Twitter data for determining the emotional responses of people to urban green spaces: A case study and critical evaluation." *Urban Studies* **56**(4): 818–835. doi:10.1177/0042098017748544.

Rode, R. (2017). The Past and Future of Indigenous Peoples' Heritage: Transforming the Legacies of Non-sustainability of Protected Areas. *Going Beyond.* Springer: 247–261.

Roe, J. and P. Aspinall (2011). "The restorative outcomes of forest school and conventional school in young people with good and poor behaviour." *Urban Forestry and Urban Greening* **10**(3): 205–212. http://dx.doi.org/10.1016/j.ufug.2011.03.003.

Schebella, M. F., D. Weber, L. Schultz and P. Weinstein (2019). "The wellbeing benefits associated with perceived and measured biodiversity in Australian urban green spaces." *Sustainability* **11**(3): 802. doi:10.3390/su11030802.

Schipperijn, J., P. Bentsen, J. Troelsen, M. Toftager and U. K. Stigsdotter (2013). "Associations between physical activity and characteristics of urban green space." *Urban Forestry and Urban Greening* **12**(1): 109–116. http://dx.doi.org/10.1016/j.ufug.2012.12.002.

Schirpke, U., A. Altzinger, G. Leitinger and E. Tasser (2019). "Change from agricultural to touristic use: Effects on the aesthetic value of landscapes over the last 150 years." *Landscape and Urban Planning* **187**: 23–35. https://doi.org/10.1016/j.landurbplan.2019.03.004.

School of Architecture (2018). "Biophilic Cities: Expanding its Global Network." *UVA Arts* **8**. Charlottesville: University of Virginia.

Schultz, W. P., C. Shriver, J. J. Tabanico and A. M. Khanzian (2004). "Implicit connections with nature." *Journal of Environmental Psychology* **24**: 31–42. https://doi.org/10.1016/S0272-4944(03)00022-7.

Schultz, W. P. and L. C. Zelezny (1999). "Values as predictors of environmental attitudes: Evidence for consistency across cultures." *Journal of Environmental Psychology* **19**: 255–265. https://doi.org/10.1006/jevp. 1999.0129.

Scopelliti, M., G. Carrus and M. Bonaiuto (2019). "Is it really nature that restores people? A comparison with historical sites with high restorative potential." *Frontiers in Psychology* **9**(2742). doi:10.3389/fpsyg.2018.02742.

Sherman, S. A., J. W. Varni, R. S. Ulrich and V. L. Malcarne (2005). "Post-occupancy evaluation of healing gardens in a pediatric cancer center." *Landscape and Urban Planning* **73**(2–3): 167–183. https://doi.org/10.1016/j.landurbplan.2004.11.013.

Shibata, S. and N. Suzuki (2002). "Effects of the foliage plant on task performance and mood." *Journal of Environmental Psychology* **22**: 265–272. https://doi.org/10.1006/jevp.2002.0232.

Simonsen, K. (2013). "In quest of a new humanism: Embodiment, experience and phenomenology as critical geography." *Progress in Human Geography* **37**(1): 10–26. doi:10.1177/0309132512467573.

Simpson, M. and J. Bagelman (2018). "Decolonizing urban political ecologies: The production of nature in settler colonial cities." *Annals of the American Association of Geographers* **108**(2): 558–568. doi:10.1080/24694452.2017.1392285.

Skår, M. (2010). "Forest dear and forest fear: Dwellers' relationships to their neighbourhood forest." *Landscape and Urban Planning* **98**(2): 110–116. http://dx.doi.org/10.1016/j.landurbplan.2010.07.017.

Smith, N. (1984). *Uneven Deveolopment: Nature, Capital and the Production of Space*. Oxford: Blackwell.

Smith, N. (1996). "The Production of Nature." *Future Natural: Nature, Science, Culture*. Melinda Mash, George Robertson, Lisa Tickner, Jon Bird, Barry Curtis and Tim Putnam. London: Routledge: 35–54.

Smith, T. S. J. and L. Reid (2018). "Which 'being' in wellbeing? Ontology, wellness and the geographies of happiness." *Progress in Human Geography* **42**(6): 807–829. doi:10.1177/0309132517717100.

Sonntag-Öström, E., M. Nordin, Y. Lundell, A. Dolling, U. Wiklund, M. Karlsson, B. Carlberg and L. Slunga Järvholm (2014). "Restorative effects of visits to urban and forest environments in patients with exhaustion disorder." *Urban Forestry and Urban Greening* **13**(2): 344–354. http://dx.doi.org/10.1016/j.ufug.2013.12.007.

Southon, G. E., A. Jorgensen, N. Dunnett, H. Hoyle and K. L. Evans (2018). "Perceived species-richness in urban green spaces: Cues, accuracy and well-being impacts." *Landscape and Urban Planning* **172**: 1–10. doi:10.1016/j.landurbplan.2017.12.002.

Stedman, R. C. (2003). "Is it really just a social construction? The contribution of the physical environment to sense of place." *Society and Natural Resources* **16**(8): 671–685. doi:10.1080/08941920309189.

Stigsdotter, U. K. and P. Grahn (2011). "Stressed individuals' preferences for activities and environmental characteristics in green spaces." *Urban Forestry and Urban Greening* **10**(4): 295–304. http://dx.doi.org/10.1016/j.ufug.2011.07.001.

Sugiyama, T., A. Carver, M. J. Koohsari and J. Veitch (2018). "Advantages of public green spaces in enhancing population health." *Landscape and Urban Planning* **178**: 12–17. https://doi.org/10.1016/j.landurbplan.2018.05.019.

Sullivan, W. C., H. Frumkin, R. J. Jackson and C.-Y. Chang (2014). "Gaia meets Asclepius: Creating healthy places." *Landscape and Urban Planning* **127**(0): 182–184. http://dx.doi.org/10.1016/j.landurbplan.2014.03.005.

Sullivan, W. C., F. E. Kuo and S. F. DePooter (2004). "The fruit of urban nature: Vital neighborhood spaces." *Environment and Behavior* **36**(5): 678–700. https://doi.org/10.1177/0193841X04264945.

Talbot, C. (1998). "The Wilderness Narrative and the Cultural Logic of Capitalism." *The Great New Wilderness Debate*. J. B. Callicott and M. P. Nelson. Athens. Georgia: University of Georgia Press: 325–333.

Taylor, A. F., F. E. Kuo and W. C. Sullivan (2001). "Coping with ADD: The surprising connection to green play settings." *Environment and Behaviour* **33**(1): 54–77. https://doi.org/10.1177/00139160121972864.

Taylor, M. S., B. W. Wheeler, M. P. White, T. Economou and N. J. Osborne (2015). "Research note: Urban street tree density and antidepressant prescription rates – A cross-sectional study in London, UK." *Landscape and Urban Planning* **136**(0): 174–179. http://dx.doi.org/10.1016/j.landurbplan.2014.12.005.

Tennessen, C. and B. Cimprich (1995). "Views to nature: Effects on attention." *Journal of Environmental Psychology* **15**(1): 77–85. https://doi.org/10.1016/0272-4944(95)90016-0Get.

Thoreau, H. D. (2004). *Walden*. New Haven and London: Yale University Press.

Thrift, N. (2005). "From born to made: Technology, biology and space." *Transactions of the Institute of British Geographers* **30**: 463–476. https://doi.org/10.1111/j.1475-5661.2005.00184.x.

Tsunetsugu, Y., J. Lee, B.-J. Park, L. Tyrväinen, T. Kagawa and Y. Miyazaki (2013). "Physiological and psychological effects of viewing urban forest landscapes assessed by multiple measurements." *Landscape and Urban Planning* **113**(0): 90–93. http://dx.doi.org/10.1016/j.landurbplan.2013.01.014.

Tuan, Y.-F. (1990). *Topophilia: A Study of Environmental Perception, Attitudes, and Values*. New York: Columbia University Press.

Tyrväinen, L., A. Ojala, K. M. Korpela, T. Lanki, Y. Tsunetsugu and T. Kagawa (2014). "The influence of urban green environments on stress relief measures: A field experiment." *Journal of Environmental Psychology* **38**: 1–9. http://dx.doi.org/10.1016/j.jenvp.2013.12.005.

Uhlmann, K., B. B. Lin and H. Ross (2018). "Who cares? The importance of emotional connections with nature to ensure food security and wellbeing in cities." *Sustainability* **10**(6): 1844. https://doi.org/10.3390/su10061844.

Ulrich, R. S. (1981). "Natural versus urban sciences: Some psycho-physiological effects." *Environment and Behaviour* **13**: 523–556. http://dx.doi.org/10.1177/0013916581135001.

Ulrich, R. S. (1984). "View through a window may influence recovery from surgery." *Science* **224**(4647): 420–421. doi:10.1126/science.6143402.

Ulrich, R. S. (1986). "Human responses to vegetation and landscapes." *Landscape and Urban Planning* **13**: 29–44. https://doi.org/10.1016/0169-2046(86)90005-8.

Ulrich, R. S. (1993). "Biophilia, Biophobia, and Natural Landscapes." *The Biophilia Hypothesis*. S. W. Kellert and Edward O. Washington, DC: Island Press**:** 73–137.

Uzzell, D. and N. Rathzel (2009). "Transforming Environmental Psychology." *Journal of Environmental Psychology* **29**(3): 340–350. https://doi.org/10.1016/j.jenvp.2008.11.005.

van den Berg, A. E., A. Jorgensen and E. R. Wilson (2014). "Evaluating restoration in urban green spaces: Does setting type make a difference?" *Landscape and Urban Planning* **127**(0): 173–181. http://dx.doi.org/10.1016/j.landurbplan.2014.04.012.

van den Berg, A. E., C. A. J. Vlek and J. F. Coeterier (1998). Group differences in the aesthetic evaluation of nature development plans: A multilevel approach. *Journal of Environmental Psychology* **18:** 141.

van den Berg, M. M., M. van Poppel, I. van Kamp, A. Ruijsbroek, M. Triguero-Mas, C. Gidlow, M. J. Nieuwenhuijsen, R. Gražulevičiene, W. van Mechelen, H. Kruize and J. Maas (2019). "Do physical activity, social cohesion, and loneliness mediate the association between time spent visiting green space and mental health?" *Environment and Behavior* **51**(2): 144–166. doi:10.1177/0013916517738563.

van der Jagt, A. P. N., T. Craig, J. Anable, M. J. Brewer and D. G. Pearson (2014). "Unearthing the picturesque: The validity of the preference matrix as a measure of landscape aesthetics." *Landscape and Urban Planning* **124**(0): 1–13. http://dx.doi.org/10.1016/j.landurbplan.2013.12.006.

van der Wal, R., D. Miller, J. Irvine, S. Fiorini, A. Amar, S. Yearley, R. Gill and N. Dandy (2014). "The influence of information provision on people's landscape preferences: A case study on understorey vegetation of deer-browsed woodlands." *Landscape and Urban Planning* **124**(0): 129–139. http://dx.doi.org/10.1016/j.landurbplan.2014.01.009.

van Dijk-Wesselius, J. E., J. Maas, D. Hovinga, M. van Vugt and A. E. van den Berg (2018). "The impact of greening schoolyards on the appreciation, and physical, cognitive and social-emotional well-being of schoolchildren: A prospective intervention study." *Landscape and Urban Planning* **180**: 15–26. https://doi.org/10.1016/j.landurbplan.2018.08.003.

Vich, G., O. Marquet and C. Miralles-Guasch (2019). "Green streetscape and walking: Exploring active mobility patterns in dense and compact cities." *Journal of Transport and Health* **12**: 50–59. https://doi.org/10.1016/j.jth.2018.11.003.

Villeneuve, P. J., M. Jerrett, J. G. Su, S. Weichenthal and D. P. Sandler (2018). "Association of residential greenness with obesity and physical activity in a US cohort of women." *Environmental Research* **160**: 372–384. doi:10.1016/j.envres.2017.10.005.

von Lindern, E., N. Bauer, J. Frick, M. Hunziker and T. Hartig (2013). "Occupational engagement as a constraint on restoration during leisure time in forest settings." *Landscape and Urban Planning* **118**(0): 90–97. http://dx.doi.org/10.1016/j.landurbplan.2013.03.001.

Wachsmuth, D. and H. Angelo (2018). "Green and gray: New ideologies of nature in urban sustainability policy." *Annals of the American Association of Geographers* **108**(4): 1038–1056. doi:10.1080/24694452.2017.1417819.

Waller, D. M. (1998). "Getting back to the Right Nature: A Reply to Cronon's 'The Trouble with Wilderness'." *The Great New Wilderness Debate.* J. B. Callicott and M. P. Nelson. Athens, Georgia: University of Georgia Press: 540–567.

Wang, C.-H., N.-W. Kuo and K. Anthony (2019). "Impact of window views on recovery: An example of post-cesarean section women." *International Journal for Quality in Health Care.* doi:10.1093/intqhc/mzz046.

Wang, D., G. Brown and Y. Liu (2015). "The physical and non-physical factors that influence perceived access to urban parks." *Landscape and Urban Planning* **133**(0): 53–66. http://dx.doi.org/10.1016/j.landurbplan.2014.09.007.

Wang, J., L. Geng, P. W. Schultz and K. Zhou (2019). "Mindfulness increases the belief in climate change: The mediating role of connectedness with nature." *Environment and Behavior* **51**(1): 3–23. doi:10.1177/0013916517738036.

Ward Thompson, C., J. Roe and P. Aspinall (2013). "Woodland improvements in deprived urban communities: What impact do they have on people's activities and quality of life?" *Landscape and Urban Planning* **118**(0): 79–89. http://dx.doi.org/10.1016/j.landurbplan.2013.02.001.

Ward Thompson, C., J. Roe, P. Aspinall, R. Mitchell, A. Clow and D. Miller (2012). "More green space is linked to less stress in deprived communities: Evidence from salivary cortisol patterns." *Landscape and Urban Planning* **105**(3): 221–229. http://dx.doi.org/10.1016/j.landurbplan.2011.12.015.

Wartmann, F. M. and R. S. Purves (2018). "Investigating sense of place as a cultural ecosystem service in different landscapes through the lens of language." *Landscape and Urban Planning* **175**: 169–183. https://doi.org/10.1016/j.landurbplan.2018.03.021.

Wells, N. M. (2000). "At home with nature: Effects of 'greenness' on children's cognitive functioning." *Environment and Behavior* **32**(6): 775–795. https://doi.org/10.1177/00139160021972793.

Whaley, L. (2018). "Geographies of the self: Space, place, and scale revisited." *Human Arenas* **1**(1): 21–36. doi:10.1007/s42087-018-0006-x.

White, R. (1995). "Are you an environmentalist or do you work for a living?" *Uncommon Ground.* W. Cronon. New York: W. W. Norton & Co.: 171–185.

Wilkie, S. and H. Clements (2018). "Further exploration of environment preference and environment type congruence on restoration and perceived restoration potential." *Landscape and Urban Planning* **170**: 314–319. https://doi.org/10.1016/j.landurbplan.2017.04.013.

Wilkie, S. and L. Clouston (2015). "Environment preference and environment type congruence: Effects on perceived restoration potential and restoration outcomes." *Urban Forestry and Urban Greening* **14**(2): 368–376. http://dx.doi.org/10.1016/j.ufug.2015.03.002.

Wilkie, S. and A. Stavridou (2013). "Influence of environmental preference and environment type congruence on judgments of restoration potential." *Urban Forestry and Urban Greening* **12**(2): 163–170. http://dx.doi.org/10.1016/j.ufug.2013.01.004.

Willems-Braun, B. (1997). "Buried epistemologies: The politics of nature in (post)colonial British Columbia." *Annals of the Association of American Geographers* **87**(1): 3–31. https://doi.org/10.1111/0004-5608.00039.

Williams, D. R. (2014). "Making sense of 'place': Reflections on pluralism and positionality in place research." *Landscape and Urban Planning* **131**(0): 74–82. http://dx.doi.org/10.1016/j.landurbplan.2014.08.002.

Williams, D. R. and M. E. Patterson (2007). "Snapshots of what, exactly? A comment on methodological experimentation and conceptual foundations in place research." *Society and Natural Resources* **20**: 931–937. https://doi.org/10.1080/08941920701537015.

Williams, D. R. and M. E. Patterson (2008). "Place, Leisure, and Well-Being." *Sense of Place, Health, and Quality of Life.* J. Eyles and A. Williams. Aldershot, UK: Ashgate: 105–119.

Williams, R. (1973). *The Country and the City.* New York: Oxford University Press.

Williams, R. (1976). *Keywords*. Glasgow: William Collins Sons and Co.

Wilson, E. O. (1984). *Biophilia*. Cambridge, Massachusetts, and London, UK: Harvard University Press.

Woodyer, T. and H. Geoghegan (2013). "(Re)enchanting geography? The nature of being critical and the character of critique in human geography." *Progress in Human Geography* **37**(2): 195–214. doi:10.1177/0309132512460905.

Wright, M. W. (2010). "Geography and gender: Feminism and a feeling of justice." *Progress in Human Geography* **34**(6): 818–827. doi:10.1177/0309132510362931.

Wu, J. (2013). "Landscape sustainability science: Ecosystem services and human well-being in changing landscapes." *Landscape Ecology* **28**(6): 999–1023. doi:10.1007/s10980-013-9894-9.

Wyles, K. J., M. P. White, C. Hattam, S. Pahl, H. King and M. Austen (2019). "Are some natural environments more psychologically beneficial than others? The importance of type and quality on connectedness to nature and psychological restoration." *Environment and Behavior* **51**(2): 111–143. doi:10.1177/0013916517738312.

Young, R. F. (2010). "Managing municipal green space for ecosystem services." *Urban Forestry and Urban Greening* **9**(4): 313–321. http://dx.doi.org/10.1016/j.ufug.2010.06.007.

Yu, K. (1995). "Cultural variations in landscape preference: Comparisons among Chinese sub-groups and Western design experts." *Landscape and Urban Planning* **32:** 107.

Zhang, H., B. Chen, Z. Sun and Z. Bao (2013). "Landscape perception and recreation needs in urban green space in Fuyang, Hangzhou, China." *Urban Forestry and Urban Greening* **12**(1): 44–52. http://dx.doi.org/10.1016/j.ufug.2012.11.001.

Zhang, J. W., R. T. Howell and R. Iyer (2014). "Engagement with natural beauty moderates the positive relation between connectedness with nature and psychological well-being." *Journal of Environmental Psychology* **38**: 55–63. http://dx.doi.org/10.1016/j.jenvp.2013.12.013.

2
ECOLOGY IN THE MARGINS
Green infrastructure and stormwater management

Introduction

Highlighting the damage to salmon runs from polluted urban stormwater runoff were some of the first – and most memorable – iterations of 'green infrastructure' for stormwater management in the U.S. Seen most often in west coast 'environmentalist' cities with a history of advocacy and environmentalism, such as Portland, Oregon, and Seattle, Washington, this link between the ways cities are designed and built and their 'ecological footprint' followed from an environmental aesthetic particular to the region: as articulated by one of Portland's leading advocates for green infrastructure: "Here in the rainy Pacific Northwest, water and nature inextricably linked to forests and salmon, each of which have deep cultural and economic roots dating back for millennia" (Liptan 2017). This approach highlighted the impact of polluted stormwater overflow on wildlife habitat (Environmental Services n.d.; Seattle Public Utilities n.d.) and advocated for a different and more harmonious approach to urban infrastructure (Liptan 2017; Environmental Services n.d.), often through innovative pilot projects. Some of the most influential projects were Seattle's ground-breaking pilot projects such as the 2nd Avenue Street Edge Alternatives (SEA) street, which took away sidewalks and integrated stormwater vegetation into a curvy street edge, or their Green Area Factor (GAF), which makes projects 'replace' or compensate for any natural land lost to development that could have absorbed stormwater, a concept originally from Germany (Senate Deparment of Urban Development in Berlin 2005). These green infrastructure (GI) initiatives have since evolved into more complex programs that aim to absorb stormwater runoff at the source; they are still used as models for other cities wanting to implement green infrastructure and are staples in green infrastructure guides (National Association of City Transportation Officials n.d.).

Now, however, many cities, and not just traditionally 'green' cities such as Portland and Seattle, are implementing innovative solutions to stormwater management and urban greening. Shifting expectations and knowledge around the socio-cultural 'co-benefits' of urban greening are changing the way cities are thinking about and addressing stormwater management strategies, the oldest form of green infrastructure. While there are many cities adopting GI in North America (Brown 2017), the case studies in this chapter exemplify the pressures to create solutions that meet both ecosystem and socio-economic goals. Philadelphia is the first city in North America to adopt a city-wide implementation of GI to meet federal and state requirements *and* socio-economic benefits. That it has managed to do this successfully with limited funds and significant socio-economic inequalities makes it an interesting example of the new innovative approaches to urban greening outlined in the introduction. Conversely, Toronto, which *does* have a long history as an environmentally progressive city (City of Toronto 2000; City of Toronto 2007c; Green Roofs for Healthy Cities n.d.) – though not necessarily for stormwater management – is also trying to balance ecological and socio-cultural concerns but is being slowed down by numerous institutional, policy, and knowledge barriers that are common to cities (and in particular Canadian cities) trying to implement GI with varying levels of success (Johns 2019b).

Both Philadelphia and Toronto are instructive examples of green infrastructure, one of the three types of urban greening currently happening in cities in North America, which also include elevated greenspace and greenspace in vacant lots and post-industrial interstitial spaces. They are also good examples of *why* small-scale urban greening (SSUG) is happening: cities are placing increased attention on the ecological benefits that urban nature can have and on the use of in-between, or interstitial, spaces, to which the addition of urban greenspace can bring multiple benefits. Philadelphia and Toronto also offer insight into both the possibilities and limitations for GI implementation under two different political systems – American and Canadian – with significant differences in power distribution between municipal, state/provincial, and federal scales (Johns 2019b). Though any comparison between American and Canadian cities should be made with caution, given the traditionally higher levels of autonomy and revenue-raising power of most U.S. cities over their Canadian counterparts (Rothblatt 1994), recent campaigns for increased fiscal and political autonomy have seen Toronto move closer to the level of power and autonomy seen in U.S. cities (Rothblatt 1994; City of Toronto 2007b). Furthermore, Pennsylvania also has a unique 'power sharing' system among different levels of government, which facilitates comparison between the cities (Stormwater PA n.d.).

Research questions and chapter structure

This chapter and the next focus on green infrastructure: this chapter will explore Philadelphia and Toronto's approaches to green infrastructure for stormwater management, while Chapter 3 will look at green roofs, using two case studies from leading cities in green roof implementation in North America (Chicago and Toronto). While each case study will cover policy and implementation (discussed again in the conclusion), the focus is more on the intersection of research and real-world implementation, and the resulting implications for SSUG and health, well-being, and sense of place. This 'research lens' links the case studies in this chapter to the research debates covered in Chapter 1, which provides context for understanding the on-the-ground issues, debates, and conflicts that are currently happening in cities implementing SSUG projects.

Key areas of inquiry framing this chapter include: (1) if, how, and by whom research is being used to justify and implement the projects detailed in the cases studies; (2) how factors around implementation (such as funding sources and larger policy goals) impact the design of the projects; (3) what key insights and results these projects yield; and (4) what gaps and current issues have been identified (see Tables 2.1 and 2.2). While this chapter will give an overview of each city's approach to stormwater, given that the majority of impervious cover in cities is often the streetscape (Philadelphia Water Department n.d.-b), and the focus of the book is greening in interstitial spaces, this chapter will examine urban greening through the lens of 'green street' guidelines, or the public right of way (ROW).

Ecosystem services, green infrastructure, and stormwater: a short history of re-thinking water in cities

There is general agreement that modern public health began in the 1840s in England, when, along with Dr. John Snow's famous cholera and water pump experiment, a series of interventions led to the Victorian sanitation movement (Youngson 1979; Ashton 1992), which dramatically reduced mortality and disease. However, along with these boons for health – and the arrival of the automobile – came the 'pave, pipe, and pump' (Knight 2017) approach to urban development. The modernist city is a legacy of this tradition, in which any evidence of 'wild' or 'dirty' nature and flows are hidden and whisked quickly out of the city via buried streams and large pipes, and through an urban façade of glass, concrete, and neatly manicured lawns (Hough 1984; Kaika 2006; Kolbert 2008). As we know now, however, as cities became increasingly paved over a host of urban environmental problems started to appear – hotter and hotter summers, a loss of habitat and greenspace, and increased flooding (Chen, Yao et al. 2014; Zhang, Xie et al. 2015; Nowak and Greenfield 2018; Du, Cheng et al.

2019). Water that would normally be absorbed by soil and plants was now being channeled into pipes and sewers that were increasingly unable to contain large storm events, leading to flooding, waterway pollution, and stream erosion (Yang, Endreny et al. 2015). The recognition of these issues coincided with a larger environmental movement in the 1990s that focused less on urban nature as a refuge against the ills of the city, and more on how to reduce harm to nature outside the city (Sinha 2014).

Bringing ecology into the city

While the earliest understanding of this problem was linked to habitat destruction and pollution of rivers and streams *outside* cities, sometimes called an 'ecological footprint' approach (Rees and Wackernagel 2008), worsening urban environmental issues due to climate change have led to a more 'ecological' approach to nature *within* cities. The increasing prominence of ecology in conceptualizing urban nature can be seen in three ways. First, researchers and city planners are recognizing the active role nature plays in cities. Historically valued and understood as a scenic, static leisure amenity outside the city – viewed from a window, or enjoyed during a Sunday afternoon stroll – nature is now seen as having agency or power on its own (Braun 2005; Thrift 2005; Braun 2008; Lorimer, Hodgetts et al. 2019). This power can be destructive – for example, flooding and eroding streambeds, streets, and basements if left unchecked – or useful – as 'ecosystem services' or 'green infrastructure' that could manage on site much of the stormwater overflow without the cost of traditional big-pipe solutions. The majority of academic research on this topic studies exactly *how* ecosystem services can be useful by mitigating extremes from climate change, particularly by reducing heat extremes, air pollution, or flooding (Ketterer and Matzarakis 2014; Netusil, Levin et al. 2014; Middel, Chhetri et al. 2015) and thereby increasing resilience (Olsson, Jerneck et al. 2015; Dhakal and Chevalier 2016; Masoudi and Tan 2019; Szota, Coutts et al. 2019; Yang and Bou-Zeid 2019). Second, the language, metaphors, and way of thinking about ecology started to influence city planning. Discussions of habitat, patches, corridors, and the interconnectedness of the parts to the whole system began to appear in city planning and international policy documents about cities (City of Philadelphia 2011; City of Toronto 2015). A key component of this work is the recognition that the city is intricately connected, and at many scales, to natural systems both inside and outside of it (Toronto and Region Conservation Authority 2014). Lastly, ecological thinking about urban nature led to the re-evaluation of traditional approaches to urban design, planning, and engineering; cities are finding ways of working *with* nature and natural systems that could compete with traditional approaches (Jim 2015; Lafortezza, Chen et al. 2018). This shift in thinking has led to an ongoing debate among researchers over the right framework with which to blend municipal policy and procedures with ecological knowledge and systems (Kattel, Elkadi et al. 2013; Ahern, Cilliers et al. 2014), to attempts to define resilience as applied to complex urban systems and people (Olsson, Jerneck et al. 2015), and to technical discussions and evaluations on how to achieve this (Gómez-Baggethun and Barton 2013; Jackson and Palmer 2015).

Green infrastructure

Green infrastructure (GI) has its roots in the concept of *ecosystem services*, an idea put forth in the late 1990s (Bolund and Hunhammar 1999) that aimed to quantify the value of ecosystems for human use and to encourage their conservation (Dick, Smith et al. 2011; Flint, Kunze et al. 2013). Ecosystem services represent an increasingly dominant paradigm – though still by and large a utilitarian one – used by both cities and international organizations to frame and guide decisions about natural resource management (Flint, Kunze et al. 2013) and is commonly defined in terms of 'benefits that humans obtain from ecosystem functions' (Millennial Ecosystem Assessment 2003) or 'direct and indirect contributions from ecosystems to human well-being' (TEEB 2011). As in the case of green infrastructure, researchers and policy makers are wrestling with how exactly to understand ecosystem services' biophysical (Escobedo, Kroeger et al. 2011; Pataki, Carreiro et al. 2011), economic (Jim and Chen 2009; Sander, Polasky et al. 2010), and socio-cultural benefits (Andersson, Barthel et al. 2007; Barthel, Folke et al. 2010; Gómez-Baggethun and Barton 2013), and how it might be integrated into policy (Kattel, Elkadi et al. 2013; Jackson and Palmer 2015; Gulsrud, Raymond et al. 2018). This ambiguity, particularly around the socio-cultural, or 'co-benefits,' of green infrastructure (Tzoulas, Korpela et al. 2007; Gómez-Baggethun and Barton 2013; Wartmann and Purves 2018), has not impeded its popularity in North America, however, particularly in dealing with stormwater (Netusil, Levin et al. 2014; Szota, Coutts et al. 2019). Faced with prohibitive costs for grey infrastructure upgrades, many cities are implementing GI strategies as an alternative means to address combined stormwater overflow (CSO) water pollution, state and federal code compliance on water quality (Meng and Hsu 2019), or local flooding issues (Tetra Tech 2010; Philadelphia Water Department n.d.-b). Common GI strategies deal with stormwater on site by filtering, absorbing, and containing stormwater during heavy rains instead of moving it quickly to existing stormwater systems, often through 'green street' vegetative strategies, green alley programs, green roofs, residential or commercial incentives for reducing impervious surfaces, or the creative retrofit of existing greenspace (such as parks, schoolyards, and playgrounds) to better manage stormwater (Gómez-Baggethun and Barton 2013; Newell, Seymour et al. 2013; National Association of City Transportation Officials n.d.) (see Table 2.1).

Table 2.1 Green infrastructure case studies: policy and implementation

City	Problem	Policy/project goals	Implementation *actors*	Implementation *funding*	Precedent	Complements (policies and programs)	Policy tools	Case study/ examples
Philadelphia (GCCW program)	Required compliance with State and Federal water quality codes High cost of grey infrastructure Pressing socio-economic needs from disinvestment	Compliance with State and Federal regulations through Green Street Infrastructure (GSI) (Consent Order and Agreement to reduce CCO over 25 years) Also provide socio-cultural and economic benefits to communities immediately Avoid huge grey-infrastructure costs	Philadelphia Water (PWD), Parks and Recreation, Streets, and Public Property departments Pennsylvania Horticultural Society (PHS) Private property owners	Stormwater ratepayer funds Public grants (i.e. Stormwater grant) Private sources, grants	*Greenworks* 2009 Best practices of other cities: Seattle, WA; Portland, OR	*Rebuild* *Green2015* *Greenworks* (2009, 2016) *LandCare* Philadelphia *2035 Comprehensive Plan* Safe Routes to Schools	Philadelphia's Green Stormwater Regulations Stormwater Incentives and fees (i.e. PWD's Stormwater grant) Planning and zoning tools, especially interdepartmental and stakeholder collaboration	Queen Lane Bumpout 53rd and Baltimore
Toronto (GSTS) and Green Streets Program	Meeting provincial stormwater guidelines and Toronto Green Standard (TGS) Manage flooding due to extreme weather events and climate change Need for holistic approach to resilience	Provide technical guidelines for the implementation of urban Green Infrastructure (GI) Align GI guidelines with municipal and provincial policies Provide pilots and case studies for Toronto-specific context Provide holistic program to address resiliency and GI	Toronto Water Civic Design (Toronto Department of Planning) Universities of Toronto and Ryerson Various departments City of Toronto Stakeholder advisory group Champions City of Toronto	Toronto Water and Planning Divisions Toronto's Engineering and Construction services Green Streets now part of capital budget	Previous stormwater management policy and legislation (i.e. TGS, WWFMP, TRCA) Green Roof by-law (2009) (for stormwater GI initiative) City of Toronto *Official Plan* Best practices of other cities: Seattle, WA; Portland, OR; Philadelphia, PA	Local: Toronto's Complete Streets Guidelines, Biodiversity, Pollinator Protection, and Ravine strategies, Tree Canopy Strategy Regional: TRCA's *Living City* policies and *STEP Low-Impact Development (LID) Guidelines*	Mix of budget, regulatory, planning instruments at municipal and provincial scale (Johns, 2018, 2019) Council-approved Implementation Plan, governance model, part of capital budget	Bioswale for Keele Street Pilot Raingarden at Fairford Bioretention Parkette

City-wide approaches to urban greening and stormwater: the case of Philadelphia

The problem

Like many cities in North America, Philadelphia faces issues with flooding, stormwater runoff quality, and aging infrastructure, some of which dates back to the nineteenth century and is a combination of combined and separate sewer systems (Philadelphia Water Department 2011; Philadelphia Water Department n.d.-b). Combined sewer systems carry both sewage and stormwater in one pipe to be treated, while separate sewer systems have separate pipes for sewage and stormwater, with sewage being sent for treatment and stormwater released into local waterways (Philadelphia Water Department n.d.-c). Both carry risks to watersheds; combined systems often get overwhelmed during heavy rain events and release raw sewage into watersheds, while stormwater often picks up surface pollutants from roads and buildings that can compromise water quality in watersheds (Philadelphia Water Department 2011). In addition, cities across the U.S. must comply with the regulations outlined in U.S. Environmental Protection Agency's (EPA) Clean Water Act (CWA), which requires municipalities to address watershed pollution from combined stormwater overflow (CSO), as well as regulations outlined by state mandates. The U.S. EPA also supports GI with funding incentives, technical leadership, and support or best practices (Johns 2019b) as well as state mandates (Chiorean 2019). Philadelphia must also align with the state's watershed-level stormwater management plans as laid out in the 1978 Pennsylvania Storm Water Management Act (Stormwater PA n.d.). Philadelphia estimated that a traditional infrastructure approach would cost them $9 billion (Chiorean 2019), a prohibitive sum and one that would have a severe negative impact on their taxpayers, 26 percent of whom live below the poverty line (The Pew Cheritable Trusts 2018). Furthermore, traditional grey infrastructure approaches did not carry any co-benefits for communities or support the goals of the City's program launched in 2009 by former Mayor Michael Nutter (City of Philadelphia 2009). This plan aimed to make Philadelphia the 'Greenest City in America' through limiting resident exposure to rising energy prices, reducing their environmental footprint, and repositioning their workforce and economic development strategy to take advantage of the green economy (Philadelphia Water Department 2011). Supported by the newly created cabinet-level Office of Sustainability and a top-down mandate, the plan set out ambitious targets on Energy, Environment, Equity, and Economy (Philadelphia Water Department 2011; Palantino 2019). The combination of economic constraint and commitment to socio-economic benefits supported Philadelphia's approach to GI.

An alternative solution: Green City, Clean Waters program and resulting projects

Given these constraints, Philadelphia looked for an alternative approach to comply with federal and state stormwater regulatory requirements while addressing complementary municipal policy goals. Referring to then published EPA guidelines on green infrastructure as a means to address water quality issues, the Philadelphia Water Department (PWD) undertook two years of economic and engineering analysis to argue that an incremental, adaptive, and multi-benefit green infrastructure (GI) approach was the best option for the city (Philadelphia Water Department 2011). These analyses, along with extensive public outreach on preferences, showed that using a GI approach would benefit the watersheds and neighbourhoods within the Combined Sewer Areas as well as Philadelphia's streams and rivers. This approach would also begin accruing benefits immediately, be adaptive, and provide multiple environmental, social, and economic benefits for the city. Furthermore, it would cost only $2.4 billion, versus the estimated $9 billion for traditional grey infrastructure solutions (Philadelphia Water Department 2011). This argument led to the 2009 proposal of the Green City, Clean Waters (GCCW) program to update the City's CSO Long Term Control Plan – and its adoption in 2011 – through agreements with the U.S. EPA and Pennsylvania Department of Environment. Specifically, PWD has a Consent Order and Agreement to reduce combined sewer overflow (CSO) in Philadelphia over the next 25 years (Noon 2019). It is the first city-wide adoption of this approach to CSO compliance and social benefits in the U.S. (Philadelphia Water Department 2011). The program aimed to capture 85 percent of CSO runoff city-wide through the management of more than one-third of the impervious area within the combined sewer area (Philadelphia Water Department n.d.-b). In its first five years, the program committed to the target implementation of 744 'greened acres' (Philadelphia Water Department n.d.-a). A greened acre refers to the acre of impervious cover within the combined sewer area that has at least the first inch of runoff managed by stormwater infrastructure, including the stormwater management feature, as well as the area that drains into it (Philadelphia Water Department n.d.-a).

Five-year later evaluation of GCCW

Five years after its creation, the 'test or pilot phase' of the policy has been considered a success. While the goals of the program aimed to 'green' 744 acres, by 2016, 837.5 acres had been greened, $51 million invested into the city from public grants and private sources, and 430 new jobs created (Philadelphia Water Department n.d.-a). Importantly, as we will see below, over 300,000 citizens were also engaged throughout the process (Philadelphia Water Department n.d.-a), 1,100 green stormwater tools have been added (Philadelphia Water Department n.d.-b), and an on-going public–private partnership with the Sustainable Business Network of Greater Philadelphia is helping to make the business case as well as provide feedback to PWD on successful implementation of GCCW (Green Stormwater Infrastructure Partners and sbn 2016; Shipp 2019). Furthermore, the 'greened acre' was adopted as a metric for progress for Philadelphia's *Green 2015* policy that aimed to increase access to greenspace for all residents, some of which is being rolled into the ambitious *Rebuild* program (City of Philadelphia 2019b). This program is one of the first urban policies in the U.S. to be successfully funded by a sweetened beverage tax (Tanenbaum 2018; City of Philadelphia 2019a) and aims to invest up to $500 million over seven years to improve Philadelphia's parks, recreation centres, libraries and playgrounds (City of Philadelphia 2019b; Gould 2019; Palantino 2019; Strong 2019; Westerman 2019). A central goal of this program is to ensure that every Philadelphian has access to good, *useable* greenspace. Their complementary grant incentive programs such as the Stormwater Management Incentive Program (SMIP) and Greened Acre Retrofit Program (GARP) have been similarly successful; so much so that the PWD has asked the Philadelphia Water, Sewer, and Stormwater Rate Board to increase their budget for those programs (Baker 2018).

Research and precedent

The Philadelphia Water Department (PWD) was able to successfully argue for the feasibility of the GCCW policy through a combination of research, demonstration projects, and alignment with concurrent municipal policies and mayoral directive. In addition to extensive research and interviews with practitioners from other cities such as Seattle and Portland (Chiorean 2019) and demonstration projects, the PWD referred to years of research demonstrating the public benefit of improvements to greenspace from the Pennsylvania Horticultural Society's (PHS) *LandCare* vacant lot improvement program (discussed in Chapter 4), including a reduction in vandalism, gun assaults, and burglary (Branas, Cheney et al. 2011; Wolfe and Mennis 2012). In fact, PWD worked with some of the same researchers examining the vacant lot program to show that there is a correlation between 'greened' streets for stormwater management and a reduction in narcotics possession within up to a half mile from GSI installations (Kondo, Low et al. 2015). This demonstration of statistically relevant public benefit – along with a long history of open space conservation and collaboration and demonstration projects with the Department of Environmental Protection and PHS – provided support for their triple bottom line research on the potential benefits. Thus when their analysis showed that implementing green infrastructure would not only cost less but also provide annual jobs (Green Stormwater Infrastructure Partners and sbn 2016), this aligned with larger equity and neighbourhood stabilization goals of *Greenworks*, *LandCare*, and the Office of Sustainability, and provided support for the development of *Green2015* and *ReBuild*, among other policies (see Table 2.2). Research was further used to argue for social benefits of green infrastructure – such as reduced heat fatalities, increased property values, and enhanced recreation – as well as the more traditional environmental benefits such as ecosystem restoration, improved air quality, and reduced energy use from cooler cities (Philadelphia Water Department 2011).

GCCW case studies

What does the GCCW look like on the ground? What benefits are expected from these projects? How is the community involved, if at all? In the following case studies, we will look at one of the first 'greened' streets that was a collaboration between the PWD and the Streets Department, as well as a more recent collaboration. Streets and sidewalks comprise roughly 40 percent of impervious surface in Philadelphia and are thus a huge opportunity for critical investment to meet PWD's greened acre targets (Philadelphia Water Department 2011; Chiorean 2019). Furthermore, given the required co-benefits for GI in Philadelphia, they provide numerous opportunities for aligning with other community benefits such as the traffic calming, bike lanes, and pedestrian amenities that are often part of complete streets or Safe Route to School interventions (Brooks 2019; Chiorean 2019). Street runoff can also be conveyed and managed on properties, such as parks or recreation centres, increasing opportunities to manage this impervious area to meet the GCCW program targets while enhancing or aligning with park goals.

Queen Lane Bumpouts

The Queen Lane Bumpouts – which 'bump' the street edge out into space previously taken up by traffic with stormwater retention interventions – were part of the first phase of the GCCW policy. PWD piloted several green street stormwater management practices around PWD facilities as a proof of concept and required close collaboration with the Philadelphia Streets Department (PSD). The completed six bumpouts now manage the first inch of runoff from an acre of drainage area, or 800,000–900,000 gallons of runoff each year (Brooks 2019). This means that it counts as a 'greened acre' under the GCCW policy. The project did not encounter any community resistance or challenges, and due to its success as a model of city department collaboration, stormwater management, and community benefits in terms of traffic calming and pedestrian safety, bumpouts have been used throughout the city (Brooks 2019) (Figure 2.1).

Table 2.2 Green infrastructure: the intersection of research, policy, and implementation

Type of SSUG	Research used to justify policy or project?	Alignment with current research	Future areas for research and implementation synergies	Suggested ways forward
Interstitial Green Infrastructure (right of way, bioswales, rain gardens)	*Precedent:* PHS and *Landcare* research connected greenspace and health (Philadelphia); municipal GI examples of other North American cities (both) *Policy:* Municipal review of best-case practices, key stakeholder interviews provided policy precedent (Toronto, Philadelphia) Technical guidance and pilots used (Toronto) *Research:* Policy documents cite human benefits of nature (environmental psychology) (Philadelphia, Toronto) University collaborations (both)	*Planning:* Need for cross-departmental collaboration Adaptive versus path dependency approach *Implementation:* Need to move beyond risk reduction framing of health to larger socio-economic and health benefits Need for community engagement	*Framework:* Call for better integration of urban ecology knowledge and urban planning Incorporation of socio-ecological, socio-economic, power dynamics and other social constructionist research insights into GI cultural benefits research Aligning sense of place research with GI, values, attitudes *Metrics:* Longitudinal studies on cultural shifts and values and GI Qualitative and quantitative research methods, approaches *Scale:* How much nature is enough to provide human and ecological benefits? For whom?	Learn-by-doing approach based on transdisciplinary collaboration and community engagement Develop better metrics that value ecological, equity, cultural, economic needs with GI Engagement with social sciences around values, perceptions, aesthetics and lived experience of urban nature and GI Use GI as a tool for connection to nature, ecological education, larger environmental values

Figure 2.1 Queen Lane stormwater bumpouts.
Source: Philadelphia Water Department.

53rd and Baltimore Rain Gardens

Another collaboration between PWD and the PSD, this project has the goal to improve the safety of a dangerous intersection while also addressing stormwater management. Slip lanes are being removed at the intersection in order both to promote multi-modal transportation (such as cyclists and pedestrians as well as cars) and to improve the safety of street crossings for local elementary school students. The project will consist of two rain gardens and a stormwater bumpout and their associated subsurface features (such as underground storage tanks). While the stormwater management is important, outreach in the neighbouring Cobbs Creek and Cedar Park communities, as well as research from the Children's Hospital of Philadelphia, pointed to the need for improved safety at that intersection, and thus the project specifically aims to also provide multiple community benefits. Because of the improved traffic safety, the project also secured funding from the Pennsylvania Department of Transportation, which increased the complexity of the standards and partners (Figure 2.2).

Figure 2.2 53rd and Baltimore Rain Garden and slip lane removal rendering.
Source: Philadelphia Water Department.

Community feedback and results

While the case studies above are small, they are good examples of the kind of urban greening Philadelphia is undertaking that combines ecological and community benefits while also potentially impacting residents' lived experience of place. While the PWD did not encounter much community resistance or conduct official post-implementation community outreach about these specific case studies, overall they have had positive responses to their GI projects. However, given the specific goals of the GCCW, they have had to re-tool how they approach the *design* of added green-space for green infrastructure in two ways that differ from traditional GI projects, and which may impact community perceptions of the projects. First, PWD does not own much of the land in the city. This, combined with a fairly limited budget and aggressive timelines and goals, has necessitated a much higher level of collaboration to both implement and fund these types of projects (Brooks 2019; Chiorean 2019). And while a partnership between the PWD and the PSD is a natural fit, new partnerships, such as collaborating with the school district, or Safe Routes to Schools initiatives, brings in stakeholders that have not traditionally dealt with stormwater infrastructure and who bring their own goals, requirements, and community partners.

Second, although the PWD has educated residents for decades, they had to develop a new notification and engagement strategy to partner with community leadership and develop resources for residents. These resources were on topics related to landscaping and the use of public spaces which would create community-supported GI projects. This shift in strategy is due to initial community consultations that made the PWD realize that the first thing on community members' minds was not stormwater, but often safety and beautification (Brooks 2019). Furthermore, as both community members and the City were interested in seeing projects that had a visible component, the PWD had to go beyond their original scope of work around GI infrastructure to include visible changes that address neighbourhood concerns, such as traffic calming, repairing cracked sidewalks, or public property improvements needed to secure future potential GI implementation. As a result, in cases where the scope of work is too large to be covered by current funding, PWD has decided to put the GI project off until more partners and funding can be found (Brooks 2019; Chiorean 2019).

The need to systematically address community concerns and engage in interdepartmental collaboration thus is a big change from a water department's traditional underground pipe work (Chiorean 2019) and has influenced the scope and design of these GI projects. For example, while a majority of PWD's activities are around green streets, they are also involved in partnerships with park, schoolyard, and vacant land projects (Chiorean 2019). The new Rebuild program for parks provides another opportunity to fold in many current policies (Gould 2019; Palantino 2019; Strong 2019; Westerman 2019) (see Plate 1). The goals of Rebuild, Green 2015, Philadelphia 2035 (their comprehensive planning document), and the updated Greenworks (2016) highlight that greenspace in Philadelphia needs to be high quality, accessible, and useable (PennPraxis 2010; City of Philadelphia 2011, 2016, City of Philadelphia 2019b), while the goals of GCCW link resilience and community vitality to ecosystem services (Philadelphia Water Department 2011). This means that aesthetically unpleasing, or mediocre, GI projects are unlikely to be approved by either Rebuild or the community. The high level of community input and the inclusion of their upgrades and improvements, then, make it harder to separate out what community members feel about the aesthetics of the vegetative part of the project versus the overall added amenities. While this generally bodes well for the success of Philadelphia's approach to stormwater and urban greening, it may miss some useful insights that can help to design these projects to maximize the potential impact on urbanites' health, well-being, and creativity given the lack of influence of socially constructed research on policy seen in Chapter 1.

How Philadelphia's approach differs from traditional GI approaches

Thus, though there have been green infrastructure approaches to urban stormwater issues for almost 30 years, what distinguishes Philadelphia's approach at an *implementation* level is the degree of interdepartmental collaboration and the focus on community benefits and engagement. The extensive interdepartmental collaboration between departments has changed how the City approaches any infrastructure investment. Instead of the more traditional public–private partnerships which can have contested outcomes in terms of public benefit (Martin 2018; Mayer 2018; Opara and Rouse 2019), this approach requires multiple public benefits and has also allowed for economic efficiencies in a city with a less-than-wealthy tax base (The Pew Cheritable Trusts 2018). The second key difference is that the community benefits are just as important drivers for implementation as the economic benefits (Chiorean 2019). In fact, the GCCW was viewed as a tool for revitalization of public health, recreation, housing, and neighbourhood values through investment in infrastructure and the addition of small-scale urban nature (Philadelphia Water Department 2011):

> But as the single largest investment in the City's environment over the next 25 years, it presents a unique opportunity to be much more than just a water quality improvement program and reverse the decline in the physical infrastructure of the City. It must be designed to provide additional benefits beyond the reduction of CSOs, so that every investment made provides a maximum return in benefits to the City.
>
> (Philadelphia Water Department 2011)

Whereas other cities are also using green infrastructure as an interstitial tool for urban greening and stormwater management, and viewing rainwater as a resource versus a liability, Philadelphia has placed as much importance on the social, health, economic revitalization, and community benefits as on the economic and environmental benefits. This emphasis is reflected in their basic principles underlying the GCCW, which explicitly refer to collaboration and energizing their citizens, or community engagement (Philadelphia Water Department 2011). It is also reflected in the updated Greenworks 2016 plan that focuses on community engagement and translating many sustainability efforts to communities (Chiorean 2019). Furthermore, though the scale is ultimately very large, as the majority of efforts are at the street level, this type of urban greening exemplifies an innovative way of adding nature to interstitial or in-between spaces in the city using nature as ecosystem *and* socio-cultural services.

Challenges

As with many complex projects, there are ongoing challenges that impact the level of success of Philadelphia's GI projects. Many of these are technical: finding environmentally suitable land that is also available for on-going maintenance by

PWD; negotiating jurisdictions on this land, monitoring and evaluating which plants are successful; and engaging in education and outreach for an organization that has traditionally focused on notification and underground technical solutions (Brooks 2019). However, the level of success Philadelphia has enjoyed, even though it does not have a wealthy tax base, is an important example of creative solutions to so-called complex, wicked problems such as economic disinvestment legacies combined with social and ecological problems (Levin, Cashore et al. 2012; Stony Brook University n.d.).

Piece-by-piece layering and conversion: urban greening and stormwater in Toronto

Introduction

Like Philadelphia, Toronto faces a host of issues around stormwater management, including severe flooding, aging infrastructure, and poor runoff quality that threatens both local watersheds that drain into Lake Ontario and the Great Lake itself (City of Toronto 2006; Toronto and Region Conservation Authority n.d.). Toronto also has multiple layers of government legislating water quality and runoff, which results in a combination of local, regional, and provincial mandates and policies (Johns 2018, Johns 2019b). While most Canadian municipalities do not have constitutional policy powers and focus mainly on implementation and service delivery, recent legislation, such as the City of Toronto Act (City of Toronto 2007b), has given Toronto some unique powers in that it is allowed to pass by-laws in some areas and levy taxes other than property taxes. Some of Toronto's policies have been very progressive; however, they have been created in fits and starts that do not always align, leading to an uneven landscape for green infrastructure until recently (Toronto Water 2015; City of Toronto 2019; Johns 2019b). This is partly why, despite Toronto's long history as an environmentally progressive city – including leadership on climate change (City of Toronto 2007a), environmental goals and guidelines (City of Toronto 2000), green roofs (City of Toronto 2009), and green development standards (City of Toronto 2007c) – it has lagged behind cities like Seattle and Portland in green infrastructure standards and has not been considered a leader in GI (Johns 2019). Until recently, in many cases, Toronto did not even meet its own or provincial guidelines for stormwater runoff during large storm events, routinely releasing pollutants into waterways, and ultimately Lake Ontario, that far exceeded provincial pollutant-level guidelines or their own Green Development Standard (City of Toronto 2007c; Livegreen Toronto, City of Toronto et al. 2017). It was one of these large storm events that officially precipitated the request for the creation of the Green Streets Technical

Standards (GSTG), which was completed in late 2017 and recently won a Canadian Society of Landscape Architects award of excellence (Canadian Society of Landscape Architects 2019), and which served as a catalyst for their new Green Streets Program (City of Toronto n.d.-a). Severe flooding events in July 2013 paralyzed the city and surrounding region, including power outages and transit delays, for days (Boudreau, Cheung et al. 2017).

The GSTG is a great example of a growing trend in which cities are creating specific technical guidelines for low-impact development and green infrastructure that both support policy mandates and provide technical guidance on how to do so (City and County of Denver 2016; City of New York 2017). In the case of Toronto, these technical guidelines also help support later innovative programs and by-laws (see Chapter 3). It is also a good example of common barriers even environmentally progressive cities face when trying to implement GI. And while Toronto's difficulties are partly unique to the Canadian constitutional-power sharing system (Dhakal and Chevalier 2016; Johns 2019b), many of the barriers addressed are also found in U.S. cities (Dhakal and Chevalier 2016). Though Toronto's stormwater issues extend beyond its street network, which is approximately 27 percent of its landmass, the GSTG and later Green Streets Program is meant to show leadership on how to successfully replicate urban green infrastructure (Boudreau 2019; Stott 2019). Toronto's experience with common bureaucratic barriers, combined with the GSTC's goal of 'weaving green infrastructure into the fabric of the city' (Boudreau 2019) and the impact this can have on community knowledge, leadership, and engagement with Toronto's water systems, makes it an interesting example of small-scale urban greening currently happening in cities in North America.

The creation of the GSTG: the role of key champions and policy gaps

In many ways Toronto's story of creating green infrastructure standards is much more common for cities than Philadelphia's level of interdepartmental integration and leadership: policy development in fits and starts, departments working in silos, community activism and push for more progressive environmental action, and dedicated action and 'side of desk' work by a few key champions. While Toronto had pieces of legislation and policies that required stormwater management prior to the creation of the GSTG, these were not always followed, did not align with one another, or needed more cross-jurisdictional support (see Table 2.1). For example, Toronto Water's Wet Weather Master Plan (WWMP) includes a policy that refers to green infrastructure practices as far back as 2003 (City of Toronto 2003; Boudreau 2019), and the subsequent 2006 Wet Weather Flow Guidelines include Low-Impact Development (LID) practices (City of Toronto 2006). Another important planning approval tool for the City is the Toronto Green Standard (TGS) (City of Toronto 2018) which incorporated the Toronto Water guidelines to mandate requirements for both stormwater retention and the quality of the runoff (Toronto and Region Conservation Authority 2016a; Livegreen Toronto, City of Toronto et al. 2017). While the City was aware that they were not meeting their own standards, they struggled with the knowledge gaps and barriers with existing planning and design for capital projects (Boudreau 2019), a common problem for complex policy-technical solutions (Murphy 2019). Understanding the key role that stormwater played in meeting these standards, and working creatively to find solutions, was in large part initiated by a former consultant who ended up working for the City in 2011.

Sheila Boudreau, whom many credit with helping to get the GSTG created, realized that the traditional engineering approach of providing soil for street trees was inadequate and did not do much to address the stormwater standards for quality and quantity in the TGS. Working with another key champion in Toronto Water, Senior Engineer Patrick Cheung, and the Planning Department she was hired into, Boudreau advocated for a different approach to greenspace and hardscape that integrated the two – green infrastructure. When it became clear during her work with the City's urban design team (Civic Design) that not all staff were aware that the City wasn't meeting the TGS, Boudreau advocated that the TGS update include the mandate that all capital projects needed to meet it in 2014 (which was approved by City Council). Using this policy mandate, Boudreau, Cheung, and other city champions attempted to apply green infrastructure to City capital projects, as well as to a number of pilot projects. However, given the need for innovation for each project, and a lack of approved construction standards on how to apply green infrastructure to difference projects, they realized they needed a different approach. Using a design-thinking, learning-by-doing approach, they began strategic outreach to key City officials, a working group, and alliances with university partners such as the Universities of Toronto and Ryerson. They began to experiment with pilot projects to come up with guidelines for green infrastructure in Toronto. With support from key officials through social media, community-initiated pilots, constant outreach and education, and the example of the extreme storm event above, Toronto Water decided to fund consultants to develop the GSTG in 2013 (Boudreau 2019). More recently, another City of Toronto champion, Barbara Gray, General Manager of Toronto's Transportation Services Division (who came from the City of Seattle), was also instrumental in helping to use the GSTG as a catalyst for the Green Streets Program (see below) (Stott 2019).

Policy support, precedent, and goals

With support from TGS staff and environmental planner Shayna Stott, Boudreau and Cheung led the hiring of an interdisciplinary consultant team to develop a user-friendly but technical handbook to guide the design and construction of GI in the right of way (ROW). Given the extensive knowledge acquired from both policy gaps and lessons learned from the pilots, the GSTG team did strategic outreach to key City figures, formed internal and external working groups, created alliances with the Universities of Guelph, Ryerson, and Toronto, did an extensive review of City policy documents and precedent manuals from other North American cities, and conducted in-depth interviews with internal staff and contacts from those municipalities (Livegreen Toronto, City of Toronto et al. 2017), and outreach to existing partners from previous and ongoing pilot work and outreach (Boudreau, Cheung et al. 2017; Boudreau 2019). Key city documents included the City of Toronto Official Plan, the Toronto Green Standards (TGS), and the Wet Weather Flow Master Plan and Guidance (WWFMP). This background research was used to identify three key things: the environmental drivers, or pressures, that Toronto faced and which needed to be addressed by the GSTG; policies that would be suited to Toronto's climate and geography; and policies that would be appropriate for Toronto's particular ROW conditions (Livegreen Toronto, City of Toronto et al. 2017). These final techniques were selected for inclusion in the GSTG and provide a comprehensive set of tools for decision makers.

In addition, the GSTG, and green infrastructure in general, was supported by a number of policy updates at multiple levels before, during, and after its creation (see Plate 2) (Livegreen Toronto, City of Toronto et al. 2017). These include a 2014 Provincial Policy Statement that defined green infrastructure and required all Ontario municipalities to promote it in their Official Plan updates, a 2015 Ontario Ministry of the Environment and Climate Change *Interpretation Bulletin* that supported site-specific performance criteria based on watershed studies and source control measures such as Low Impact Development, and a 2016 Ministry of Municipal Affairs and Housing Official Plan amendment 262 that included green infrastructure as part of larger environmental strategies to address climate change, energy, and the natural environment (Livegreen Toronto, City of Toronto et al. 2017). At a local level, a Toronto Official Plan update in 2014 defined and supported green infrastructure as a means to address climate change mitigation and energy conservation, and required it for future development initiatives (Livegreen Toronto, City of Toronto et al. 2017). The GSTG is meant to work in alignment with both local and regional policies and initiatives, which include Toronto's Complete Streets

Guidelines and their Biodiversity, Pollinator Protection, and Ravine strategies (Livegreen Toronto, City of Toronto et al. 2017; Boudreau 2019) at the local level and, at the regional level, the Toronto and Region Conservation Authority's (TRCA) Living City policies and Sustainable Technologies Evaluation Program (STEP), which provide policy and technical guidance and training on LID practices (Livegreen Toronto, City of Toronto et al. 2017; Boudreau 2019). Most importantly, the GSTG catalyzed the creation of the Green Streets Program, in 2017 which created a governance structure that mandates key decision makers must address green streets as a whole (Stott 2019). The Green Streets Program and the GSTG also align and support Toronto's new Resilience Strategy as part of the 100 Resilient Cities program (City of Toronto 2019; City of Toronto n.d.-a).

The official goals of the GSTG, and more recently, the Green Streets Program, in contrast to those of Philadelphia, are mainly environmental, and focus on climate change resilience and the mitigation of poor urban environmental quality, particularly around air, water, and ecology (City of Toronto 2017; Livegreen Toronto, City of Toronto et al. 2017). This makes sense, given that the GSTG was intended to align with the TGS and environmental goals of the Official Plan. The GSTG is also meant to align policy-wise with the Complete Streets policy in Toronto, a gap that has plagued older examples of green infrastructure in the U.S. (Boudreau 2019) and is now being addressed by the Green Streets Program. Unofficially, however, the GSTG is also meant to provide technical guidance and leadership to encourage green infrastructure across the city, which seems to have been successful. In addition, the GSTG supports a larger groundswell of community activism, connection to the symbolic, Indigenous, and historic sense of place of the watersheds in the Toronto region, and provides a living example of shifting attitudes and understanding through integrating greenspace into city life (Boudreau 2019). These underlying goals come from both champions at the City and grassroots activists, as we will see below in some case studies that were enabled by the GSTG.

GSTG case studies

The use of pilots as an attempt to bypass inaction and uncertainty around specific technical guidance at the City level was a key enabler of the development of the GSTG. This 'learning-by-doing' experimental approach to problem-solve specifically for Toronto's streets was supported by its creators' engagement with research and best practice. Just as importantly, the development of the GSTG is a story of the power of engaging community members and inspiring them to connect with the history of local watersheds, biodiversity, and community space.

Keele Avenue pilot bioswale

This was the first official pilot in the right of way (ROW) using green infrastructure in Toronto, with the aim of understanding what was involved in implementing green infrastructure techniques like bioretention cells (stormwater underground holding tanks) and bioswales (vegetated retention and filtration installations) in Toronto. Keele Avenue is a busy north–south arterial road in Toronto that is prone to flooding. While the City officially did not have any guidelines on how to design bioretention cells, Boudreau and Cheung's outreach referred to the Sustainable Technologies Evaluation Program (STEP) Low-Impact Development (LID) guidelines (Toronto and Region Conservation Authority 2016b), backed by pilots and research for their effectiveness. The experience with the Keele pilot informed a model for future projects based on the identification of gaps in knowledge, practices, and processes. This model includes: form a cross-divisional working group; gain the support of the local Councillor; aim to monitor and evaluate the performance of the pilot; and look for education and outreach opportunities to position a pilot as a learning opportunity or living lab, versus a project that was seen as risky due to unfamiliarity (Boudreau 2019).

RESULTS

At the time of installation and up to the time of writing, the City did not have a formal monitoring or evaluation process but used a visual inspection for ponding, or sitting water, and plant health (Boudreau 2019). The plants at the lower end of the project that benefited from the bioswale have done very well, indicating that some water is being retained by the bioswale. However, due to a lack of maintenance, weeds have overtaken many of the original plants. Coordination issues during construction and the lack of maintenance demonstrate the need for departments to work differently than 'business as usual' in order to develop, install, and maintain green infrastructure projects. These issues are beginning to be addressed through changes with the Green Streets Program. While Transportation Services, which was officially in charge of the project, knew there needed to be a maintenance program, staff and resources were not assigned to work on it until a full-time Green Streets Project Manager was hired, though this is still only one person for the entire program (Stott 2019). Even Toronto Water, the official 'asset' owner, does not traditionally deal with components of green infrastructure that need maintenance, such as cleaning out trench drains or maintaining the plants. This may be solved soon, however, as an MOU (memorandum of understanding) is currently being developed to determine roles and responsibilities (Boudreau 2019) and all Green Streets projects will be monitored for effectiveness in a more consistent manner to demonstrate that the City meets the proposed Provincial stormwater volume control standards (Boudreau 2019), which are currently on hold (Johns 2019a).

Raingarden at Fairford Parkette

This raingarden is an example of bottom-up activism in Toronto around green infrastructure in the right of way (ROW). Opened in late 2015, the parkette is situated at the south-west corner of Fairford Avenue and Coxwell Avenue in an area of mixed residential and small business properties. The $320,000 Cdn project took over a turning lane and turned it into a popular raingarden with bicycle parking spaces, a trench drain system for bioretention, and two seating areas for up to 22 people (Sustainable Technologies Evaluation Program 2017) (See Figures 2.3 and Plate 3).

THE ROLE OF COMMUNITY ACTIVISM

The local community had approached their City councillor in 2012 and complained that the intersection was unsafe. They got Transportation, one of the four major divisions involved in green infrastructure (the others are City Planning, Toronto Water, and Engineering and Construction Services) to evaluate the intersection to see if it could be realigned, and when the answer was yes, did a community-led pilot. Similar to many tactical urbanism initiatives, the community worked with the local councillor and used Jersey barriers to 'remove' the turning lane, had kids draw on the street to reclaim it as community space, and when the 'sky didn't fall down' (Boudreau 2019) got the City to redesign the space as a public realm. When Boudreau was asked to

Figure 2.3 Raingarden at Fairford Parkette, 1.

Source: © Chrystelle Maechler, from documentary series "Urban Resilience Toronto" by Chrystelle Maechler and Andreas Krätschmer.

design the project, she proposed a bioretention parkette with two seating areas framed by low curved walls, a central pollinator garden, and wood-trimmed pedestrian lighting (Boudreau 2019). Urban Design suggested the site be used as a pilot to test the implementation of green infrastructure in a ROW and secured the participation of numerous city departments, landscape architects, and water resources engineers. The project got funding from Toronto's Engineering and Construction services, and the community was heavily involved in the design. The goals of the project include *public benefit goals*, such as enhancing the pedestrian environment and the aesthetics of the area, and promoting multi-modal transportation; *green infrastructure goals*, such as piloting bioretention techniques that support policy goals and reduce flooding; and *educational goals*. These latter include incorporating lessons learned from the Keele Avenue Pilot, documenting construction, developing evaluation criteria, and identifying regional coordination issues (Toronto and Region Conservation Authority 2019). A key component of the approach for the parkette is multifunctionality. In this case that means that the park is valuable and attractive community space, provides biodiversity for pollinators, and improves stormwater management (Toronto and Region Conservation Authority 2019).

CHALLENGES

While the project in the end has been a success, there were numerous challenges around construction and maintenance. Because it required interdisciplinary and interdepartmental coordination, as well as staff training on low-impact development practices, the project took longer to complete than expected. In addition, the City had trouble securing qualified contractors to do the work and maintenance; it had to go through two contractors for the construction and, eventually, because the maintenance was sub-par, reverted the maintenance back to different departments in the City (Toronto and Region Conservation Authority 2019). These include Toronto Transportation services for the maintenance of the infrastructure and planting beds, and Urban Forestry for the trees (Sustainable Technologies Evaluation Program 2017). A particular barrier was finding contractors willing and able to create the right bioretention media, as well as regular maintenance while the plants were being established (Toronto and Region Conservation Authority 2019). Interestingly, it was not the perceived lack of research that was a barrier, but the translation of research into practice and practical, locally adaptable standards.

RESULTS

As green infrastructure, the raingarden is a success, draining even heavy rain events within 24 hours (Sustainable Technologies Evaluation Program 2017). The parkette as a whole has also been very popular with the local community. One local Master Gardener wrote in her blog that she 'makes an effort to cross the street to walk through that park space. I did not do that before' (Battersby 2017), while another man approached Boudreau and Cheung to explain how the park was a different kind of space, that it actually was about stormwater, and a new direction the City was taking (Boudreau 2019). While there is an interpretive sign for the project, the decorative trench drain grate also makes visible the normally hidden water processes of the city, bringing to light the long-buried streams and rivers. This melding of biodiversity, community involvement, and the elevation of the role of water in cities through 'integrating green infrastructure into the urban fabric' (Boudreau 2019) makes the parkette successful on many levels, despite the ongoing challenges with maintenance. What is perhaps more instructive is that another planned green infrastructure pilot garden proposed by Boudreau, the Raindrop Plaza, draws on the lessons learned from both Keele Avenue and the Fairford Coxwell parkette as well as going even further. The Raindrop Plaza – a planned permeable parkette to replace a traffic island and turning lane at the corner of Coxwell and Dundas Streets slated for construction in the summer of 2019 – has also involved community engagement to help design the space (Boudreau 2019). However, it has gone a step further in co-designing the storytelling art and symbolism of the space with local artists and Indigenous and other schoolchildren, thus bringing symbolism, values, and history into the space (Boudreau 2019). The high visibility of the green infrastructure pilots, in addition to sustained outreach and education, has also supported the creation of community-led raingardens and a non-profit in the east end of the city (RaingardensUnited.com), led by a former graduate student Marc Yamaguchi (Draaisma 2016; Yamaguchi 2016).

These case studies also helped shape specific lessons learned from a City perspective. For example, it became apparent that the City needed to fit projects into partners' schedules; with university partnerships, this became clear because by the time the City got the permissions the students involved had finished their classes and moved on. In addition, the City recognized the need to create special task forces to manage all of the work involved, including efforts to increase visibility and education for elected officials through exposure to the pilots (Boudreau 2019). This is especially important since the problem, as mentioned above, is less the lack of research or examples of successful green infrastructure, but that councillors rely upon the expertise of City engineers who are trained in and comfortable with grey infrastructure, and who often do not believe that GI can manage flooding and see it as an 'extra' to implement when there are resources (Dhakal and Chevalier 2016; Johns 2018; Murphy 2019). Lastly, it also demonstrated the need for a cohesive approach and helped catalyze the Green Streets program.

How Toronto's approach differs from traditional GI approaches

While there has been policy support for low-impact development and green infrastructure for 15 years in Toronto, most notably in their Wet Weather Flow Master Plan (2004), Green Roof By-law (2009), and Green Development Standard (GDS, 2007), the GSTG, combined with championing by Barbara Gray, catalyzed the most comprehensive attempt to integrate green infrastructure into the fabric of the city and systemically change how things are done through the Green Streets Program. Officially aimed at interventions in the ROW, it is also meant to provide a learning-by-doing, hands-on experience for both community members and policy officials.

Like Toronto's green roof by-law, the GSTG and the Green Streets Program has the potential to change the lived experience of place of local communities by integrating greenspace into the in-between spaces of the city and reclaiming them for public use. While it is too early to tell how a widespread shift from grey to green through green infrastructure would be perceived by local urbanites, given the popularity of both the Coxwell parkette and the community raingardens, it is likely to be positive. Much of this projected success presupposes extensive community engagement and outreach, however, which has been shown in both cities to be an effective way to get community buy-in, acceptance, and potentially help with maintenance. It should also be noted that the pilot projects so far have been done in fairly well-established, stable, and centre-city neighbourhoods. Unlike many American cities, Canadian cities, and Toronto in particular, tend not to have been hollowed out by flight to the suburbs in the last century. Toronto also has a high level of ethnic diversity (more than half the population identify as visible minorities (Statistics Canada 2017, Whalen 2017, City of Toronto n.d.-b), and while newer immigrant neighbourhoods tend to have more poverty, this is not as true for older, more established neighbourhoods (Hulchanski 2010; Monsebraaten 2011). In light of these factors, many neighbourhoods in the city proper are highly desirable, often have good access to transit, and more recently, sustain high enough housing prices to push out more disadvantaged populations. Furthermore, the Coxwell parkette in particular has been designed to be a lush raingarden versus more traditional utility-based green infrastructure, with flowers, benches, and custom-designed storm grates (see Plate 3). Many of the surrounding neighbourhoods have their own gardens, and thus it is not surprising that the parkette is preferred to the pavement and pedestrian-unfriendly turning lane.

What all of this means in practice is that the acceptance of projects like the Coxwell parkette are unlikely to be opposed by local communities, who see it as a garden amenity that they can use as they walk or bike by it with the added benefit of being environmentally friendly. What is less clear is how green infrastructure projects would be perceived in lower-income, ethnically diverse communities. While there is a broad acceptance of a 'wilder' nature aesthetic associated with cottage country north of the city and environmental initiatives in Toronto, some research has shown that some immigrant communities, even well-established ones, prefer manicured, paved-over residential lots to 'wilder,' heavily-treed lots (Fraser and Kenney 2000), and visitors to cottage country are still predominantly white (Jiménez 2006). On the other hand, Toronto's long history with environmentally progressive policies, focus on biodiversity, and community support may make it easier to push biodiversity, native plants (as seen with the Coxwell parkette), and links to symbolism and native history than it would be in some of the more disadvantaged neighbourhoods in Philadelphia where many of their green infrastructure improvements are occurring.

Challenges: shifting from grey to green

Some of the key challenges facing Toronto's GSTG and the successful implementation of GI are typical of many cities: resistance from traditional infrastructure departments that do not see GI as a viable alternative to pure grey infrastructure and business-as-usual (Dhakal and Chevalier 2016; Johns 2019b); cross-jurisdictional issues in which mandates from one level of government contradict or are not supported by another; and a lack of capacity, support, and training for staff (Boudreau 2019; Johns 2019a, 2019b; Murphy 2019). These issues show the difficulty of city-wide transformative change, both in actual policy and practice, and in mindset. While there are many dedicated champions and some progressive policies, researchers have found that there has been less of a 'shift occurring from grey to green' and more of a 'layering of green infrastructure policies and instruments on top of a very well entrenched system of grey' (Johns 2019a). This is partly because of a lack of motivation and knowledge on the part of those who need to implement green infrastructure – Toronto Water in particular (Johns 2019b) – and a focus on maintaining adequate, if not great, infrastructure in the immediate future, versus making major changes (Murphy 2019). It is also partly due to an entrenched belief among many engineers that 'while low-impact development plays a role in environmental stewardship and good urban development, it has limited impact and (they) prefer traditional centralized infrastructure to convey water' (Murphy 2019). This may be changing somewhat with the Green Streets Program, whose governance model and formal structure with key decision makers in the room mimics the success of Philadelphia's model and which also supports the City's new Resilience Strategy (Stott 2019). Combined with the proposed increase in stormwater requirements from the Ministry of Environment and Climate Change, and the new Chief Resilience Officer hire (Johns 2019b) as part of

Toronto's selection as one of the Rockefeller Foundation's 100 Resilient Cities (100 Resilient Cities 2019; Rockefeller Foundation n.d.) recipients, this may provide some of the needed cohesion and staffing. Hopefully these changes will address ongoing issues of implementation and support. For example, while Toronto Water initially expected industry to be innovative in developing GI solutions, city staff was not trained on how to review site plan applications including LID, and no construction standards existed at the time by which to compare project submissions (Boudreau 2019). While this is not unusual, a perceived lack of leadership and cross-departmental outreach from Toronto Water on GI is considered an ongoing barrier to GI progress (Johns 2019b). This is not entirely unexpected, given that the majority of staff working at Toronto Water are engineers trained in grey infrastructure, and unlike City Planning, which is seen as more progressive and familiar with cross-jurisdictional outreach, are not familiar with or trained in that kind of policy work (Johns 2019b). Toronto also faces a continuing lack of staff capacity. While cities such as Seattle and Philadelphia have understood that support and outreach are essential components of their GI implementation plans (one Seattle consultant noting that a full 30 percent of their budget is set aside for outreach) (Boudreau 2019), the City of Toronto has largely (barring one Transportation Services staff who is now the Green Streets Project Manager) left the implementation to a few employees who work on it as a 'side of desk' project. Furthermore, there is ongoing internal resistance to spending time and money on outreach and education, since these are viewed as extraneous to the technical guideline development (Boudreau 2019; Murphy 2019). This is not a surprising outcome of classic path dependency and institutional historicalism, wherein policy change is seen as a gradual layering onto existing policy that may eventually lead to change (Mahoney and Thelen 2009; Johns 2019b), versus a dramatic shift in institutional paradigms or operations. While this mindset is extremely common, it does pose a challenge for large-scale change; in the words of Boudreau: 'How are we going to move any of this forward if we have people who don't understand what low impact development means?'

A larger challenge may be the realization of the goal of 'using GI to build communities, not deliver widgets' (Boudreau 2019), in part because of the historical implementation and aligned leadership issues outlined above, which are common with many cities trying to implement complex environmental policy and practice (Mahoney and Thelen 2009; Loder 2011). Canadian cities lack the regulatory mandates of many U.S. cities with the Clean Water Act, and must therefore argue for co-benefits and alignment (Stott 2019), which both the Green Streets Program and the new Resilience Strategy address. However, it may still be difficult to attain the larger goal of community building, in part to the grounding of the GSTG and the Green Streets Program in mainly environmental goals, and the perceived lack of dire social inequalities and economic distress (unlike in Philadelphia). While Toronto certainly has social inequality, often focused in the inner, older suburbs with poor transit access (Hulchanski 2010; Allen 2018; Varghese 2018; Vendeville 2019), it does not have the level of inequality and disinvestment seen in some of its southern neighbours. While positive overall, this fact does reduce some of the urgency to link community well-being and cohesiveness to environmental initiatives, though this may change with their new Resilience Strategy. Additionally, the proximity of high-value 'nature' to the city (in this case the highly desirable cottage country just a short drive to the north) can make it difficult for even the most progressive cities to make urban environmental initiatives seem an urgent policy directive, regardless of their popularity.

Small-scale urban greening and green infrastructure: reflections

The case studies above reflect the recognition in many North American cities that environmental issues alone are no longer adequate drivers for GI prioritization, implementation, or successful maintenance. And while long-time leaders in green infrastructure such as Seattle and Portland are still held up as some of the most advanced examples of successful GI policy and implementation, 'newer' cities implementing GI are using slightly different drivers and framing to help them adapt green infrastructure to the particular needs of their cities. These drivers, along with varying levels of political support, have strongly influenced the effectiveness of their green infrastructure programs.

Philadelphia's commitment to equity and the improvement of greenspace, combined with state and federal policy mandates to meet water quality standards, has provided strong drivers for implementing green infrastructure. Without leadership from the mayor and cabinet-level support, however, their innovative and very effective approach to implementation would not have been nearly as successful. The requirement that all major decision makers must meet regularly to evaluate any capital project for potential green infrastructure implementation, as well as set yearly targets, has enabled Philadelphia to avoid many of the problems that cities face when trying to implement urban greening programs (including silo-ing of departments and a lack of coordination and responsibility for maintenance and funding for projects that have cross-departmental benefits). However, even this governance alignment for GI implementation would not be effective or politically palatable if it did not weave equity and socio-cultural and economic benefits into both the framing and implementation of the ROW projects. Furthermore, Philadelphia was able to build on their successful history of community outreach on urban greening projects through their Pennsylvania Horticultural Society

(PHS) work on vacant land (see Chapter 4) and has provided support and a positive approach to re-thinking community outreach for even more traditional engineering departments such as the Philadelphia Water.

The case of Toronto is much more typical of many cities in North America: despite strong environmental policy and leadership at multiple levels of government (Dhakal and Chevalier 2016), their lack until recently of a unified cross-departmental approach, ongoing lack of leadership from the province and federal government (Johns 2019b), and strong, but not urgent, environmental drivers, Toronto struggled to integrate street-level green infrastructure effectively into its policy and programs. Furthermore, while Toronto certainly has economic disparities, the lack of urgent (at least as generally perceived) socio-economic disparities and disinvestment, as seen in Philadelphia, has meant that while public outreach is encouraged, there is significant municipal resistance to seriously funding or supporting this with staff and resources, though hopefully this will change as the new programs get off the ground. The result may be some lost opportunity for designing green infrastructure that is the most effective at supporting urbanites' health, well-being, and sense of place.

Links to research and moving forward

Green infrastructure, in its balance between nature and the more mechanical workings of a city, can provide insight into dominant paradigms, or idea frameworks, about the relationship between urban nature, ecology, and public benefits. By comparing current academic debates with real-world implementation, we can approach some key questions such as: where do the case studies align, and where do they differ? And what can we learn from the gaps and synergies between theory and practice about the potential for green infrastructure to positively impact urbanites' sense of place, health, and well-being? While the majority of research on ecosystems is aimed at a more quantitative measurement of greenspace and technical guidelines (Moseley, Marzano et al. 2013; Kim, Miller et al. 2015; Van Mechelen, Van Meerbeek et al. 2015; Sookhan, Margolis et al. 2018; Kim and Miller 2019), there are five key areas of research that align with the insights from the case studies above that may be instructive for other cities and researchers.

Urban planning, theory, and ecological knowledge: negotiating competing frameworks

As we can see from the case studies above, the movement to re-integrate nature into cities as an ecological service, while promising, is not without complications. While integrating urban nature into the city through ecosystem services and green infrastructure is no longer new, it still suffers from the same difficulties that many urban environmental initiatives face: a fundamental mismatch between natural and built systems and the accounting and mindset that keep the two separated. Both urban planning and ecosystem research have their own language, frameworks, and paradigms that can make integration difficult, even when both sides agree on the need to integrate. For example, municipal policy documents are recognizing that natural systems are potentially valuable inputs that can reduce risks from extreme weather events from climate change while also reducing grey infrastructure costs (Philadelphia Water Department 2011; City of Chicago and Department of Water Management 2014). Ecosystem terminology has also begun to infiltrate policy documents, with Philadelphia, Toronto, and Seattle all using terms like *natural corridors*, *habitat*, *patches*, and *connectivity* in their public-facing documents (City of Toronto 2015). However, while researchers agree on the need to better integrate urban ecology into urban planning, particularly given climate change pressures, they argue that a new framework that urban planners and practitioners can use as a model for integration is needed (Kattel, Elkadi et al. 2013; Haase, Haase et al. 2014; Fischer 2018). Most of these discussions critique the lack of integration of solid *ecological* knowledge in urban planning (Wang, Tan et al. 2014; Brown, Vanos et al. 2015), and the lost opportunities (Huber, Shilling et al. 2012), risks, and problems this can cause, citing for example the need for horticultural knowledge of specific species' water needs (Norton, Coutts et al. 2015), or the limits of ecosystems in dealing with possible contamination (Nassauer 2012). Others focus on differences in definitions of resilience (Olsson, Jerneck et al. 2015); the difficulty of exactly *how* to measure, implement and integrate ecosystem services (Dempsey and Robertson 2012; Van Mechelen, Van Meerbeek et al. 2015; Scholte, Daams et al. 2018); and technicalities of how to achieve integration (Huber, Shilling et al. 2012; Kattel, Elkadi et al. 2013; Steiner 2014; Hoversten and Swaffield 2019). Lastly, while not as common, some researchers are moving beyond a mainly technical approach to integration and pointing to the separate logic and importance of social, political, and economic factors that influence outcomes (Gómez-Baggethun and Barton 2013; Niemelä 2014; Jackson and Palmer 2015; Wartmann and Purves 2018). While there is certainly a need for more ecological knowledge to inform urban planning, it is these last approaches that may provide the most promise for long-term sustainability of GI projects, due to their acknowledgement of the need for cultural-ecological integration.

The difficulty of integrating ecological knowledge into policy can be seen in our case studies. For example, Toronto's GSTG deliberately references policy precedents (North American best case practice and local policy) and ecological imperatives (Toronto's climatic and policy goals) as a means to justify and make locally relevant its guidelines. It also references multiple layers of policy in Ontario that support the guidelines and provides technical guidance on how to implement green infrastructure in the ROW in Toronto. And it is based on lessons learned from local pilots, countless hours of outreach, and was supported by extensive political messaging and outreach by its key authors. However, despite this level of innovation, local stakeholder analysis described less of an integration of ecosystem services into Toronto's policy, and more of a 'layering green over grey' (Johns 2019a), reflecting academic discussions of the problems of *path dependency* and hard-to-change institutional frameworks that are resistant to the kind of change needed for green infrastructure implementation (Matthews, Lo et al. 2015). The mirroring of academic debates with on-the-ground implementation is also reflected in the engineering mindset of 'technical fixes' for GI (Chiorean 2019) that do not integrate with other complementary policies, such as complete street guidelines (Boudreau 2019).

While these ongoing issues of alignment, leadership, and implementation across multiple scales of government continue to play an important role, especially for Toronto, in GI leadership, the lesson from Philadelphia points to another component necessary for success. Seen in both of the above case studies, there is the realization of the need to more fully integrate community values, feedback, and needs for the site into the process. While it is exactly these 'co-benefits' for communities that have enabled many cities to justify the use of green infrastructure instead of big-pipe solutions in the first place – seen most clearly in the case of Philadelphia and supported in international documents such as the Millennial Ecosystem Assessment (Millennial Ecosystem Assessment 2003) – the actual integration of community involvement in a previously technical process has been anything but simple. Even in Philadelphia – which has the most explicit support for public benefits from green infrastructure in its policy documents – the Water Department has admitted that the learning curve for how to do public outreach and integrate it into their process is steep, and yet it has to be done intentionally and is critical to the success of these programs (Chiorean 2019). In other cities where the social benefits have not been as heavily promoted – such as Toronto – the need to support public outreach with staff time and resources has been heavily resisted from personnel entrenched in a technological-fix mindset of implementation (Boudreau 2019).

An alternative approach: an adaptive proposal

Faced with this 'policy standoff' between traditional and green infrastructure implementation, some researchers have called for a more adaptive approach that is more closely related to design thinking and workshops than to traditional ecosystem knowledge or policy precedent (Ahern, Cilliers et al. 2014; Grose 2014;

Steiner 2014). By employing a 'learning-by-doing' model of transdisciplinary collaboration, both ecological and socio-political approaches are called upon to work in a 'safe to fail' framework that includes experimental design guidelines, monitoring and assessment of outcomes, and protocols and strategies for revising initial concepts to be more adaptive and flexible to local community needs (Ahern, Cilliers et al. 2014; Luo, Liu et al. 2018). Proponents of such an approach also emphasize that a revised perspective on data from both sides will be an essential component, such that ecological knowledge does not always trump local needs and perspectives, but rather sits in the context of *constructed* ecologies that balance human and ecological needs (Grose 2014).

In this model, implementing green infrastructure is not a one-way street, where ecologists tell communities what they need using a universal, but abstract, understanding of science and nature (Davison 2008); rather, a successful green infrastructure project includes the recognition that community values, needs, and local lived experience of nature and place are also essential components and that this more complex approach has greater likelihood of success (Flint, Kunze et al. 2013; Ahern, Cilliers et al. 2014; Wartmann and Purves 2018). The more multidimensional approach also recognizes that the language and frameworks of ecology are perhaps not as neutral as previously believed, arguing for example that ecological terms such as *resilience* can mean stability and engineering solutions, change and adaptation, or even have political meaning (Dempsey and Robertson 2012; Olsson, Jerneck et al. 2015). It could be argued that Philadelphia is trying this more adaptive approach through its cross-departmental collaborative mandate that challenges the status quo and the silo-ing of departments, and which focuses on elevating and legitimizing the needs of community as equal to ecological imperatives. While they are not there yet, activists in Toronto are aware of the need for and are calling for this more adaptive approach in order to overcome bureaucratic and political hurdles (Boudreau 2019; Murphy 2019) as well as ensure more multidimensional successes. These activists recognize that communities need to be engaged in order to gain political acceptance of green infrastructure projects, especially when competing social priorities are argued to be more important. Similar calls for greater integration of means and goals can be seen even in traditionally environmental focused cities. This can be seen in Seattle, with the increasing elevation and integration of community priorities and partnerships in green infrastructure approaches that were historically constrained by more narrowly scoped measures of success such as quantifiable ecological benefit, regulatory compliance, and cost per unit of stormwater system benefit (Emerson 2019). It can also be seen in the recognition that without regular experience of the projects, there is less likelihood of community acceptance (Jim, Lo et al. 2015). While perhaps not yet a relational approach to the human relationship to nature seen in Chapter 1, this hybrid approach is moving away from a purely utilitarian or adaptive model more traditionally seen in ecosystem services literature.

Human health and green infrastructure: moving from risk-reduction to socio-cultural co-benefits

A second theme that emerges from both the case studies and research debates focuses on how ecosystem services and green infrastructure may influence human health and well-being. While traditional ecosystem services and green infrastructure policy work focused more on *reducing risks* to ecosystems and human health, more recent policy positions at multiple scales have recognized that green infrastructure may offer potentially *positive* or health *promoting* 'socio-cultural' or 'co-benefits' to human health and well-being (Millennial Ecosystem Assessment 2003; Gómez-Baggethun and Barton 2013; Lachowycz and Jones 2013). This multi-benefit framing around green infrastructure and health can be seen in all the case studies, though it is most clearly articulated by Philadelphia, which places ecological and human health on equal footing. The research used to justify the co-benefits of GI reflects a variety of paradigms and interests, ranging from environmental psychology on the positive health impacts of access to nature; to social values around ecosystem services (Riechers, Barkmann et al. 2018; Bubalo, van Zanten et al. 2019); to econometric valuations of nature – such as the increased real estate value of projects close to urban nature (Kovacs 2012); to a health and well-being perspective on the role of greenspace in quality of life at a community or population scale (Ward Thompson, Roe et al. 2012).

Not surprisingly given the increased policy uptake from environmental psychology research discussed in Chapter 1, most of these policy documents imply a connection between green infrastructure and human health and well-being, and they also assume that any added greenspace counts as a universal, generally accepted, and positive idea of nature. This reflects the tendency for ecology to adopt a utilitarian or adaptive paradigm around the human relationship to nature, wherein 'nature' is an input to a neutral human object with a measurable, and predictable, output (Flint, Kunze et al. 2013; Kolinjivadi, Van Hecken et al. 2019). While such a conceptualization of the nature–human relationship – and of what 'nature' *is*, even more fundamentally – more easily lends itself to inclusion in urban policy, it is unlikely to address the complex lived experience of urbanites, or be easily integrated into the adaptive planning model advocated by both policy activists and researchers alike. That the utilitarian ecological services model can be a limiting factor can be seen most clearly when human needs are contrasted to ecological needs, and where an ecological risk-reduction model without the larger socio-cultural context is not readily accepted by the public or political leaders.

This tension between ecological and human needs can be seen in Chicago, where ongoing issues with gun violence and poverty have created a new approach to GI that recognizes that in cities with significant social and economic problems *resilience* must take a different meaning:

> ... within the City of Chicago how do you ensure that all communities are at the same level of resilience?... How do we do that and what does it mean? It's not just our sewer system and putting green infrastructure in.... How are we going to get jobs back in those neighbourhoods? How are we going to improve the school system in those neighbourhoods? How are we going to combat crime in those neighbourhoods?
>
> (Berkshire 2019)

Given these difficulties, some researchers are advocating for a more relational approach to understanding the link between ecosystem services (ES) and human health and well-being (Flint, Kunze et al. 2013), arguing that a more flexible model is needed to understand the mechanisms between exposure to green infrastructure and human health. Researchers have pointed to the clear need for longitudinal studies, but other gaps in current research have been identified as well. For instance, there is a need for research that considers the influence of cultural shifts and values on perceptions of ES, similar to work that has been done around wilderness and which can re-politicize ES (Dahmus and Nelson 2014; Uren, Dzidic et al. 2015; Finewood, Matsler et al. 2019; Kolinjivadi, Van Hecken et al. 2019). Other researchers have called for more attention around issues of scale – i.e. how much 'nature' in ES is enough to impact health and well-being? (Flint, Kunze et al. 2013) – and the link between ES, psychosocial variables, subjective well-being (Jennings, Larson et al. 2016). There have also been calls for research that can lead to a better understanding of the complex interactions between urbanites and ecosystems (Tzoulas, Korpela et al. 2007); of the role that stress plays in urbanites' perceptions of urban greenspace (Peschardt and Stigsdotter 2013; Samuelsson, Giusti et al. 2018); and the role that place identity plays in restoration outcomes or GI projects (Wilkie and Clouston 2015; Verbrugge and van den Born 2018). While these recent studies are promising, the limited evidence to date from resident perceptions of green infrastructure – and the paradigm-altering example of Chicago's recent GI resilience project that include equity and economic factors (see below) (Berkshire 2018) – indicate that these modified approaches to GI implementation may need to be even further developed. These modified approaches may address, in addition to ecological services, issues such as equity, aesthetics, biodiversity, and inherited values around wildness, health, and urban nature (Macdonald and King 2018; Finewood, Matsler et al. 2019).

Aesthetics and biodiversity

A key component of green infrastructure projects such as green streets that emerges from a more adaptive model of design and implementation versus an engineering approach is the role that aesthetics plays in urbanites' attitudes and values. Research from the social constructionist paradigm, described in Chapter 1, has shown that aesthetics plays a key role in participant attitudes, values, and perceptions of nature (Gobster, Nassauaer et al. 2007; Heft 2010), and that these perceptions directly influence the projects' perceived health impact (Hunter 2015). Furthermore, while most research on urban greening has focused on more traditional types of nature, such as parks and trees (Nordh and Østby 2013; Sugimoto 2013; Palmer and English 2019), the rise of small-scale urban greening in interstitial spaces raises questions about urbanites' perceptions of nature that is woven into the daily fabric of their city. Do green roofs (discussed in Chapter 3), elevated greenspaces (Chapter 4), or green streets 'count' as nature to the urbanites who live among them? If these small-scale urban nature projects *are* considered 'nature,' then they also likely provide benefits similar to those associated with traditional urban nature: improved concentration (Loder 2014), recovery from stress (Jiang, Chang et al. 2014; Hazer, Formica et al. 2018), and improved mood (Beute and de Kort 2014; Li, Deal et al. 2018). Because ecological processes have long been hidden from view under the engineering big-pipe model (Hough 2004), and public outreach for green infrastructure projects is still in its infancy, it is unclear whether communities recognize these projects as ecology or 'nature,' or what role aesthetics plays in public perceptions of green infrastructure such as green streets.

What we do know is that so-called 'wild' nature in the city – such as naturalized medians – whose messy, unkempt aesthetic has been linked to perceived disorder and perceived increased crime (Wang, Tan et al. 2014), is not always appreciated or understood by urbanites (Jorgensen and Tylecote 2007; Loder 2014), and in many cases is associated with disease, ill-health, poverty, and poor moral values (Kaika 2006; Poškus and Poškienė 2015). This underlying influence on urbanites' perception has meant that previous well-meaning urban greening initiatives – such as ecological lawns – have been seen as a sign of either progress or decay (Robbins and Sharp 2003; Dahmus and Nelson 2014; Ignatieva, Ahrné et al. 2015). We also know that areas that have 'cues to care' such as straight lines, mowed areas, and flowers that show deliberate human presence (Nassauer 1995) are often preferred to 'wilder' areas of urban greenspace such as buffer zones that are rated as unattractive if perceived as ill-maintained (Panduro and Veie 2013). This raises questions about the human impact of green infrastructure that is designed for ecological, versus human, benefits, specifically around the role of perceived maintenance, biodiversity, climate-specific aesthetics, and ecological knowledge.

For example, while not all of the case studies have clear data on community perceptions of them, it is not surprising that highly designed 'rain gardens' with abundant colour and flowers – seen in the Coxwell rain garden in Toronto– are generally less contentious and more well liked than green streets that were more ambiguously designed or unclear in their goals. In a qualitative study done in Portland, Oregon, participants were ambivalent about whether green streets were nature and unclear on the goals of the project, but they liked them better than nothing (Church 2015) – similar to results found on office workers' perceptions of green roofs (Loder 2014) (see Chapter 3). However, environmental aesthetics is also one of the few areas of human perception and behaviour that has responded well to environmental education (Gobster, Nassauaer et al. 2007; Junker and Buchecker 2008; Goleman, Bennett et al. 2012). For example, after environmental education in a Toronto pilot project helped residents to understand the complex role of the 'wild' aesthetics of the gardens, many changed their 'neatening up' behaviour in their raingardens (Yamaguchi 2016).

Also unclear is the role beauty and emotion play in urbanites' perceptions of SSUG such as GI. Research conducted in Mississauga, Ontario on resident perceptions and readiness for more sustainable GI landscaping emphasized the need to tap into resident's emotional connection to the landscape and their need for peace and beauty (Freeman Associates 2008), supporting research that has shown that the role of beauty in urban nature may be a crucial element in ensuring acceptance, connection, and stewardship (Zhang, Howell et al. 2014; Lumber, Richardson et al. 2017; Wyles, White et al. 2019).

What is less clear is the role of biodiversity in aesthetic perceptions of small-scale urban nature projects such as green streets. Some research has linked increased biodiversity to increased acceptance and potential attention restoration from urban nature (Loder 2014; Carrus, Scopelliti et al. 2015; Southon, Jorgensen et al. 2018; Ramer, Nelson et al. 2019; Schebella, Weber et al. 2019), and to increased property values (Netusil, Levin et al. 2014) and ecological benefits (Weber, Kowarik et al. 2014). Other research is less clear on the benefits of biodiversity and human health, however (Qiu, Lindberg et al. 2013; Korpela, Pasanen et al. 2018), and participant recognition of biodiversity is also highly variable, with participants assuming colour indicated higher levels of biodiversity (Hoyle, Norton et al. 2018; Southon, Jorgensen et al. 2018). Given that participants are often unsure of the ecological benefits of green infrastructure but have greater acceptance of 'wilder' aesthetics if they feel that the project is meant to benefit others, especially wildlife (Garbuzov, Fensome et al. 2015; Unterweger, Schrode et al. 2017; Ramer, Nelson et al. 2019), including environmental education and outreach as part of implementation of green infrastructure would very likely increase community – and thus political – acceptance.

What remains to be seen is the role of aesthetics in arid climates, particularly since research has shown that xeriscaped landscapes – those designed to need little irrigation – are less preferred than water-loving landscapes. Furthermore, both landscapes are highly symbolic and can influence urbanites' acceptance of urban greening projects (Neel, Sadalla et al. 2014). For example, cities that are arid but suffer from periodic flooding, such as Denver, Colorado, may need to engage directly with the aesthetic preferences of residents – many of whom grew up in wetter climates – and may need to address different expectations and values around green streets than cities dealing with wetter climates, such as Philadelphia or Seattle. Lastly, the role of beauty and sense of place in small-scale urban nature – a burgeoning trend in research on the human relationship to nature touched on in Chapter 1 – is important to watch as green infrastructure becomes more commonly integrated into the urban fabric of the city. Similarly, understanding cultural differences will prove essential for the success of green street projects, particularly in communities with high cultural and economic diversity, such as Toronto. Extensive community outreach will be needed to understand community perceptions that may influence the design of green infrastructure interventions that could impact urbanites' well-being and sense of place.

Sense of place and lived experience: issues of mobility, ecological knowledge, and collective experience

As more small-scale urban greening projects are integrated into the fabric of cities, and in particular, the ROW, larger questions arise about how these projects might impact urbanites' sense of place and lived experience. The obvious answer draws on research from environmental psychology and other disciplines that have shown the positive impact on urbanites from contact with nature. Most of this research has focused on individual benefits, such as improved attention restoration (Korpela, Ylen et al. 2008; Tyrväinen, Ojala et al. 2014; Weber and Trojan 2018) and decreased mental fatigue and respite for stressed individuals (discussed in Chapter 1) (Ulrich, Simons et al. 1991; Stigsdotter and Grahn 2011; Hazer, Formica et al. 2018). Certainly, green infrastructure that has been co-designed with community members, as in Philadelphia and Toronto, has a higher chance of being accepted and liked by the community and providing these restorative moments, especially if woven into the fabric of the city such that there is easy access and more chance of contact. What remains to be seen is the issue of scale and mobility – or how contact with nature is impacted by size and location in urbanites' daily lives – a limitation acknowledged by many researchers on the human–nature relationship (Flint, Kunze et al. 2013; Lachowycz and Jones 2013; Li, Deal et al. 2018). How much nature is enough to counteract the acknowledged stressors of traffic and concrete? Are ribbons along roadsides enough to give that restorative sense of 'being away' from daily stressors central to the Kaplan's Attention Restoration Theory? What about mobility? People do not experience the city from only one vantage point or at one point in time, and some researchers have started to explore what role experiencing nature throughout the city has on their well-being, preferences, and perceptions (Bamberg, Hitchings et al. 2018). The need for the evaluation of nature as experienced through mobility and action is a central argument behind the utilitarian paradigms' affordances approach which argues that nature is liked and beneficial in terms of how many opportunities for recreation and restoration it provides (Heft 2010; Hooper, Boruff et al. 2018).

What may help here is a less quantitative approach to discovering the socio-cultural benefits of nature, which can run directly counter to the technical and ecological goals of most green infrastructure. For example, there has been some work that has argued that the benefits of contact with nature may be more linked to a larger sense of place than previously realized (Korpela, Ylen et al. 2009; Lachowycz and Jones 2013; Baptiste, Foley et al. 2015; Wilkie and Clements 2018), meaning that outreach may also need to address sense of place around GI projects, not just community aesthetic or activity preferences and technical infrastructure needs. Furthermore, there is debate on what exactly is meant by sense of place. For those working from an adaptive or utilitarian model, sense of place can be measured by constructs such as satisfaction and attachment, and is influenced by the characteristics of the place itself (Stedman 2003). From this perspective, engaging community in outreach to determine their level of satisfaction and place attachment would help to design green infrastructure that is also potentially more restorative and impactful on communities' daily lived experience than assuming a one-size-fits all technical approach. Other researchers have expanded the list of constructs believed to influence sense of place to include rootedness, belonging, and emotional attachment (Williams, Heidebrecht et al. 2008), while still working from a psychometric approach. This expanded understanding of sense of place parallels work around the human relationship to nature and the role that emotion plays in attachment, loss, and mood around human–nature outcomes (Pearce, Davison et al. 2015; Knez, Butler et al. 2018; Knez, Sang et al. 2018). Linking green infrastructure to local lost ecological history – such as the buried streams in the proposed Raindrop Plaza in Toronto (Mutrie 2018), or salmon runs they are trying to bring back in Seattle (Sullivan and Simson 2019) – is a way of making it more meaningful to inhabitants and can link them to their local 'place.' Researchers found not only that the restoration of a salmon stream brought stakeholders together who were at a standstill, but that it helped the community rediscover a local ecological identity, with even the schoolchildren becoming involved and drawing salmon all facing the same way after working in the streams (Mills 2000).

Because most urbanites are distant from natural processes of the landscape around them, making ecological processes visible, such as 'daylighting' hidden streams and waterways, increases the likelihood of their acceptance and understanding of green infrastructure (Hough 2004; Baptiste, Foley et al. 2015). Bringing more visibility to ecological processes in the city can also draw attention to larger ecological systems outside the city, which can help provide a sense of scale, awe, and so-called glacial time (i.e. ecological time) versus chronological time, or human-time (Castells 2010a, 2010b). This awareness of the larger rhythms and time-scale of nature has been shown to reduce stress (Kaplan 1984; Hazer, Formica et al. 2018), and reflects some of the perspectives of the phenomenological approach to sense of place (discussed in Chapter 3), which argues being in or experiencing nature is an effective way to engage in meditative versus calculative thinking (Stefanovic 2008). Lastly, encouraging local experience of nature, here in the form of green infrastructure in the ROW, can help to make the more abstract, scientific understanding of nature used to justify the technical capacities of GI more meaningful, and thus have the potential to positively impact urbanites' sense of place and well-being.

However, implementing GI also needs to address collective experiences of place that can impact resident perceptions. Those working from a social constructionist model have discussed the role social and historical processes have played in constructing, negotiating, and contesting sense of place, showing through work with women and fear that sense of place can be collectively experienced (Valentine 1990; Manzo 2008). This approach may be useful when designing and implementing green infrastructure in vulnerable neighbourhoods, or near specific populations. This is particularly important for vulnerable groups or communities that do not always feel welcome in or have time to spend in more traditional greenspaces, or who live in neighbourhoods with a negative sense of place. In Denver, for example, where the Globeville neighbourhood suffers from both ongoing health, economic, and social insecurity as well as constant flooding from multiple sources, different groups are working with members of the community to re-frame the notion of the neighbourhood – moving from the historic dumping ground of the city's waters to a place of key ecological importance, with possibilities for environmental education and training (Vogelsang 2018). Thinking about the particular needs of a community may also influence the design of a green infrastructure project. What might green infrastructure look like near a school? A senior home? A community of recent immigrants or refugees? A recent, and promising, example of a place-based and locally sensitive approach was taken by the City of Chicago with their 100 Cities Rockefeller Resilience stormwater project, which identified areas where flooding and socio-economic and health problems were the worst, and then took city-owned vacant land and turned it into working stormwater landscapes for the city's most vulnerable. Recognizing this socio-economic and ecological approach to resilience, they co-developed the design and location with local community organizations which will then maintain them (Berkshire 2019). The goals are not only to reduce flooding and heat stress, but also to improve economic stabilization and social cohesion, which is demonstrated in their aggressive local hiring policy. This kind of combined socio-economic, health and well-being approach to GI, which acknowledges a collective experience of place, can be transformative and empowering for communities.

As seen from the above case studies and discussion of current gaps and promising areas for future exploration, implementing GI in North American cities is gaining traction as a legitimate means to address urban environmental problems. For some cities, combining socio-economic and environmental benefits from GI has enabled these projects to gain more acceptance and community support; other cities have recognized the need to include community input but are still navigating the shift from an engineering to a combined engineering/socio-ecological approach. While documentation of community response is limited given the newness of these projects, research on the benefits of increased contact with nature offers insight into possible human and ecological benefits from these SSUG projects. When combined with further work around adaptive planning, aesthetics and biodiversity, and sense of place, this newer approach to GI may provide opportunities to benefit urbanites' health, well-being, and sense of place while also reducing negative ecological impact.

References

100 Resilient Cities. (2019). "100 Resilient Cities." Retrieved May 10, 2019, from https://100resilientcities.org.

Ahern, J., S. Cilliers and J. Niemelä (2014). "The concept of ecosystem services in adaptive urban planning and design: A framework for supporting innovation." *Landscape and Urban Planning* **125**(0): 254–259.

Allen, J. (2018). *Mapping Inequalities of Access to Employment and Quantifying Transport Poverty in Canadian Cities*. Master of Arts, University of Toronto.

Andersson, E., S. Barthel and K. Ahrné (2007). "Measuring social-ecological dynamics behind the generation of ecosystem services." *Ecological Applications* **17**(5): 1267–1278.

Ashton, J. (1992). "The Origins of Healthy Cities." *Healthy Cities*. J. Ashton. Milton Keynes and Philadelphia, Open University Press: 1–12.

Baker, A. R. (2018). "Philadelphia's Green City, Clean Waters Needs Funding to Achieve Goals." *PennFuture Blog: Our Perspectives on the Latest Issues* Retrieved June 5, 2019, from https://pennfuture.org/Blog-Item-Philadelphias-Green-City-Clean-Waters-Needs-Funding-to-Achieve-Goals.

Bamberg, J., R. Hitchings and A. Latham (2018). "Enriching green exercise research." *Landscape and Urban Planning* **178**: 270–275.

Baptiste, A. K., C. Foley and R. Smardon (2015). "Understanding urban neighborhood differences in willingness to implement green infrastructure measures: A case study of Syracuse, NY." *Landscape and Urban Planning* **136**(0): 1–12.

Barthel, S., C. Folke and J. Colding (2010). "Social–ecological memory in urban gardens – Retaining the capacity for management of ecosystem services." *Global Environmental Change* **20**(2): 255–265.

Battersby, H. (2017). "Pilot Rain Garden Parkette at Fairford and Coxwell." *Toronto Gardens*, www.torontogardens.com/2017/06/pilot-rain-garden-parkette-at-fairford-and-coxwell.html/2019.

Berkshire, M. (2018). *Resilient Corridors*. Chicago: Greenbuild.

Berkshire, M. (2019). Green Projects Administrator, Department of Planning and Development, City of Chicago. Interview with A. Loder.

Beute, F. and Y. A. W. de Kort (2014). "Natural resistance: Exposure to nature and self-regulation, mood, and physiology after ego-depletion." *Journal of Environmental Psychology* **40**(0): 167–178.

Bolund, P. and S. Hunhammar (1999). "Ecosystem services in urban areas." *Ecological Economics* **29**(2): 293–301.

Boudreau, S. (2019). Former Senior Landscape Architect, Special Projects and Design Services, Project Management Office, Toronto and Region Conservation Authority, and Urban Designer, City of Toronto. Interview with A. Loder.

Boudreau, S., P. Cheung and K. Nelischer (2017). Green infrastructure: The right way for the right-of-way in Toronto. *Municipal World*, November.

Branas, C. C., R. A. Cheney, J. M. MacDonald, V. W. Tam, T. D. Jackson and T. R. Ten Have (2011). "A difference-in-differences analysis of health, safety, and greening vacant urban space." *American Journal of Epidemiology* **174**(11).

Braun, B. (2005). "Environmental issues: Writing a more-than-human urban geography." *Progress in Human Geography* **29**(5): 635–650.

Braun, B. (2008). "Environmental issues: Inventive life." *Progress in Human Geography* **32**(5): 667–679.

Brooks, J. (2019). Director, Green Stormwater Infrastructure Unit, Philadelphia Water Department. Interview with A. Loder.

Brown, H. J. (2017). "Green infrastructure: Best practices for cities." *Advocacy and Policy*. Retrieved May 2, 2019, from www.usgbc.org/articles/green-infrastructure-best-practices-cities.

Brown, R. D., J. Vanos, N. Kenny and S. Lenzholzer (2015). "Designing urban parks that ameliorate the effects of climate change." *Landscape and Urban Planning* **138**(0): 118–131.

Bubalo, M., B. T. van Zanten and P. H. Verburg (2019). "Crowdsourcing geo-information on landscape perceptions and preferences: A review." *Landscape and Urban Planning* **184**: 101–111.

Canadian Society of Landscape Architects (2019). CSLA Announces the Recipients of the 2019 Awards of Excellence: Rooted in Clay – WY Garden (Winnipeg, MB) by Straub Thurmayr Landscape Architects is awarded the Jury's Award of Excellence.

Carrus, G., M. Scopelliti, R. Lafortezza, G. Colangelo, F. Ferrini, F. Salbitano, M. Agrimi, L. Portoghesi, P. Semenzato and G. Sanesi (2015). "Go greener, feel better? The positive effects of biodiversity on the well-being of individuals visiting urban and peri-urban green areas." *Landscape and Urban Planning* **134**(0): 221–228.

Castells, M. (2010a). The Greening of the Self: The Environmental Movement. *The Power of Identity*. Oxford, UK, Malden, MA.: Wiley-Blackwell. **2**: 168–191.

Castells, M. (2010b). *The Rise of the Network Society*. Oxford, Malden, MA: Wiley-Blackwell.

Chen, A., X. A. Yao, R. Sun and L. Chen (2014). "Effect of urban green patterns on surface urban cool islands and its seasonal variations." *Urban Forestry and Urban Greening* **13**(4): 646–654.

Chiorean, S. (2019). Environmental Scientist and Planner, Philadelphia Water Department. Interview with A. Loder.

Church, S. P. (2015). "Exploring Green Streets and rain gardens as instances of small scale nature and environmental learning tools." *Landscape and Urban Planning* **134**(0): 229–240.

City and County of Denver. (2016). "Ultra-Urban Green Infrastructure." *Wastewater Management*. Retrieved May 2, 2019, from www.denvergov.org/content/denvergov/en/wastewater-management/stormwater-quality/ultra-urban-green-infrastructure.html.

City of Chicago and Department of Water Management (2014). Green Stormwater Infrastructure Strategy. Chicago.

City of New York (2017). Standard Designs and Guidelines for Green Infrastructure Practices. New York.

City of Philadelphia (2009). Greenworks Philadelphia. Mayor Michael A. Nutter. Philadelphia, Mayor's Office.

City of Philadelphia (2011). Citywide Vision: Philadelphia2035. P. C. P. Commission. Philadelphia.

City of Philadelphia (2016). Greenworks: A vision for a sustainable Philadelphia. Office of Sustainability, Philadelphia: 38.

City of Philadelphia. (2019a). "Philadelphia Beverage Tax." *Business taxes*. Retrieved June 5, 2019, from www.phila.gov/services/payments-assistance-taxes/business-taxes/philadelphia-beverage-tax.

City of Philadelphia. (2019b). "Rebuild." Retrieved May 2, 2019, from www.phila.gov/programs/rebuild.

City of Toronto (2000). Clean, Green and Healthy: A Plan for an Environmentally Sustainable Toronto. Environmental Task Force. Toronto.
City of Toronto (2003). Wet Weather Flow Management – Policy. Toronto.
City of Toronto (2006). Wet Weather Flow Management – Guidelines. Toronto.
City of Toronto (2007a). Change is in the Air: Climate Change, Clean Air and Sustainable Energy Action Plan: Moving from Framework to Action: Phase 1. Toronto: 16.
City of Toronto. (2007b). "January 1, 2007: City of Toronto Act 2006 Proclaimed Ontario's Capital City Begins New Era." Retrieved February 9, 2007, from www.toronto.ca/mayor_miller/torontoact.htm.
City of Toronto (2007c). The Toronto Green Development Standard January 2007. City Planning and Development Policy and Research, City of Toronto: 1–27.
City of Toronto (2009). By-law to Require and Govern the Construction of Green Roofs in Toronto. Chief Planner and Executive Director, Chief Building Official and Executive Director, City Planning. Toronto.
City of Toronto (2015). Toronto Official Plan. Toronto.
City of Toronto (2017). Toronto Green Streets Technical Guidelines. Toronto.
City of Toronto (2018). Toronto Green Standard Version 3. Toronto.
City of Toronto (2019). "Resilience Strategy." Retrieved July 30, 2019, from www.toronto.ca/services-payments/water-environment/environmentally-friendly-city-initiatives/resilientto.
City of Toronto (n.d.-a). "Green Streets." Retrieved July 30, 2019, from www.toronto.ca/services-payments/streets-parking-transportation/enhancing-our-streets-and-public-realm/green-streets.
City of Toronto (n.d.-b). "Toronto at a Glance." *Data, Research and Maps*. Retrieved May 2, 2019, from www.toronto.ca/city-government/data-research-maps/toronto-at-a-glance.
Dahmus, M. E. and K. C. Nelson (2014). "Nature discourses in the residential yard in Minnesota." *Landscape and Urban Planning* **125**(0): 183–187.
Davison, A. (2008). "The trouble with nature: Ambivalence in the lives of urban Australian environmentalists." *Geoforum* **39**(3): 1284–1295.
Dempsey, J. and M. M. Robertson (2012). "Ecosystem services: Tensions, impurities, and points of engagement within neoliberalism." *Progress in Human Geography* **36**(6): 758–779.
Dhakal, K. and L. R. Chevalier (2016). "Urban stormwater governance: The need for a paradigm shift." *Environmental Management* **57**(5): 1112–1124.
Dick, J. M., R. I. Smith and E. M. Scott (2011). "Ecosystem services and associated concepts." *Environmetrics* **22**(5): 598–607.
Draaisma, M. (2016). "Rain gardens pretty and functional, says Toronto resident." *CBC News*, August 15.
Du, J., L. Cheng, Q. Zhang, Y. Yang and W. Xu (2019). "Different flooding behaviors due to varied urbanization levels within river basin: A case study from the Xiang River Basin, China." *International Journal of Disaster Risk Science* **10**(1): 89–102.
Emerson, P. (2019). Green Infrastructure Planner, City of Seattle. Interview with A. Loder.
Environmental Services (n.d.). "Green Infrastructure." *What We Do*. Retrieved May 2, 2019, from www.portlandoregon.gov/bes/34598.
Escobedo, F. J., T. Kroeger and J. E. Wagner (2011). "Urban forests and pollution mitigation: Analyzing ecosystem services and disservices." *Environmental Pollution* **159**(8): 2078–2087.
Finewood, M. H., A. M. Matsler and J. Zivkovich (2019). "Green infrastructure and the hidden politics of urban stormwater governance in a postindustrial city." *Annals of the American Association of Geographers* **109**(3): 909–925.
Fischer, A. P. (2018). "Forest landscapes as social-ecological systems and implications for management." *Landscape and Urban Planning* **177**: 138–147.
Flint, C. G., I. Kunze, A. Muhar, Y. Yoshida and M. Penker (2013). "Exploring empirical typologies of human–nature relationships and linkages to the ecosystem services concept." *Landscape and Urban Planning* **120**(0): 208–217.
Fraser, E. D. G. and W. A. Kenney (2000). "Cultural background and landscape history as factors affecting perceptions of the urban forest." *Journal of Arboriculture* **26**(2): 106–112.
Freeman Associates (2008). *Market Research and Marketing Strategy: Lot-level Stormwater Control in the Residential Sector – City of Mississauga*. Whitby, Ontario.
Garbuzov, M., K. A. Fensome and F. L. W. Ratnieks (2015). "Public approval plus more wildlife: Twin benefits of reduced mowing of amenity grass in a suburban public park in Saltdean, UK." *Insect Conservation and Diversity* **8**(2): 107–119.

Gobster, P. H., J. Nassauaer, T. C. Daniel and G. Fry (2007). "The shared landscape: What does aesthetics have to do with ecology?" *Landscape Ecology* **22**(7): 959–972.

Goleman, D., L. Bennett and Z. Barlow (2012). *Ecoliterate: How Educators Are Cultivating Emotional, Social, and Ecological Intelligence*. San Francisco: Jossey-Bass.

Gómez-Baggethun, E. and D. N. Barton (2013). "Classifying and valuing ecosystem services for urban planning." *Ecological Economics* **86**: 235–245.

Gould, D. (2019). Deputy Director of Community Engagement and Communications, Rebuild, City of Philadelphia. Interview with A. Loder.

Green Roofs for Healthy Cities (n.d.). "City of Toronto." *Government/Non-Profit*. Retrieved June 6, 2019, from https://greenroofs.org/members/city-of-toronto.

Green Stormwater Infrastructure Partners and sbn (2016). *The Economic Impact of Green City, Clean Waters: The First Five Years*. Philadelphia.

Grose, M. J. (2014). "Gaps and futures in working between ecology and design for constructed ecologies." *Landscape and Urban Planning* **132**(0): 69–78.

Gulsrud, N. M., C. M. Raymond, R. L. Rutt, A. S. Olafsson, T. Plieninger, M. Sandberg, T. H. Beery and K. I. Jönsson (2018). "'Rage against the machine'? The opportunities and risks concerning the automation of urban green infrastructure." *Landscape and Urban Planning* **180**: 85–92.

Haase, D., A. Haase and D. Rink (2014). "Conceptualizing the nexus between urban shrinkage and ecosystem services." *Landscape and Urban Planning* **132**(0): 159–169.

Hazer, M., M. K. Formica, S. Dieterlen and C. P. Morley (2018). "The relationship between self-reported exposure to greenspace and human stress in Baltimore, MD." *Landscape and Urban Planning* **169**: 47–56.

Heft, H. (2010). "Affordances and the Perception of Landscape: An Inquiry into Environmental Perception and Aesthetics." *Innovative Approaches to Researching Landscape and Health: Open Spaces: People Space 2*. C. Ward Thompson, P. Aspinall and S. Bell. Abingdon, UK: Routledge.

Hooper, P., B. Boruff, B. Beesley, H. Badland and B. Giles-Corti (2018). "Testing spatial measures of public open space planning standards with walking and physical activity health outcomes: Findings from the Australian national liveability study." *Landscape and Urban Planning* **171**: 57–67.

Hough, M. (1984). "Introduction, and Urban Ecology, a Basis for Design." *City Form and Natural Process*. London and Sydney: Croom Helm: 1–4, 5–27.

Hough, M. (2004). *Cities and Natural Process: A Basis for Sustainability*. London; New York: Routledge.

Hoversten, M. E. and S. R. Swaffield (2019). "Discursive moments: Reframing deliberation and decision-making in alternative futures landscape ecological planning." *Landscape and Urban Planning* **182**: 22–33.

Hoyle, H., B. Norton, N. Dunnett, J. P. Richards, J. M. Russell and P. Warren (2018). "Plant species or flower colour diversity? Identifying the drivers of public and invertebrate response to designed annual meadows." *Landscape and Urban Planning* **180**: 103–113.

Huber, P. R., F. Shilling, J. H. Thorne and S. E. Greco (2012). "Municipal and regional habitat connectivity planning." *Landscape and Urban Planning* **105**(1–2): 15–26.

Hulchanski, J. D. (2010). *The Three Cities within Toronto: Income Polarization among Toronto's Neighbourhoods, 1970–2005*. Toronto, Cities Centre, University of Toronto.

Hunter, M. (2015). *Developing Design Guidelines for Urban Spaces in Support of Mental Wellbeing Using Theoretical Frameworks from Environmental Psychology and Aesthetics*. Los Angeles: Environmental Design and Research Association.

Ignatieva, M., K. Ahrné, J. Wissman, T. Eriksson, P. Tidåker, M. Hedblom, T. Kätterer, H. Marstorp, P. Berg, T. Eriksson and J. Bengtsson (2015). "Lawn as a cultural and ecological phenomenon: A conceptual framework for transdisciplinary research." *Urban Forestry and Urban Greening* **14**(2): 383–387.

Jackson, S. and L. R. Palmer (2015). "Reconceptualizing ecosystem services: Possibilities for cultivating and valuing the ethics and practices of care." *Progress in Human Geography* **39**(2): 122–145.

Jennings, V., L. Larson and J. Yun (2016). "Advancing sustainability through urban green space: Cultural ecosystem services, equity, and social determinants of health." *International Journal of Environmental Research and Public Health* **13**(196): 1–15.

Jiang, B., C.-Y. Chang and W. C. Sullivan (2014). "A dose of nature: Tree cover, stress reduction, and gender differences." *Landscape and Urban Planning* **132**(0): 26–36.

Jim, C. Y. (2015). "Assessing climate-adaptation effect of extensive tropical green roofs in cities." *Landscape and Urban Planning* **138**(0): 54–70.

Jim, C. Y. and W. Y. Chen (2009). "Ecosystem services and valuation of urban forests in China." *Cities* **26**(4): 187–194.

Jim, C. Y., A. Y. Lo and J. A. Byrne (2015). "Charting the green and climate-adaptive city." *Landscape and Urban Planning* **138**(0): 51–53.

Jiménez, M. (2006). "Why they call cottage country the Great White North: Minorities are rarely visible, but it's often because they just don't get the attraction." *Globe and Mail*, May 20. Toronto.

Johns, C. M. (2018). *Green Infrastructure and Stormwater Management in Toronto: Policy Context and Instruments*, Centre for Urban Research and Land Development.

Johns, C. M. (2019a). Associate Professor, Department of Politics and Public Administration, Ryerson University. Interview with A. Loder.

Johns, C. M. (2019b). "Understanding barriers to green infrastructure policy and stormwater management in the City of Toronto: A shift from grey to green or policy layering and conversion?" *Journal of Environmental Planning and Management* **62**(8): 1–25.

Jorgensen, A. and M. Tylecote (2007). "Ambivalent landscapes: Wilderness in the urban interstices." *Landscape Research* **32**(4): 443–462.

Junker, B. and M. Buchecker (2008). "Aesthetic preferences versus ecological objectives in river restorations." *Landscape and Urban Planning* **85**(3): 141–154.

Kaika, M. (2006). "The political ecology of water scarcity: The 1989–1991 Athenian drought." *In the Nature of Cities: Urban Political Ecology and the Politics of Urban Metabolism*. N. Heynen, M. Kaika and E. Syngedouw. New York: Routledge: 157–172.

Kaplan, R. (1984). "Wilderness perception and psychological benefits: An analysis of a continuing program." *Leisure Sciences* **6**(3): 271–290.

Kattel, G. R., H. Elkadi and H. Meikle (2013). "Developing a complementary framework for urban ecology." *Urban Forestry and Urban Greening* **12**(4): 498–508.

Ketterer, C. and A. Matzarakis (2014). "Human-biometeorological assessment of heat stress reduction by replanning measures in Stuttgart, Germany." *Landscape and Urban Planning* **122**(0): 78–88.

Kim, G. and P. Miller (2019). "The impact of green infrastructure on human health and well-being: The example of the Huckleberry Trail and the Heritage Community Park and Natural Area in Blacksburg, Virginia." *Sustainable Cities and Society* **48**: 101562.

Kim, G., P. A. Miller and D. J. Nowak (2015). "Assessing urban vacant land ecosystem services: Urban vacant land as green infrastructure in the City of Roanoke, Virginia." *Urban Forestry and Urban Greening* **14**(3): 519–526.

Knez, I., A. Butler, Å. Ode Sang, E. Ångman, I. Sarlöv-Herlin and A. Åkerskog (2018). "Before and after a natural disaster: Disruption in emotion component of place-identity and wellbeing." *Journal of Environmental Psychology* **55**: 11–17.

Knez, I., Å. O. Sang, B. Gunnersson and M. Hedblom (2018). "Wellbeing in urban greenery: The role of naturalness and place identity." *Frontiers in Psychology* **9**: 491.

Knight, S. (2017). "What would an entirely flood-proof city look like?" *The Guardian*, September 25.

Kolbert, E. (2008). "Turf War: Americans can't live without their lawns – but how long can they live with them?" *The New Yorker*, July 14, Conde Nast.

Kolinjivadi, V., G. Van Hecken, D. V. Almeida, J. Dupras and N. Kosoy (2019). "Neoliberal performatives and the 'making' of Payments for Ecosystem Services (PES)." *Progress in Human Geography* **43**(1): 3–25.

Kondo, M. C., S. C. Low, J. Henning and C. C. Branas (2015). "The impact of green stormwater infrastructure installation on surrounding health and safety." *American Journal of Public Health* **105**(3): e114–e121.

Korpela, K. M., T. Pasanen and E. Ratcliffe (2018). "Biodiversity and Psychological Wellbeing." *Urban Biodiversity: From Research to Practice*. A. Ossola and J. Niemelä. Abingdon, UK and New York: Routledge: 134–149.

Korpela, K. M., M. Ylen, L. Tyrvainen and H. Silvennoinen (2008). "Determinants of restorative experiences in everyday favorite places." *Health and Place* **14**: 636–652.

Korpela, K. M., M. Ylen, L. Tyrvainen and H. Silvennoinen (2009). "Stability of self-reported favourite places and place attachment over a 10-month period." *Journal of Environmental Psychology* **29**(1): 95–100.

Kovacs, K. F. (2012). "Integrating property value and local recreation models to value ecosystem services from regional parks." *Landscape and Urban Planning* **108**(2–4): 79–90.

Lachowycz, K. and A. P. Jones (2013). "Towards a better understanding of the relationship between greenspace and health: Development of a theoretical framework." *Landscape and Urban Planning* **118**(0): 62–69.

Lafortezza, R., J. Chen, C. K. van den Bosch and T. B. Randrup (2018). "Nature-based solutions for resilient landscapes and cities." *Environmental Research* **165**: 431–441.

Levin, K., B. Cashore, S. Bernstein and G. Auld (2012). "Overcoming the tragedy of super wicked problems: Constraining our future selves to ameliorate global climate change." *Policy Sciences* **45**(2): 123–152.

Li, D., B. Deal, X. Zhou, M. Slavenas and W. C. Sullivan (2018). "Moving beyond the neighborhood: Daily exposure to nature and adolescents' mood." *Landscape and Urban Planning* **173**: 33–43.

Liptan, T. (2017). "Sustainable stormwater management: We should invest in a landscape-driven approach." *Living Architecture Monitor*, Green Roofs for Healthy Cities **19**: 35.

Livegreen Toronto, City of Toronto and 311 (2017). Toronto Green Standard for New Mid to High-Rise Residential and All Non-Residential Development, Version 2.1. Toronto.

Loder, A. (2011). *Greening the City: Exploring Health, Well-being, Green Roofs, and the Perception of Nature in the Workplace*. Doctor of Philosophy, University of Toronto.

Loder, A. (2014). "'There's a meadow outside my workplace': A phenomenological exploration of aesthetics and green roofs in Chicago and Toronto." *Landscape and Urban Planning* **126**: 94–106.

Lorimer, J., T. Hodgetts and M. Barua (2019). "Animals' atmospheres." *Progress in Human Geography* **43**(1): 26–45.

Lumber, R., M. Richardson and D. Sheffield (2017). "Beyond knowing nature: Contact, emotion, compassion, meaning, and beauty are pathways to nature connection." *PLOS ONE* **12**(5): e0177186.

Luo, F., Y. Liu, J. Peng and J. Wu (2018). "Assessing urban landscape ecological risk through an adaptive cycle framework." *Landscape and Urban Planning* **180**: 125–134.

Macdonald, E. and E. G. King (2018). "Novel ecosystems: A bridging concept for the consilience of cultural landscape conservation and ecological restoration." *Landscape and Urban Planning* **177**: 148–159.

Mahoney, J. and K. Thelen (2009). "A Theory of Gradual Institutional Change." *Explaining Institutional Change: Ambiguity, Agency, and Power*. J. Mahoney and K. Thelen. Cambridge: Cambridge University Press: 1–37.

Manzo, L. C. (2008). "The Experience of Displacement on Sense of Place and Well-being." *Sense of Place, Health and Quality of Life*. J. Eyles and A. Williams. London, Routledge.

Martin, L. L. (2018). *Public-Private Partnerships (P3s): What Local Government Managers Need to Know*. Washington, DC: International City/County Management Association.

Masoudi, M. and P. Y. Tan (2019). "Multi-year comparison of the effects of spatial pattern of urban green spaces on urban land surface temperature." *Landscape and Urban Planning* **184**: 44–58.

Matthews, T., A. Y. Lo and J. A. Byrne (2015). "Reconceptualizing green infrastructure for climate change adaptation: Barriers to adoption and drivers for uptake by spatial planners." *Landscape and Urban Planning* **138**(0): 155–163.

Mayer, J. (2018). "P3s Can Be Bad for Racial Equity – But They Don't Have to Be." *Living Cities Blog*. Retrieved May 12, 2019, from www.livingcities.org/blog/1262-p3s-can-be-bad-for-racial-equity-but-they-don-t-have-to-be.

Meng, T. and D. Hsu (2019). "Stated preferences for smart green infrastructure in stormwater management." *Landscape and Urban Planning* **187**: 1–10.

Middel, A., N. Chhetri and R. Quay (2015). "Urban forestry and cool roofs: Assessment of heat mitigation strategies in Phoenix residential neighborhoods." *Urban Forestry and Urban Greening* **14**(1): 178–186.

Millennial Ecosystem Assessment (2003). Washington, DC: Island Press.

Mills, S. (2000). "Salmon Support." *Environmental Restoration*. W. Throop. Amherst, New York: Humanity Books: 39–52.

Monsebraaten, L. (2011). Toronto's poor concentrated in aging highrises. *The Star*, Toronto.

Moseley, D., M. Marzano, J. Chetcuti and K. Watts (2013). "Green networks for people: Application of a functional approach to support the planning and management of greenspace." *Landscape and Urban Planning* **116**(0): 1–12.

Murphy, A. (2019). Manager, Research and Partnerships, Ryerson Urban Water, Faculty of Science, Ryerson University. Interview with A. Loder.

Mutrie, E. (2018). "A new park pays tribute to Toronto's lost waterways." *Designlines* **3**, last edited November 7, Designlines Magazine.

Nassauer, J. (1995). "Messy ecosystems, orderly frames." *Landscape Journal* **14**(2): 161–170.

Nassauer, J. I. (2012). "Landscape as medium and method for synthesis in urban ecological design." *Landscape and Urban Planning* **106**(3): 221–229.

National Association of City Transportation Officials (n.d.). "Urban Street Stormwater Guide." Retrieved May 2, 2019, from https://nacto.org/publication/urban-street-stormwater-guide.

Neel, R., E. Sadalla, A. Berlin, S. Ledlow and S. Neufeld (2014). "The social symbolism of water-conserving landscaping." *Journal of Environmental Psychology* **40**(0): 49–56.

Netusil, N. R., Z. Levin, V. Shandas and T. Hart (2014). "Valuing green infrastructure in Portland, Oregon." *Landscape and Urban Planning* **124**(0): 14–21.

Newell, J. P., M. Seymour, T. Yee, J. Renteria, T. Longcore, J. R. Wolch and A. Shishkovsky (2013). "Green Alley Programs: Planning for a sustainable urban infrastructure?" *Cities* **31**: 144–155.

Niemelä, J. (2014). "Ecology of urban green spaces: The way forward in answering major research questions." *Landscape and Urban Planning* **125**(0): 298–303.

Noon, J. (2019). Strategic Partnerships Supervisor, Green Stormwater Infrastructure Unit, Philadelphia Water Department. Interview with A. Loder.

Nordh, H. and K. Østby (2013). "Pocket parks for people: A study of park design and use." *Urban Forestry and Urban Greening* **12**(1): 12–17.

Norton, B. A., A. M. Coutts, S. J. Livesley, R. J. Harris, A. M. Hunter and N. S. G. Williams (2015). "Planning for cooler cities: A framework to prioritise green infrastructure to mitigate high temperatures in urban landscapes." *Landscape and Urban Planning* **134**(0): 127–138.

Nowak, D. J. and E. J. Greenfield (2018). "Declining urban and community tree cover in the United States." *Urban Forestry and Urban Greening* **32**: 32–55.

Olsson, L., A. Jerneck, H. Thoren, J. Persson and D. O'Byrne (2015). "Why resilience is unappealing to social science: Theoretical and empirical investigations of the scientific use of resilience." *American Association for the Advancement of Science* **1**: e1400217.

Opara, M. and P. Rouse (2019). "The perceived efficacy of public-private partnerships: A study from Canada." *Critical Perspectives on Accounting* **58**: 77–99.

Palantino, A. (2019). Deputy Commissioner, Philadelphia Parks and Recreation. Interview with A. Loder.

Palmer, J. F. and D. B. K. English (2019). "An index of viewer sensitivity to scenery while engaged in recreation activities on U.S. National Forests." *Landscape and Urban Planning* **189**: 91–98.

Panduro, T. E. and K. L. Veie (2013). "Classification and valuation of urban green spaces: A hedonic house price valuation." *Landscape and Urban Planning* **120**(0): 119–128.

Pataki, D. E., M. M. Carreiro, J. Cherrier, N. E. Grulke, V. Jennings, S. Pincetl, R. V. Pouyat, T. H. Whitlow and W. C. Zipperer (2011). "Coupling biogeochemical cycles in urban environments: Ecosystem services, green solutions, and misconceptions." *Frontiers in Ecology and the Environment* **9**(1): 27–36.

Pearce, L. M., A. Davison and J. B. Kirkpatrick (2015). "Personal encounters with trees: The lived significance of the private urban forest." *Urban Forestry and Urban Greening* **14**(1): 1–7.

PennPraxis (2010). Green2015: An Action Plan for the First 500 Acres. Philadelphia Parks and Recreation. Philadelphia: 144.

Peschardt, K. K. and U. K. Stigsdotter (2013). "Associations between park characteristics and perceived restorativeness of small public urban green spaces." *Landscape and Urban Planning* **112**(0): 26–39.

Philadelphia Water Department (2011). Amended – Green City Clean Waters – The City of Philadelphia's Program for Combined Sewer Overflow Control – Program Summary. Philadelphia.

Philadelphia Water Department (n.d.-a). "5 down, 20 to go: Celebrating 5 years of cleaner water and greener neighborhoods." www.phila.gov/water/sustainability/greencitycleanwaters/Pages/default.aspx.

Philadelphia Water Department (n.d.-b). "Green City, Clean Waters." *What We're Doing*. www.phila.gov/water/sustainability/greencitycleanwaters/Pages/default.aspx.

Philadelphia Water Department (n.d.-c). "Stormwater management." *Watershed Issues*. www.phila.gov/water/sustainability/greencitycleanwaters/Pages/default.aspx.

Poškus, M. S. and D. Poškienė (2015). "The Grass is Greener: How Greenery Impacts the Perceptions of Urban Residential Property." *Social Inquiry into Well-Being* **1**(1): 22–31.

Qiu, L., S. Lindberg and A. B. Nielsen (2013). "Is biodiversity attractive? On-site perception of recreational and biodiversity values in urban green space." *Landscape and Urban Planning* **119**(0): 136–146.

Ramer, H., K. C. Nelson, M. Spivak, E. Watkins, J. Wolfin and M. Pulscher (2019). "Exploring park visitor perceptions of 'flowering bee lawns' in neighborhood parks in Minneapolis, MN, US." *Landscape and Urban Planning* **189**: 117–128.

Rees, W. and M. Wackernagel (2008). "Urban Ecological Footprints: Why Cities Cannot be Sustainable – and Why They are a Key to Sustainability." *An Introduction to Urban Ecology as an Interaction between Humans and Nature*. J. Marzluff, W. Endlicher, G. Bradley, U. Simon, E. Shulenberger, M. Alberti, C. Ryan and C. ZumBrunnen. Boston, MA: Springer. **16:** 537–555.

Riechers, M., J. Barkmann and T. Tscharntke (2018). "Diverging perceptions by social groups on cultural ecosystem services provided by urban green." *Landscape and Urban Planning* **175**: 161–168.

Robbins, P. and J. Sharp (2003). "Producing and consuming chemicals: The moral economy of the American lawn." *Economic Geography* **79**: 425–451.

Rockefeller Foundation (n.d.). "100 Resilient Cities." *Our Work*. Retrieved May 10, 2019, 2019, from www.rockefellerfoundation.org/our-work/initiatives/100-resilient-cities.

Rothblatt, D. N. (1994). "North American metropolitan planning: Canadian and U.S. perspectives." *Journal of the American Planning Association* **60**(4): 501–522.

Samuelsson, K., M. Giusti, G. D. Peterson, A. Legeby, S. A. Brandt and S. Barthel (2018). "Impact of environment on people's everyday experiences in Stockholm." *Landscape and Urban Planning* **171**: 7–17.

Sander, H., S. Polasky and R. G. Haight (2010). "The value of urban tree cover: A hedonic property price model in Ramsey and Dakota Counties, Minnesota, USA." *Ecological Economics* **69**(8): 1646–1656.

Schebella, M. F., D. Weber, L. Schultz and P. Weinstein (2019). "The wellbeing benefits associated with perceived and measured biodiversity in Australian urban green spaces." *Sustainability* **11**(3): 802.

Scholte, S. S. K., M. Daams, H. Farjon, F. J. Sijtsma, A. J. A. van Teeffelen and P. H. Verburg (2018). "Mapping recreation as an ecosystem service: Considering scale, interregional differences and the influence of physical attributes." *Landscape and Urban Planning* **175**: 149–160.

Seattle Public Utilities (n.d.). "Current GSI Projects." *Green Stormwater Infrastructure*. Retrieved May 2, 2019, from www.seattle.gov/utilities/environment-and-conservation/projects/green-stormwater-infrastructure/current-gsi-projects.

Senate Department of Urban Development in Berlin (2005). "Environment: BAF Biotope area factor." Retrieved March 15, 2005, from www.stadtentwicklung.berlin.de/umwelt/landschaftplanung/bff/index_en.shtml.

Shipp, A. (2019). Executive Director, The Sustainable Business Network of Greater Philadelphia. Interview with A. Loder.

Sinha, A. (2014). "Slow landscapes of elevated linear parks: Bloomingdale Trail in Chicago." *Studies in the History of Gardens and Designed Landscapes* **34**(2): 113–122.

Sookhan, N., L. Margolis and J. Scott MacIvor (2018). "Inter-annual thermoregulation of extensive green roofs in warm and cool seasons: Plant selection matters." *Ecological Engineering* **123**: 10–18.

Southon, G. E., A. Jorgensen, N. Dunnett, H. Hoyle and K. L. Evans (2018). "Perceived species-richness in urban green spaces: Cues, accuracy and well-being impacts." *Landscape and Urban Planning* **172**: 1–10.

Statistics Canada (2017). Toronto [Census metropolitan area], Ontario and Ontario [Province] (table). *Census Profile, 2016 Census*. Ottawa, Statistics Canada Catalogue.

Stedman, R. C. (2003). "Is it really just a social construction? The contribution of the physical environment to sense of place." *Society and Natural Resources* **16**(8): 671–685.

Stefanovic, I. L. (2008). "Holistic Paradigms of Health and Place: How Beneficial are they to Environmental Policy and Practice?" *Sense of Place, Health and Quality of Life*. J. Eyles and A. Williams. London: Routledge.

Steiner, F. (2014). "Frontiers in urban ecological design and planning research." *Landscape and Urban Planning* **125**(0): 304–311.

Stigsdotter, U. K. and P. Grahn (2011). "Stressed individuals' preferences for activities and environmental characteristics in green spaces." *Urban Forestry and Urban Greening* **10**(4): 295–304.

Stony Brook University (n.d.). "What's a Wicked Problem?" *About*. Retrieved June 5, 2019, from www.stonybrook.edu/commcms/wicked-problem/about/What-is-a-wicked-problem.

Stormwater PA (n.d.). "Regulations." *How*. Retrieved May 2, 2019, from www.stormwaterpa.org/swm-regs.html.

Stott, S. (2019). Environmental Planner, City of Toronto. Interview with A. Loder.

Strong, K. (2019). Deputy Director of Design and Construction, Rebuild, City of Philadelphia. Interview with A. Loder.

Sugimoto, K. (2013). "Quantitative measurement of visitors' reactions to the settings in urban parks: Spatial and temporal analysis of photographs." *Landscape and Urban Planning* **110**(0): 59–63.

Sullivan, J. and C. Simson (2019). "Green Stormwater Infrastructure." *2017–2018 Overview and Accomplishment Report*, King County Seattle Public Utilities.

Sustainable Technologies Evaluation Program (2017). "Fairford Parkette, Toronto Green Streets." *Low Impact Development*, Toronto and Region Conservation for The Living City.

Szota, C., A. M. Coutts, J. K. Thom, H. K. Virahsawmy, T. D. Fletcher and S. J. Livesley (2019). "Street tree stormwater control measures can reduce runoff but may not benefit established trees." *Landscape and Urban Planning* **182**: 144–155.

Tanenbaum, M. (2018). "Philadelphia releases searchable database for public to track soda tax revenue, spending." *PhillyVoice*.

TEEB – The Economics of Ecosystems and Biodiversity (2011). *TEEB Manual for Cities: Ecosystem Services in Urban Management*. Geneva.

Tetra Tech (2010). "2010 CSO Reduction Plan Amendment." *Combined Sewer Overflow Program*, Seattle Public Utilities.

The Pew Cheritable Trusts (2018). "Overview." *Philadelphia 2018 – The State of the City*. Philadelphia.

Thrift, N. (2005). "From born to made: Technology, biology and space." *Transactions of the Institute of British Geographers* **30**: 463–476.

Toronto and Region Conservation Authority (2014). The Living City Policies for Planning and Development in the Watersheds of the Toronto and Region Conservation Authority Summary Document.

Toronto and Region Conservation Authority (2016a). The Living City Report Card 2016: A Progress Report on Environmental Sustainability in the Toronto Region, Toronto and Region Conservation: 100.

Toronto and Region Conservation Authority (2016b). Low Impact Development Stormwater Management Practice Inspection and Maintenance Guide. Vaughn, Ontario, Sustainable Technologies Evaluation Program.

Toronto and Region Conservation Authority (2019). "Sustainable Technologies Evaluation Program." Retrieved May 2, 2019, from https://sustainabletechnologies.ca.

Toronto and Region Conservation Authority (n.d.). "Stormwater Management." *Conservation*. Retrieved May 2, 2019, from https://trca.ca/conservation/stormwater-management.

Toronto Water (2015). Funding Options for Paying for Toronto Water's Stormwater Management Capital Program. Toronto.

Tyrväinen, L., A. Ojala, K. M. Korpela, T. Lanki, Y. Tsunetsugu and T. Kagawa (2014). "The influence of urban green environments on stress relief measures: A field experiment." *Journal of Environmental Psychology* **38**: 1–9.

Tzoulas, K., K. M. Korpela, S. Venn, V. Yli-Pelkonen, A. Kaźmierczak, J. Niemela and P. James (2007). "Promoting ecosystem and human health in urban areas using Green Infrastructure: A literature review." *Landscape and Urban Planning* **81**(3): 167–178.

Ulrich, R. S., R. F. Simons, B. D. Losito, E. Fiorito, M. A. Miles and M. Zelson (1991). "Stress recovery during exposure to natural and urban environments." *Journal of Environmental Psychology* **11**: 201–230.

Unterweger, P. A., N. Schrode and O. Betz (2017). "Urban nature: Perception and acceptance of alternative green space management and the change of awareness after provision of environmental information. A chance for biodiversity protection." *Urban Science* **1**(3): 24.

Uren, H. V., P. L. Dzidic and B. J. Bishop (2015). "Exploring social and cultural norms to promote ecologically sensitive residential garden design." *Landscape and Urban Planning* **137**(0): 76–84.

Valentine, G. (1990). "Women's fear and the design of public space." *Built Environment (1978-)* **16**(4): 288–303.

Van Mechelen, C., K. Van Meerbeek, T. Dutoit and M. Hermy (2015). "Functional diversity as a framework for novel ecosystem design: The example of extensive green roofs." *Landscape and Urban Planning* **136**(0): 165–173.

Varghese, S. (2018). "The cold hard truth about Toronto's transport network." *CityMetric*, January 12.

Vendeville, G. (2019, January 10, 2019). "Stranded without transit? Researchers say one million urban Canadians suffer from 'transport poverty'." *News*. Retrieved May 10, 2019, from https://utsc.utoronto.ca/news-events/breaking-research/stranded-without-transit-researchers-say-one-million-urban-canadians-suffer.

Verbrugge, L. and R. van den Born (2018). "The role of place attachment in public perceptions of a re-landscaping intervention in the river Waal (The Netherlands)." *Landscape and Urban Planning* **177**: 241–250.

Vogelsang, B. (2018). Principal and Owner, OV Consulting. Interview with A. Loder.

Wang, Z., P. Y. Tan, T. Zhang and J. I. Nassauer (2014). "Perspectives on narrowing the action gap between landscape science and metropolitan governance: Practice in the US and China." *Landscape and Urban Planning* **125**(0): 329–334.

Ward Thompson, C., J. Roe, P. Aspinall, R. Mitchell, A. Clow and D. Miller (2012). "More green space is linked to less stress in deprived communities: Evidence from salivary cortisol patterns." *Landscape and Urban Planning* **105**(3): 221–229.

Wartmann, F. M. and R. S. Purves (2018). "Investigating sense of place as a cultural ecosystem service in different landscapes through the lens of language." *Landscape and Urban Planning* **175**: 169–183.

Weber, A. M. and J. Trojan (2018). "The restorative value of the urban environment: A systematic review of the existing literature." *Environmental Health Insights* **12**. doi:10.1177/1178630218812805.

Weber, F., I. Kowarik and I. Säumel (2014). "A walk on the wild side: Perceptions of roadside vegetation beyond trees." *Urban Forestry and Urban Greening* **13**(2): 205–212.

Westerman, N. (2019). Executive Director, Rebuild, City of Philadelphia. Interview with A. Loder.

Whalen, J. (2017). "Census 2016: More than half of Torontonians identify as visible minorities." *CBC News*, October 25.

Wilkie, S. and H. Clements (2018). "Further exploration of environment preference and environment type congruence on restoration and perceived restoration potential." *Landscape and Urban Planning* **170**: 314–319.

Wilkie, S. and L. Clouston (2015). "Environment preference and environment type congruence: Effects on perceived restoration potential and restoration outcomes." *Urban Forestry and Urban Greening* **14**(2): 368–376.

Williams, A., C. Heidebrecht, L. DeMiglio, J. Eyles, D. Streiner and B. Newbold (2008). "Developing a Psychometric Scale for Measuring Sense of Place and Health: An Application of Facet Design." *Sense of Place, Health and Quality of Life*. J. Eyles and A. Williams. London: Routledge.

Wolfe, M. K. and J. Mennis (2012). "Does vegetation encourage or supress urban crime? Evidence from Philadelphia, PA." *Landscape and Urban Planning* **108**: 112–122.

Wyles, K. J., M. P. White, C. Hattam, S. Pahl, H. King and M. Austen (2019). "Are some natural environments more psychologically beneficial than others? The importance of type and quality on connectedness to nature and psychological restoration." *Environment and Behavior* **51**(2): 111–143.

Yamaguchi, M. (2016). Project Manager, Rain Gardens United. Interview with A. Loder. Denver.

Yang, J. and E. Bou-Zeid (2019). "Scale dependence of the benefits and efficiency of green and cool roofs." *Landscape and Urban Planning* **185**: 127–140.

Yang, Y., T. A. Endreny and D. J. Nowak (2015). "Simulating the effect of flow path roughness to examine how green infrastructure restores urban runoff timing and magnitude." *Urban Forestry and Urban Greening* **14**(2): 361–367.

Youngson, A. J. (1979). *The Scientific Revolution in Victorian Medicine*. New York: Holmes & Meier Publishers.

Zhang, B., G.-D. Xie, N. Li and S. Wang (2015). "Effect of urban green space changes on the role of rainwater runoff reduction in Beijing, China." *Landscape and Urban Planning* **140**: 8–16.

Zhang, J. W., R. T. Howell and R. Iyer (2014). "Engagement with natural beauty moderates the positive relation between connectedness with nature and psychological well-being." *Journal of Environmental Psychology* **38**: 55–63.

3
MEADOWS IN THE SKY
A green roof case study

Introduction

While much of the green infrastructure (GI) in North America has been implemented for stormwater management, increasingly hot summers from climate change have spurred municipal interest in urban greenspace as an adaptation and mitigation strategy for the urban heat island effect (UHI) (Vailshery, Jaganmohan et al. 2013; Emmanuel and Loconsole 2015; Eisenman, Churkina et al. 2019). Though most of the relevant research on climate change mitigation is on existing types of urban greenspace (Armson, Stringer et al. 2012; Ketterer and Matzarakis 2014; Mueller, Soder et al. 2019), unconventional greenspace is receiving more attention, for the same reasons outlined in the previous chapter – lack of space to add parks (Thwaites 2001; City of Chicago 2012; Perini and Magliocco 2014; Norton, Coutts et al. 2015). One form of GI that has been increasing in popularity in North America is green roofs, mainly due to their numerous benefits such as the reduction of stormwater overflow and the urban heat island effect (Chih-Fang 2008; Bliss, Neufeld et al. 2009). Green roofs are unique and relatively novel, which makes them interesting case studies both from a policy perspective – because their placement on the tops of buildings requires different policies and incentives – as well as from a research perspective – due to their potential to provide insight into what urbanites think and feel about them.

This chapter explores the implications of different approaches to the health and well-being of cities and communities through urban greening projects. It does so by examining a case study on office workers and green roofs from two cities that are leaders in implementation of this form of GI – Toronto, Ontario, and Chicago, Illinois. In addition to providing insights into office workers' perceptions and attitudes to a relatively new – but increasingly influential – form of urban greening, this chapter also explores the impact of different research methods on the kind of knowledge that is generated. With this in mind, this chapter can be read on three levels: first, as an overview of the implementation of green roof policy in two cities that are similar but that had different initial results; second, as an exploration into research findings that can help us understand the impact of urban greening projects on urbanites' sense of health, place, and well-being; and third, as a continued discussion of the importance of research methods and how their underlying paradigms shape our knowledge and understanding of these relationships.

Current research on green roofs

Due to the environmental drivers pushing green roof implementation (see below), most of the research on green roofs focuses on their environmental performance, such as the reduction of stormwater overflow and the urban heat island effect (Chih-Fang 2008; Bliss, Neufeld et al. 2009; Chow, Bakar et al. 2018; Yang and Bou-Zeid 2019). More recently, there is also interest in the potential for green roofs to mimic native habitat such as prairie (Butler, Butler et al. 2012), as well as their potential to provide urbanites, and in particular office workers, with social and health benefits such as psychological restoration (Lee, Williams et al. 2014; Lee, Williams et al. 2015; Mesimäki, Hauru et al. 2019). While this work has been promising in its exploration of aesthetic preferences (Jungels, Rakow et al. 2013; Vanstockem, Vranken et al. 2018) and green roofs' potential for enhancing well-being and providing a feeling of restoration (White and Gatersleben 2011), there has been scant qualitative research that examines *why* office workers have these aesthetic preferences, or what the underlying cultural and contextual factors are that influence perceptions of green roofs, restoration, and urban nature. There has also been scant work that examines perceptions of real-world green roofs (versus images) in downtown central business districts (Nooriati, Aldrin et al. 2010). As seen in Chapter 1, qualitative work in this area is much needed, given previous conflicts between popular urban aesthetics and ecological goals, which have resulted in residents' ambivalent responses to naturalized urban areas (Gobster 2000; Spears 2005) and which can inhibit the success of urban greening projects. We also saw that affective, emotional responses to nature may be key to understanding the role nature plays in sense of place and well-being (Hinds and Sparks 2008; Korpela, Ylen et al. 2009; Wyles, White et al. 2019), but that they are difficult to capture with quantitative methods (Perrin and Benassi 2009). While green roofs are not uncontroversial (Henry and Frascaria-Lacoste 2012) and are not always the best urban greening option, they make an interesting case study through which to explore the human relationship with nature. This is because they challenge the traditional nature/city divide (Cronon 1995), they lack existing symbolism such as the kind associated with mountains or forests (Saito 2002b), and there is a current trend to use them to mimic native habitat.

To explore these themes, the research conducted in downtown Toronto and Chicago used three different methods to examine office worker perceptions of green roofs: two qualitative methods – interviews using a phenomenology and social constructionism lens – and one quantitative method – a survey and statistical analysis. After a brief overview of the policy development and implementation by Chicago and Toronto, the majority of the chapter reports on the findings of the qualitative analysis,[1] which is followed by a comparison of these findings to the results of the quantitative analysis.

Qualitative research on perceptions of green roofs: the interviews

A phenomenological approach was used to analyze the results of 55 semi-structured interviews that included the following key research questions: (1) What do participants think and feel about green roofs? (2) How does their lived experience influence their perceptions of aesthetics and urban nature? (3) What are the design implications for a more sustainable city? Key themes that emerged from the research include: increased fascination and creative thinking with 'wilder' green roofs, even if these are not always preferred aesthetically; the conflict between 'messy' ecological aesthetics and the modernist city; and the difference between cognitive or intellectual and felt or affective responses to the green roofs. These findings can help us to understand how we value and think about green roofs, provide insights for urban greening and policy development, and contribute to our understanding of how nature affects our lived experience of cities, an issue of increasing importance as the world becomes more urbanized.

What do we know about green roofs, health, and well-being?

Research on green roofs has tended to fall into four main approaches: the ecosystems approach, the human benefit approach (or the adaptive and utilitarian paradigms outlined in Chapter 1), the social constructionist approach, and, intertwined throughout, research that examines the role aesthetics plays in human–nature interactions. Research on green roofs has predominantly followed the ecology or ecosystems approach to studying urban nature, focusing on technical performance and ecosystem services (Blank, Vasl et al. 2013; Liu and Chui 2019; Yang and Bou-Zeid 2019). This ecology approach (discussed in Chapter 2), which underlies the policy impetus for urban greening programs, looks at how greenspace, and what types of greenspace, can be preserved or added to the city to reduce the urban heat island effect, manage stormwater overflow, and provide habitat for urban wildlife, among other benefits (Lundholm 2006; Lee, Moon et al. 2013; Peng and Jim 2013; Imran, Kala et al. 2018; Hirano, Ihara et al. 2019). Conflicts resulting from negative public perceptions of ecological restoration projects (where damaged or destroyed ecosystems are restored by human intervention) (Gobster 2000; Junker and Buchecker 2008) or green roofs (Francis and Lorimer 2011; Henry and Frascaria-Lacoste 2012) have contributed to a growing recognition of the importance of aesthetics to the success of these projects (Gobster, Nassauer et al. 2007; Peck 2017; Souto, Listopad et al. 2019).

While the ecological approach remains dominant, the empirical results of research following the adaptive or utilitarian paradigms have increased interest in the human benefit potential of additional urban greenspace (such as green roofs). This can be seen in references to improved health and well-being in policy documents on urban greenspace and in recent grants promoting greenspace projects in underserved neighbourhoods (see case studies in Chapter 4). Similarly, the claim in environmental values research that humans have an implicit connection or emotional affinity toward nature that influences our motivations to protect it (Kals, Schumacher et al. 1999; Schultz, Shriver et al. 2004; Korpela, Borodulin et al. 2014) has raised the potential for urban greening to be linked to larger urban ecological goals.

As we saw in Chapter 1, research following a social constructionist paradigm has offered important insights into explaining conflicts over ecological restoration and naturalization projects (Nassauer 1995; Gobster 2000; Simpson and Bagelman 2018) that are relevant to green roofs. Work in aesthetics has also deconstructed seemingly 'innate' landscape preferences, arguing that cultural and artistic factors promote the visual or touristic appreciation of dramatic, distant, 'scenic' landscapes over nearby, messy, everyday landscapes (Saito 2002a; Urry 2005). Of particular relevance to this chapter are two key arguments. The first, from social constructionists, is that 'nature' is a complex phenomenon and that bringing 'nature' back to cities first begs the question of 'which nature, and where?' This complexity has been seen in idealizations of 'wildness' outside the city, for example rural cottage country, that contrast with its rejection as an aesthetic paradigm within the city, for example in naturalized lawns (Wilson 1991; Hough 2004). Second, from aesthetics comes the argument that aesthetic valuations of nature are not superficial but are influenced by cognitive information – such as ecological knowledge and abstract thinking – and deeper emotional and psychological connections to nature (Hepburn 1993). Hence, an understanding of both cognitive and emotional factors is necessary to shift public perception towards the ecological aesthetic.

Though interest is growing, only a small number of studies have looked at perceptions of green roofs. Some studies have recognized that the aesthetics of a green roof have positive psycho-physiological benefits in general (assumed to be from the general appreciation of plants) (Sutton 2014; Kotzen 2018), but most have looked at mediating factors on preference. For example one study found that scale and distance affected perceptions and evaluations of green roofs (Lee and Koshimiz 2004), while another found that green roofs on residential buildings were seen to increase the perception of beauty and psychological restoration for participants, particularly for meadow-type or ivy roofs (White and Gatersleben 2011). Office workers in downtown central business districts also prefer tall grasses, preferably green and flowering, over lower-growing red and succulent vegetation such as sedums, but prefer moderate versus high diversity in vegetation (Lee, Williams et al. 2014). In contrast, sedum-dominated or mixed-perennial green roofs were preferred over grasses on botanic garden and university green roofs, with grasses seen as 'messy' and not fitting in as well with their surroundings. These green roof preferences were found to be positively correlated with attitudes and knowledge of green roof benefits (Jungels, Rakow et al. 2013). In general participants tended not to like 'weedy' aesthetics: one study found that gaps in green roof vegetation and weedy species are less preferred (Vanstockem, Vranken et al. 2018), while suburban residents disliked the 'messy' look of green roofs that contrasts with the standard suburban lawn aesthetic and have little interest in installing green roofs (Smith and Boyer 2007). Students and residents in Spain also disliked messier green roof aesthetics, preferring a more careful design similar to a garden. They also tend to rate green roof aesthetics lower if they grew up in forested areas (Fernandez-Cañero, Emilsson et al. 2013). A few studies have looked at levels of awareness around green roofs given their novelty, finding low levels of awareness and knowledge about the benefits of green roofs among suburban residents (Kuper 2009), citizens (Lee, Huh et al. 2016), and landscape professionals (Calkins 2005; Rahman, Ahmad et al. 2013). Despite the call for more qualitative methodology to go beyond scenic preferences of nature commonly found in research following the adaptive paradigm (Gobster 1999; Wilkie and Stavridou 2013), only two studies have used qualitative methods (Yuen and Hien 2005; White and Gatersleben 2011). Yuen and Hien (2005) used focus groups, surveys, and interviews to assess resident perceptions about a green roof on the deck of their building, finding that they used it to get away, have a place for children to play, and access greenspace (Yuen and Hien 2005). White and Gatersleben (2011) complemented their questionnaire with a small number of interviews, finding that interview participants were polarized in their aesthetic preferences, viewing lawn as neat or boring, and grasses as untidy or natural. Only Lee, Williams et al. (2014) examined the workplace, and none have looked at perceptions of respondents who both look out at a green roof and/or can access it physically.

By reporting on what office workers think and how they feel about real green roofs from their daily lived experience, this research addresses the current lack of qualitative research by enabling respondents to discuss how they feel about the green roof over time and different seasons, how the green roof fits (or not) into their ideas of nature – and thus whether nature studies can be applied to green roofs – and what cultural valuations and attitudes may be influencing their perception. This kind of qualitative data can provide more meaningful information for policy makers than likes and dislikes and contributes to our understanding of the human relationship to nature, and urban nature in particular – an important area of research given the proximity of workplaces to many downtown green roofs and the current interest in workplace health and well-being (Lottrup, Grahn et al. 2013; Bjornstad, Patil et al. 2015; Chan and Liu 2018; Cinderby and Bagwell 2018).

Methods

Research paradigm

A phenomenological approach was chosen for the study because it considers the world as we experience it in an everyday way, not as we conceptualize or theorize it (Husserl 1970, cited in Orbe 2000). Such a perspective is useful when examining something as complex as our relationship to nature, which, as we saw in Chapter 1 from research following a social constructionist paradigm, is replete with cultural, social, and historical values that may seem inherent and natural. Phenomenology has also been used to explore health and well-being (McNamara 2005; Ortiz-Dowling, Der Ananian et al. 2018; Adams 2019) and sense of place (Relph 1976; Vandenberg, Ball et al. 2018; Ryfield, Cabana et al. 2019), themes relevant to experiences of nature. Finally, phenomenology can be used to help explain aesthetic preferences by uncovering the essential, underlying thread or structure that unifies the lived experience of the phenomenon (Moustakas 1994; Cresswell 1998). Phenomenological methods emphasize: a reflexive awareness of the practitioner's experience, philosophical framework and biases, called bracketing; in-depth interviews that aim to understand underlying factors influencing participants' experience but which may not be articulated yet; and both textural (what) and structural (how) descriptions of the experience (Cresswell 1998).

Following this method, a matrix of the ontological, axiological, and methodological assumptions (or paradigms) of literature relevant to the human relationship to nature in cities was developed which helped define topic areas and a conceptual framework for the interview guide, provided a basis for the literature review for the project, and helped promote awareness and reflexivity about my own biases, assumptions, and ontological frameworks (Cresswell 1998; Padgett 2008). An interview guide was developed with a combination of open-ended questions and standardized questions (such as health and stress measures modified from

Canadian census surveys), allowing for later comparisons with the survey responses (Padgett 2008). The interview guide had five main sections covering: (a) green roofs; (b) perceptions, attitudes, and experiences of nature; (c) nature and health; (d) workplace environment; and (e) health. The goal of the interviews was to allow participants to respond in their own words and to draw out their narratives and lived experiences of nature, nature in the city, green roofs, and their health and well-being.

Case studies: Chicago and Toronto's green roof policies

Toronto and Chicago were chosen as case studies for their green roof leadership and similarities. Both cities have been promoting green roofs since 2000 (City of Chicago: Mayor's Office 2006; City of Toronto 2006), and they are frequently compared for their urban greening policies given their similar population size, climate, Great Lakes environmental problems, and green roof policies (Rothblatt 1994; City of Toronto 2007b; Gorrie 2007). Though similar, the cities have a few differences relevant to this study. As outlined in Chapter 2, while Toronto has recently obtained some power to create by-laws and raise taxes (City of Toronto 2007a), it has nowhere near the constitutional power of many American cities, Chicago included. Toronto also has a consensus-based political system (City of Toronto n.d.; Florida and Broadbent 2018), which means that the city is not able to pass legislation nearly as quickly as Chicago, with the latter's strong top-down mayor system (Los Angeles Times 2005). As we will see below, Chicago's green roof policies developed quickly through mayoral initiatives and were highly publicized (City of Chicago 2010), while Toronto's consensus-based process only really took off when their green roof by-law was passed in 2009 (City of Toronto 2009). Chicago's architecture, with repeated sightlines to the lake, extensive lakeshore parkland, and swimmable beaches make Chicagoans much more connected, symbolically and physically, to Lake Michigan than Torontonians are to Lake Ontario, which is separated from the city by an elevated expressway. Though Toronto has a few Blue Flag beaches (internationally certified for water quality) most of the population remains suspicious of Lake Ontario's water quality and few residents swim in it. Furthermore, the strong iconic presence of forested cottage country and a much-loved provincial park just north of Toronto, both classic symbols of Canadian wilderness, strengthens cultural associations and valuations of 'nature' as something immersive and distant – 'up north' – for many Torontonians. For Chicagoans, in contrast, despite attempts to make the prairie native again (Meine 2008), this long-lost 'nature' lacks the symbolic value of forests. The sections below give a brief overview of how each city approached their green roof policy before focusing on the results from the interviews and survey.

Chicago

The infamous heat wave that killed over 700 people in 1995 in Chicago (Klinenberg 2002) spurred then-Mayor Daley to seek ways to reduce the UHI (urban heat island); he settled on green roofs as a strategy after seeing successful municipal leadership on green roofs on a visit to Germany (Koehler and Keeley 2003; Keeley 2004). Chicago then used traditional strategies to encourage the uptake of green roofs, such as incentives, or 'carrots,' like a green roof grant program (City of Chicago n.d.; City of Chicago 2006) and publicity around the green roof on City Hall to show municipal support (American Society of Landscape Architects 2002). Their success can be traced more to a combination of a strong mayoral system, extensive publicity and education, and policies and programs that were financially supported and sustainable (Loder 2011) (see Plate 4). While Mayor Daley was able to command interdepartmental collaboration on green roofs, his use of green roofs as a key symbolic centrepiece for a larger program of urban revitalization, investment, and beautification enabled green roofs to become a key component of his drive to make Chicago 'the greenest city.' This high-publicity profile for a new urban greening typology was supported by research evaluating the success of the program and the environmental benefits (with satellite data and the EPA respectively) (Yocca and Berkshire 2019), as well as partnerships with other public institutions showcasing examples, demonstration projects, and research around green roofs. While Daley himself, education, and research were key components of Chicago's success, the single biggest factor was the *Green Matrix* (now called *Sustainability Matrix*) (City of Chicago 2012), part of their *Chicago Sustainable Development Policy* (Berkshire 2006). The *Green Matrix* meant that private projects seeking public assistance, or who had proximity to Lake Michigan or the Chicago River, had to meet minimum green building requirements, with green roofs as one of the options (City of Chicago 2012). Crucially, the *Green Matrix* was simultaneously supported by multiple TIF (tax incremental financing) districts (the highest number in the U.S.) (Healy and McCormick 1999) (see Tables 3.1 and 3.2). These districts earmarked money specifically for green development such as green roofs or LEED (Leadership in Energy and Environmental Design) buildings based on future projected property value increases (often a way to encourage development in underserved areas), and could not be used for other municipal projects, thus ensuring a reliable source of income for green roof implementation. While Washington, DC, has overtaken Chicago as the U.S. leader in green roof implementation (Living Architecture Monitor 2018), Chicago's leadership on environmental issues, and green roofs in particular, along with moving former Mayor Daley's green initiatives into policy (Berkshire 2008), have cemented their position as a forward-

Table 3.1 Green roof case studies: policy and implementation

City	Problem	Policy/project goals	Implementation		Precedent	Complements	Policy tools	Case study/ examples
			Actors	Funding				
Chicago *Green Matrix/ Chicago Sustainable Development Policy (CSDP)*	Poor air quality UHI Stormwater runoff	Improve urban environmental quality, climate change adaptation and mitigation (UHI, stormwater) Urban revitalization through greening: to become "the greenest city" Beautification, habitat, and "soft" benefits	Mayor Daley's office Chicago Department of Planning and Development Private businesses	*Green Roof Grant Program* *Green Permit Program* Private businesses Density-bonusing and TIF districts *Green Roof Improvement Fund* (discontinued in 2008) *Pilot*: Settlement money from CommEd from heat wave deaths	Germany's green roofs	*Green Urban Design guidelines* *Chicago Climate Action Plan* *Green Building Agenda* Stormwater Policy and Ordinances *2015 Sustainable Chicago Action Agenda*	Incentives (grants, TIFs) Incorporating green roofs into other legislation Requiring private developments seeking public assistance for certain projects to meet green building or roof requirements (CSDP) Publicity and education, collaboration with stakeholders	Chicago's City Hall Other green roofs through the CSDP and TIFF

Toronto Green Roof By-Law (GRBL) (2009)	Poor air quality UHI Stormwater runoff	Mitigate stormwater runoff and UHI Cost-savings Meet climate change adaptation and mitigation initiatives	Former Mayor Miller Deputy Mayor Pantalone Green Roofs for Healthy Cities	Toronto Water for Eco-Roof Incentive Program *Pilots:* Combination of departments Incorporation of green roof requirements into new public buildings or retrofits (city budget) Labour and material donations	City of Toronto Act (COTA) 2007 Some private green roofs, other city examples U.S. and European examples	*Environmental Plan* *Official Plan* *Wet Weather Flow Master Plan* *Toronto Green Standard* *Toronto Clean Air and Climate Change Action Plan* *Toronto Green Roof Construction Standards*	*Eco-Roof Incentive program* (grants) Requiring buildings that meet certain criteria to install a green roof (GRBL) Must meet *Toronto Green Roof Construction Standards* Incorporation of green roofs in planning documents and public building retrofits Publicity and education	Toronto's City Hall Other green roofs through GRBL

Table 3.2 Green roofs: the intersection of research, design, and implementation

Type of SSUG	Research used to justify policy or project?	Alignment with current research	Future areas for research and implementation synergies	Suggested ways forward
Green Roofs	Both cities used European research and precedent *Chicago:* EPA and satellite data evaluated environmental benefits and success of the green roof program *Toronto:* Ryerson University and the National Research Council conducted studies on the benefits of green roofs for Toronto	*Planning:* Ecological justification aligns with top reasons for inclusion in policies, planning Beginning to recognize health and wellbeing benefits in green roof policy *Implementation:* Aligns with interest on technical performance, ecosystem services, climate change mitigation and adaptation *Research:* Role of aesthetic preferences, environmental values on restoration and other benefits as applied to green roofs Access to nature and workplace benefits: concentration, restoration, creativity	Qualitative research examining cultural and contextual factors that affect perceptions of green roofs Perceptions of real-world green roofs versus only virtual/laboratory Include studies with diverse populations, contexts	Include both human and environmental considerations in green roof policy Incorporate region-specific cultural and contextual views of nature and aesthetic preferences in the design and promotion of green roofs Increase physical access to or visual intrigue in green roof design

thinking, progressive city (at least environmentally), in contrast to other Midwestern cities suffering from de-industrialization.

Toronto

While Toronto also had issues with UHI and stormwater management, the initial driver came from a local green roof non-profit that lobbied then-Deputy Mayor Pantalone to pursue green roofs as a climate change adaptation and mitigation strategy (S. Peck, personal communication October 17, 2003). Like Chicago, Toronto showed leadership by putting two test plots on their city hall and partnered with a federal governmental research agency to study the benefits (Green Roofs for Healthy Cities 1999; 2000; Deputy Mayor Pantalone and Burton 2006). They also had incentive programs to defray the cost of green roofs and encourage implementation. Unfortunately, the test plots were not well maintained, and Toronto lacked a cohesive strategy to promote or integrate green roofs into their policy. Within a consensus-based system, green roofs limped along for a while, with small policy changes and funding drawn from different departments (not very successfully since the costs of green roofs were higher than single-source environmental benefits, such as stormwater relief from Toronto Water). This changed with the election of a more environmentally minded mayor (Mayor Miller) who, along with persistent lobbying from a green roof non-profit, promoted a retrofitted city hall green roof that was bigger and better (City of Toronto 2011). This new green roof was used more effectively in publicity campaigns, and helped to gradually integrate support for green roofs into municipal policy: first with the strong encouragement for green roofs to be considered for all new municipal buildings and roof replacements (unless not technically feasible) (J. Welsh, personal communication, September 26, 2011), and eventually into the first mandated green roof by-law in North America (City of Toronto 2009b). This legislation was supported crucially by two things: the commissioning of another study on the benefits of green roofs for Toronto in partnership with Ryerson University (Doshi, Baniting et al. 2005); and an adjustment to provincial policy (the *City of Toronto Act*) that allowed Toronto to set higher green building standards than the province (City of Toronto 2007a) (see Plate 2, Chapter 2). Thus, while the consensus method was slower for Toronto, they did manage to eventually create strong SSUG implementation policy, albeit with the addition of stronger leadership (both mayoral and in their green roof), legislative change, and the support of research for 'new' urban greening. Unlike their current approach to GI, their green roof policy is fairly well publicized and supported and the green roof legislation has spurred other cities, such as San Francisco (2017) and, more recently, Denver (2018), to adopt similar legislation (San Francisco Planning Department 2017; City and County of Denver 2019).

Case study selection

For the case studies, green roofs were chosen that were viewable by and/or physically accessible to office workers in a downtown district and that had similar vegetation. Determining which buildings overlooked or had access to the green roofs was done by a combination of archival research such as real estate databases and site visits. The Chicago City Hall green roof (see Figure 3.1) – which is a

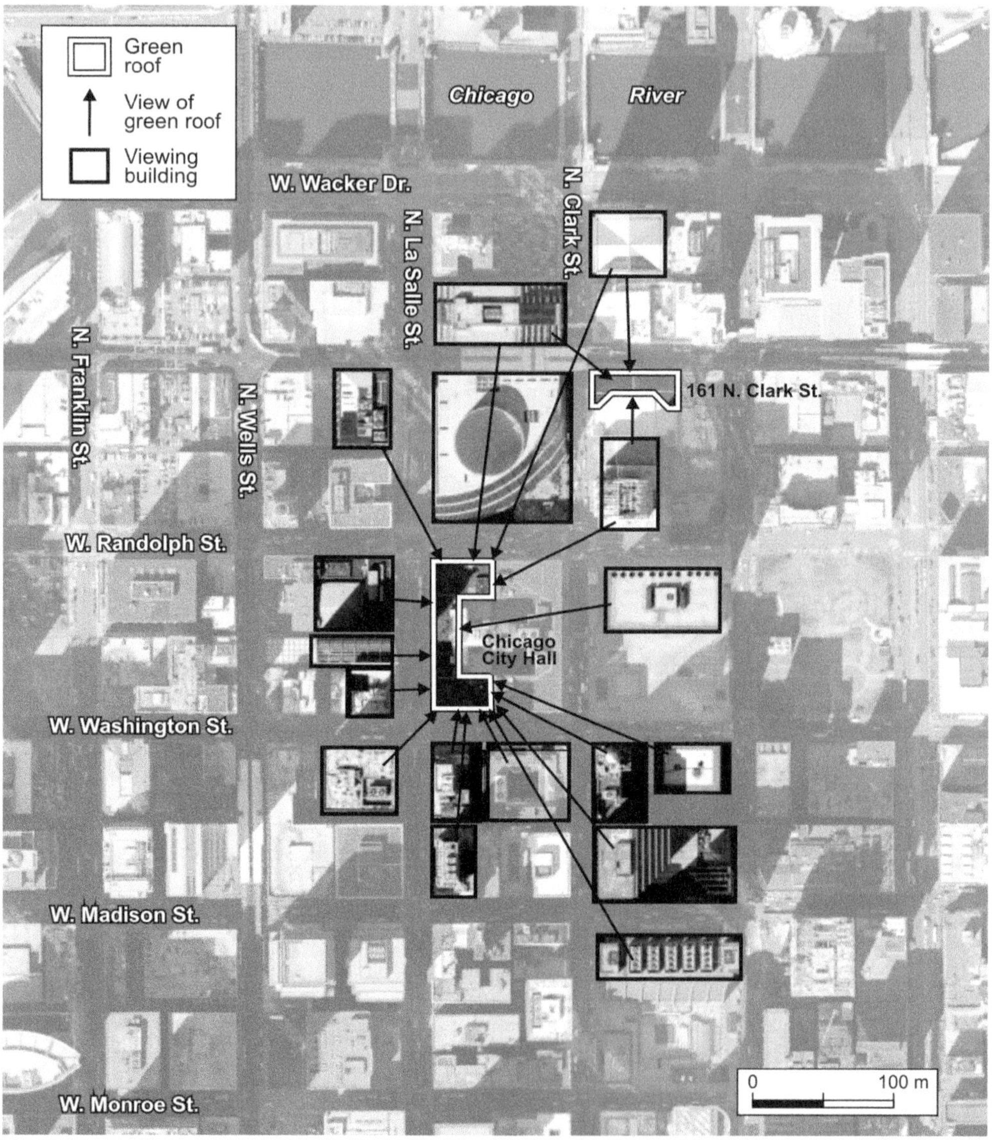

Figure 3.1 Map of Chicago City Hall green roof, green roof on 161 N. Clark and sightlines of participating buildings who could see the green roof(s).

prairie-style green roof, well-known and directly viewed by thousands of office workers – and a sedum roof also visible to office workers (161 N. Clark, see Figure 3.2), were chosen as the Chicago case studies. The 20,300 sq. ft. Chicago City Hall green roof was completed in 2001 and was planted with mostly prairie plants native to the region (City of Chicago 2010) (see Plate 5). In Toronto, the green roofs on the Mountain Equipment Co-op, 401 Richmond, and 215 Spadina (the Robertson Building) were chosen, as they were well known and viewable by office workers, and the latter two are accessible (see Figure 3.3). The 4,000 sq. ft.

Figure 3.2 Sedum green roof on parking garage, 161 N. Clark, Chicago.

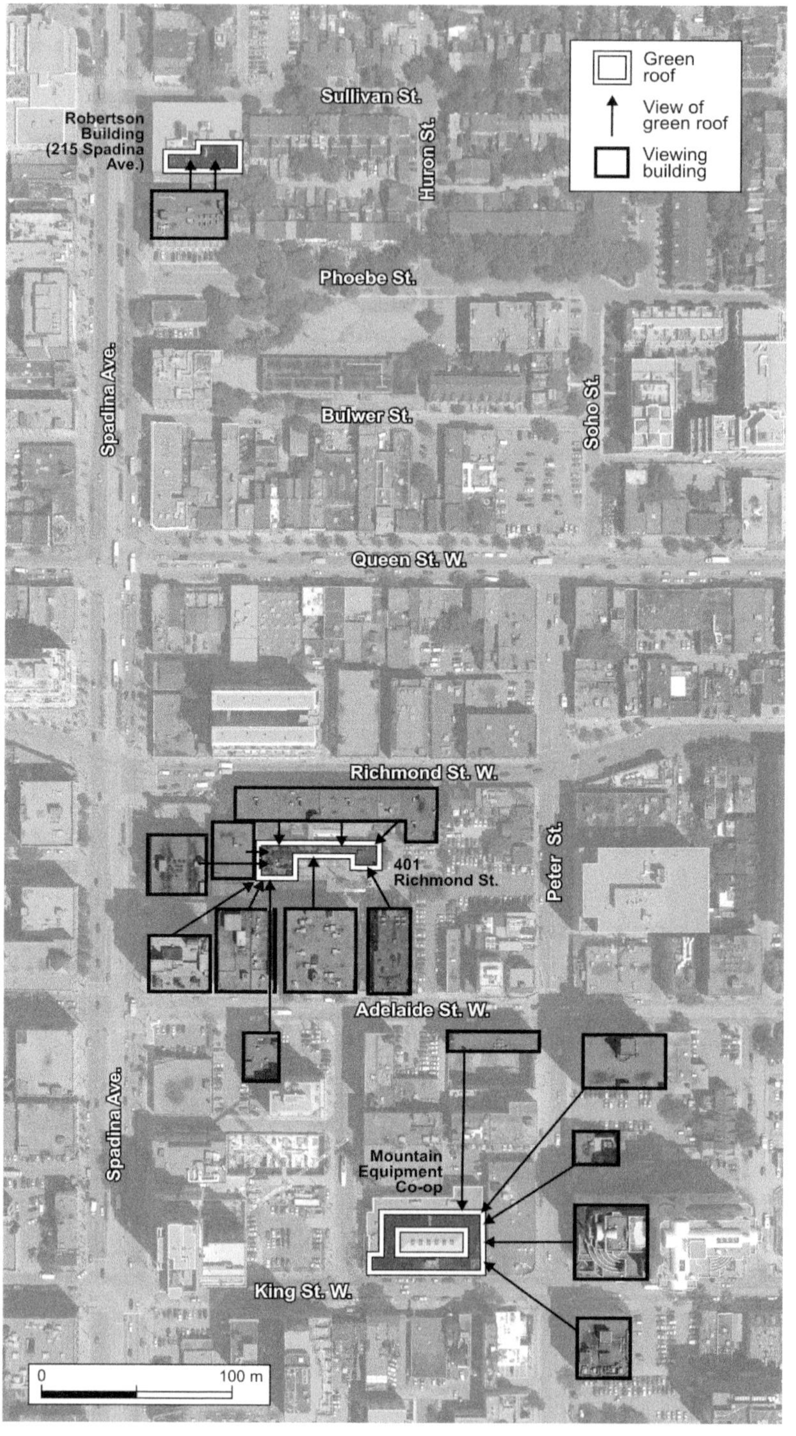

Figure 3.3 Map of three case study green roofs in Toronto and sightlines of participating buildings who could see the green roof(s).

green roof on 215 Spadina was completed in 2004 and was designed to showcase biodiversity with Ontario native perennials (Robertson Building 2010) (see Plate 6). The 10,000 sq. ft. green roof on the Mountain Equipment Co-op was also designed to mimic a prairie environment and was built in 1998 (Mountain Equipment Co-op 2009) (see Figure 3.4). Since 1995, 401 Richmond has had some sort of accessible roof garden; the current 2,600 sq. ft. extensive green roof, planted mainly with sedums, was added in 2005 (401 Richmond 2010) (see Figure 3.5). According to Michael Berkshire, who helped to develop green roof policy in Chicago, the City Hall green roof is meant to show municipal leadership, while the sedum roof was the first green roof required by municipal policies. In Toronto the green roofs were voluntary and meant to showcase private environmental leadership.

As the research was exploratory and phenomenological, a broad range of participants over many buildings was targeted. Combined with a survey of the same population discussed below, the interviews provided a baseline of office workers' perceptions of green roofs in each downtown area. Participants were selected based on their visual or physical access to one of the case study green roofs and recruited

Figure 3.4 Green roof on Mountain Equipment Co-op.

Figure 3.5 Green roof on 401 Richmond.

until the same themes kept emerging, with 26 participants in Toronto, 29 in Chicago, and approximately equal numbers of men and women. Though participants were sought across a representative range of income and ethnicity, the populations in each case study are predominantly white and middle to upper income, which is representative of these work neighbourhoods but less wealthy and diverse than Toronto or Chicago's populations. Interview participants were found from most of the 34 participating buildings, however, giving a broad range of participant access and experience of the green roofs.

It was difficult to solicit participation from those who did not have access to the green roof or who were less interested in urban greening, and thus the participant sample may be somewhat more 'green' than the general population, particularly in Toronto where the offices tend to be used by non-profits and arts media businesses. Multiple site visits over a year resulted in 55 semi-structured interviews, lasting anywhere from 20 to 60 minutes. Full details on the transcription, analysis, and coding (looking for themes that emerged) is not reported on here but can be found in Loder 2014.

Results: what did they think and feel about green roofs?

In general, most participants associated green roofs with some sort of environmental benefit, mainly due to the association of plants and greenery with the mitigation of air pollution. Green roofs were also generally thought to be a good idea. In addition to aesthetics, the size, scale, and distance of the green roof from participants strongly mediated their responses. For example, those who looked out directly onto a green roof, particularly at eye level, indicated that the green roof made much more of an impact on their daily experience than if they could only see a small sliver in the distance. The environmental values of the participants and political context also influenced their perception of the green roofs, though not always in the same way. These mitigating factors influenced the responses and the five themes that emerged from participant perceptions of green roofs: aesthetics, fascination, green roofs as part of 'nature' (or not), symbolism, and well-being. All participants have been given pseudonyms to protect their identity, and Toronto and Chicago are discussed together unless the responses warrant separate treatment.

Aesthetics

What role does aesthetics play in mediating office workers' perceptions of green roofs and urban nature? Results from the interviews indicate the key influence the following themes or concepts have on aesthetic perceptions: native habitat (the green roof's relation to this in the region); expectations (about what nature 'should' look like and whether it could coexist with or be located in a city); control ('nature' seen as something outside of human control); access (either visual or physical); and close observation (participants' watching and noticing changes over time). All of the participants agreed that the green roof was visually preferable to a black tar or gravel roof, but there was considerable ambiguity on whether participants liked the aesthetics of the roof. Though the prairie is long gone for most of the Midwest, except in neglected patches (Gobster 2001), most Chicago participants recognized the City Hall green roof as a prairie aesthetic: "…this one gives the appearance of you're driving down a country road and there's that prairie and it's completely overgrown and it's very wild and very – it's just very wild-looking" (Zsolt, Chicago). The Mountain Equipment Co-op (MEC) green roof in Toronto also has a prairie aesthetic, but this was really only recognized by participants who had grown up in the prairies: "…but I'm sure every time that I see it subconsciously, it reminds me of a natural prairie setting" (Tom, Toronto). While some participants found the prairie aesthetic wild, beautiful, and intriguing, many also found it messy, unkempt, and too 'wild looking':

> It seems not very well maintained, not very well landscaped, but I'm no expert…. This particular green roof it seems weedy, it seems almost like

> they're just letting it grow naturally and not really putting a lot of care in it, but then who knows? … Just looking at it, it looks like a bit of an overgrown prairie that's not being maintained properly.
>
> (Zsolt, Chicago)

This acknowledgement that the 'natural' aesthetic, while intentional, was not preferred, was common among participants, especially in Chicago. The green roof was contrasted less favourably with the bright colours and order of the median planters that were part of former Mayor Daley's urban revitalization in the loop business district. Chicago participants who only experienced the green roof visually found the more manicured aesthetic common to a sedum green roof – especially at a distance – not nearly as interesting or appealing, despite these same participants' dislike of the messy quality of the 'prairie' green roof. The green roof on 161 N. Clark was thought to be half-finished, unappealing, and less intriguing:

> …it doesn't entice you to dig further and deeper into it to understand the system. So for that green roof over on the parking garage, it doesn't invoke anything. It's just 'eh,' where it just looks like someone spit up carpet or grass on a roof and that's about it, whereas at least the one on City Hall, yeah it's not accessible, but from those that can view it, at least evokes something.
>
> (Bethany, Chicago)

Thus, though the prairie aesthetic was not always understood or liked, participants found it more interesting and engaging than a manicured, or lawn, aesthetic.

Participants' dislike of the messy aesthetics of the prairie-style green roof may be partly explained by what kind of 'nature' participants expect in the city, and where:

> And I suppose if I'm in the wilds, I don't expect – maybe it's based on expectation. If I'm in the wilds, I don't expect to see a beautiful cultivated garden or plants or everything in perfect order … but I do love being out in the wilderness and in there, that's what I expect…. In the city, I'm thinking more about what's uniform and again, what I find to be beautiful … flowers to look at and I don't see that up there.
>
> (Mark, Chicago)

This idea of expectation also brings up the issue of control in the city:

> I think there's a lot of ways to control a city environment, and I think that's one of the reasons why it's not as conducive to clear thought because you're

> always thinking, "If that person would just shut off their iPod then I'd maybe be able to focus on what I need to read … here," or something like that. Where you don't have any control over that cricket. You can't turn off that cricket, so you accept it and it becomes part of your environment.… If you accept that crickets have to be chirping and the stars have to be out and that the wind has to be blowing at whatever speed it's blowing, then it just becomes part of you with what's around you and essentially part of what you are.
>
> (Tim, Chicago)

Interestingly, participants who had physical access to a green roof with a similar aesthetic or who had close visual access said that they started to understand why it was left natural:

> At first, I thought it was kind of weird that they don't really … tend to it or have it like a garden and I'm like, "Well, I guess it's not a roof then," like a green roof where … but now I do understand. Letting it.… It's just more natural.
>
> (Jane, Toronto)

The relative ease and type of access to the green roof also influenced participants' perceptions. Those who were farther away from the green roof could not see much detail, colour, or variation, but were surprised when they subsequently visited the roof:

> And then to come up and see all this diversity of plants and the 'nature' that's using it, then it kind of connects for them. They go, "Oh, this is just like a wild lands in a park" or some cottage area where they go to or something. They can connect that. They see, "Oh, nature would use this as a stopping place to get to the lake or to continue on somewhere, bees for pollinating" and that sort of thing.
>
> (Robert, Toronto)

This direct experience of the variety of plant and animal life that exists on the roof usually resulted in more appreciation and understanding of the purpose and rhythm of the naturalized green roof, particularly if birds or bees used it as habitat. This appreciation was particularly apparent in participants who had strong environmental awareness, expressed as concern about and interest in environmental issues.

Environmental education also influenced participant perceptions. Those participants who assumed or had heard the green roof was installed for energy efficiency or stormwater management reasons also assumed that the naturalized aesthetic had some environmental rationale and was not intended to be pretty. This was true in Chicago where green roofs were more widely promoted as helping to reduce energy costs by the City and in Toronto where the green roof was assumed to reflect the environmental values of the building owners.

Surprise and fascination

The relative novelty of green roofs in the North American urban aesthetic landscape was reflected in participants' surprise over the green roof when they first saw it – surprise that vegetation could exist in a landscape of mostly glass, steel, and concrete:

> Well, it's just like this piece of concentrated vegetation existing.... I see just looking out the window right now, I see a few trees, but mostly I just see concrete, metal, cars, buildings and stuff, but I don't really see any vegetation out there, right? So it's hard to believe that it can exist where there's really no – what's the word I'm looking for? It doesn't seem this type of environment would be conducive for vegetation to exist in.
>
> (John, Toronto)

Many participants, particularly those who saw any sign of nature in the city as a sign of hope or progress, also viewed the green roof with delight:

> When I look ... to the Mayor's garden, it's a positive experience. I just feel a certain sense of delight and a little bit of smugness that, here we are in the middle of the city and yet we get to see this green thing. So, I think psychologically it certainly is a positive thing.
>
> (Peter, Chicago)

On a daily basis many participants found themselves attracted to the green roof almost unconsciously. They would be chatting on the phone, or looking out over the cityscape, and would find their eyes drawn to the roof:

> What always will happen is when you're on the phone and you have a chair that has wheels on it, just by force of habit, you'll be – you know, your mind will be elsewhere, but you'll happen to just kind of – when I find myself noticing it, I instinctually am drawn to it or continue to look at it without

> thinking about it, with my head completely somewhere else, but I will stay focused on it just out of some, I think, truly, just natural, instinctive pleasure that I derive from plants and nature.
>
> (Zsolt, Chicago)

This fascination and pleasure in viewing nature led many participants to actively observe the green roof out of curiosity – was anything different? Had anything changed? For many office workers, the green roof was one of the only cues to seasonal change they could see from their windows. For those with close access to the green roof, the view proved particularly fascinating: "Even when it's windy and raining, it's – there's something going on across the roof ... just staring at it, it's just beautiful, you know, and the colors" (Jennifer, Chicago). This close watching strongly influenced whether or not participants felt that the green roof was part of nature.

Is a green roof 'nature'?

Whether or not green roofs were considered part of nature revealed the ambiguity many participants felt about the human relationship with nature. While some felt that the presence of wildlife or plants – something 'wild' – meant that it was nature – "Oh, of course! They've got bees!" (Melanie, Chicago) – others felt that the obvious role of humans in creating a green roof moderated the 'nature' aspect of green roofs. For these participants, green roofs were seen as an approximation of or simulacrum for nature, but not as the real thing: "... um ... I want to say yes, but I feel it's implemented nature" (Judy, Toronto). This reaction reflects the ambiguity of 'nature' as both a place and a thing, or ideological 'Nature' versus everyday 'nature':

> Um.... Is the green roof part of nature? ... Yeah. I mean, it's, it's trees and plants. It's not nature for me in terms of being my vision – when you say what does nature evoke visually for you, nature is the untouched world. If you say, "I'm going out into nature," that doesn't mean I'm coming out to the green roof. That means I'm going out into, you know, camping or out into the woods. If I'm coming out to the green roof, that's a man-made construct. That, um, it's nice. It's lovely. It's green and everything, but that, to me, isn't nature.
>
> (June, Toronto)

Central to this perspective is the aesthetic experience of the juxtaposition of the green roof with densely clustered urban built form, which some participants felt reduced its immersive, natural effect:

> So, is that like nature? A little bit, but it's hard for me to say, "Oh, yeah. I feel like I'm in a nature preserve." because I can't look at that without seeing concrete all around me and buildings.
>
> (Mark, Chicago)

For these participants, nature is something you immerse yourself in, can touch, smell, and experience more than visually, a sentiment echoed by Joe: "… would I consider it part of nature? I think, you know what, if I went up there and sat down in the grass and read a book and enjoyed it, then yes, I would consider it part of nature" (Joe, Toronto). Though much of this confusion centres on the influence of scale and access, the ambivalence for many participants arose from how they *felt* versus *thought* about the green roof:

> It feels like it is (part of nature). I think that there's this conscious separation for me that says it's not specifically nature probably because I knew it was constructed and planned and put together rather than just happening on its own. But I think the end result feeling is that it's a part of nature when it's all done.
>
> (Dolores, Chicago)

Lastly, participants with strong environmental knowledge and values either saw the green roof as mitigating or compensating for environmental damage wrought by humans, or as not nearly enough given the destruction of wilderness and habitat outside the city. In this sense green roofs were symbolic of larger environmental values.

Green roofs and symbolism

Green roofs do not evoke the traditionally iconic concepts of nature, like forest or lakes. Instead, participants viewed green roofs as symbolic of the values and intention of the person or organization assumed to be responsible for their implementation. In Chicago, this was former Mayor Daley, and the City Hall green roof was often referred to as "… the Mayor's garden" (Anna, Chicago). This association is due largely to the high level of publicity around green roofs as a mayoral initiative, but also to the larger program of urban greening and revitalization in Chicago, of which green roofs were assumed to be a part: "So when I saw the green roof, it just was another extension of what seemed like all these wonderful things that Chicago was doing to bring flowers and green and trees into the city" (Dolores, Chicago). This greening was strongly associated with a sense of pride that the mayor was promoting environmental initiatives that improved both the public experience of the city and showcased Chicago to the world as progressive and green:

> And I think people are more proud today to be Chicagoans in no small part because of the greening of the city. I mean, it is a *beautiful* city.... I think they enjoy the experience more because it's greener. I know I do. I know I, you know, I can't put my finger on the tangible effects of it, but you just *feel* different when you can run around the city and see these greening initiatives. It's, it's great. People *love* to come here, and you want to be proud of your city as a Chicagoan. We've always been proud of Chicago as an architectural landmark and architectural template ... and to be able to wed that to greenery that lives up to that standard of architectural ... excellence is nice. It really makes Chicago a global city, and as a citizen, you always want to be proud of your city.
>
> (Donald, Chicago)

Green roofs and other greening initiatives thus became symbolic of the City's caring about the community's aesthetic lived experience of the city and sharing their environmental values.

In Toronto, green roofs were also associated with the organization assumed to be responsible for their implementation, in this case the Mountain Equipment Co-op (MEC) or the owners of 401 Richmond and 215 Spadina: "...I thought that the MEC Building, which has, I guess, a green roof ... was something unique to them in that it was part of their, I guess, motif or branding to be environmentally friendly" (Matthew, Toronto). As in Chicago, participants saw the green roof as reflecting their own environmental values, and in particular as compensation for and recovery from human destruction of the environment:

> Well, my understanding about green roofing and all of that is it's a sustainability project that many cities have adopted, and it's like a replacement.... Because we are expanding our cities quite a bit and there is a lot of greenery that is being lost and, and/or not preserved within the city.
>
> (Elaine, Toronto)

This association of green roofs with recovery and the organization which installed them reflects green roofs as emblematic of the environmental values of the participants. This was often linked to a sense of hope and well-being.

Green roofs and well-being

The ambiguity around whether green roofs are part of nature, as well as around the differentiation between health and well-being, complicated the responses to questions about the relationship between green roofs and well-being. For those participants who felt that 'nature' needed to be immersive and large-scale to be beneficial, or that nature was a place, green roofs were not generally viewed as affecting their health. These participants expressed the desire for the green roof to be accessible, and for more green roofs, before any health benefits might be felt. They interpreted both health and green roofs in a very literal, scale-oriented way: one green roof will not clean the air as much as many green roofs, and clean air impacts one's physical health. While many of the participants found the green roof made them feel better, this scale-based and physical interpretation kept them from associating this experience with health:

> It made you feel better. I don't want to say it influenced my health.... But, yes... – if it reduces your stress, I guess it would affect your health. I never thought of it in those terms. But it definitely made you feel better.
>
> (Hugo, Chicago)

However, it is in these more qualitative, affective responses where some of the more interesting perceptions about green roofs and well-being emerge. For example, most participants found that the green roof broke up the aesthetic monotony and hardness of the concrete city:

> Breaking the grayness, the hardness of the city ... these rooftop gardens would be a part of that.... So, I respond to aesthetics. Something that looks nice, something that breaks the monotony, something that is intriguing that'll have me stop for a moment and look at something.
>
> (Peter, Chicago)

This softening of the city provided a balancing and release against the stress of the central business district: "It's a balancing and kind of emotional release to look out and see a garden versus concrete everywhere" (Iris, Chicago). Participants also often mentioned the calming effect of the presence of the green roof: "I do believe that having green roofs, or having trees on top of buildings brings a bit of a calmness to people, and that reality check of not just buildings, and coldness, and corporate world" (Jackie, Toronto). Though participants who had access to the green roof found more stress relief, even looking out the window at the green roof provided an escape from the stresses of long hours at the office and numerous demands on participants' time:

> Um, it just kind of gives me just a sense, like a few minutes of quiet. I can, you know, – I find it easier to reflect looking at something, some tree or a

> plant or flowers, a field and that's kind of what it reminds me of. It reminds me of a meadow or something.
>
> (Elaine, Toronto)

This ability of the green roof to evoke other nature experiences, for example reminding them of a meadow, brought participants back to a happier time, often in childhood:

> I think that it exudes the same feelings of that I would've gotten when I went out into the woods when I was growing up. When I enjoy the green roof, when I enjoy the Chicago planters, it's that same sort of happy, free spirit feeling that things are good, things are beautiful.
>
> (Dolores, Chicago)

Gazing out at the green roof also helped them gain perspective in their work and creatively solve problems. Participants mentioned that the green roof helped them to "get back to basics" (Melanie, Chicago), put things into perspective (Maurice, Chicago), and clear their head to better approach their work (Jane, Toronto). Lastly, the presence of the green roof gave many participants a sense of hope about a re-balancing of the natural and human-made world: "But I feel hope. I guess I feel hope when I come up here. I think people are making an effort to try and reintegrate environmental considerations into our built world and that makes me feel hopeful" (June, Toronto). These more affective, nuanced perceptions of the relationship between green roofs and participants' health and well-being point to possible ways to understand how aesthetics mediates participants' relationship with nature in cities.

Implications for policy, research, and the human relationship to nature

Implementing green roofs: comments on policy and leadership

Implementing green roofs is even more difficult than other types of GI as it often requires private as well as public action, and thus a different suite of tools. The differing initial success rates of green roof implementation in Chicago and Toronto point to the important role played by not only political structure (such as a strong mayor versus a consensus system) but also leadership and publicity. Chicago's strong mayor system, well-maintained, researched, and publicized City Hall green roof, and carrot/stick policy combination enabled the city's ten-year lead in green roof implementation in North America. Toronto, on the other hand, had not only changes in leadership, but a poorly maintained and publicized city hall green roof and only 'carrot' incentives, which meant that they lagged behind Chicago for years even though on paper they had similar strategies. It wasn't until they had stronger leadership (and some legislative changes that allowed them to go further than the province) and a well-designed and publicized case study, that they were able to build momentum to create North America's groundbreaking first green roof by-law. Throughout this process the importance of using the symbolism of green roofs as an emblem of a larger, consistent environmental vision is an important lesson learned from both cities. While the policy and leadership context is important for understanding the relative success and acceptance of green roofs in these particular cities, the case studies uncover the underlying personal and cultural themes of urbanites' response to green roofs.

Insights from social constructionism and phenomenology

How can the frameworks of social constructionism and phenomenology help us to (1) understand how these office workers' responses contribute to literature on perceptions and preferences of green roofs and SSUG more generally; (2) point to possible cultural factors influencing these preferences; and (3) offer insight into key components of their daily lived experience that shape their perceptions of aesthetics and their relationship to urban nature?

Participant's mixed reactions to the aesthetics of the green roofs echo the differing aesthetic preferences found by recent green roof studies where either grasses (White and Gatersleben 2011; Lee, Williams et al. 2014) or sedums (Jungels, Rakow et al. 2013) were preferred. While other studies have linked socio-demographic and group variables to aesthetic preferences (van den Berg, Vlek et al. 1998), these did not emerge as important factors in the interviews. Participant responses, however, point to possible cultural influences on these aesthetic perceptions and challenge the idea that these preferences are either innate or only individual variations, echoing the social constructionist critiques seen in Chapter 1. The recurring association of prairie-style vegetation with ecological restoration supports work that argues aesthetic preferences are malleable and influenced by education (Gobster, Nassauer et al. 2007; Shume 2016), particularly since participants' knowledge of the environmental benefits of green roofs often led to an increased acceptance of a prairie aesthetic. Conversely, the association of prairie-style green roofs with messiness and a lack of maintenance may point to the Victorian legacy of public health and sanitation which has linked 'messiness' and 'wildness' with neglect and ill-health (Nassauer 1995; Hough 2004) and the subsequent association of straight lines and order with the modernist city ideals of planning, beautification, economic progress, and control (Kaika 2006). Participants' expectation of 'wild' nature outside the city, but neat, colourful nature within it also reflects the elevation of the scenic or tourist aesthetic instrumental to North American nation building – and in particular the control over the 'wild west' over local, lived, and messy nature (Merchant 1995; Saito 2002b; Urry 2005). Thus, a green roof turning brown during a dry season can signal neglect and death, rather than the normal changes of grassland. In this way the prairie aesthetic in the city seems to challenge the expectation of 'nature' as 'out there,' far away and unchanging, a hyperreal scenic frozen ideal that lacks the in-depth, intimate knowledge of the lived experience of place and ecological processes (Cronon 1995; Foster 2000; Gobster, Nassauer et al. 2007). Though sedums can also have visual interest, they lack an association with native habitat and their detail is often not visible from a distance, making them stand out less among a mass of tall buildings. This may explain participants' lukewarm or neutral reactions to their aesthetics, particularly in Chicago.

Participant ambivalence over whether 'nature' that is clearly manipulated by humans (i.e. planted on a roof) could count as 'real' 'Nature' also mirrors ecological restoration debates in which preservationists believe real 'Nature' is outside the city, ideally untouched by humans and not replicable once destroyed, while restorationists imagine a more reciprocal, active relationship between humans and nature through care and labour (Elliot 2000; Hull and Robertson 2000). Thus, though current urban greening goals are to bring 'nature' back to the city, this may conflict with an inherited Anglo-American ideology in which the nature/city separation is necessary for the goals of economic progress and human and ecological health.

The phenomenological perspective also offers different insights about participants' aesthetic experiences and perceptions of green roofs and urban nature. Central to participants' experiences are the concepts of fascination over time, wildness, and intention. Participant fascination with green roofs – even when they were unsure about, or even disliked, the aesthetics – supports work in environmental psychology, biophilia, and environmental values that argues that humans are not indifferent to the natural world and are implicitly drawn to it, even in dense urban settings (Ulrich 1993; Wilson 1993; van den Berg, Koole et al. 2003; Schultz, Shriver et al. 2004). A phenomenological perspective, however, reveals the role that close watching over time played in participant perceptions. Participants who watched the green roof over time and who were close enough to notice detail and seasonal change expressed recognition of otherness and wildness, separate from the concrete and glass buildings. This watching over time often led them to let go of ideas about what the green roof should or should not be, what it should look like, what it should do; in short, participants who could observe the details allowed the green roof to *be as it is*, paralleling a more phenomenological way of viewing the world that tries to let things unfold in their own way, while letting the categories we impose on things fall away (Heidegger 1971). This kind of knowing has been called a meditative thinking (Heidegger 1966; Stefanovic 1991), and is in direct contrast with the kind of calculative thinking required in many workplaces and encouraged by sharp-edged, efficient urban landscapes. However, meditative thinking *is* conducive to creative work and problem solving and may help to develop an ecological aesthetic that blends knowledge with aesthetics and fosters a closer, deeper relationship with nature (Leopold 1971; Gobster 1999). If research shows that other urbanites have similar lived experiences from close contact with green roofs or other ecologically oriented urban greening projects, then green roofs or other similar 'local' nature projects may provide opportunities to shift aesthetic preferences from a remote scenic or tourist aesthetic and increase the chance of success for greening projects (Carlson 2010; Varandas 2015). Furthermore, meditative thinking challenges the expectation of control expressed by participants and returns agency to nature (Brady 2006; Lorimer, Hodgetts et al. 2019) which can lead to a sense of calmness and peace and thus well-being. Insights from those participants who were able to watch the green roof closely over time therefore support some suggestions in phenomenology that nature can serve as a possible vehicle, or cue, to this kind of knowing and awareness (Stefanovic 1991).

Meditative versus calculative thinking also seems to be key in participant's perceptions of whether or not green roofs are nature and have the same benefits as 'Nature.' While environmental knowledge can affect aesthetic preferences, it often did not alter participants' conscious, fixed idea of nature as a place untouched by humans and thus 'wild,' even when their more affective, immediate perception of the green roof that came from a more meditative watching shifted their experience of it as a kind of nature. This kind of knowing supports work in aesthetics that argues we understand aesthetics and nature through both cognitive and affective pathways (Hepburn 1993; Saito 2007; Moore 2008; Toadvine 2010), but it also speaks to the importance of implicit, felt connections to nature that are mediated, but not determined, by aesthetics and culture. Participants who watched the green roof over time were more likely to 'feel' that the green roof was part of nature, that it influenced their health and well-being, and associated green roofs with the sense of connection, calm, and a mental break commonly associated with large-scale, immersive experiences in nature highlighted by environmental psychologists (Kaplan 1995; Krenichyn 2006). Though urban greening projects do not have the scale, remoteness, or ideological heft of forests or mountains, awe and inspiration can be found in the hiddenness and minute details of 'nature' (Wilson 1993). This understanding of different ecological scales and processes can deepen the human relationship to nature (Hepburn 1993; Gobster, Nassauer et al. 2007; Carlson 2019). In this sense the experience of otherness, or wildness, in nature may be key in whether or not urban greening projects are perceived to have health benefits similar to those of 'Nature.' This perspective avoids the nature/city dualism and highlights the key role of emotion in the human relationship to nature in the city.

Lastly, a phenomenological analysis reveals the sensitivity of participants to the perceived *intention* behind the green roof. This may help to explain why for Chicago participants, though the sedum green roof fit into their expectations of control and order in the city, it was less liked due to the perception that not as much effort was put into it. While this feeling may have been influenced by the modular style of sedum roof on 161 N. Clark, it also seems to be due to aesthetics and perceived effort. The sedum green roof had to cover at least 50 percent of the roof under Chicago's policies, and according to Michael Berkshire from the City of Chicago, the building owners installed only the minimum required. This minimal effort was picked up on by almost all the Chicago participants. Toronto participants who had physical access to the roof and who associated it with environmental initiatives were less negative about the sedum roof. However, though the prairie-style green roofs were seen as 'messy' and possibly not as maintained as they 'should' be, they also had visibly more detail (even from a distance), design work, and ongoing maintenance, whether from path patterns as on the Chicago City Hall, physical access and terracing, as on the Robertson building, or regular tours and maintenance crews on all three. The reference to prairie ecologies outside the city also seems to have influenced many participants' perception of green roofs as a symbol of restoration, hope, and care, even if mismanaged by the City; the green roofs signalled the thought and effort the City had put into the quality of urban public life, public health, and larger environmental issues. This sense of hope and restoration, and of pride in their city, is linked to larger debates around the quality of life and public space in cities and of a collective well-being and sense of place. The fatigue from concrete, glass, and steel, from long hours with little to no access to fresh air and greenspace, and the view of tar roofs, dead birds, and mechanical equipment, all shape the context in which these participants experience green roofs in the city, and how the unexpected presence of meadows in the sky can give some of them a sense of calmness, hope, and respite.

Limitations of the research

Phenomenology as a method looks for essential underlying themes that can provide insight into the human condition – in this case the human relationship with and aesthetics of urban nature. Though previous research on the human relationship to nature has found commonalities across socio-economic and ethnic lines (Kaplan and Talbot 1988; Gobster 1998), the limited ethnic and socio-economic characteristics of the sample population, and the possibility of self-selection by those who tend to be more interested in nature and 'green' issues, means that the insights resulting from the research may only be applicable to similar populations until further research can test these themes on different populations. However, the case studies do nonetheless offer compelling insight into *why* urbanites feel the way they do about small-scale urban greening projects that do not fit into well-known symbolic or cultural understandings.

Asking the same questions in a different way: a survey

As we saw in Chapter 1, different methods, and the paradigms behind them, can lead to different results, so the findings from the interview responses were subsequently tested out with a larger population. Over 900 office workers in Chicago and Toronto who could see or had access to the green roofs used as case studies for the interviews were surveyed; while the full study is not reported on here, key findings are highlighted, particularly those that differed from the interview response results.

Methods and case study selection

Through a combination of visits to the green roofs themselves and to the buildings overlooking them, the study population was identified as those who had offices within the identified buildings (Figures 3.1 and 3.3), with 17 buildings chosen in Chicago and 14 chosen in Toronto.[2] The online survey was completed by 903 respondents in total: 624 in Chicago and 279 in Toronto. Given the multiple constraints of working with numerous public and private companies in each building, and the gatekeepers at most of the Chicago buildings, it was impossible to fully assess the sampling frame and do a randomized sample, so the results of the survey cannot be assumed to be statistically representative of that population. However, the distribution of occupations and industries in the sample was fairly representative of these office populations, and as the research was intended to be exploratory (given that there was almost no research of its kind at the time), the goals were less to be statistically representative and more to explore possible significant relationships and themes for future research.

The online survey asked participants questions about: their access to and awareness of green roofs, with access defined as visual, physical, or both; if they felt green roofs were beneficial to the city, and why; the importance of nature in their work neighbourhood and to their health; whether they associated green roofs with 'nature'; and whether they felt green roofs influenced their health. The survey used standard socio-demographic and environmental attitude questions, while questions on participants' perception of the level and importance of nature near their workplace, and their health, stress, and concentration were adapted from existing measures (answered on a 5-point Likert scale). In addition to basic attitudes and perceptions about green roofs, the survey was particularly interested in exploring possible significant relationships between three key areas: (1) access to the green roof and self-reported responses to participants' health, stress, and concentration levels; (2) participant's *perception* that the green roof influenced their health and green roof access; and (3) possible links between the association of green roofs with environmental benefits, green roofs with nature, and the participant's own health.

Results

The sample populations in Toronto and Chicago were better educated and more white than each city's general population, and, barring almost twice as many women responding as men, fairly representative of the workforce in those office buildings. Chicago's respondents tended to work in professional, legal, or financial services – which is unsurprising given the proximity to City Hall – while Toronto's population tended to work in the non-profit, arts, and media professions. This likely influenced the higher-than average incomes for Chicago and slightly lower than average incomes for Toronto. Most respondents spent most of their day in the office, had been in their office between one and ten years, and were divided between being very and somewhat satisfied with their jobs. Most respondents (65 percent) rated their health as excellent or very good, and roughly half rated their life as stressful (54 percent) or indicated they had difficulty concentrating at work (51 percent).

What did this larger survey population think or know about green roofs? The vast majority of respondents knew what a green roof was (90 percent) and felt that it was beneficial (84 percent), though this likely reflects the self-selection to participate. Of those who thought green roofs were beneficial, three-quarters thought green roofs were nice to look at, saved money for buildings that had them, and/or added greenspace to the city. Those who didn't think they were beneficial thought they were too expensive or were unsure of the benefits. Around 60 percent associated green roofs with the specific environmental benefits of cooling the city and reducing stormwater overflow.

Almost half of the respondents were aware of a green roof outside or on their workplace (48 percent). This number was far higher for the Toronto respondents than the Chicago respondents, and might be explained by the larger floor plans of the Chicago offices – workers on the opposite side of the building or in the centre offices may never see the green roof. Of those who *were* aware of a green roof (56 percent in both cities combined), far more respondents in Chicago (71 percent) than in Toronto (33 percent) could see the green roof from their workplace. This is also likely due to the fact that the Toronto green roofs were on smaller buildings and in some cases accessible.

What did the survey respondents feel about nature near their workplace and green roofs? A small majority (61 percent) of respondents felt that it was very important or important to have nature near their workplace, with 31 percent feeling it was somewhat important. Three-quarters (78 percent) felt that there wasn't enough 'nature' near their workplace, while the vast majority of respondents (80 percent) felt that having nature near their workplace influenced their health and well-being. Interestingly, while 80 percent associated green roofs with 'nature,' just over half of the respondents felt that the green roof influenced their health (52 percent), while 34 percent were unsure.

Was access to a green roof linked to a difference in health, stress, or concentration status? For the survey population, only concentration showed a significant relationship. Specifically, participants' self-rated concentration and the perception that green roofs influenced their health both had a significant relationship to green roof access (χ^2 (1) = 5.50, $p<.05$). In addition, there was a significant association between respondents' perception that green roofs were beneficial to the city, those who associated green roofs with 'nature,' and their belief that they influenced his or her health (χ^2 (4) = 3.31, $p<.001$) and (χ^2 (4) = 7.90, $p<.001$) respectively. Conversely, if respondents did *not* associate green roofs with nature, they were also more likely to feel that green roofs did not influence their health. Lastly, respondents who associated green roofs with 'nature' were more likely than expected to feel that the green roofs were beneficial to the city (χ^2 (4) = 5.52, $p<.001$), though a large percentage of respondents who did not associate green roofs with nature still felt that green roofs were beneficial to the city.

Lessons learned from quantitative versus qualitative methods

How do these results add to our understanding of small-scale urban greening projects such as green roofs and their impact on urbanites, and how they challenge or support the results of the interviews?

As mentioned above, different methods and underlying paradigms influence what kinds of questions we ask and how we interpret the results. Most surveys aim to find out *what*, not *how* or *why*, people think or behave the way they do, which is very useful for policy work. The goals of this online survey were on the surface similar to those of the interviews: to discover what office workers knew and thought about green roofs, whether they thought green roofs were 'nature,' and whether they felt that the green roofs influenced their health and well-being. Nuances, however, or instances in which people are themselves unsure of how they feel, can be lost in quantitative surveys.

The results for the most part supported the findings from the interviews. Office workers in Toronto and Chicago generally felt that nature near their workplace and in their city was important for their health and well-being and that green roofs were beneficial to the city both for ecological and aesthetic reasons, and they associated green roofs with specific environmental benefits like managing stormwater and the urban heat island. This was most notable in Chicago, which at the time had promoted green roofs far more heavily than Toronto. Participants who had access to a green roof were also more likely to feel that green roofs were beneficial to the city, influenced their health, and were associated with nature. Visual access to a green roof was also associated with better concentration, regardless of how participants felt about green roofs. This kind of information is very useful for policy makers; it allows them to understand if their target population knows about their small-scale urban greening projects, if their communication campaign is effective, how urbanites value or what they think about them, and possible benefits to their residents. The larger sample population also allows them to justify spending public dollars on investments, and the quantifiable data can be used more persuasively because it feels more 'true' to the general public than qualitative findings.

What is less clear from the survey, and what came through in the interviews, particularly using a phenomenological approach, is how office workers thought or felt green roofs influenced them. In the survey responses, this is seen in participants' uncertainty about whether or not green roofs influenced their health, even though they associated green roofs with nature and nature with influencing their health. Results of the interviews shed some light on this ambiguity. Interview participants often had difficulty self-evaluating their health; they tended to quantify their health, and therefore tried to quantify how much 'green' they would need in order to have it impact their health. Similarly, interview participants were unsure about whether or not green roofs counted as 'nature,' since this came up against inherited values that nature is something found outside the city, untouched by humans (mirroring ecological restoration debates). They also had difficulty with linking aesthetics that may have been 'messy' with their health, again coming up against inherited Victorian values about sanitation and health in the city. However, when participants began to talk about how they *felt* about the green roof, and how they watched it over time, many of them found that it felt like nature, and that it influenced their health, well-being, concentration, creativity, and perspective. Furthermore, they began to associate it with larger nature outside the city, especially if the aesthetics were 'wilder.' These kinds of insights can help explain the ambiguity survey respondents had around whether or not the green roofs influenced their health.

Though less often used in policy, the added nuance of the findings above strongly suggest that the inclusion of qualitative research can be extremely helpful for city planners in understanding possible resistance to, or appreciation of, small-scale urban greening projects. It can highlight where cultural values may influence likes or dislikes and use these insights in their design and promotion of urban greening programs and projects. And qualitative research can help bring insight to the sought-after but elusive concept of sense of place, or the lived experience of the city, which can make or break new or revitalized developments.

Conclusion

While green roofs are a new form of nature in cities, we have seen from the research studies discussed above that participant experiences of them are highly mediated by aesthetics, previous experiences of and preconceptions about nature, and narratives about progress, modernity, and native habitat. In Chicago, these factors led to participants recognizing the City Hall green roof as prairie-style, while in Toronto only participants familiar with the prairie recognized this. Such associations also carry cultural values. For Chicago, the remnants of prairie outside of the city evoked both the unconstrained explorations of childhood and wild beauty and neglect, messiness, and a resistance to the narrative of progress, control, and cultivation of the Midwest. For Toronto, many participants viewed real 'Nature' as up north, with forests and lakes, and while many found the prairie-style green roofs beautiful, they were not seen necessarily as 'Nature,' which they conceived as a place they retreat to. These findings have implications for the public acceptance and appreciation of both green roofs and urban greening projects in general. They also suggest that, if done carefully, SSUG may open up possibilities for re-connecting urbanites with the native habitat of their region.

The research also points to promising possibilities for the acceptance of SSUG in cities, if they are implemented with an awareness of the expectations urbanites have of their daily lived experience of downtown central business districts, and the role of expectation of their daily lived experience. Certainly, control of nature, and a lack of outdoor places to eat lunch and take a break, can be read from the hardness of concrete, glass, and steel. The narrative such a setting supports is one of work and control, not comfort and rest. However, participants often spent eight to ten hours a day at work and expressed the need for even a five-minute mental break to help them be more productive and in a better head space at work. Given participant expressions of gratitude and hope over the placement of green roofs within visual or physical access of their workplace, placing green roofs or other small greening projects may signal care of the whole person, versus just the worker, and may start to change the lived experience of place in central business districts. This may be particularly relevant as many central business districts are experiencing booms in condominium construction and have people living in them for the first time in their history. These new residents will have different expectations of comfort, dwelling, and place than office workers.

Lastly, participant responses to green roofs raise the issue of access, scale, and distance which influenced participant perceptions of green roofs and the level of importance they had in their workday. The sensuous aspect, whether through touch, smell, sound, or visual cues, is an important part of the human experience with nature. If only the visual aspect is available to office workers in central business districts, then perhaps urban greening projects can be designed to maximize interest, a sense of play, and exploration to mimic participant memories of childhood nature experiences. Combined with a more ecological aesthetic, and juxtaposed with the built form of central business districts, these urban greening projects may prove to be beneficial both ecologically and psychologically for the city and its workers.

Notes

1 For the full report, please see Loder 2014.

2 Respondents were recruited through a combination of building manager cooperation, cold calling, or visiting businesses where possible. The interview respondents discussed above were also used as contacts for their offices. To promote the survey, an email describing it was sent to the main contact to forward to their offices or buildings (for building managers) that contained a link to the online survey.

References

401 Richmond (2010, August 19). "401 Richmond green roof." Retrieved August 19, 2010, from www.401richmond.net/gardens.

Adams, M. L. (2019). "Step-counting in the 'health-society': Phenomenological reflections on walking in the era of the Fitbit." *Social Theory and Health* **17**(1): 109–124.

American Society of Landscape Architects (2002). "2002 Award Winners: Chicago City Hall Green Roof." Retrieved December 5, 2007, from www.asla.org/meetings/awards/awds02/chicagocityhall.html.

Armson, D., P. Stringer and A. R. Ennos (2012). "The effect of tree shade and grass on surface and globe temperatures in an urban area." *Urban Forestry and Urban Greening* **11**(3): 245–255.

Berkshire, M. (2006). *Fast Track Permitting and Incentives for Residential Green Roofs in Chicago*. Greening Rooftops for Sustainable Communities, Boston, Green Roofs for Healthy Cities.

Berkshire, M. (2008). (Green Projects Administrator, City of Chicago, Department of Planning). Interview with A. Loder.

Bjornstad, S., G. G. Patil and R. K. Raanaas (2015). "Nature contact and organizational support during office working hours: Benefits relating to stress reduction, subjective health complaints, and sick leave." *Work* **53**(1): 9–20.

Blank, L., A. Vasl, S. Levy, G. Grant, G. Kadas, A. Dafni and L. Blaustein (2013). "Directions in green roof research: A bibliometric study." *Building and Environment* **66**(0): 23–28.

Bliss, D. J., R. D. Neufeld and R. J. Ries (2009). "Storm water runoff mitigation using a green roof." *Environmental Engineering Science* **26**(2): 407–417.

Brady, E. (2006). "The aesthetics of agricultural landscapes and the relationship between humans and nature." *Ethics, Place and the Environment* **9**(1): 1–19.

Butler, C., E. Butler and C. M. Orians (2012). "Native plant enthusiasm reaches new heights: Perceptions, evidence, and the future of green roofs." *Urban Forestry and Urban Greening* **11**(1): 1–10.

Calkins, M. (2005). "Strategy use and challenges of ecological design in landscape architecture." *Landscape and Urban Planning* **73**(1): 29–48.

Carlson, A. (2010). "Contemporary environmental aesthetics and the requirements of environmentalism." *Environmental Values* **19**(3): 289–314.

Carlson, A. (2019). "Environmental Aesthetics." *The Stanford Encyclopedia of Philosophy*, Center for the Study of Language and Information, Stanford University.

Chan, I. Y. S. and A. M. M. Liu (2018). "Effects of neighborhood building density, height, greenspace, and cleanliness on indoor environment and health of building occupants." *Building and Environment* **145**: 213–222.

Chih-Fang, F. (2008). "Evaluating the thermal reduction effect of plant layers on rooftops." *Energy and Buildings* **40**(6): 1048–1052.

Chow, M. F., M. F. A. Bakar and L. M. Sidek (2018). "A review on the controlling factors that affecting the stormwater retention performance of green roof." *IOP Conference Series: Earth and Environmental Science* **159**: 012045.

Cinderby, S. and S. Bagwell (2018). "Exploring the co-benefits of urban green infrastructure improvements for businesses and workers' wellbeing." *Area* **50**(1): 126–135.

City and County of Denver. (2019). "Denver's Green Buildings Ordinance." *Denver Development Series* Retrieved June 11, 2019, from www.denvergov.org/content/denvergov/en/denver-development-services/commercial-projects/green-roof-initiative.html.

City of Chicago (n.d.). "Green and Solar Permit Incentives." *Buildings*. Retrieved June 1, 2019, from www.chicago.gov/city/en/depts/bldgs/provdrs/permits/svcs/green-permits.html.

City of Chicago (2006, 2010). "Green Roof Grant Program 2006." Retrieved November, 2006, from www.cityofchicago.org/city/en/depts/doe/supp_info/green_roof_grantsprograms.html.

City of Chicago (2010, August 19). "Chicago City Hall Green Roof." Retrieved August 19, 2010, from www.explorechicago.org/city/en/about_the_city/green_chicago/Green_Roofs_.html.

City of Chicago (2012, 2011). "Building Green/Green Roof Matrix." Retrieved March 12, 2012, from www.cityofchicago.org/city/en/depts/zlup/supp_info/sustainable_development.html.

City of Chicago: Mayor's Office (2006). "Mayor Daley Dedicates Cultural Center Green Roof." Retrieved December 12, 2006, from http://egov.cityofchicago.org/city/webportal/portalContentItemAction.do?blockName=Content&topChannelName=HomePage&contentOID=536944504&Failed_Reason=Invalid+timestamp%2C+engine+has+been+restarted&contenTypeName=COC_EDITORIAL&com.broadvision.session.new=Yes&Failed_Page=%2Fwebportal%2FportalContentItemAction.do&displayBack=null&context=Recent+News.

City of Toronto (n.d.). "City of Toronto's Governance System." *Introduction to Toronto's Government*. Retrieved June 11, 2019, from www.toronto.ca/city-government/accountability-operations-customer-service/get-involved-how-government-works/torontos-governance-system.

City of Toronto (2006). "Making Green Roofs Happen." Policy and Finance Committee, City of Toronto: 1–41.

City of Toronto (2007a). "January 1, 2007: City of Toronto Act 2006 Proclaimed Ontario's Capital City Begins New Era." Retrieved February 9, 2007, from www.toronto.ca/mayor_miller/torontoact.htm.

City of Toronto (2007b). The Toronto Green Development Standard January 2007. City Planning Division, Policy and Research, City of Toronto: 1–27.

City of Toronto (2009a). By-law to Require and Govern the Construction of Green Roofs in Toronto. Chief Planner and Executive Director, Chief Building Official and Executive Director, City Planning. Toronto, City of Toronto.

City of Toronto (2009b, August 12). "Overview of the Green Roof By-law." Retrieved August 12, from www.toronto.ca/greenroofs/overview.htm.

City of Toronto (2011). "Green Roofs around Toronto." Retrieved April 11, 2011, from www.toronto.ca/greenroofs/experience.htm.

Cresswell, J. W. (1998). *Qualitative Inquiry and Research Design: Choosing among Five Traditions*. Thousand Oaks, California: SAGE Publications.

Cronon, W. (1995). "The Trouble with Wilderness: or, Getting back to the Wrong Nature." *Uncommon Ground*. W. Cronon. New York: W. W. Norton & Co.: 69–90.

Deputy Mayor Pantalone, J. and L. Z. Burton (2006). "Making Green Roofs Happen." *Greening Rooftops for Sustainable Communities*. Boston, Green Roofs for Healthy Cities. **1**: 7.

Doshi, H., D. Baniting, J. Li, P. Missios, A. Au, B. A. Currie and M. Verrati (2005). *Report on the Environmental Benefits and Costs of Green Roof Technology for the City of Toronto*. Toronto: Ryerson Univeristy.

Eisenman, T. S., G. Churkina, S. P. Jariwala, P. Kumar, G. S. Lovasi, D. E. Pataki, K. R. Weinberger and T. H. Whitlow (2019). "Urban trees, air quality, and asthma: An interdisciplinary review." *Landscape and Urban Planning* **187**: 47–59.

Elliot, R. (2000). "Faking Nature." *Environmental Restoration*. W. Throop. Amherst, New York: Humanity Books: 71–82.

Emmanuel, R. and A. Loconsole (2015). "Green infrastructure as an adaptation approach to tackling urban overheating in the Glasgow Clyde Valley Region, UK." *Landscape and Urban Planning* **138**(0): 71–86.

Fernandez-Cañero, R., T. Emilsson, C. Fernandez-Barba and M. Á. Herrera Machuca (2013). "Green roof systems: A study of public attitudes and preferences in southern Spain." *Journal of Environmental Management* **128**(0): 106–115.

Florida, R. and A. Broadbent (2018). What is the most democratic and effective way to govern a city the size and economic import of Toronto? *The Globe and Mail.* Toronto.

Foster, C. (2000). "Restoring Nature in American Culture: An Environmental Aesthetic Perspective." *Restoring Nature: Perspectives from the Social Sciences and Humanities.* P. H. Gobster and R. B. Hull. Washington, D.C.: Island Press: 71–94.

Francis, R. A. and J. Lorimer (2011). "Urban reconciliation ecology: The potential of living roofs and walls." *Journal of Environmental Management* **92**(6): 1429–1437.

Gobster, P. H. (1998). "Urban parks as green walls or green magnets? Interracial relations in neighborhood boundary parks." *Landscape and Urban Planning* **41**(1): 43–55.

Gobster, P. H. (1999). "An Ecological Aesthetic for Forest Landscape Management." *Landscape Journal* **18**(1): 54–64.

Gobster, P. H. (2000). "Introduction: Restoring Nature: Human Actions, Interactions, and Reactions." *Restoring Nature: Perspectives from the Social Sciences and Humanities.* P. Gobster and Bruce Hull. Washington, D.C.: Island Press: 1–19.

Gobster, P. H. (2001). "Human dimensions of early successional landscapes in the eastern United States." *Wildlife Society Bulletin* **29**(2): 474–482.

Gobster, P. H., J. I. Nassauer, T. C. Daniel and G. Fry (2007). "The shared landscape: What does aesthetics have to do with ecology?" *Landscape Ecology* **22**(7): 959–972.

Gorrie, P. (2007). "Study in Contrasts: As they vie to lay claim to the 'greenest' city, one mayor talks while the other acts." *The Toronto Star.* Toronto: 1, 20.

Green Roofs for Healthy Cities (1999). "TAF Funds Roof Greening Study for Toronto City Hall." *Green Roof Infrastructure Monitor.* Toronto. **1:** 4.

Green Roofs for Healthy Cities (2000). "Toronto Green Roof Demonstration Projects- Implementation Has Begun." *Green Roof Infrastructure Monitor.* Toronto. **2:** 4.

Healy, L. and J. F. McCormick. (1999, December). "Urban Revitalization and Tax Increment Financing in Chicago." *Government Finance Review.* Retrieved December 17, 2008, from www.cdfa.net/cdfa/cdfaweb.nsf/fbaad5956b2928b086256efa005c5f78/817c2f758fa7a4ca8625714c00777c79/$FILE/UrbanRevitalizationandTIFinChicago.pdf.

Heidegger, M. (1966). *Discourse on Thinking. A Translation of Gelassenheit, by John M. Anderson and E. Hans Freund. With an Introduction by John. M. Anderson. Heidegger, Martin, 1889–1976.* New York: Harper & Row.

Heidegger, M. (1971). "Building, Dwelling, Thinking." *Poetry, Language, Thought.* New York: Harper & Row: 143–159.

Henry, A. and N. Frascaria-Lacoste (2012). "The green roof dilemma: Discussion of Francis and Lorimer (2011)." *Journal of Environmental Management* **104**(0): 91–92.

Hepburn, R. W. (1993). "Trivial and Serious in Aesthetic Appreciation of Nature." *Landscape, Natural Beauty and the Arts.* S. Kemal and I. Gaskell. Cambridge, UK: Cambridge University Press: 65–80.

Hinds, J. and P. Sparks (2008). "Engaging with the natural environment: The role of affective connection and identity." *Journal of Environmental Psychology* **28**(2): 109–120.

Hirano, Y., T. Ihara, K. Gomi and T. Fujita (2019). "Simulation-based evaluation of the effect of green roofs in office building districts on mitigating the urban heat island effect and reducing CO2 emissions." *Sustainability* **11**(7): 2055.

Hough, M. (2004). *Cities and Natural Process: A Basis for Sustainability.* London; New York: Routledge.

Hull, B. R. and D. P. Robertson (2000). "The Language of Nature Matters: We Need a More Public Ecology." *Restoring Nature: Perspectives from the Social Sciences and Humanities.* P. H. Gobster and R. Bruce. Washington D.C.: Island Press: 97–118.

Imran, H. M., J. Kala, A. W. M. Ng and S. Muthukumaran (2018). "Effectiveness of green and cool roofs in mitigating urban heat island effects during a heatwave event in the city of Melbourne in southeast Australia." *Journal of Cleaner Production* **197**: 393–405.

Jungels, J., D. Rakow, S. B. Allred and S. M. Skelly (2013). "Attitudes and aesthetic reactions toward green roofs in the Northeastern United States." *Landscape and Urban Planning* **117**: 13–21.

Junker, B. and M. Buchecker (2008). "Aesthetic preferences versus ecological objectives in river restorations." *Landscape and Urban Planning* **85**(3): 141–154.

Kaika, M. (2006). "The Political Ecology of Water Scarcity: The 1989–1991 Athenian Drought." *In the Nature of Cities: Urban Political Ecology and the Politics of Urban Metabolism*. N. Heynen, M. Kaika and E. Syngedouw. New York: Routledge: 157–172.

Kals, E., D. Schumacher and L. Montada (1999). "Emotional affinity toward nature as a motivational basis to protect nature." *Environment and Behavior* **31**: 178–202.

Kaplan, R. and J. F. Talbot (1988). "Ethnicity and preference for natural settings: A review and recent findings." *Landscape and Urban Planning*. **15:** 107.

Kaplan, S. (1995). "The restorative benefits of nature: Toward an integrative framework." *Journal of Environmental Psychology* **15**(3): 169–182.

Keeley, M. (2004). *Green Roof Incentives: Tried and True Techniques from Europe*. Greening Rooftops for Sustainable Communities, Portland, Oregon: Green Roofs for Healthy Cities.

Ketterer, C. and A. Matzarakis (2014). "Human-biometeorological assessment of heat stress reduction by replanning measures in Stuttgart, Germany." *Landscape and Urban Planning* **122**(0): 78–88.

Klinenberg, E. (2002). *Heat Wave: A Social Autopsy of Disaster in Chicago*. Chicago, University of Chicago Press.

Koehler, M. and M. Keeley (2003). "The Green Roof Tradition in Germany: The Example of Berlin." *Earthpledges Handbook: Green Roofs*. New York: Earthpledge.

Korpela, K. M., K. Borodulin, M. Neuvonen, O. Paronen and L. Tyrväinen (2014). "Analyzing the mediators between nature-based outdoor recreation and emotional well-being." *Journal of Environmental Psychology* **37**: 1–7.

Korpela, K. M., M. Ylen, L. Tyrvainen and H. Silvennoinen (2009). "Stability of self-reported favourite places and place attachment over a 10-month period." *Journal of Environmental Psychology* **29**(1): 95–100.

Kotzen, B. (2018). "Green Roofs Social and Aesthetic Aspects." *Nature Based Strategies for Urban and Building Sustainability*. G. Pérez and K. Perini, London: Butterworth-Heinemann**: 4.2** 273–281.

Krenichyn, K. (2006). "'The only place to go and be in the city': Women talk about exercise, being outdoors, and the meanings of a large urban park." *Health and Place* **12**: 631–643.

Kuper, R. (2009). "What's up? Examining the awareness of green roofs in suburbia." *Journal of Soil and Water Conservation* **64**(5): 145A–149A.

Lee, H. and H. Koshimiz (2004). *Research on the Scenic Meaning of Rooftop Greening with Semantic Differential Measure and Join-Count Statistics*. Greening Rooftops for Sustainable Communities, Boston: Green Roofs for Healthy Cities.

Lee, J. W., K. Y. Huh and J. Park (2016). "Awareness and satisfaction of citizens on green roof projects (GRPs) in Changwon City, South Korea." *Journal of Korean Society for People, Plants, and Environment* **19**(6): 605–614.

Lee, J. Y., H. J. Moon, T. I. Kim, H. W. Kim and M. Y. Han (2013). "Quantitative analysis on the urban flood mitigation effect by the extensive green roof system." *Environmental Pollution* **181**(0): 257–261.

Lee, K. E., K. J. H. Williams, L. D. Sargent, C. Farrell and N. S. Williams (2014). "Living roof preference is influenced by plant characteristics and diversity." *Landscape and Urban Planning* **122**(0): 152–159.

Lee, K. E., K. J. H. Williams, L. D. Sargent, N. S. G. Williams and K. A. Johnson (2015). "40-second green roof views sustain attention: The role of micro-breaks in attention restoration." *Journal of Environmental Psychology* **42**: 182–189.

Leopold, A. (1971). *A Sand County Almanac with other essays on conservation from Round River*. New York: Oxford University Press.

Liu, X. and T. F. M. Chui (2019). "Evaluation of green roof performance in mitigating the impact of extreme storms." *Water* **11**(4): 815.

Living Architecture Monitor (2018). "2017 Green Roof Industry Survey Shows Washington, DC in Top Spot for Most Green Roofs Installed." Toronto.

Loder, A. (2011). *Greening the City: Exploring Health, Well-being, Green Roofs, and the Perception of Nature in the Workplace*. Doctor of Philosophy, University of Toronto.

Loder, A. (2014). "'There's a meadow outside my workplace': A phenomenological exploration of aesthetics and green roofs in Chicago and Toronto." *Landscape and Urban Planning* **126**: 94–106.

Lorimer, J., T. Hodgetts and M. Barua (2019). "Animals' atmospheres." *Progress in Human Geography* **43**(1): 26–45.

Los Angeles Times (2005). "What makes a strong mayor." *Los Angeles Times*.

Lottrup, L., P. Grahn and U. Stigsdotter (2013). "Workplace greenery and perceived level of stress: Benefits of access to a green outdoor environment at the workplace." *Landscape and Urban Planning* **110**: 5–11.
Lundholm, J. T. (2006). "Green roofs and facades: A habitat template approach." *Urban Habitats* **4**(1): 87–97.
McNamara, M. (2005). "Knowing and doing phenomenology: The implications of the critique of 'nursing phenomenology' for a phenomenological inquiry. A discussion paper." *International Journal of Nursing Studies* **42**: 695–704.
Meine, C. (2008). "Conservation, Chicago Style." *Chicago Wilderness* **11:** 16–17.
Merchant, C. (1995). "Reinventing Nature: Western Culture as a Recovery Narrative." *Uncommon Ground.* W. Cronon. New York: W. W. Norton & Company: 132–159.
Mesimäki, M., K. Hauru and S. Lehvävirta (2019). "Do small green roofs have the possibility to offer recreational and experiential benefits in a dense urban area? A case study in Helsinki, Finland." *Urban Forestry and Urban Greening* **40**: 114–124.
Moore, R. (2008). *Natural Beauty: A Theory of Aesthetics beyond the Arts*. Peterborough: Broadview Press.
Mountain Equipment Co-op. (2009, August). "Mountain Equipment Coop green roof." Retrieved August 2009, from www.mec.ca/Main/content_text.jsp?FOLDER%3C%3Efolder_id=2534374302887037.
Moustakas, C. (1994). *Phenomenological Research Methods*. Thousand Oaks, California: Sage Publications.
Mueller, J. M., A. B. Soder and A. E. Springer (2019). "Valuing attributes of forest restoration in a semi-arid watershed." *Landscape and Urban Planning* **184**: 78–87.
Nassauer, J. (1995). "Messy ecosystems, orderly frames." *Landscape Journal* **14**(2): 161–170.
Nooriati, T., A. Aldrin, S. Syed Fadzil and S. Y. Foong (2010). "An assessment of thermal comfort and users' perceptions of landscape gardens in a high-rise office building." *Journal of Sustainable Development* **3**(4): 154–164.
Norton, B. A., A. M. Coutts, S. J. Livesley, R. J. Harris, A. M. Hunter and N. S. G. Williams (2015). "Planning for cooler cities: A framework to prioritise green infrastructure to mitigate high temperatures in urban landscapes." *Landscape and Urban Planning* **134**(0): 127–138.
Orbe, M. P. (2000). "Centralizing diverse racial/ethnic voices in scholarly research: The value of phenomenological enquiry." *International Journal of Intercultural Relations* **24**: 603–621.
Ortiz-Dowling, E. M., C. Der Ananian, L. K. Larkey and S. P. Hooker (2018). "Health-seeking behaviors and health information gathering in older Mexican American males." *Psychology of Men and Masculinity* **20**(4): 564–574.
Padgett, D. K. (2008). *Qualitative Methods in Social Work Research*. Thousand Oaks, California: Sage Publications.
Peck, S. W. (2017). "Interview with Charlie Miller." *Living Architecture Monitor*, Green Roofs for Healthy Cities. **19:** 29–30.
Peng, L. L. and C. Y. Jim (2013). "Green-roof effects on neighborhood microclimate and human thermal sensation." *Energies* **6**(2): 598–618.
Perini, K. and A. Magliocco (2014). "Effects of vegetation, urban density, building height, and atmospheric conditions on local temperatures and thermal comfort." *Urban Forestry and Urban Greening* **13**(3): 495–506.
Perrin, J. L. and V. A. Benassi (2009). "The connectedness to nature scale: A measure of emotional connection to nature?" *Journal of Environmental Psychology* **29**(4): 434–440.
Rahman, S. R. A., H. Ahmad and M. S. F. Rosley (2013). "Green roof: Its awareness among professionals and potential in Malaysian market." *Procedia – Social and Behavioral Sciences* **85**: 443–453.
Relph, E. (1976). *Place and Placelessness*. London: Pion.
Robertson Building. (2010, August 19). "Robertson building green roof." Retrieved August 19, 2010, from www.robertsonbuilding.com/roofgarden.
Rothblatt, D. N. (1994). "North American metropolitan planning: Canadian and U.S. perspectives." *Journal of the American Planning Association* **60**(4): 501–522.
Ryfield, F., D. Cabana, J. Brannigan and T. Crowe (2019). "Conceptualizing 'sense of place' in cultural ecosystem services: A framework for interdisciplinary research." *Ecosystem Services* **36**: 100907.
Saito, Y. (2002). "Ecological design: Promises and challenges " *Environmental Ethics* **24**(3): 243–261.
Saito, Y. (2002). "Scenic national landscapes: Common themes in Japan and the United States." *Essays in Philosophy* **3**(1): article 5.
Saito, Y. (2007). "The Role of Aesthetics in Civic Environtmentalism." *The Aesthetics of Human Environments*. A. Berleant and A. Carlson. Peterborough: Broadview Press: 203–219.

San Francisco Planning Department. (2017). "San Francisco Better Roofs." *Plans and Programs*. Retrieved June 11, 2019, from https://sfgov.org/sfplanningarchive/san-francisco-better-roofs.
Schultz, W. P., C. Shriver, J. J. Tabanico and A. M. Khanzian (2004). "Implicit connections with nature." *Journal of Environmental Psychology* **24**: 31–42.
Shume, T. (2016). "Teachers' Perspectives on contributions of a prairie restoration project to elementary students' environmental literacy." *International Journal of Environmental and Science Education* **11**(12): 5331–5348.
Simpson, M. and J. Bagelman (2018). "Decolonizing urban political ecologies: The production of nature in settler colonial cities." *Annals of the American Association of Geographers* **108**(2): 558–568.
Smith, C. and M. Boyer (2007). "Who wants to live with a living roof?" *Green Places* **October**: 24–27.
Souto, L. A., C. M. C. S. Listopad and P. J. Bohlen (2019). "Forging linkages between social drivers and ecological processes in the residential landscape." *Landscape and Urban Planning* **185**: 96–106.
Spears, J. (2005). "Is it a jungle out there? Neighbours take flowers vs. weeds fight to council." *Toronto Star*. Toronto: 18.
Stefanovic, I. L. (1991). "Evolving sustainability: A re-thinking of ontological foundations." *Trumpeter* **8**(4): 194–200.
Sutton, R. K. (2014). "Aesthetics for green roofs and green walls." *Journal of Living Architecture* **2**.
Thwaites, K. (2001). "Experiential landscape place: An exploration of space and experience in neighbourhood landscape architecture." *Landscape Research* **26**(3): 245–255.
Toadvine, T. (2010). "Ecological Aesthetics." *Handbook of Phenomenological Aesthetics*. H. R. Sepp and L. Embree. Dordrecht, Netherlands: Springer: 85–91.
Ulrich, R. S. (1993). "Biophilia, Biophobia, and Natural Landscapes." *The Biophilia Hypothesis*. S. W. Kellert and Edward O. Wilson. Washington, D.C.: Island Press: 73–137.
Urry, J. (2005). "The Place of Emotions within Place." *Emotional Geographies*. J. Davidson, L. Bondi and M. Smith. Aldershot, UK and Burlington, Vermont: Ashgate: 77–86.
Vailshery, L. S., M. Jaganmohan and H. Nagendra (2013). "Effect of street trees on microclimate and air pollution in a tropical city." *Urban Forestry and Urban Greening* **12**(3): 408–415.
van den Berg, A. E., S. L. Koole and N. Y. van der Wulp (2003). "Environmental preference and restoration: (How) are they related?" *Journal of Environmental Psychology* **23**(2): 135–146.
van den Berg, A. E., C. A. J. Vlek and J. F. Coeterier (1998). Group differences in the aesthetic evaluation of nature development plans: A multilevel approach. *Journal of Environmental Psychology* **18**: 141.
Vandenberg, A. E., M. M. Ball, C. L. Kemp, P. J. Doyle, M. Fritz, S. Halpin, L. Hundley and M. M. Perkins (2018). "Contours of 'here': Phenomenology of space for assisted living residents approaching end of life." *Journal of Aging Studies* **47**: 72–83.
Vanstockem, J., L. Vranken, B. Bleys, B. Somers and M. Hermy (2018). "Do looks matter? A case study on extensive green roofs using discrete choice experiments." *Sustainability* **10**(2): 309.
Varandas, M. J. (2015). "The Land Aesthetic, Holmes Rolston's insight." *Environmental Values* **24**(2): 209–226.
White, E. V. and B. Gatersleben (2011). "Greenery on residential buildings: Does it affect preferences and perceptions of beauty?" *Journal of Environmental Psychology* **31**(1): 89–98.
Wilkie, S. and A. Stavridou (2013). "Influence of environmental preference and environment type congruence on judgments of restoration potential." *Urban Forestry and Urban Greening* **12**(2): 163–170.
Wilson, A. (1991). *The Culture of Nature: North American Landscapes from Disney to the Exxon Valdez*. Toronto: Between the Lines.
Wilson, E. O. (1993). "Biophilia and the Conservation Ethic." *The Biophilia Hypothesis*. S. R. Kellert and E. O. Wilson. Washington, D.C.: Island Press: 31–41.
Wyles, K. J., M. P. White, C. Hattam, S. Pahl, H. King and M. Austen (2019). "Are some natural environments more psychologically beneficial than others? The importance of type and quality on connectedness to nature and psychological restoration." *Environment and Behavior* **51**(2): 111–143.
Yang, J. and E. Bou-Zeid (2019). "Scale dependence of the benefits and efficiency of green and cool roofs." *Landscape and Urban Planning* **185**: 127–140.
Yocca, D. and M. Berkshire (2019). "Commemorative Case Study: Chicago City Hall Green Roof – A 20-Year Retrospective." *Living Architecture Monitor*, Green Roofs for Healthy Cities **21:** 16–20.
Yuen, B. and W. N. Hien (2005). "Resident perceptions and expectations of rooftop gardens in Singapore." *Landscape and Urban Planning* **73**: 263–276.

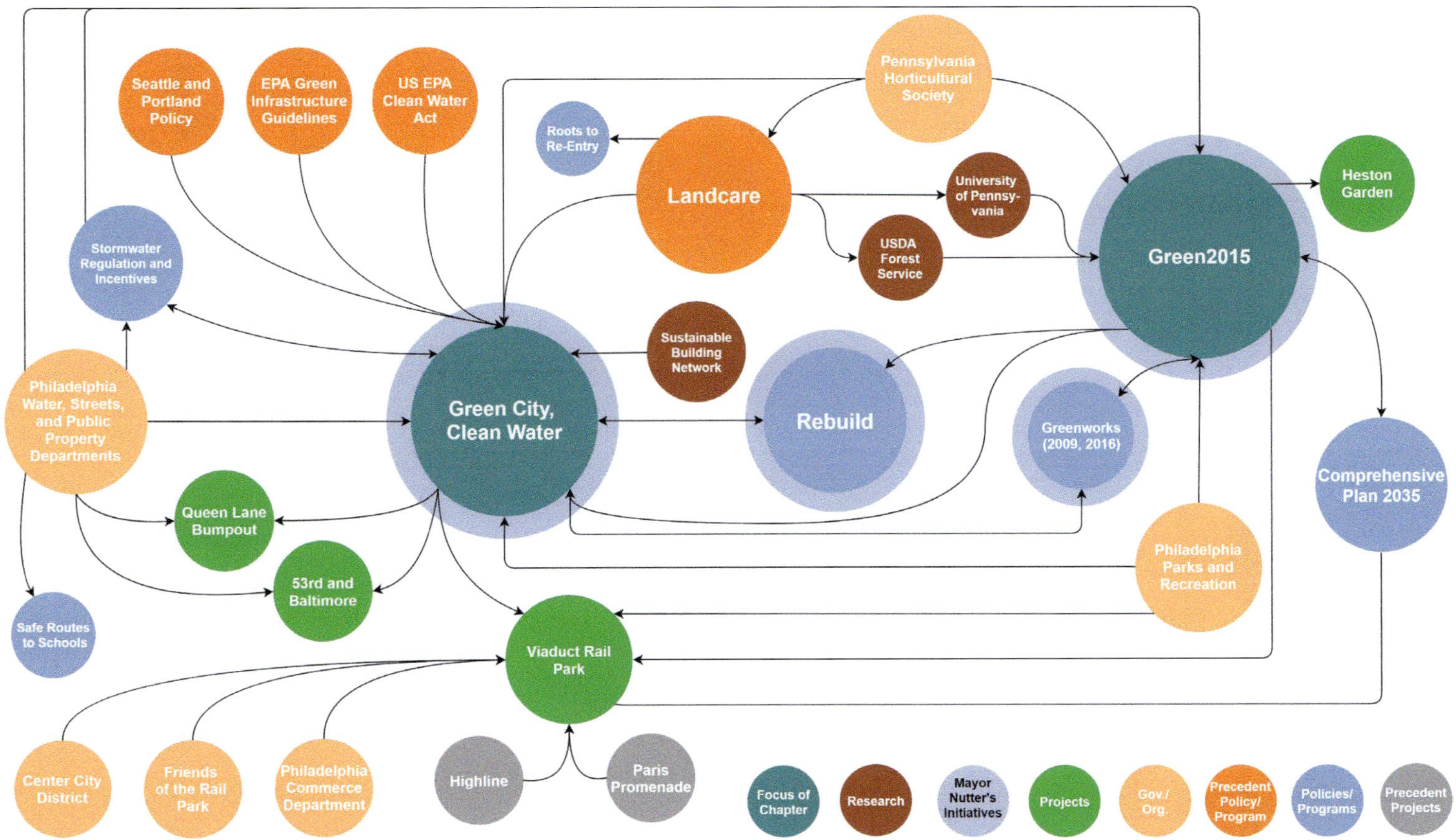

Plate 1 Philadelphia Policy SSUG Map.

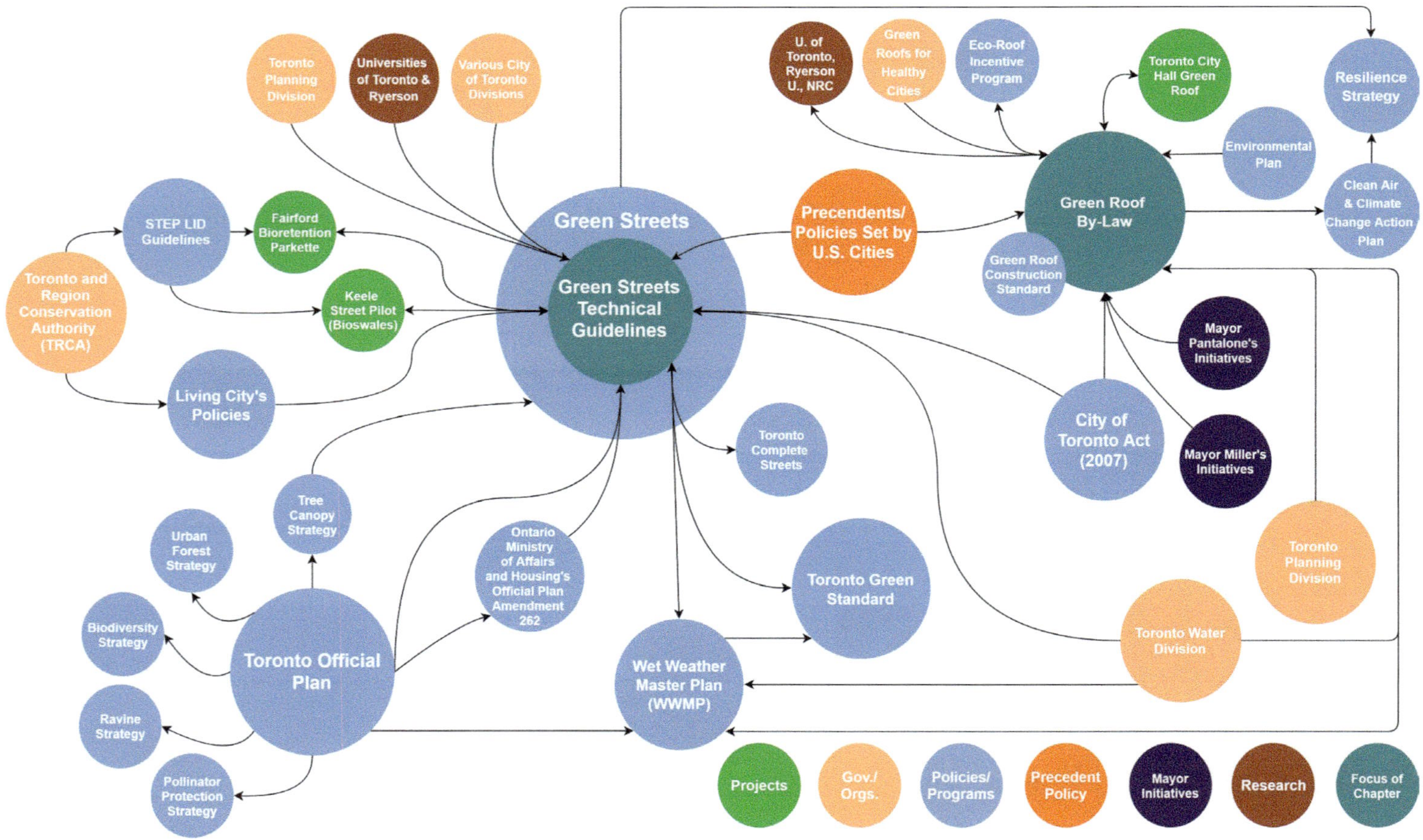

Plate 2 Toronto Policy SSUG Map.

Plate 3 Raingarden at Fairford Parkette, 2.

Source: © Sheila Boudreau.

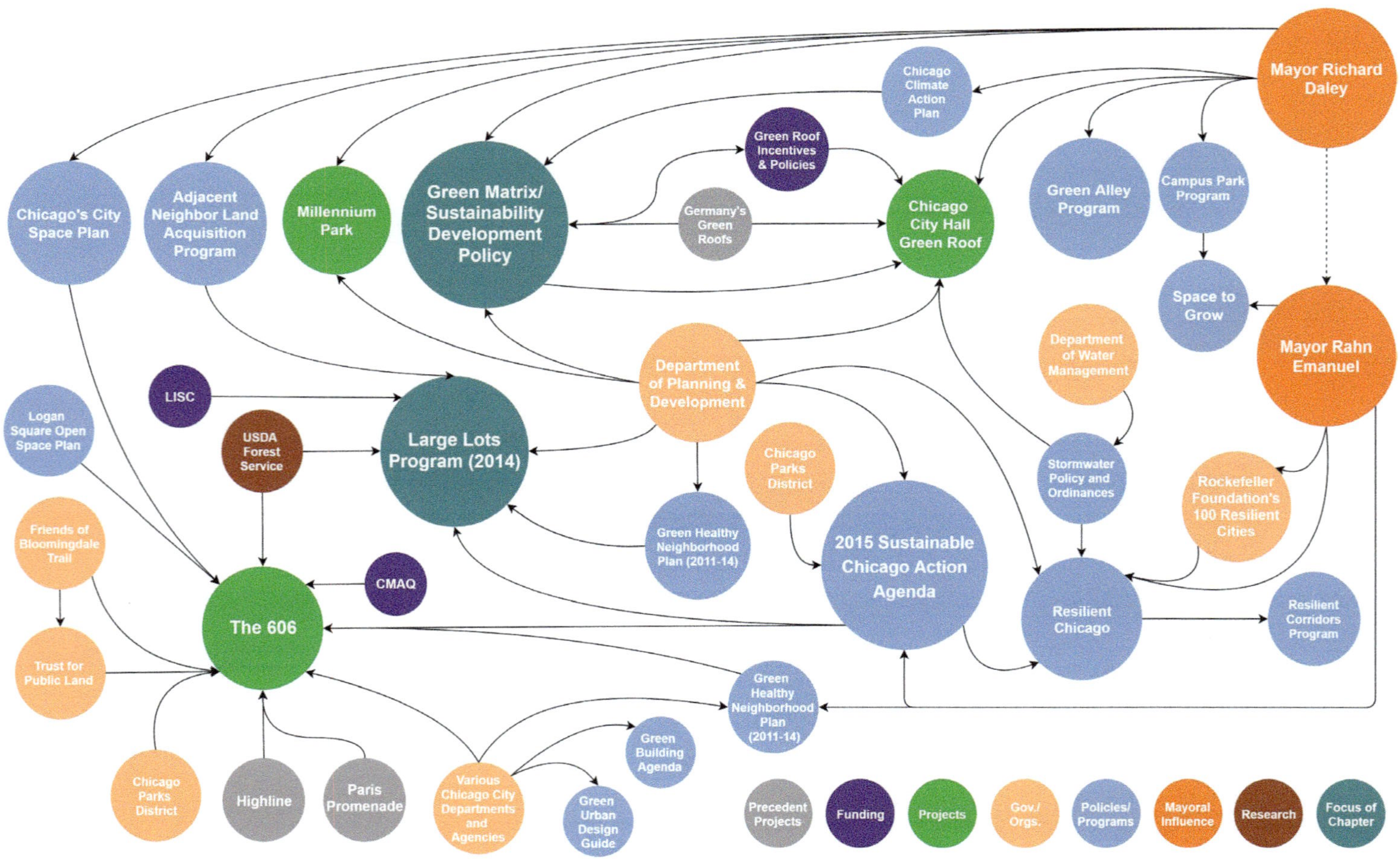

Plate 4 Chicago Policy SSUG Map.

Plate 5 Chicago City Hall green roof.

Plate 6 Green roof on 215 Spadina.

Plate 7 Green 2015: Heston Rain Garden, vacant lot, after, Philadelphia.

Source: Philadelphia Water Department.

Plate 8 Rail Park: Section showing plant selection and pathway, Philadelphia.

Source: © Bryan Hanes.

4

RECLAIMING THE CITY

Vacant lots and post-industrial corridors

Introduction

The transformation of an abandoned rail line into an elevated, leafy, blooming trail in New York City not only captured the imagination of the public but helped frame the city and its possibilities in a new light: it re-imagined the role that de-industrialized spaces, and the 'wild' nature within them, could play. Thus it could be argued that the New York City High Line, which has become one of the most popular tourist destinations in North America (Higgins 2014), catalyzed the trend for innovative approaches to urban greening through the increased attention – in both urban policy initiatives and academic research – to abandoned, neglected, or underused urban greenspaces. In the context of de-industrialization, disinvestment, and increased awareness of the link between environmental justice and urban greenspace (Pearsall 2010; Pearsall, Lucas et al. 2014; Jennings, Browning et al. 2019) many cities and researchers are looking at these spaces in a new light. While the High Line has catalyzed this new perspective on city spaces, it is no longer the only example, as seen with the case studies in this chapter.

This focus on 'marginal' (Jorgensen and Tylecote 2007) or informal urban greenspace (Ward Thompson 2002) fits into the second two types of urban greening outlined in the introduction: vacant lots (Rupprecht and Byrne 2014; Kim, Miller et al. 2018), and interstitial or marginal spaces (Gobster 2001), and post-industrial and elevated spaces (hereafter referred to as post-industrial spaces) (see Table 4.1). Both types of urban greening are becoming more popular, but it is unusual to find examples of both in the same city, which is what makes Philadelphia and Chicago interesting case studies for comparison. Philadelphia has a series of policies and programs that address vacant land in the city, and they have also recently opened up the first spur of their own version of the High Line – the

Table 4.1 Vacant lots and post-industrial corridors case studies: policy and implementation

City	Problem	Policy/project goals	Implementation		Precedent	Complements	Policy tools	Case study/ examples
			Actors	Funding				
Chicago *(Large Lots Program,* 2014)	Vacant lots, largely city-owned Community disinvestment, safety concerns, and neighbourhood destabilization Inequitable distribution of and access to quality greenspace	Social and economic: neighbourhood stabilization Reduced municipal costs of maintenance	Mayor Emmanuel and staff City of Chicago Department of Planning and Development City of Chicago Chicago Metropolitan Agency for Planning (CMAP) Community Member	LISC (Local Initiatives Support Corporation) Chicago and foundation grants	Daniel Burnham and Jens Jensen legacies *Adjacent Neighbor Land Acquisition Program* *Green Healthy Neighborhood Plan (2011-14)*	*2015 Sustainable Chicago Action Agenda* *Space to Grow* *Campus Park Program* New biodiversity-supporting parks along lakeshore *NeighborSpace* *100 Resilient Cities (Rockefeller Foundation, 2019)*	Subsidized land Zoning laws with technical assistance and public information documents for residents Collaboration with non-profits (LISC Chicago, etc)	Philadelphia *LandCare* program
Philadelphia *(Green2015)*	40,000+ vacant lots, many in disadvantaged neighbourhoods $21 million of public funds spent on maintaining and responding to vacant lots Inequitable distribution and access to quality greenspace	Useable and minimal maintenance infrastructure and greenspace in high-need areas	Philadelphia Parks and Recreation (PPR) Pennsylvania Horticultural Society (PHS) Philadelphia Water (PWD) and Streets Departments (PSD)	*Rebuild:* Sugar Sweetened Beverage (SSB) Tax A line-item in the city's budget	*LandCare* *GreenWorks (2009)* Mayor Nutter's sustainability initiatives	*Green City Clean Waters (2011)* *Comprehensive Plan 2035* *GreenWorks (2016)* *Rebuild*	Green Stormwater regulations Interdepartmental and stakeholder alignment and planning	Heston Garden

Philadelphia (post-industrial elevated parks)	Skipped over economic development Callow Hill and Chinatown neighbourhoods Lack of neighbourhood green space	Provide useable greenspace to communities with little local access Economic development and neighborhood stabilization *Community Goals:* Preservation of the area's history, native plants; provision of community space, environmental education	Friends of the Rail Park Center City District Philadelphia Commerce Department Department of Parks and Recreation Community stakeholders	City Center District and foundation grants Department of Parks and Recreation	New York City's High Line Paris' Promenade Plantée Philadelphia's other greening programs provide precedent for urban greening as economic stimulant	*Green 2015* *Greenworks 2016* Green Stormwater Incentives and Regulation	Comprehensive Plan 2035 Green Stormwater Incentives and Regulation	Viaduct Rail Park
Chicago (post-industrial elevated parks)	Lack of adequate greenspace in Logan Square, Wicker Park, Bucktown and Humboldt Park neighbourhoods, especially active greenspace	Increase access to greenspace Be an active transportation corridor Address stormwater, the UHI effect, and other ecological goals	City of Chicago (Department of Planning and Development and other agencies) *Congestion Mitigation and Air Quality Program (CMAQ)* Chicago Parks District Residential groups Non-profits (i.e. Friends of the Bloomingdale Trail, Trust for Public Land)	Federal CMAQ funds Trust for Public Land fundraising	New York City's High Line Paris' Promenade Plantée	*2015 Sustainable Chicago Action Agenda* Chicago's *City Space Plan* *Logan Square Open Space Plan*	CMAQ *Green Healthy Neighborhood Plan* (GHNP) (2011-14)	The 606

Philadelphia Rail Park – both of which also link with their stormwater initiatives (discussed in Chapter 2). In Chicago, there is a vacant lot program and a recently opened elevated post-industrial 'park,' The 606, and they have started to link vacant lot revitalization with stormwater management.

The case studies described in the following pages are also good examples of *why* small-scale urban greening is happening, as outlined in the introduction: (1) urban greening that is small-scale, tactical, and sometimes temporary, often called tactical urbanism or biophilic urban acupuncture (Unt and Bell 2014; Lydon and Garcia 2015; Walker 2015; Reinhold 2018), and (2) the explicit linking of urban greenspace and public health, both physical health in terms of increased rates of physical activity and active transportation (Kaczynski, Potwarka et al. 2009; Branas, Cheney et al. 2011; Su, Dadvand et al. 2019) with access to greenspace, and mental health and well-being, particularly for disadvantaged neighbourhoods (Ward Thompson, Roe et al. 2012; Campbell and Gabriel 2016; Tsai, McHale et al. 2018).

Research questions and chapter structure

This chapter will explore how the greening of marginal spaces and the creative re-use of post-industrial spaces helps to exemplify these trends through the examination of case studies for each type in each city. The chapter also aims to understand the increasingly prominent role that equity plays in decision making and execution of these projects. As in Chapter 2, the focus will be on connecting research with real-world implementation issues. The same areas of inquiry frame this chapter: (a) how (and if) research is being used to justify and implement the cases studies, and by whom; (b) how factors around implementation (such as funding sources and larger policy goals) impact the design of the projects; (c) key insights and results from these projects; and (d) gaps and current issues (see Table 4.2). While green roofs are elevated and are sometimes retrofits on older buildings, they are distinct from the elevated parks created from disused rail lines discussed in this chapter in both their goals and execution, and are thus not dealt with here (see Chapter 3). Examining these intersections of research and implementation around real-world case studies can bring insight into how cities in North America are approaching small-scale urban greening, how these projects differ from traditional urban greening, and how ideas on public space, health and well-being, sustainability, and approaches to equity are shifting.

Marginal spaces: re-greening neglected urban spaces

As we will see below, cities have become involved in these spaces and associated small-scale urban greening (SSUG) projects for reasons of health, environmental justice, economic revitalization, and community empowerment. And while some

Table 4.2 Vacant, marginal, and post-industrial SSUG: the intersection of research, design, and implementation

Type of SSUG	Research used to justify policy or project?	Alignment with current research	Future areas for research and implementation synergies	Suggested ways forward
Vacant Lots	*Chicago:* CMAP data was used to determine vacant lot demographics USDA Forest Service: assessing social and environmental benefit of the policy Resident feedback (Both cities) *Philadelphia:* *Landcare* data supports urban greening benefits (community, health, economic) USDA Forest Service, University of Pennsylvania: assess social, economic, health benefits of precedent program (*Landcare*); current program	*Planning:* Need to engage with stakeholders, co-creation with communities *Implementation:* Urban greenspace as complex value: social, economic, ecological *Research:* Role of aesthetics, socio-economic context, benefits around health/well-being, community cohesion, reduction in violence	Role of social, aesthetic, scale on perceptions of SSUG Impact of scale, clustering of SSUG on daily lived experience, health, wellbeing Longitudinal studies on impacts of 'improved' vacant lots: individual, community, health, socio-economic Value, use of 'vacant' land and space for non-traditional groups (youth, prostitutes, homeless)	*Research:* Integration of social-constructionist or phenomenological approach to greenspace research *Policy development:* Continued socio-economic and ecological approach Alignment/use of research from diverse perspectives *Implementation:* Continued focus on equity, community empowerment
Elevated Parks	USDA Forest Service assessing the benefits of The 606 (Chicago) Promenade Plantée and High Line showed feasibility and economic, social, and community benefits of elevated parks (Both)	*Planning:* Landscape urbanists: industrial remnants as greenspace opportunities *Research:* Explicit linking of greenspace, health, equity; greenspace as public good *Implementation:* Perceptions/values of SSUG impacted by aesthetics, social, economic contexts SSUG role in economic revitalization/ development, gentrification	Impact of elevated parks on gentrification, community, expectations of place Role of active transportation corridors, equity, gentrification Greenspace as public good but with aesthetics, design, community considerations, especially new vs existing residents	*Research:* Integration of social-constructionist or phenomenological approach to greenspace research *Policy development:* Shift towards more nuanced understanding to SSUG benefits Alignment/use of research from diverse perspectives *Implementation:* Pairing research with community investment and stewardship Co-community stewardship and maintenance

of these initiatives are fairly large-scale, more often than not there is the recognition that large-scale interventions are not always possible or desired, and that the initiatives that may find most success are those temporary and/or small-scale projects that empower community members and local non-profits to co-design and manage these spaces (PennPraxis 2010; Unt and Bell 2014). Furthermore, the interstitial nature of *where* these projects are being implemented distinguishes them significantly from the large-scale urban greening initiatives of the nineteenth century, such as the creation of Fairmount Park in Philadelphia or Central Park in New York City, or the development of miles of parkland along the waterfront in Chicago (Burnham, Bennett et al. 1909), which create a more immersive, versus interstitial, experience. From a research perspective, there is increasing collaboration around understanding and evaluating the public benefits that come from revitalizing vacant or underused land (Bucchianeri, Gillen et al. 2012; Garvin, Cannuscio et al. 2012). This is particularly true in the recognition from researchers and city officials that these greenspaces are social *and* ecological (City of Philadelphia 2009; Wang, Tan et al. 2014; City of Philadelphia 2016; Anderson and Minor 2017; Riley, Perry et al. 2018), a notable departure from traditional ecosystem services approaches which have tended to address human factors in a general, and often abstract, way with little participation from those directly affected by the greenspaces (Flint, Kunze et al. 2013; Kolinjivadi, Van Hecken et al. 2019). However, researchers' focus and approach to these new small-scale urban greenspaces have some key differences from those of urban officials. These include: attention to both positive and negative valuations of aesthetics; ecology; marginal spaces; and design (Jorgensen and Tylecote 2007; Rupprecht and Byrne 2014; Hunter 2015; Riley, Perry et al. 2018); power dynamics for those living near the space versus those making decisions about the space (Palardy, Boley et al. 2018); and tensions between revitalization and gentrification (Wolch, Byrne et al. 2014; Rupprecht and Byrne 2018). It is in these tensions or gaps where we see some of the most promising opportunities for advancing our understanding of what kind of SSUG can bring the most benefits to urbanites.

Case studies: Chicago and Philadelphia

Chicago and Philadelphia provide interesting opportunities to compare case studies, because both cities have post-industrial spaces, aging infrastructure, similar urban environmental issues, such as stormwater management and the urban heat island (UHI) effect, as well as areas of long-term disinvestment and poverty. They have similar population sizes, and are often compared in policy documents on their urban greening initiatives (PennPraxis 2010). In addition, though they both have famously designed parks as a commitment to public space and a fairly high per capita amount of greenspace per resident (City of Philadelphia 2011), both cities have publicly recognized that not all of their residents enjoy equal access to high-quality greenspace and that this negatively impacts their communities, economy, and environment (City of Philadelphia 2011; Sustainability Council 2015a; City of Philadelphia 2016). While the case studies below are influenced by specific programs or policies for each city, it is important to understand that these programs are increasingly being integrated into an overall vision of, or approach to, urban greening that is often linked with sustainability for each city (see the conclusion, policy section). Understanding how each case study fits into these approaches to urban greening can therefore be helpful for other cities facing similar issues.

Vacant lots: Chicago

Background

Chicago's built and natural environment legacy includes the visionary work of both famous architects, such as Daniel Burnham, and landscape architects, such as Jens Jensen, who laid out a vast system of public parks, boulevards and 26 miles of lakeshore parkland to beautify the city and provide public amenity space at the turn of the twentieth century (Sustainability Council 2015a). As with many U.S. cities, however, years of disinvestment, racism, and car-oriented development began to take a toll on the quality, safety, and maintenance of the parks, culminating in the Chicago Park District being sued in the early 1980s for discrimination in its allocation of recreational and park services which had left many black and Hispanic neighbourhoods without equitable access to high-quality greenspaces (Rotenberk 2015). As seen in Chapter 3, it was under the former mayor Daley in the 1980s that things began to turn around for the city's approach to urban greening. After numerous visits to Europe, Mayor Daley began a program of urban greening and beautification that included planted boulevards, a comprehensive and aggressive green roof program, and ultimately Millennium Park, a huge multi-million dollar lakeshore park that connected the downtown loop to the existing lakeshore parkland, bringing in 12.9 million guests in the second half of 2016 alone and being a highly successful, albeit initially controversial, addition to Chicago's greenspace (Mayor's Press Office and Chicago 2017). While these initiatives helped to beautify and green the city, many neighbourhoods in the south and west still suffered from a lack of quality greenspace. At the same time, the presence of many vacant lots negatively impacted communities already suffering from a poor housing market, lack of employment opportunities, and years of population decline (Chicago Metropolitan Agency for Planning 2016; Chandler and City of Chicago 2019). Furthermore, it became apparent from community outreach by the city that current programs, such as the *Adjacent Neighbor Land Acquisition Program*, were not meeting residents' needs; though residents had tried to buy vacant lots in their neighbourhood they often did not meet the requirements of the program and had faced resistance from local aldermen (Chandler 2019).

To address these issues the City developed a *Large Lot* program (Sustainability Council and City of Chicago 2014; Chandler 2019) of which the case study below is a part. This program was part of the continued efforts by then-mayor Rahm Emanuel and staff to promote Chicago as the nation's most sustainable city and falls under their *2015 Sustainable Chicago Action Agenda* (see Figure 3.1). The *Action Agenda* recognizes the social, environmental, and economic value of Chicago's greenspace and the legacy of being a 'City in a Park for 175 years, while also acknowledging the need for improvement in quality, quantity, and equitable access' (City of Chicago 2012; Sustainability Council and City of Chicago 2014). As part of this program Mayor Emanuel pushed for the creation of 800 new acres of parkland, recreation areas, and greenspaces throughout Chicago with the Beyond Burnham plan, The 606 (discussed below), and the *Large Lot* program as signature initiatives. The *Large Lot* and The 606 are also highlighted as a key success under their Parks, Open Space, and Healthy Food focus in the *Action Agenda* (Sustainability Council 2015b; Mayor's Press Office 2016). These initiatives complement other Chicago urban greening initiatives such as the Campus Park Program and Space to Grow initiative, which created new play and landscaped areas in former school parking lots and integrated stormwater management, respectively (Healthy Schools Campaign and Openlands 2016; City of Chicago n.d.), and new parks supporting biodiversity along the lakeshore (Mayor's Press Office 2016). They also complement the continued support of and sometimes integration with community-managed small-scale open greenspace through the non-profit *NeighborSpace* (Helphand 2019). Lastly, the *Large Lot* program complements Chicago's recent designation as one of *100 Resilient Cities* from the Rockefeller Foundation, which includes funding and support to hire a Chief Resiliency Officer (Berkshire 2016; City of Chicago, 100 Resilient Cities Team et al. 2019). Through the *Large Lot* program, any homeowner can buy one or two vacant lots on their street for one dollar and look after them for five years, after which they can keep them if desired (LISC Chicago and Latentdesign 2015; Chandler 2019).

Impetus for the program

According to Jeanne Chandler, from the City of Chicago Department of Planning and Development, the impetus for *Large Lot* program (which came into effect in 2014), was from the three-year public outreach and engagement process, as well as data from the Chicago Metropolitan Agency for Planning (CMAP), that led to the *Green Healthy Neighborhood Plan* (GHNP) planning document (CMAP 2013; Chicago Department of Planning and Development 2014). The document examined a 13.1 square mile section of the city, and includes the neighbourhoods of Englewood, Woodlawn, Washington Park, and Greater Grand Crossing. Green space revitalization is a key component of the 20-year plan, and includes green infrastructure, agriculture, and parks (Chicago Metropolitan Agency for Planning 2016). The GHNP planning document found that there were 11,000 vacant lots in those neighbourhoods, about half of which were city owned. Furthermore, demographic and economic projections indicated that the population of those neighbourhoods was not projected to increase substantially over the next 30 years, and that even taking into account future developer needs for housing infill, there was more than enough housing and land to meet projected needs (Chicago Department of Planning and Development 2014; Chandler 2019). Throughout the planning process, city officials consistently heard from residents about the negative impacts of the vacant lots in their neighbourhood. These included viewing the vacant lots as a security risk from unwanted activity and frustration with current City maintenance programs that failed to address what residents viewed as blight, with the following resident quote fairly typical of how many residents felt: "if you are not going to maintain (them) then I'd like to because it's right next to my house and it's a throughway for activity that is not really supported by residents in our community" (Chandler 2019). Based on community input and a three-year planning process, three key recommendations emerged from the GHNP that influenced the *Large Lot* program:

> a) give local residents greater control over the vacant land in their neighbourhood; b) dispose of some of the city-owned vacant land efficiently, which returns the land to the tax rolls; and c) increase safety, build community, and raise home values by creating more neighbourhood-level investment.
>
> (Chandler 2019)

How Chicago's approach differs from traditional urban greening approaches

Though City officials recognize the positive value of greenspace for the health and well-being of both residents and the environment, the primary goals for the *Large Lot* program are social and economic:

> That [the *Large Lot* program] was not a green space issue. The origins of the *Large Lot* has everything to do with stabilizing the neighborhood and

> creating wealth and taking control of your neighborhood.... I mean, it's land and it can be greened but it's not a green space goal ... in fact some people don't even like the idea that you are letting people take land when it should be housing.... The reason the sustainable development division is managing the program is because it is a land community goal, a social goal not just an environmental goal. How the land ends up to being used, we are not trying to direct that.
>
> (Dickhut 2019)

As such, the program's aims are to empower community at a residential level in order to stabilize the neighbourhood, and to be able to replicate the program in other similarly challenged neighbourhoods as a *land community* versus greenspace goal. The City does have other ecological services programs, such as their *Green Alley Program* that aims to reduce stormwater runoff, flooding, and pollution of Lake Michigan through modifications such as permeable pavement (City of Chicago 2012), as well as their recent *Resilient Corridors* program (City of Chicago, 100 Resilient Cities Team et al. 2019) (see Chapter 2). However, due to the need to stabilize these neighbourhoods and the fact that the City does not mandate landscaping on private residential property, the City does not require residents to meet ecological goals such as stormwater management (Dickhut 2019). While residents can undertake any activity on the lot that is allowed by zoning (LISC Chicago and Latentdesign 2015), and the City has provided an extensive public information document and technical assistance to help residents navigate different types of improvement projects, most residents have created a side yard as a lush recreation space for their children, and sometimes all the children on the block (Chandler 2019). This ability to beautify previously 'blighted' space into something that can be enjoyed by their children and extended family, many of whom still own their childhood home, has given many residents a feeling of empowerment over their daily lives and a more positive view of the City's responsiveness to their needs:

> [W]e've gotten a lot of feedback from residents in the community about how much this means to them and I think that is something we weren't really realizing the magnitude (of), that the selling of a lot for a dollar would really have on people's everyday lives and the way they viewed the city.
>
> (Chandler 2019)

In particular, the ability to beautify the vacant lots has given residents an increased feeling of security and nostalgia. As one woman told city officials: "you don't understand and I can't convey to you what this means to me because it was such an eyesore. It was such a security risk for me on a daily basis" (Chandler 2019). When she was given the lot and allowed to fence it, she told officials, she no longer had that fear. Lastly, as many residents still owned their childhood home, even if they no longer lived there, they felt that investing in the community through the *Large Lot* program allowed them to help bring the community back to what it was when they were growing up:

> In many instances they rent it out to other family members and they are very tied to that property and that land, and they want to see the community come back to what it was when they were growing up, and the opportunity to invest more in that community means so much to them because it's their home.
>
> (Chandler 2019)

Research and precedent

A key component of this work is the support of the City, which has recognized the need to involve community partners, researchers, and residents at a very fine scale in order to make the program successful (Chandler 2019; Gobster 2019). For example, while the City did not rely on academic research per se to develop or justify the program, their Department of Planning and Development asked Paul Gobster at the USDA Forest Service in Evanston (in partnership with colleagues at the University of Illinois) to evaluate the social and environmental assessment of the benefits of the program, the initial results of which are outlined below (Gobster, Stewart et al. 2018).[1] Key aspects of the study included both visual and social assessments. The social assessment included focus groups, a mail survey, and selected in-depth interviews (Stewart 2016; Gobster 2017; Stewart, Gobster et al. 2019). The study also used visual assessments, which are an increasingly popular method to more quickly evaluate physical landscape features at the neighbourhood level on everything from social disorder (Gobster, Stewart et al. 2017; Marco, Gracia et al. 2017) and perceived safety (Naik, Philipoom et al. 2014; Gobster, Stewart et al. 2017) to urban ecology metrics of urban greenery (Li, Zhang et al. 2015) and urban agriculture (Taylor and Lovell 2012). The visual assessment examined the condition of the lot using photo assessments, Google Earth and street view, and property information from the Cook County Tax Assessor Office. Key research questions the team examined include testing whether the condition and adjacency of the previously owned property, previous unofficial appropriation of the lot (called blotting), and the condition of the block, influenced or predicted the improvements made to the *Large Lot* after their purchase (Gobster, Stewart et al.

2017; Gobster, Stewart et al. 2018). Following the greening hypothesis by Krusky and colleagues from work on vacant lots in Philadelphia (Krusky, Heinze et al. 2015), the prediction would be that blocks with higher levels of care would motivate new *Large Lot* owners to go to greater lengths to improve their newly acquired lot. This follows the line of inquiry of some researchers doing work on Philadelphia's greening of vacant lots (discussed below), which argue that SSUG can lead to a sort of spatial contagion (the greening hypothesis) which both 'improves' adjacent properties and has been shown to lead to reductions in crime (see below) (Wolfe and Mennis 2012; Kondo, Keene et al. 2015).

The second hypothesis tested focused on whether there were signs of 'cues to care' that influenced the level of lot improvement. As discussed in Chapters 1, 2, and 3, 'cues to care,' developed by Nassauer (Nassauer 1995), have been linked to perceptions of attractiveness and stewardship of landscapes and often include fencing, mowing around 'wilder' areas, and signage (Gobster, Nassauer et al. 2007). Cues to care have also been used to evaluate vacant land and have "been shown to be important indicators of attractiveness across many types of landscapes" (Nassauer 2011; Dewar, Nassauer et al. 2013; Gobster, Stewart et al. 2017). The difference between the above work and that happening in Chicago is that the scale is much smaller, localized initially to one neighbourhood over time (Englewood), and includes both environmental and social assessments and multiple methods (Gobster 2019).

Results

Initial results of the visual assessment (conducted between 2014 and 2018) show significant improvements (especially around better kept turf grass and lack of clutter, i.e. cars, junk, etc.) in the first year after implementation, with smaller continued improvements thereafter (Gobster, Stewart et al. 2018; Gobster, Hadavi et al. 2019) (see Figures 4.1 and 4.2). Initial results of the study would also seem to support the contagion hypotheses tested, and showed that blocks with higher levels of care, and proximity to the owners' property, influenced the number of lots purchased, and that the biggest change was seen in the first year after purchase (Gobster, Hadavi et al. 2019; Gobster, Rigolon et al. 2019). Interestingly, the aesthetic preferred by residents differs slightly from aesthetic norms reported in the literature (Nassauer, Wang et al. 2009; Gobster, Stewart et al. 2017). While researchers found neatly mown lawns (partly to adhere to Chicago's weed ordinance), an increase in flower gardens, and trimmed trees from the *Large Lot* program, they also found paved over turf for parking, decreases in woody vegetation, especially large tree or 'weed tree' removal, and brightly coloured fencing (Gobster, Stewart et al. 2017; Gobster, Stewart et al. 2018).

Figure 4.1 East Garfield Park Neighbourhood, vacant lot, Chicago, before.
Source: U.S. Forest Service photo, Google Street View.

Figure 4.2 East Garfield Park Neighbourhood, vacant lot, Chicago, after.
Source: U.S. Forest Service photo, Google Street View.

This desire for a 'neater, cleaner' and more colourful aesthetic contrasts with the research discussed in Chapters 1 and 2, in which vegetation that has more interest and biodiversity has been linked to increased attention restoration, well-being, and creativity (Loder 2014; Carrus, Scopelliti et al. 2015; Wood, Harsant et al. 2018). However, it does support some research that shows a public preference for 'neater' landscapes (Qiu, Lindberg et al. 2013; Uren, Dzidic et al. 2015), as well as public debates and conflicts that have happened over ecological restoration projects and urban greening that have a wilder aesthetic without concurrent education (Gobster 2000; Junker and Buchecker 2008). It also supports research that has linked the perception of disorder and lack of maintenance with fear of crime and neighbourhood satisfaction (Hur and Nasar 2014), as well as actual reductions in crime after urban greening (Garvin, Cannuscio et al. 2012). Initial results of the study would seem to support this research; Gobster and colleagues found that there were statistically significant negative associations between the levels of care and urban greening and rates of crime. In other words, urban greening can reduce crime even at a block level, and the quality of the urban greening matters (Hadavi, Gobster et al. 2019).

Initial results from the interviews found that residents also mentioned beautification, using the space as a resource and for growing food, and family identity as key reasons for purchasing the lots (Stewart, Gobster et al. 2019). For example, in reflecting the desire to beautify the neighbourhood, one resident commented they wanted "a lot that is developed so that when people walk by, it makes you and to stop and reflect" (Stewart, Gobster et al. 2019). Residents also felt that there was a decrease in undesirable activity, it was quieter and safer, they had decreased fear of mortality, and increased social interaction with their neighbours:

> What a powerful difference the lot has made on the block. It's about beautification where people know that good things are possible. We're not just bottom-feeders who live here. [These gardens that were once vacant lots] change culture. The mother who has a picnic in the garden is overjoyed. It's become theirs and they treat it like it's theirs. People look out for one another now.
>
> (Stewart, Gobster et al. 2019)

This case study on Chicago's *Large Lot* program reveals a complex understanding of the role, meaning, and benefits of marginal land in these neighbourhoods. The socio-economic value (or liability) of the vacant lots is clearly understood by both the City and the community. Left untouched, these lots are a threat to the safety, stability, and viability of these neighbourhoods, leaving residents feeling vulnerable and powerless against unwanted activity and economic and social decline, and to the City, with communities that are slipping into further instability and marginalization. Letting residents take control over vacant lots on their street to improve them is thus a smart move on the part of the City: it reduces the burden of maintenance, stabilizes the community, and increases property values. It can also help with psychological restoration, particularly where flower beds and trees are added (Lindal and Hartig 2015; Wyles, White et al. 2019). For residents, having ownership of spaces close to their homes has given them a sense of control, pride, and a sense that they are investing and protecting the community they grew up in. It can also provide safe places for children to play, which has been shown to increase physical activity and provide a host of social and emotional benefits, including self-esteem, self-discipline, and cognitive function, all which tend to be at risk in vulnerable, stressed populations (Mårtensson, Jansson et al. 2014; King, Litt et al. 2015; Schutte, Torquati et al. 2017; van Dijk-Wesselius, Maas et al. 2018).

What is less clear is the role that this 'small-scale nature,' or the greenspace itself, plays in resident's perceptions and sense of community. While the desire for 'cleanliness' and 'neatness' in the formerly abandoned lots reflects the desire for stability against chaos and unpredictability, and the signaling that the community is active and watching against unwanted activity (not to mention city code compliance), the removal of mature trees contradicts the conclusions of most research on mature trees: that they provide multiple benefits and are highly valued (Meier and Scherer 2012; Peckham, Duinker et al. 2013; Clemens 2015; Kardan, Gozdyra et al. 2015) including better recovery from stress (at least for men) (Jiang, Chang et al. 2014), and a reduction in crime rates (Troy, Morgan Grove et al. 2012). However, most of this research has also been done on white, Anglo-American college-age students, not vulnerable communities of colour, which may partly explain the difference. Certainly, research on the urban forest in the highly multicultural Toronto has shown that communities of Portuguese, Italian, and Chinese descent prefer highly manicured yards and tend to cut down mature trees (Fraser and Kenney 2000). And while the need for neighbourhood stabilization is understandable in these communities, research has shown that marginal urban lands tend to have a higher rate of biodiversity than more 'tended,' mainstream parks and urban greenspace (Cohen, Baudoin et al. 2012; Bonthoux, Brun et al. 2014; Müller, Bøcher et al. 2018; Twerd and Banaszak-Cibicka 2019). Given that higher levels of biodiversity have been linked to increased restoration and reduction in stress (though partly dependent on individual perceptions of 'naturalness') (van den Berg, Jorgensen et al. 2014; Carrus, Scopelliti et al. 2015; Wood, Harsant et al. 2018), this leaves the link between health, aesthetics, and community vitality far more complex than simply 'cleaning and greening' marginal land.

Vacant lots: Philadelphia

Background

Like Chicago's, Philadelphia's built and natural environmental legacy includes a famous park system, as well as a greenbelt and a planned grid system that included open space and watershed protection (PennPraxis 2010; Milroy 2016). Many of the parks were originally acquired as a health and sanitation measure, particularly to safeguard the city's drinking water after a series of epidemics in the eighteenth century (Philadelphia Water Department 2015). Philadelphia also benefits from close collaboration between the famous Pennsylvania Horticultural Society and the historic Parks and Recreation department, as well as a long history of interest and promotion of horticulture and gardening (Lovell 2019; Palantino 2019). Like Chicago however, de-industrialization, car-oriented development, and population loss after the 1950s have made it difficult for the city to maintain public facilities designed for 2.5 million people instead of the current 1.5 million (City of Philadelphia 2011), and many are in need of updating and repair (City of Philadelphia 2019). Furthermore, while there is less vacant land than there was in the 1970s at the peak of population decline (City of Philadelphia 2011), there are still over 40,000 vacant lots, representing 10 percent of land in Philadelphia (City of Philadelphia 2011; Ortega 2019), many of which are located either in post-industrial areas (City of Philadelphia 2011; Ortega 2019) or neighbourhoods and employment centres that have seen high losses of population and jobs (City of Philadelphia 2011). While 78 percent of these vacant lots are privately owned, the City recognizes that the problems associated with vacancy fall on the City's shoulders, including increased rates of crime (Branas, Cheney et al. 2011; Branas, South et al. 2018), gun violence (Branas, Cheney et al. 2011; Berger 2018; Branas, South et al. 2018), and over $21 million in public funds spent annually responding to and maintaining vacant land (Econsult Corporation, Penn Institute for Urban Research et al. 2010; Ortega 2019):

> [E]ven though the city doesn't own all the vacant lots, a lot of them are tax delinquent private properties or just … negligent owners. The city recognized that they own the problems that come from the vacancy and the blighted lots … problems like increased gun violence or things like children … are nervous to walk next to a lot that is covered in trash so they will walk down the middle of the street in order to get to school. So the city says we don't own all the vacant lots but we own the problems that come from the vacancy.
>
> (Ortega 2019)

At the same time, while fully 13 percent of Philadelphia is open space (City of Philadelphia 2011; Geeting 2015), access to the large formal parks is not equitably distributed among residents, and nearby 'green' spaces may be of poor quality and accessibility and therefore rarely used (Palantino 2019). Most of these neighbourhoods are also economically disadvantaged, have poor health, and have poor access to healthy food and safe areas for physical activity (City of Philadelphia 2011). In examining Philadelphia's approach to urban greening, this socio-economic and historical context is key to understanding their approach.

Origins of their vacant lot programs

In addition to Philadelphia's *Green City, Clean Waters* (GCCW) stormwater plan outlined in Chapter 2, their most comprehensive approach to urban greening is the Department of Parks and Recreation's planning document *Green2015* (PennPraxis 2010). The document grew out of the Office of Sustainability's *Greenworks Philadelphia* plan (2009, 2016), which came out of former mayor Nutter's larger sustainability initiative. This sustainability initiative was supported by the creation of a cabinet-level Office of Sustainability that also required the regular participation of all departments (Palantino 2019). Of relevance to Philadelphia's approach to urban greening is the Equity goal in their *Greenworks Philadelphia* plan that calls for a target of creating 500 greened public acres to address the 200,000 Philadelphia residents who do not have access to a park within a ten-minute walk from their home (City of Philadelphia 2016). As with Chicago's *Large Lot* program, the City also did extensive community outreach that informed the goals of *Green2015* (PennPraxis 2010). The target of 500 acres of greened public space was considered the minimum needed to advance the City's goal of becoming more fair, livable, and competitive (PennPraxis 2010), and the *Green2015* action plan sets out the goals, justification, and criteria for selection for potential sites to achieve this goal. While this chapter will be interested mainly in the goals and objectives of the *Green2015* plan below, the plan is designed to work seamlessly with the most recent comprehensive plan for the City of Philadelphia, its land use prioritization based on environmental, demographic, economic, and population predictions (City of Philadelphia 2011); the updated *GreenWorks* (2016) plan (City of Philadelphia 2016); the *Green City, Clean Waters* stormwater plan (Philadelphia Water Department 2011); and the new *Rebuild* plan (City of Philadelphia 2019) (see Plate 1, Chapter 2). As mentioned in Chapter 2, the Rebuild plan is a $500 million program to reinvigorate Philadelphia's parks, libraries, playgrounds, and recreation centres, which is being paid for by a *Sweetened Beverage* tax, the first major city that has successfully (if contentiously) done so (Tanenbaum 2018; Briggs 2019). As part of the City's efforts at collaborative partnerships and efficiencies, many parts of *Green2015* are being moved under the *Rebuild* mandate (Palantino 2019).

Policy and research precedents

The *Green2015* plan also builds on the success of long-standing programs to deal with urban blight and vacant lots (Ortega 2019; Pennsylvania Horticultural Society n.d.-a) and the evidence that has come out of research partnerships evaluating the programs. For example, a program developed out of a demonstration project called *LandCare* by the Pennsylvania Horticultural Society (PHS) in collaboration with the City (Pennsylvania Horticultural Society n.d.-a) has 'cleaned and greened' 12,000 of 40,000 vacant lots in Philadelphia. Ongoing research and evaluation from this program has demonstrated the positive community, health, and economic benefits from even minimal greening efforts (usually the clearing of debris, installation of sod and trees, and a fence around the perimeter) (Garvin, Cannuscio et al. 2012; Branas and MacDonald 2014) (see Figures 4.3 and 4.4). These benefits include increased food security through potential community gardens, land value increases, reductions in crime, and neighbourhood revitalization (Bucchianeri, Gillen et al. 2012; The Center for High Impact Philanthropy 2013; Branas, South et al. 2018). Maintenance, the need to replicate the program at a city-wide scale, and the need to provide training and employment in these neighbourhoods were key factors in the choice of a "park-like setting that could be implemented at a city-wide scale" which provides good sight-lines for safety, employment for private contractors and community organizations, and visual indicators that "someone is taking care of this space" (Ortega 2019). The PHS hires local landscape contractors to do the initial clean-up and twice-monthly maintenance, and then works with

Figure 4.3 Landcare: 8th and Berks East, before.
Source: Pennsylvania Horticultural Society.

Figure 4.4 Landcare: 8th and Berks East, after.
Source: Pennsylvania Horticultural Society.

community partners to hire and train local workers to maintain the lots (Ortega 2019), including ex-offenders through the *Roots to Re-Entry* program (Pennsylvania Horticultural Society n.d.-b). Depending on city funding (the program is a line-item in the city's budget), PHS brings on another 300–500 lots a year (Ortega 2019).

Collaborations with the USDA Forest Service and the University of Pennsylvania have used these vacant lot greening case studies to do city-wide statistical analysis to show a 29 percent reduction in gun violence (Branas, South et al. 2018), a 41.5 percent decrease in feelings of depression (69 percent in the lowest income neighbourhoods), and 63 percent decrease in self-reported poor mental health (South, Hohl et al. 2018). Research also showed significant increases in housing wealth for every dollar invested in these areas: "We have demonstrated that every dollar invested to clean and green the vacant lots increases housing wealth by $224 with … a 22,000% return on investment, which is pretty amazing" (Bucchianeri, Gillen et al. 2012; Ortega 2019). Furthermore, some recent research has indicated that benefits of these types of urban greening initiatives can create a positive spatial contagion; in other words properties near 'cleaned and greened' lots have also demonstrated increased maintenance and upkeep (Krusky, Heinze et al. 2015), which is considered to be indicative of improved social and community benefits from increased collective efficacy and a sense of empowerment and control for residents (Hunter and Brown 2012; Wang, Tan et al. 2014). This seems to be particularly true when the cleaned and greened lots are grouped relatively close together (Ortega 2019). Lastly, these lots are meant to improve local spaces in the interim for communities rather than provide a permanent public greenspace (though this has also happened), given the projected population and economic health increases for the region (City of Philadelphia 2011).

Goals and targets of the plan

The urban greening goals outlined in *Green2015* build on this history and demonstrated success with urban greening. For example, the Primary Indicators (PennPraxis 2010) for site selection also target areas of high need in terms of lack of quality greenspace and population density, particularly the neighbourhoods of South, West, and North Philadelphia, Lower Northeast Philadelphia, and East and West Oak Lane (PennPraxis 2010). Aligning with this work, lots under the *LandCare* program have given approximately 45,000 residents access to greenspace within a half mile of their home who wouldn't otherwise have access to greenspace (Ortega 2019). They have as their design goals sites that are basic, useable, easy to maintain and have minimal infrastructure so as to lower the initial and ongoing costs for installation and maintenance (PennPraxis 2010). However, depending on the viability of recent land trusts, funding, and community partner involvement, the plan does lay out the possibility for more extensive greening options, and many of the envisioned plans include more 'ecological' options such as meadows, increased tree coverage, and rain gardens (PennPraxis 2010; City of Philadelphia 2016).

How the plan differs from previous urban greening initiatives

Despite having some similarities with more traditional urban greening plans that address park use and access, *Green2015* differs from previous urban greening initiatives in a few key ways. First, the primary indicators set out for land to target for urban greening indicate a recognition both that most new public greenspace will not be in the form of a new large park, and that innovative use of existing marginal spaces will be necessary (PennPraxis 2010). Key areas that the plan targets for access include recreation centres and underused Philadelphia Parks and Recreation

(PPR) sites, public underused land, schoolyards, and private underused land (PennPraxis 2010). These target areas support the goals of the new and ambitious *Rebuild* program that aims to improve recreation and park facilities through prioritization and coordination to use resources efficiently (Walljasper 2017; City of Philadelphia 2019; Palantino 2019). Second, the plan recognizes the need to align with the larger goals set out in the *2035* plan and the *Green City, Clean Waters* (GCCW) plan (see Chapter 2) which also impact the scale and type of site targeted. For example, in contrast to Chicago's *Large Lot* program, under the plans' primary indictors lots smaller than a quarter-acre are not considered viable for this urban greening program since they are not seen to provide adequate environmental or recreational benefits (PennPraxis 2010). This effective exclusion of small lots is primarily due to criteria for stormwater catchment set by the Philadelphia Water Department in their GCCW plan that determines what counts as a 'greened acre' (Philadelphia Water Department 2011). In addition, lots that meet the linear connection, transit, and service-based centre goals set out in the 2035 plan are also considered to be primary indicators of site viability (PennPraxis 2010; Palantino 2019). Third, while falling under secondary indicators, sites are preferred that directly link to the larger vision set out in the comprehensive plan for a *Green Network* of public greenspace that connects residents to existing watershed parks, the waterfront, streams, river and creeks, and existing rail corridors (PennPraxis 2010). This vision marks another distinction from Chicago's *Large Lot* program, which is considered part of a larger urban greening program but is mainly focused on community empowerment and safety.

Use of research

The *Green2015* plan builds on the success and history of the *LandCare* program's research on economic and social benefits of urban greening to justify the program (PennPraxis 2010), including increased food security through potential community gardens, land value increases, reductions in crime, and neighbourhood revitalization. They also highlight regional economic and public health benefits, particularly reductions in heat-related and air-quality mortality, increased opportunities for active living, and the economic benefits of public greenspace (PennPraxis 2010). Not surprisingly given the plans' link to other municipal plans, environmental benefits are highlighted, such as climate change adaptation and mitigation and the City's sustainability goals (PennPraxis 2010; City of Philadelphia 2016). Lastly, the city uses research to justify targeting vulnerable populations, such as children under 18, seniors over 65, and low-income residents, as particularly needing additional nearby public greenspace. The plans' complexity and ambitious balancing of basic urban greening upgrades and ecological goals, targeted investment and long-term visioning of connectivity and watersheds, and economic, health, and social research provide a rich case study of approaches to targeted urban greening.

Case study: Heston Garden

In the following case study, an example of the 're-greening' or 'improvement' of a parcel of vacant land that also manages stormwater, we will consider questions such as: What does the *Green2015* look like on the ground? What benefits are expected from these projects? How is the community involved, if at all? Heston Garden was a parcel of vacant land on a former industrial site in a residential row home community of Hestonville in West Philadelphia. The impetus for improvement came from the community and local councilman Jones, who approached PWD staff for assistance to transform the open lot into a formal amenity space for the neighbourhood. PWD's public affairs team carried out extensive outreach for the project during the design phase, including attending multiple community meetings, gathering input, and presenting plans to community members. The end result is a rain garden at the corner of the vacant lot that acts as a front door to the neighbourhood (Philadelphia Water n.d.). The garden provides passive relief from the largely hardscaped neighbourhood for residents while managing over an acre of stormwater runoff from the surrounding streets, preventing over 430,000 gallons annually from being dumped quickly into the Schyulkill River watershed (Philadelphia Water n.d.). Additional improvements include a council-funded perimeter sidewalk, an internal walkway, benches, a gazebo, a mural installed by *Mural Arts*, and a new fence from the Pennsylvania Horticultural Society (PHS) (see Figures 4.5 and Plate 7) (Philadelphia Water n.d.). Both the PWD and partners and the community see the garden as providing health benefits to residents from passive viewing of nature, while providing an alternative activity and 'eyes on the street' to mitigate local drug activity, which is common in the area. Since the completion of site improvements, members of the community have taken meticulous care of the site and hold community meetings and events there in the summertime.

In this way Heston Garden is a good example of Philadelphia's approach to urban greening in its blend of ecological, social, and economic goals (through revitalization of a 'blighted' area). In other words, 'greened' spaces need to provide multiple benefits, and they need to involve the community since the success of these projects depends in large part on community stewardship and acceptance. In providing multiple benefits, such greenspaces are considered an asset and a path to investment and revitalization, not a 'nice to have' amenity for already privileged neighbourhoods. This framing represents a profound shift from the way cities have traditionally approached urban infrastructure and greening, as we will see below.

Figure 4.5 Green 2015: Heston Rain Garden, vacant lot, before.
Source: Philadelphia Water Department.

The addition of the stormwater management mandate also brings some challenges, however. Unlike vacant lot greening under the *LandCare* program that is meant to 'green' or improve vacant lots as a temporary measure, stormwater infrastructure needs to be established for 45 years. Thus vacant lands that are targeted for GI need to be set aside as permanent green spaces and not sold off for future development by the City. In addition, stormwater infrastructure is maintained by PWD, but the overall site is not, so while the rest of the site is currently being maintained by the community and the councilman through grants and a PHS contract, if priorities change site maintenance could be a major issue (Noon 2019) .

The case study of Heston Garden and Philadelphia's *Green2015* program thus describes an approach to urban greening that explicitly links green infrastructure goals and metrics with social and health benefits that are backed up by local, case-study specific data, which differs from traditional municipal justifications for the benefits of public greenspace (often parks). The novelty of Philadelphia's approach is not in making these linkages but in drawing them *all together* as a coherent, city-wide plan. Also new is the focus on improving the *quality* of urban greenspace, and on integrating *useable* greenspace into the fabric of the city on a foundation of community stewardship. This focus on community stewardship is so strong that according to Aparna Palantino with the PHS, the "goal is not only to rebuild just the amenities and the infrastructure but the communities ... because when communities participate they take ownership and ultimately then they become the stewards of these amenities" (Palantino 2019) – a necessary component when the tax base is too small to maintain all the improved greenspaces and amenities.

Furthermore, the stormwater mandate, which focuses on spaces larger than a quarter-acre, bring to these urban greenspaces an ecological component and justification. Thus, urban greening in Philadelphia has explicit social, financial (in terms of neighbourhood investment), and ecological goals that shape the size, location, and aesthetics of the revitalized spaces. This multi-dimensionality reflects the city's recognition that while urban greenspace *can* be valuable, its value is highly dependent on the social, economic, and aesthetic contexts, a viewpoint supported by the work of social constructionists, as seen in Chapter 1. This is particularly true for areas of prolonged disinvestment, where research has shown negative community perceptions of 'wild' and 'neglected' greenspace, perceptions that are reflected in community members' perceptions of disempowerment and a lack of safety (Wang, Tan et al. 2014; Palardy, Boley et al. 2018). As in Chicago, the focus to date has been mostly on 'cleaning and greening' lots to give the appearance of care and maintenance. Given the results so far of the *LandCare* program and the case study above, this has been very successful on key metrics of safety, reduced stress, and reduced crime. It is also clearly popular with some communities, who are advocating for it and maintaining it, as seen with Heston Garden.

What is less clear is the role that scale and clustering play in impacting the health and well-being of those in the community, as well as the impact of community-led versus city-led initiatives. Clearly the grouping together of these 'tidied' pockets of greening would seem to support the contagion hypothesis, possibly through a mechanism of social empowerment and pride (Krusky, Heinze et al. 2015). This scale and clustering would also support the advocacy seen by community members versus only a top-down approach. While research from social constructionists on the symbolism, power dynamics, and cultural values around nature caution against a pure quantification of benefits – i.e. this many greened acres in a square mile will give this health result (Kolinjivadi, Van Hecken et al. 2019) – the integration of 'improved' greenspace into the fabric of the city raises interesting questions on how this may impact residents' experience of place and their health and well-being. This is particularly true given *Green2015*'s goals and alignment with green corridors, transit-oriented development, and other amenities. For example, will linking 'tidy' greened spaces with green corridors with a more ecological, and possibly 'wilder' aesthetic, provide the kind of 'edging' and 'framing,' or cues to care, which make the wilder greenspace less threatening? How might these impact residents' restoration and well-being, given what we know about biodiversity and mental health and well-being? These questions become even more interesting as the *Green2015* program moves beyond the initial goals of the *LandCare* program, and are also seen in the greening of post-industrial, elevated parks, discussed below.

Post-industrial urban greening: elevated parks

Background

The second key theme seen in small-scale urban greening projects is the creative use of post-industrial spaces. While the 'capping' of expressways, such as the Big Dig in Boston and the Woodall Rodgers freeway in Dallas, are also re-thinking previous transportation infrastructure, repurposing abandoned rail lines into elevated parks is producing something quite different. While both types of projects re-imagine and revitalize previous infrastructure and examples of planning into something new, the elevated rail lines "emphasize the intertwining of landscape and industry" (Saval 2016), blending the relics of the early twentieth-century industrial economy with urban nature in a kind of nature–city hybrid that is becoming iconic for this age, a kind of "post-post-industrial planning" (Saval 2016), for the twenty-first century. The most famous examples of these are the Promenade Plantée in Paris, completed in 1993 (Saval 2016), and New York City's High Line, completed in 2013 and which has become their number one tourist attraction (Bliss 2017; NYC The Official Guide n.d.). Both famous examples provided direct inspiration for the case studies below: Philadelphia's Rail Park, started in late 2016, and Chicago's The 606, completed in 2015. While each elevated park differs in its design and goals, common themes include the provision of useable greenspace for communities that did not have adequate amounts, as well as design goals that differ somewhat from ground-level parks and greenspace. Understanding the goals of these elevated parks, and how they differ and are similar to other small-scale urban greening projects, can help us to understand how cities are re-imagining urban nature and its public benefits, where they are facing successes and challenges, and how they might impact health, well-being, and sense of place.

Case study: Philadelphia's Rail Park

Why it started

While some areas of Philadelphia are still economically depressed, other areas are undergoing an economic revitalization. This development has not been even, however, with some pockets being passed over for revitalization. One example of this uneven development is the historic Callow Hill neighbourhood in the Center City district. Traditionally an industrial area made up of industrial buildings and rail lines, along with a historically Chinese district (Chinatown North), the area remained economically stagnant despite being within walking distance of the now-desirable Center City, a thriving artist community, and some of the industrial buildings being converted into residential lofts. The lack of development was largely considered to be due to the abandoned V-shaped Reading Railroad Viaduct that ran through the area (Goldenberg 2019) with 32 percent of land around the viaduct remaining vacant (Center City District n.d.).

> Development of an expanded City Center skipped over the Callow Hill area, creating this "hole in the donut." So we – the downtown business development district – were looking at how to spur economic growth and development while improving quality of life here.
>
> (Goldenberg 2019)

The viaduct transported people and freight in and out of the city for almost a century before declines in manufacturing led to the cessation of any train traffic in the 1980s (Center City District n.d.; Studio Bryan Hanes n.d.) and had been vacant since.

Impetus for starting and community outreach

Like the High Line project in New York City, the impetus for development into an elevated park came from a few dedicated long-time residents who started the Friends of the Rail Park community organization. In 2010 they partnered with the Center City District, the City's Commerce Department, and the Department of Parks and Recreation to evaluate options for two of the segments that run through the Callow Hill neighbourhood. After visiting the High Line, the Center City District agreed that the elevated steel and masonry structure with great views of the city offered an opportunity to both spur economic development and "create an exciting new greenspace in a neighborhood that has no greenspace" (Goldenberg 2019):

> Historically, Philadelphia is a city of neighborhoods with row houses; people sit on their front stoops and talk to neighbors. Some may have small back yards where they can run around and walk the dog. But Callowhill was historically an industrial hub, so it lacked greenspace. There was no sense of a civic commons where neighbors could talk with each other or where workers could sit down and share lunch.
>
> (Goldenberg 2019)

While there was some disagreement over what should be done about the abandoned line – particularly from a community organization representing Chinatown residents who wanted it torn down for low and mid-range housing – initial seed funding for community engagement and planning found that capping contaminated soil and renovating the Viaduct was far less expensive than demolishing it for the 1.4-mile elevated spur that was the subject of the initial study (Goldenberg 2019; Center City District n.d.). Furthermore, the study found that providing additional greenspace would be more beneficial for development than demolition, while affordable housing could be constructed on triangular parcels adjacent to the Viaduct (Goldenberg 2019; Center City District n.d.). After community consultation, a design was approved in 2012, and the Center City District took on the fundraising and construction portion of the first 1.4-mile elevated spur section (also called the Reading viaduct). Construction began October 31, 2016, and the first section opened June 14, 2018 (Schmidt 2019).

Design goals

Mimicking some of the aesthetics of the Promenade Plantée and the High Line, key community-driven design goals for the project included the preservation of the historic and gritty industrial character of the area, a place for community to come and socialize with each other, the provision of environmental education, and the use of native plants (Goldenberg 2019) (see Figures 4.6 and Plate 8). Making sure that the park was not too 'designer-y,' and that it reflected the authenticity of the area, was also a key concern; in other words the residents were very concerned that the project did not morph into something aimed at tourists, or non-residents (though these are certainly welcome to visit), and was really a local amenity (Goldenberg 2019):

> We wanted to preserve that history and the authenticity.... Philadelphia is a city of history and authenticity. We wanted it (the Rail Park) to capture the grittiness of the neighborhood. So our intent is not to turn Callowhill into a Disneyland. We want it to reflect the historic industrial Nature of the community, reflective of the landscape and creating its own identity ... a place where those who now live and work can feel comfortable coming out, talking to their neighbors, looking out over the skyline of downtown Philly ... where workers can eat their lunch and nearby schoolchildren can hold outdoor classes.
>
> (Goldenberg 2019)

Figure 4.6 Rail Park: Education mural.
Source: © Bryan Hanes.

Native plants were desired from the beginning, and residents also wanted to ensure the design was of a high quality and the space would be well maintained, so they offered to do additional fundraising to cover the costs of higher-quality materials such as hardwood benches and regular manicuring of the vegetated areas. In a nice twist, some of the plants that were so loved by the community and which they wanted preserved were themselves remnants of the industrial past: Pawlonia trees that dot the viaduct grew from the pistachio shell-shaped seeds that were used as packing material for Chinese porcelain in the nineteenth century and which dropped out of the packing crates (Saval 2016).

The use of community art and future directions

While the Rail Park represents a successful partnership between community organizations and multiple levels of city government, the project also mimics other small-scale urban greening projects, particularly in the framing and programing around the project. For example, while the City of Philadelphia requires 1 percent of their contributed funding to go towards an art program or installation in the project, the heavy involvement of local artists, combined with programming from

PHS, enabled this project to have a pop-up, artistic, authentic feel while still being fairly large in scale. A collaboration between PHS and artists led to the use of a pop-up beer garden to promote the project, which included drawings of native plants found on the site and educational initiatives around it (Etchells 2016; Klein 2016). A mural arts program also linked the area's history as a red light district with much-needed lighting under some of the bridges:

> Although just one night, the art was a wonderful narrative of what it was like for some of the women who historically lived and struggled in this area. The projections of these powerful stories onto the thick masonry walls of the tunnel with fog swirling all around was quite moving.
>
> (Goldenberg 2019)

Lastly, while framed by the city largely as a development and revitalization opportunity, the stewardship and activism of the residents around what they wanted for the space mimics other urban acupuncture projects and interventions that aim to make local neighbourhoods safer, build community, and create a sense of place (Lydon and Garcia 2015) through temporary installations and art projects. While health was not a key justification, the project is situated in the larger context of Philadelphia's greening programs. These programs frame greenspace as providing multiple community and city-wide benefits, some of which include improved health and well-being for communities.

While it is early to tell how the residents will react over the long term to the built-out space, the response so far has been positive, with the project featured in the *New York Times* as an example of the current trend of urban greening (Schmidt 2019), and an on-going study on resident perceptions being conducted with Penn State University (Sheu 2019). A survey conducted in late 2018 on evaluating the creation of a business improvement district in the area also found that the first phase of the Rail Park ranked first on what people liked about their neighbourhood, and that expanding the Rail Park was third on their list of priorities (after enhanced cleanliness and safety) for desired improvements (Center City District 2018; Levy 2019). This support seems to have found financial backing; there are plans underway to develop two more sections of the three-mile long viaduct (Friends of the Rail Park n.d.).

The Rail Park represents an interesting evolution of how cities, and residents within them, are envisioning small-scale urban greenspace. If the Promenade Plantée and the High Line opened up the possibility of transforming relics of an industrial past into an 'authentic' amenity and public space, the Rail Park represents a hybrid of greenspace as economic development with neighbourhood identity and stabilization, more akin to the local garden or pocket park than the touristy, high-profile experience of the High Line. This focus on the lived experience is reflected in the desire of the community to have high-quality materials that felt good to sit on and spend time in rather than cheap materials that are less welcoming but may look good for photos:

> We're choosing a high-quality hard wood for our benches rather than metal, which can be hot and uncomfortable. The maintenance cost may be higher, but we find wood much more welcoming and in keeping with the aesthetic of the park.
>
> (Goldenberg 2019)

Similarly, the emphasis on native plants speaks to a desire to focus on the history and identity of the space and a re-visioning of the role that plants and greenspace play in it, while keeping the wildness, or unmanicured aspects, in check. It is interesting to note that many of the residents did not grow up in the community and that those who did, mainly the older Chinese population, were less enthused about the project at its onset. This might speak to changing expectations about the neighbourhood that was never intended to be residential, as well as the role that a higher level of socio-economic stability plays in perceptions of wildness and aesthetics for urban greenspace. It may be that greater stability enables a bit more freedom and even empowerment to enjoy 'wilder,' 'abandoned' industrial relics without feeling that one is also at risk of becoming similarly neglected. While the neighbourhood currently has enough vacant lots not to be as worried about gentrification, it will be interesting to see how this changes with changing demographics and investment.

Case study: Chicago's The 606

Background

Chicago's The 606, which opened in June 2015, has both similarities and differences with Philadelphia's Rail Park. The highly popular 2.7-mile elevated trail runs between the streets of Ashland and Ridgeland and connects the neighbourhoods of Logan Square, Humboldt Park, Wicker Park, and Bucktown (The Trust For Public Land n.d.-b). It has become a popular bike and walking route, having hit over 1 million users on the west end, and 2 million on the east end by the fall of 2016, only a year after opening (Gobster 2019). Design features include public art, a landscape designed to feel like a series of 'rooms' from end to end (Simone 2016), and four newly acquired, upgraded, or expanded parks adjacent to the trail meant to increase greenspace and provide access. Two new grade level (or on-the-ground) access parks are also anticipated in the future (Simone 2016) (see Figures 4.7 and 4.8).

Figure 4.7 606: Trail, showing active transportation.
Source: US Forest Service.

Figure 4.8 606: Trail, showing plant selection.
Source: US Forest Service.

Impetus for development

According to Kathy Dickhut, Deputy Commissioner at the City of Chicago Department of Planning and Development, the impetus for The 606 came from Chicago's *City Space Plan* that was adopted in 1998. The City Space Plan was a joint effort between the Chicago Park District, the Forest Preserve District of Cook County, and Chicago Public Schools that aimed to quantify the amount of open space per community area ('community area' refers to census-block parcels on which the City collects socio-economic data for planning purposes) with a goal of two acres of open space per 1,000 residents (Dickhut 2019). Logan Square and another community area were found to have the least amount of open space, and much of the open space in Logan Square was passive green-space in the historic boulevard system (Dickhut 2019). As the community was already established, there was little to no vacant land to add more greenspace, but there was the elevated Bloomindale Rail Line at the southern end of it, which by the 1990s had very little freight traffic (Simone 2016; The Trust For Public Land n.d.-b).

As in Philadelphia, city officials were aware of the success of the Promenade Plantée in Paris and knew they "couldn't really create big parcels of land anywhere so ... were looking for different innovative types of spaces and they saw ... this elevated three-mile long stretch of abandoned rail" (Gobster 2019). The potential of an elevated rail park line was bolstered through research on the Promenade Plantée, and in 2004 the City adopted the *Logan Square Open Space Plan* which, among other recommendations, suggested the Bloomingdale Rail Line as an opportunity to provide open space to those communities and help fulfill the goals of the *City Space Plan*. The Bloomingdale Rail Line as open space was also mentioned in the *Quality of Life Plans* for Logan Square and Humboldt Park (the neighbourhood at the other end of the line) in 2005 and 2006 (Bickerdike Redevelopment Corporation and LISC/Chicago's New Communities Program 2005; Logan Square Neighborhood Association and LISC/Chicago's New Communities Program 2005). These plans were put together by the Local Initiatives Support Corporation (LISC), which is part of a nation-wide non-profit corporation that helps both community-based and for-profit development organizations transform distressed neighbourhoods into healthy ones and which also works on the Large Lot program (LISC Chicago n.d.). The recommendation of the Bloomingdale Rail Line transformation as a way to achieve the open space goals of numerous City planning documents helps to explain the constant support from the City for residential groups who advocated for the trail for over a decade (Simone 2016).

Implementation

Like the Rail Park's, the eventual success of The 606[2] trail is due to a combination of top-down, governmental support, as well as ongoing community activism and the support of non-profit partners. Around the same time the Logan Square *Open Space Plan* was being put together, a local non-profit advocacy group called Friends of the Bloomingdale Trail was launched, with leadership from Ben Helphand, who also runs NeighborSpace. It was this group that built initial support for the vision and helped to maintain momentum during the economic downturn (Helphand and Lawson 2011; Friends of the Bloomingdale Trail n.d.), worked with elected officials and residents, and eventually recommended that a key non-profit partner – the Trust for Public Land (TPL) – be engaged in the project to help manage its development and assist with fundraising (Simone 2016). This combination of partners, including key roles for the Chicago Park District and the City of Chicago (with numerous agencies involved), as well as initial collaboration and funding that came from federal CMAQ (Congestion Mitigation and Air Quality) funds helped to shape the design goals and type of community engagement for the project in ways that differ from Philadelphia's Rail Park (Gobster 2019).

Funding and goals

Since the initial funding for some of the preliminary design and engineering and final construction for the project came from CMAQ, a key requirement of the project was that it be used at least partly as an active transportation corridor, and in particular for bicycles (Gobster 2019). This focus on active transportation has helped to shape the overall design goals of the project, which have needed to address things like on and off ramp access and bike-friendly surfaces in order to support active transportation, versus the more lush, manicured, passive-recreation style of the High Line (Simone 2016): "We had to temper expectations that it wasn't going to be as highly manicured and pristine let's say as the High Line.... The 606 was always meant to be more recreational" (Simone 2016). And while the project needed to address stormwater management and the urban heat island effect, as well as the overall goal of re-use of existing materials, ecological goals were not as high a priority in the design process (Thompson 2015; Simone 2016).

The role of research

The role of active transportation also shaped the kind of research commissioned for the project. The Trust for Public Land (TPL) came to the USDA Forest Service research branch in Evanston, and in particular Paul Gobster, who has a long history of working on the social dimensions of urban greenspace, and asked them to assess the benefits of The 606. In contrast to the goals of the *Large Lot* program, initial research goals for The 606 focused primarily on understanding how many people were using the trail, and also whether residents from the less wealthy and largely Hispanic Humboldt Park western end of the trail use it as much as residents from the more hip, wealthy neighbourhoods of Wicker Park and Bucktown (Gobster 2019). The strong partnership with key City of Chicago agencies and the Chicago Park District also helped to acquire or upgrade the adjacent parks to the trail. As such, The 606 was considered a signature project for Mayor Emanuel's goal to create 800 new acres of park, recreation areas, and greenspaces discussed above (The 606 n.d.; The Trust For Public Land n.d.-b).

The role of community partners

The selection of the TPL as an "honest broker … that could be the intermediary between government and the average citizen" (Simone 2016) to be the public face of the project also influenced the design goals and community engagement component of the project, and here The 606 aligns more closely with the goals of the Rail Park. For example, the TPL had far more time to devote to community outreach than overburdened city and park district staff, and its intermediary role allowed for more public trust and engagement than traditional community hall meetings (Simone 2016):

> We were able to build up trust in the community in a way that I think government … just doesn't have that kind of track record that they build up a lot of trust in the community … people don't feel like they are going to get what they need.
>
> (Simone 2016)

This extensive process helped to allay existing resident concerns about privacy (since the trail abuts numerous private residences) through installing varied railing heights, and it helped generate the idea that the trail could be a "living work of art" (Simone 2016). As in the case of the Rail Park, an artist was a key part of the design team, but it was through extensive public engagement that the idea that the trail could be an active community art space arose: "(It was a) desire from the community that there be opportunity for art on the trail as well as along the wall of the embankment and in the access park" (Simone 2016). A planned 'Community Curators' is being undertaken by TPL to train and hire residents in the community to be curators of temporary installations on the trail and to further take ownership of the trail (Simone 2016).

With 80,000 people living within walking distance to The 606, and one acquired park serving 4,000 children under the age of 12 alone, the involvement of TPL also fulfills the mandates of both TPL and the City; TPL's mandate is to make sure that everyone in America (some 80–85 percent of the population) live within a 10-minute walk of a park (Simone 2016). The 606 work also supports their Climate-Smart Cities initiative *Connect* goal to connect transportation, health, and community through greenspaces (Gobster 2019; The Trust For Public Land n.d.-a).

Discussion

While it is too soon to predict long-term outcomes of The 606, initial findings from the USDA Forest Service and partners suggest that The 606 is highly used, with an average daily traffic of 3,550–4,000 users (and on peak days upwards of 10,000) (Gobster, Sachdeva et al. 2017; Lindsey, Qi et al. 2019). As the TPL coordinator for the project, Jamie Simone, commented: "It's amazing to see, particularly in the summer months, all the use and you just wonder 'where were all these people before?'" (Simone 2016). The predominance of pedestrians also indicates that while bike traffic is substantial, many users are taking advantage of the uninterrupted and traffic-safe trail as an alternative place for walking (Gobster, Sachdeva et al. 2017; Lindsey, Qi et al. 2019). Anecdotally, there appears to be great diversity both in the population of users of the trail and in their activities (Simone 2016; Gobster 2019), but there is higher use on the east end (1.2 million users counted) than on the less wealthy west end (1 million users counted), even though the population density is higher there (Lindsey, Qi et al. 2019). This is not surprising given historically lower usage of parks and active recreation facilities by those from lower socio-economic areas, often from a lack of access (Powell, Slater et al. 2004; Moore, Diez Roux et al. 2008; Cohen, Han et al. 2012), and may also be a reflection of fears expressed by residents during community outreach of increased connectivity between the ethnically and economically disparate neighbourhoods (Simone 2016). However, the east end is closer to major commercial hubs and bike lanes, which may explain some of the difference, and anecdotally the fairly high level of use, even at the east end, suggests that there was a need for active recreation space away from the street, particularly for Hispanic users. This can be seen in this story told to the researchers:

> [A]n Hispanic older woman had said that she wanted to exercise outside but that is something you don't do in her culture. But up on the trail it is almost like you've got leeway there and not only can you dress more athletically but she went out and bought a whole outfit just to go up there.
>
> (Gobster 2019)

Interestingly, the disparity seems to be lessened when the temperatures rise, i.e. the 'trendier' users tend to drop off but the rate of Hispanic users stays the same (Gobster 2019).

Ongoing issues

Ongoing issues and areas of research for The 606 include evaluating the impact of the trail on gentrification and housing prices, as well as the impact on community cohesiveness and identity (Institute for Housing Studies at DePaul University, Smith et al. 2016; Harris 2018; Rigolon and Németh 2018). As the design of the trail occurred during a major recession, there was not much concern at the time about the large public investment pushing people out due to rising housing prices (as has happened with the High Line) (Rodkin 2018). Now that the neighbourhoods (in particular Wicker Park and Bucktown) have bounced back, this concern has been raised and reflects the tension between large public investment and the vulnerability of some residents to gentrification (Simone 2016; Madhani 2017). As seen throughout the case studies, this is far from a simple case of investment equaling displacement:

> When you see a $95 million investment come to your neighbourhood and you feel like people are being displaced because rents are going up or because people are buying multiunit buildings and converting them to single family homes, it's a lot easier to point to a $95 million investment than to try and solve a complex story of a neighbourhood undergoing change. These neighbourhoods were experiencing change and reinvestment years before the trail opened, but projects were delayed or fell apart due to the recession. The timing of The 606 happened to coincide with the resurgence of the real estate market.
>
> (Simone 2016)

However, the fact remains that in some formerly affordable neighbourhoods, housing prices have jumped by 48.2 percent with an increasing share of investors and developers buying them, prompting a proposal by some in Chicago's city council that would penalize developers and help fund an affordable housing trust (Madhani 2017). This concern over gentrification is happening nationally, with even the High Line proponents admitting that it has primarily benefited tourists and real estate developers over the black and Latino residents nearby (Friedrich 2017; Madhani 2017), and the resignation from the Atlanta Belt Line board of Ryan Gravel who wanted more focus on subsidies for affordable housing as another sign (Saval 2016).

This tension is also seen between existing residents, whom the investment is aimed to help, and those who move in after the investment. For example, there was a marked difference between the concerns of the existing residents, who had lived next to the abandoned rail line and were often concerned about safety and light criminal activity, and residents who moved to the neighbourhood after the trail opened, and who viewed the trail as an amenity and wanted to maximize their access (Simone 2016). This raises interesting questions about expectations of place from those living in the neighbourhood and their socio-economic status versus those who view the project from the birds-eye view of city planning and greenspace acquisition, with no easy answers on either side. While the transformation of abandoned industrial relics into public greenspace amenities can connect neighbourhoods and provide the health and well-being benefits associated with access to nature, they have also been critiqued as "exud(ing) the priorities of a new Gilded Age, even as they cover up the eyesores of the old one" (Saval 2016). Initial results from research on the *Large Lots* program has confirmed this, finding that in some cases urban greening follows gentrification, with higher numbers of white and educated property owners buying the lots, and a higher chance of lots being bought close to downtown (Gobster, Stewart et al. 2018). However, while it is too early to tell the impact of ongoing arts and event programming, as well as of the inclusion of The 606 in the City's larger environmental and park goals, the arts aspect of the trail is promising given the input the community had on the design and programming of the space.

Small-scale urban greening, interstitial, and post-industrial space: reflections and moving forward

What do these case studies tell us about how cities in North America are approaching small-scale urban greening? How do they differ from traditional urban greening programs? What do they tell us about shifting ideas on public space, health and well-being, sustainability, and approaches to equity? How do they align with current research, and how do they differ? And lastly, does the use of current research impact their design and implementation? In reviewing these case studies, the following insights stand out that may be instructive for other cities and researchers.

The case studies represent current approaches to a pernicious problem in many cities: the boom and bust cycles of capitalism and technology, along with racism and disinvestment, have left an uneven trail of development and high-quality public greenspaces. This is not new; the City Beautiful movement at the turn of the last century also recognized the need for better urban public space in the form of high-quality parks, and gave birth to great parks like Central Park (Central Park

Conservancy n.d.), Chicago's lakeshore park system (Chicago Park District n.d.), and Philadelphia's Fairmont park (The Fairmount Park Conservancy n.d.). What is new is the creative use of pilots, interstitial spaces, and widespread community engagement and collaboration to bypass traditional funding and bureaucratic hurdles in establishing greenspaces.

Using tactics similar to those used by proponents of active transportation and complete streets, both the *Large Lot* and *LandCare* programs started as pilots, the success of which enabled expansion of the program as seen in Chicago (WLS-TV Chicago 2016), or the development of a larger, more comprehensive program, as seen in Philadelphia. While the infrastructure investment required to safely develop The 606 and the Rail Park made them unsuitable as pilots per se, the elevated parks used the success of the High Line and the Promenade Plantée to support their proposal as both feasible and providing multiple economic, social, and community benefits. Furthermore, the use of artists in both elevated parks, strong community involvement through an intermediary organization, and even the pop-up beer gardens for the Viaduct, demonstrate the tactical urbanism approach applied to the projects even when their scale is somewhat large. This bottom-up approach reflects the recognition by these cities that citing academic research without community investment and stewardship of the projects is unlikely to lead to a successful outcome, particularly in the disadvantaged neighbourhoods the projects are meant to serve. This may also reflect a recognition that greenspace involves living plants that have an element of wildness and agency on their own, and which require ongoing maintenance to continue their support of the initial vision of the designer.

In a similar vein, though the cumulative scale of the projects is quite large, the approach by city officials and community partners to finding vacant, underused, or corridor spaces in which to add local greenspace reflects a shift in thinking from the City Beautiful movement and the influence of the ecological park model – and it's use of 'green' or habitat corridors – of the late 1990s (Sinha 2014) to something new. This new approach aligns with the vision of landscape urbanists, who see industrial relics as opportunities for the integration of landscape and urban life. It also challenges our ideas of cities with their traditional separation of 'green' or 'nature' areas and densely built urban infrastructure (Heynen, Kaika et al. 2006; Kaika 2006; Soga and Gaston 2016): "Monuments to ways of life and work that we no longer require are being converted, one by one, into promenades and playgrounds, changing what we think cities are for and how they ought to be used" (Saval 2016).

Greenspace for whom?

How exactly these public spaces should be used, and by whom, is at the core of the second difference from previous urban greening movements. In this new iteration, there is the explicit linking of greenspace, health, and equity, and the selective use of research collaborations to evaluate and justify the continued funding and possible expansion of these projects or programs. There seems to be widespread consensus among policy makers in these cities that access to greenspace is a public good, and that this public good is not equitably accessible to all of their residents (PennPraxis 2010; City of Philadelphia 2011). However, there is some discrepancy as to what constitutes a public good in terms of greenspace, aesthetics, and design.

In Philadelphia, greenspace as a public good varies depending on the type of urban greening, particularly between vacant land cleaning and greening or upgrading, and the creation of new post-industrial parks like the Rail Park. For the original *Land Care* program, greenspace is a public good if it conveys messages of care, cleanliness, and order; 'wild' or disorderly nature is threatening and represents "blight and unwanted activities," poor economic performance, and distressed neighbourhoods (Wang, Tan et al. 2014). Research done in collaboration with the City (and used to justify the program) supports this view of greenspace as a public good: it has been for the most part large-scale, quantitative, and generalizable. The work of Charlie Branas and colleagues at the University of Pennsylvania in particular has shown reductions in violent crime (gun assaults) and vandalism (though less common), reduced stress, and more exercise in sections of the city that have benefited from the *LandCare* program (Branas, Cheney et al. 2011; Kreeger 2011; Branas, South et al. 2018; South, Hohl et al. 2018; Moyer, MacDonald et al. 2019). This supports related research showing that minor improvements to vacant properties in Philadelphia (specifically a program to install new windows and doors in abandoned buildings) has also resulted in reductions city-wide for overall crimes, total assaults, gun assaults, and nuisance crimes (Kondo, Keene et al. 2015), and fits in well with arguments by the City on their high costs to deal with so-called blighted lots (Ortega 2019). For the *Green2015* program, greenspace is a public health *and* ecological good, providing public health amenities such as reduced stress, opportunities for physical activity, and reduced vulnerability to extreme environmental conditions such as flooding and extreme heat. It also explicitly provides environmental benefits (or ecological services), in the form of stormwater mitigation through green infrastructure. Other public health benefits, such as restoration, which are beginning to be used as justification for increased access to nature in cities (often as a 'Nature prescription') are not as promoted (Carpenter 2013; Root 2017; Klass 2018; Kallen n.d.), possibly due to time and budgetary constraints on the design of these spaces, though they are recognized by the City. For the Rail Park, greenspace is a public good if it reflects the industrial, 'gritty' history of the neighbourhood, is well-maintained and manicured, and isn't too 'designery,' or not reflective of the ethos and culture of the neighbourhood. In both of these cases, greenspace 'improvement' is also a key component of economic revitalization and development (Goldenberg 2019).

For Chicago, the public good benefits from urban greenspace are similar for the *Large Lot* program and Philadelphia's *LandCare* program, both of which focus on the social benefits of 'cleaned and greened' vacant lots and reversing some of the negative social and economic effects of blight. Though Chicago has stormwater programs, namely their *Sustainability Matrix*, which has helped create over 500 green roofs, and their *Green Alley* program (City of Chicago and Chicago Department of Transportation n.d.), the focus for the *Large Lot* program is mainly social and economic – in other words, the aim is empowering vulnerable communities to improve their neighbourhood in ways that they feel are appropriate (within a menu of options set by the city) (LISC Chicago and Latentdesign 2015), rather than prescriptive environmental or restoration goals. Like the vacant land programs in Philadelphia, 'improved' vacant lots often mean signs of order (such as neat lawns) and fences, and resident improvements reflect this 'neat' aesthetic. For The 606, the public benefits focused mainly on providing equitable access to greenspace for areas that did not have much per capita, and on health benefits such as increased opportunities for active transportation, which provided much of the initial funding (Gobster 2019). Like the *Green2015* program and the *Rail Park*, the benefits of The 606 are also strongly linked to increased connectivity to existing parks or amenities (such as the waterfront), and thus closely associated with current urban planning goals around connectivity, access, and high-quality public space (Sustainability Council 2015a).

Despite the variations on what counts as a public good, particularly around aesthetics and social metrics, the case studies above all emphasize the central role that equity, economic stabilization, and health play in their promotion and justification. Thus while urban greenspace has generally been recognized as a public good in the form of parks, explicitly calling out the *lack* of high-quality greenspace through the perspective of public health and equity, and using data on crime, stress, and neighbourhood-level disempowerment and poverty to back it up, shows the increasing influence of a socio-ecological approach to public health and its connection to urban greenspace, as well as the need to include environmental justice in urban greening discourse and policy. The socio-ecological approach, as will be seen below, is in itself a blend of academic research and on-the-ground experience and testing of the efficacy of public health interventions (County Health Rankings 2011; Robert Wood Johnson Foundation n.d.).

The socio-ecological approach to public greenspace

The socio-ecological approach (sometimes called eco-epidemiology (Susser and Susser 1996)) to health recognizes that only a small fraction of an individual's health status comes from genetic factors, and that two-thirds are from community-level factors – or social determinants of health – such as neighbourhood quality and amenities, social support, and easy access to opportunities to be physically active and make healthy food choices (McGinnis, Williams-Russo et al. 2002). This is in profound contrast to the biomedical approach that has dominated ideas of health in the last 50 years. The biomedical approach focuses on individual behaviour change and often defines health in mechanistic terms and in a context- and place-neutral manner (Carpenter 2013; Smith and Reid 2018). In contrast, the socio-ecological approach acknowledges that environmental modification and programmatic changes at a community level have longer-lasting impacts than exhortations for individual change, particularly for vulnerable populations, and are now commonly the backbone of many regional public health assessments (County Health Rankings 2011; McCullough and Leider 2017). This approach has been seen most commonly in public health work on physical activity such as the *Surgeon General's Call to Action for Walkability* (U. S. Department of Health and Human Services 2015) or New York City's *Active Design Guidelines* (City of New York 2010). These policy documents acknowledge the role the built environment plays in levels of physical activity, marking a significant departure from previous recommendations to simply exercise more regardless of barriers to doing so (Frumkin 2003; Williams 2007; Kärmeniemi, Lankila et al. 2018). Similar to the paradigm-shifting work recognizing the impact of car-oriented development on walkability and physical activity by Howard Frumkin and colleagues (Frumkin, Frank et al. 2004), this recognition of the role of the *natural* urban environment in health status seems to be legitimizing long-standing work from many environmental psychologists (see Chapter 1) – formerly dismissed by some as 'subjective' and therefore not 'real science' – on the health and well-being benefits of access to greenspace, which for many years was considered 'nice to have' but was often cut in times of budgetary constraint.

Research to implementation: real-world implications

How this research is used, however, directly influences on-the-ground implementation of small-scale or interstitial urban greening projects. For example, the real-world policy impacts of adopting a socio-ecological approach to urban greenspace initiatives can be seen in three key ways in Chicago and Philadelphia. First, the approach explicitly acknowledges that urban greenspace is both ecological and social (Rupprecht and Byrne 2014; Wang, Tan et al. 2014; Simpson and Bagelman 2018; Kolinjivadi, Van Hecken et al. 2019), a recognition that seems to have particular traction in their policy work on vacant and post-industrial land. Adopting this approach means that any initiatives to address existing or new urban greenspace need to acknowledge the consistent relationship found by researchers between perceived disorder and perceived risk of crime (Wang, Tan et al. 2014; Troy, Nunery et al. 2016). In this frame, greenspace is part of a complex system at both a neighbourhood and city scale that includes social components and issues of access, connectivity, economic stability, and sense of place, which often take primacy over ecological goals. This prioritization can be seen directly in the preferences of *Large Lot* owners who actually removed vegetation that is normally associated with increased property values and psychological restoration, such as large trees, or paving over greenspace in an effort to create a clean, neat, and well-ordered space in the midst of vacancy, uncertainty, and safety concerns. Understanding that aesthetic perceptions of urban greenspace are influenced by social ties, context, and values is in contrast to much dominant research in environmental psychology and in the Nature Rx movement which still often views nature in a somewhat reductionist, neutral manner – i.e. the impact on individual health and well-being can be measured by reducing nature (and the individual's values and socio-economic status) to a mechanistic relationship of exposure and reaction (Carpenter 2013).

Second, the socio-ecological approach can be seen in the explicit recognition by cities that providing urban greenspace in areas that lack them – i.e. providing environmental changes – can have positive impacts on health and well-being. For The 606 this was seen through increased physical activity rates, particularly for vulnerable populations, while for the Rail Park this was seen through increased social interactions and community cohesion. Lastly, Philadelphia's use of census-level statistical data on crime and greenspace supports their continued budgetary and policy backing for greenspace initiatives such as *LandCare*, while enabling more ambitious types of green initiatives to be implemented, such as *Green2015* and *ReBuild*. The influence of the research on crime and greening from Philadelphia's *LandCare* program (among others) can also be seen in the City of Chicago's request for research over time studying the possible positive social benefits of the *Large Lot* program, while the influence of the socio-ecological approach as evidence can be seen in TPL's request for data on increased rates of physical activity from The 606. This shift towards a more nuanced understanding of the impact and benefits of urban greenspace bodes well for the negotiation of the conflicts that are arising from their implementation.

Research and the real-world: opportunities for collaboration and change

How does the use of research outlined above relate to current debates around access to nature, health, well-being, and sense of place? Where does it complement current work, and where is it challenged? What can we learn from both about how new types of urban greening are supporting these goals or have room for improvement?

Complementary work

Some academic work has used the socio-ecological approach to support urban greening initiatives such as the ones outlined above, but much of this research is not yet widely known or adopted in policy circles. For example, new but promising work by Viniece Jennings and colleagues attempts to flesh out the social side of ecosystem services (often called Cultural Ecosystem Services) (Millennial Ecosystem Assessment 2003) and link them to equity and social determinants of health (Jennings, Larson et al. 2016). They argue that ecosystem services are nature-based health amenities, and that while traditionally undervalued in ecosystem services calculations, these 'amenities' are the next frontier in environmental justice and public health. They argue this is particularly important around uneven access and distribution to urban nature, and that this needs to be better integrated into policy and economic calculations. Their approach is compelling because they explicitly link traditional social determinants of health categories such as education, economic stability, neighbourhood context, and health care with the equivalent research on the health benefits of access to nature. For example, they link the idea of spending time in nature (or the Nature Rx mentioned in the Introduction and Chapter 1) with preventative medicine, improved academic and cognitive performance from time in nature with education, and the stress-buffering and social cohesion promotion of nature with social and community determinants of health (Jennings, Larson et al. 2016).

Other researchers have used theories of collective efficacy to explain why 'cleaning and greening,' such as the *Large Lot* and *LandCare* programs, can positively impact communities without being locked into the environmental determinism popular in the 1940s in North America (Judkins, Smith et al. 2008; Wang, Tan et al. 2014; Krusky, Heinze et al. 2015). This type of research looks at how the breakdown of community bonds, accountability, and cohesion, as seen in areas with systematic poverty and unemployment, are influenced by perceived blight, disorder, and lack of care in urban greenspace. They argue that positive examples of care and aesthetic norms of surveillance, seen for example in community gardens or 'improved' vacant lots, help reduce crime and stress through improved collective efficacy and cues to care that signify surveillance and thus deter criminal activity (Wang, Tan et al. 2014; Krusky, Heinze et al. 2015; Troy, Nunery et al. 2016; Branas, South et al. 2018). While differing slightly from older work on the buffering effects of greenspace on stress and anti-social activity from Chicago's now-torn down public housing complexes (Kuo, Bacaicoa et al. 1998; Kuo and Sullivan 2001; Sullivan, Kuo et al. 2004), there are some indications that this explanatory hypothesis is gaining more traction in both academic work (Ward Thompson, Roe et al. 2012; Honold, Lakes et al. 2016; Hazer, Formica et al. 2018) and policy

(PennPraxis 2010). Framing small-scale urban greening as stress-buffering also parallels new work in environmental epigenetics that has shown how persistent environmental stressors can impact the expression of phenotypes for generations, influencing the ability to cope with stress, make decisions, delay gratification, and even process body fat (Crews, Gillette et al. 2012; Guthman and Mansfield 2013; Zucchi, Yao et al. 2013; Lecoutre, Petrus et al. 2018). While such research is not yet common, some researchers are arguing that the impacts of this so-called 'toxic stress' associated with systemic poverty (and often accompanied by a lack of quality nearby greenspace) may be mitigated by access to good-quality, SSUG projects and that this may help to explain the reduction in crime and anti-social behaviour in greened areas (Little 2015; Little and Derr 2018).

The implications of this research around community cohesion and environmental epigenetics are profound. First, they support research showing that stressed-out people tend to seek out nature more often than non-stressed-out people (Stigsdotter and Grahn 2011; Colley, Brown et al. 2017). They also support research on the benefits of access to nature generally: improvements in heart rate variability, the enhancement of mood, reduction in stress, increased self-regulation (Beute and de Kort 2014; Ewert and Chang 2018; Li, Deal et al. 2018; Twohig-Bennett and Jones 2018), residential attachment and satisfaction (Hofmann, Westermann et al. 2012; Knez, Ode Sang et al. 2018; Stewart, Gobster et al. 2019), improved health outcomes (Kondo, Fluehr et al. 2018; Twohig-Bennett and Jones 2018), and levels of physical activity from nearby nature (Korpela, Borodulin et al. 2014; Wolf and Wohlfart 2014; Kondo, Fluehr et al. 2018). These positive benefits of access to nature have been long known but not always supported by policy, especially in the context of tough budgetary decisions. Second, it supports the more traditional idea of nearby urban parks as important for health and social outcomes and the importance of paying attention to the way the body engages in landscape (Cranz 1982; Heft 2010; Cranz, Lindsay et al. 2014; Sinha 2014) – in other words, the research supports the recognition that merely viewing nature passively does not encompass the full interactive lived experience of most urbanites, particularly those whose embodied experience is one of regular vulnerability and threat. This focus on nearby experiences of nature and day-to-day life – seen most clearly in the goals of the new elevated parks such as The 606 and the Rail Park – contrasts with the traditional focus in environmental circles on scenic, un-touched nature preserved outside the city (Foster 2000; Saito 2002; Davison 2008) versus local, interstitial greenspace. Lastly, while not dismissing the valid concerns of those displaced by investment in public greenspace (see below), this type of research might provide more evidence for the need for good-quality greenspace, *particularly* for those most vulnerable to displacement, especially when combined with research showing increased concentration and fascination with greenspace that has better biodiversity and is designed to invite fascination (Loder 2014; Carrus, Scopelliti et al. 2015; Schebella, Weber et al. 2019).

Research that questions current categories and assumptions: what we can learn from it

While the research above aims to generally support urban greening, other newer work challenges the benefits of these small-scale urban greening projects by pointing out the dangers of exclusion, gentrification, and unequal power dynamics they argue are inherent in the design and execution of the projects (Byrne and Wolch 2009; Byrne 2012; Immergluck and Balan 2018; Rigolon and Németh 2018; Simpson and Bagelman 2018). These researchers also examine urban greening as an issue linked to environmental justice but use the lenses of political ecology and community-based natural resources management (CBRM) to examine how communities – and certain groups within these communities – become marginalized and excluded from decisions that impact them, how governance occurs with or without them, and how local knowledge can empower communities (Pearsall 2010; Campbell and Gabriel 2016; Immergluck and Balan 2018; Rigolon and Németh 2018; Loftus 2019). Of particular importance for SSUG projects are the ideas of Wolch et al. (Wolch, Byrne et al. 2014) and Curran and Hamilton (Curran and Hamilton 2012) who argue that because efforts to provide more greenspace to marginalized communities often end up either unused due to exclusionary practices, or pushing out through gentrification the very people they were supposed to help, that SSUG projects should aim for 'just green enough' as a design goal .

This approach argues that remediation of polluted areas to reduce risks to health, rather than health-promotion through restorative, aesthetically pleasing environments (Curran and Hamilton 2012), should be the design goal of these projects. Curran and Hamilton use the example of Newtown Creek in Brooklyn, New York as a case study of how locals rejected a LEED, green, 'upscale' vision for urban greening and instead wanted a less-pretty basic version that respected and reflected the industrial nature of the area, while Wolch et al. cited a Toronto case study where locals wanted productive urban agriculture rather than more ecological 'wilding.' This research approach reflects tensions between the post-industrial spaces and communities that need high-quality small-scale urban greening the most, and economic and cultural forces that can work to exclude them from the very spaces they need. Certainly the design goals of the Rail Park in Philadelphia reflect this concern – even the newer loft residents and artists did not want something that was too 'designer-y' and which would make them feel excluded from their own space, while the older Chinese population wanted low and mid-range housing instead of the park and have agreed to not oppose it, but are not promoting it, either (Goldenberg 2019).

This recognition of the complex social and economic factors that influence perceptions and use of urban greenspace is a direct critique of some of the Nature Rx and environmental psychology research that has been the most influential in municipal policy. While the evidence is solid that contact with nature generally has a positive impact on human health and well-being, nature is not a magic bullet that is immune to social barriers, context, or values (Carpenter 2013), a fact seen in the relatively low use of the High Line by low-income and minority residents even though they are within walking distance of the trail (Bliss 2017), or the paving over or cutting down of mature trees in the *Large Lots* program. Understanding the embodied experience of place – whether this is pleasant and safe or, in the context of many disadvantaged communities, stigmatized, unwelcoming, and unsafe (Byrne 2012; Boyd, White et al. 2018; Romolini, Ryan et al. 2019) – requires a more nuanced and place-based perspective that is often not captured in the psychometric research that is the most influential in municipal policy (Eyles and Williams 2008; Manzo 2008; Relph 2008; Cox, Shanahan et al. 2018). If cities wish to directly address some of the conflicts that are arising out of their urban greenspace investments, or find ways to blend ecological, health, and well-being benefits with social and economic stability goals, including interdisciplinary research that uses a social constructionist or phenomenological approach, which may include work from environmental epigenetics, may help to fill in these gaps.

However, some researchers, while sympathetic to the concerns of equity and exclusion, have argued that lowering the standards for small-scale urban greenspace for marginalized communities – i.e. by doing the 'minimum' instead of well-designed greenspace – only serves to further marginalize them; in other words they don't get to have the high-quality, restorative spaces that they needed in the first place (Gobster 2019). As seen in Chapter 3, urbanites can be sensitive to the amount of effort put into urban greening, and less effort indicates a lack of care, something that these communities already feel. This pitting of poverty and basic needs over health promotion and restoration has shadowed 'green' work for years in both the built and natural urban environments. In other words, it creates a false dichotomy between *either* food and jobs *or* nice amenities like greenspace, when creative thinking, such as that seen with the *Chicago Resilient Corridors* project, can combine both. While there are real problems with equity and exclusion, this can sometimes slip into a 'poor people don't deserve or appreciate nice things' rhetoric, no matter how well-meaning (Loder 2014; Florida 2019; Hamilton and Curran 2019), with serious implications for health and well-being. In addition to the potential to mediate toxic stress through greenspace, as seen throughout this book, there is plenty of evidence that access to nature can help with mood regulation, recovery from stress, and self-control, all issues strongly felt amongst vulnerable populations – in other words, they need high-quality greenspace the most. Lastly, the privileging of social benefits over ecological benefits can put residents' health at risk through a lack of knowledge about the risks that some of these vacant and post-industrial lots can have on public health – such as contaminated soil and impacts on water quality (Wang, Tan et al. 2014).

Lastly, not all researchers view marginal, vacant, and post-industrial land as purely negative, or 'dead' land waiting for economic investment, and they question who benefits from the 'cleaned and greened' spaces, and who is left out. The rise of interest and action around non-traditional urban greenspaces in urban policy has thus also spurred interest from researchers around these spaces (Kamvasinou 2011; American Planning Association 2015; Kim 2016; Gobster, Stewart et al. 2017; Rodriguez 2019). As discussed above, while some researchers have worked closely with city officials to measure positive and negative social, economic, and environmental outcomes of action or inaction around these spaces, many have chosen a different approach, looking instead at the history and valuation of marginal spaces and vacant land, the role of aesthetics, and how these spaces are used and by whom (Jorgensen and Tylecote 2007; Rupprecht and Byrne 2014). Insights from these ways of looking at vacant, post-industrial, and interstitial urban land can both challenge and support the current design of SSUG projects meant to promote ecological and human health goals.

Central to this academic work is the evaluation and historical understanding of what we mean by marginal or vacant land (Jorgensen and Tylecote 2007; Rupprecht and Byrne 2014). In a manner that aligns with the critiques of wilderness examined in Chapter 1, researchers have begun to unpack the assumption that 'vacant' or 'marginal' land is vacant at all, or that it does not play an integral role in the modern city. Focusing more on land that is in the margins of the city versus vacant lots from disinvestment, these researchers question the view that this marginal land is a wasteland in between developed and purposeful urban space – particularly under capitalism's short cycles of creation and ruin. Instead, these researchers argue that this land has historically provided many of the same experiences as wilderness: mystery and fear, complexity and the sublime, and spaces of freedom for those who do not fit easily into established identities and roles – children, youth, thieves, prostitutes, the homeless (Tuan 1979; Jorgensen and Tylecote 2007; Edensor, Evans et al. 2012; DeSilvey and Edensor 2013; Vuscan and Feng 2018). In short, these liminal spaces can provide a more readily available experience of the 'other' of nature than wilderness, particularly in spaces long-overgrown and somewhat wild (Foster 2014).

In their blend of nature taking over human artifacts and the legacy of economic and sometimes cultural ruin, marginal spaces can also represent both resistance to the sometimes overly designed urban planning landscapes of leisure and consumption in which nothing unpredictable is expected to occur, as well as uncomfortable experiences of fear, death, ruin, and decay (Lefebvre 1991; Edensor, Evans et al. 2012; DeSilvey and Edensor 2013; Riley, Perry et al. 2018; Vuscan and Feng 2018). For example, this tension is seen in the desire for the Rail Park not to be too 'designer-y' and aimed at tourists. However, while they can provide spaces of freedom and play for some segments of the population, and children and youth in particular (Edensor, Evans et al. 2012; Gobster 2012; Heatherington 2012), they can also exacerbate feelings of disempowerment and isolation (Wang, Tan et al. 2014), seen with those living next to vacant lots. This might be especially true when residents feel already disempowered and isolated; they desire safety and control, not spaces of freedom and wildness. Understanding this context may help to explain the aesthetic preferences of the residents under study in Chicago, whose improvement of the lot often included reducing otherwise highly valued natural assets like mature trees. It also provides some context for the landscape urbanism movement that views post-industrial relics as opportunities, not liabilities, and which seeks to highlight and transform these relics into monuments for a new way to use and value cities.

Insights and moving forward

What do the case studies above tell us about how cities are approaching urban greening and its impact on health, well-being, and sense of place? How do these case studies accord with or differ from the academic debates described in Chapter 1?

These case studies reflect an approach to urban greening that recognizes equity and health are as important as sustainability for cities, and initiatives are most effective when they blend both goals. The case studies also reflect the reality that cities are having to be somewhat creative in their implementation – both spatially, in existing, interstitial spaces – and as a process, using both academic research and community input to ensure success. This creativity reflects a more tactical urbanist approach to policy change, as well as the recognition of the role that the built and natural environments play in public health and community vitality. While the dominant research being used to justify these projects still comes from more traditional quantitative work – often from environmental psychology – on-the-ground tensions around vacant land and gentrification are forcing social values and economic considerations into the design and goals of these projects. While some of these issues are ones of economic displacement and policy, many of them centre on the values, symbolism, and aesthetics of urban greenspace. What is considered 'wild,' and where? When is wild an ecological benefit that also improves mental health, and when is it a sign of decay, marginalization, and social disorder? What role do these pockets and corridors of greenspace play in re-imagining the city, and for whom? What difference does it make that these projects are interwoven into the fabric of daily life, versus being large park-like expanses in the city?

While there is little evidence that cities are as ready to adopt or use a social constructionist or political ecology understanding of nature – which includes cultural values and power dynamics – as they are statistics from epidemiology or environmental psychology, their recognition of these greened spaces as both social *and* ecological, and the need for integrated community engagement to ensure the success of these projects, reflects a shift towards a more nuanced and adaptive approach to urban greening. This is good news, given the tensions over gentrification from these projects despite the best intentions by those implementing them. The inclusion of mixed methods in some of the projects – such as interviews and focus groups for the *Large Lot* program – is promising in that it has the potential to provide insight into the lived experience of place for those near these urban greening projects. This is particularly important given evidence that contact with nature is not a one-off neutral experience, but ongoing, shifting, and place-based.

We saw in Chapter 3 the impact that quiet watching, seasonal change, and biodiversity can have on mental health and well-being, creativity, and sense of place. Drawing from more diverse academic research and perspectives can offer some insight into why some populations do not use nearby greenspace (Hitchings 2013; Boyd, White et al. 2018), and how greenspace can be designed to engage diverse populations with differing values, experiences, and health states (Heynen 2018; Keith, Larson et al. 2018; Palardy, Boley et al. 2018). This includes place-based work that starts from the understanding that sense of place is a mixture of social, historical, economic, and other factors that create both shared and individual experiences of place (Manzo 2008; Relph 2008; Williams and Patterson 2008). It also includes urban planning work on community, walkability, and sense of place, particularly for those in-between spaces and lived experience (Gobster 2001; Kwan 2018; Stewart, Gobster et al. 2019). Thus while 'clean and green' nature projects are clearly beneficial for community stability and investment, assuming that those are the only benefits to be expected (or aimed for) risks missing opportunities for nuanced mental and emotional health benefits. Further engaging the neighbouring community to understand and co-create how biodiversity and industrial history can influence these spaces is one way to thoughtfully create spaces that address both social and ecological benefits (Rotherham 2012; Tylecote and Dunnett 2012; Finewood, Matsler et al. 2019). This is particularly true for vulnerable populations and transitional areas, given evidence showing the particular needs of the marginalized, vulnerable, and stressed population for restoration. Lastly, understanding the role that biodiversity plays in perceptions of nature in the city, and how this can impact health and creativity outcomes, can help to create spaces that are more engaging, inclusive, and health promoting.

Notes

1 In order to respect individual property owner's privacy results have been aggregated.
2 The 606 is technically a parks and trail network, with the elevated trail line portion formed by The Bloomingdale Trail, which links four existing and two planned at grade parks. The network together is The 606 (Helphand 2019; www.the606.org/resources/frequently-asked-questions).

References

American Planning Association (2015). "2015 Reclaiming Vacant Properties Conference." *Educational Events*. Retrieved May 31, 2019, from www.planning.org/events/eventmulti/3030120.

Anderson, E. C. and E. S. Minor (2017). "Vacant lots: An underexplored resource for ecological and social benefits in cities." *Urban Forestry and Urban Greening* **21**: 146–152. https://doi.org/10.1016/j.ufug.2016.11.015.

Berger, M. W. (2018). "Cleaning up vacant lots makes neighborhoods safer." *Penn Today*, University of Pennsylvania.

Berkshire, M. (Chicago's greening policies update). Interview with A. Loder. 2016.

Beute, F. and Y. A. W. de Kort (2014). "Natural resistance: Exposure to nature and self-regulation, mood, and physiology after ego-depletion." *Journal of Environmental Psychology* **40**(0): 167–178. http://dx.doi.org/10.1016/j.jenvp.2014.06.004.

Bickerdike Redevelopment Corporation and LISC/Chicago's New Communities Program. (2005). *Humboldt Park: Staking Our Claim*. Chicago, IL: L. Chicago.

Bliss, L. (2017). "The High Line's next balancing act." *CityLab*, The Atlantic Monthly Group.

Bonthoux, S., M. Brun, F. Di Pietro, S. Greulich and S. Bouché-Pillon (2014). "How can wastelands promote biodiversity in cities? A review." *Landscape and Urban Planning* **132**(0): 79–88. http://dx.doi.org/10.1016/j.landurbplan.2014.08.010.

Boyd, F., M. P. White, S. L. Bell and J. Burt (2018). "Who doesn't visit natural environments for recreation and why: A population representative analysis of spatial, individual and temporal factors among adults in England." *Landscape and Urban Planning* **175**: 102–113. https://doi.org/10.1016/j.landurbplan.2018.03.016.

Branas, C. C. and J. M. MacDonald (2014). "A simple strategy to transform health, all over the place." *Journal of Public Health Management and Practice* **20**(2): 157–159. doi:10.1097/PHH.0000000000000051.

Branas, C. C., R. A. Cheney, J. M. MacDonald, V. W. Tam, T. D. Jackson and T. R. Ten Have (2011). "A difference-in-differences analysis of health, safety, and greening vacant urban space." *American Journal of Epidemiology* **174**(11). https://doi.org/10.1093/aje%2Fkwr273.

Branas, C. C., E. South, M. C. Kondo, B. C. Hohl, P. Bourgois, D. J. Wiebe and J. M. MacDonald (2018). "Citywide cluster randomized trial to restore blighted vacant land and its effects on violence, crime, and fear." *Proceedings of the National Academy of Sciences* **115**(12): 2946–2951. doi:10.1073/pnas.1718503115.

Briggs, R. (2019). Lobbying war over Philly soda tax still waged by the millions. *WHYY*.

Bucchianeri, G. W., K. C. Gillen and S. M. Wachter (2012). *Valuing the Conversion of Urban Greenspace*. Philadelphia: University of Pennsylvania.

Burnham, D. H., E. H. Bennett and Commercial Club of Chicago (1909). *Plan of Chicago*. Chicago: Commercial Club of Chicago.

Byrne, J. (2012). "When green is White: The cultural politics of race, nature and social exclusion in a Los Angeles urban national park." *Geoforum* **43**(3): 595–611. doi:10.1016/j.geoforum.2011.10.002.

Byrne, J. and J. Wolch (2009). "Nature, race, and parks: Past research and future directions for geographic research." *Progress in Human Geography* **33**(6): 743–765. doi:10.1177/0309132509103156.

Campbell, L. K. and N. Gabriel (2016). "Power in urban socio-ecological systems: Processes and practices of governance and marginalization." *Urban Forestry and Urban Greening*. https://doi.org/10.1016/j.ufug.2016.05.005.

Carpenter, M. (2013). "From 'healthful exercise' to 'nature on prescription': The politics of urban green spaces and walking for health." *Landscape and Urban Planning* **118**(0): 120–127. http://dx.doi.org/10.1016/j.landurbplan.2013.02.009.

Carrus, G., M. Scopelliti, R. Lafortezza, G. Colangelo, F. Ferrini, F. Salbitano, M. Agrimi, L. Portoghesi, P. Semenzato and G. Sanesi (2015). "Go greener, feel better? The positive effects of biodiversity on the well-being of individuals visiting urban and peri-urban green areas." *Landscape and Urban Planning* **134**(0): 221–228. http://dx.doi.org/10.1016/j.landurbplan.2014.10.022.

Center City District (2018). *Callowhill BID Survey: Results – November 2018*. Philadelphia.

Center City District (n.d.). "Rail Park." *CCD Services*. Philadelphia. Retrieved May 26, 2019, from https://centercityphila.org/ccd-services/streetscape/rail-park.

Central Park Conservancy (n.d.). "Park History." Retrieved May 27, 2019, from www.centralparknyc.org/visit/park-history.html.

Chandler, J. (Formerly Project Coordinator, Department of Planning and Development, City of Chicago). Interview with A. Loder. 2019.

Chandler, J. and City of Chicago (Chicago's Large Lot Program). Interview with A. Loder. October 2016, 2019.

Chicago Department of Planning and Development (2014). "Green Healthy Neighborhoods." Chicago: 59.

Chicago Metropolitan Agency for Planning (2016). "Planning for Green and Healthy Chicago Neighborhoods." Chicago.

Chicago Park District (n.d.). "History of Chicago's Park." *About Us*. Retrieved May 27, 2019, from www.chicagoparkdistrict.com/about-us/history-chicagos-park.

City of Chicago (2012). "Sustainable Chicago 2015: Action Agenda." Office of the Mayor. Chicago: 40.

City of Chicago (n.d.). "Campus Parks Program." *Sustainable Development*. Retrieved May 20, 2019, from www.chicago.gov/city/en/depts/dcd/supp_info/campus_park_program.html.

City of Chicago, 100 Resilient Cities Team and Resilient Chicago Steering Committee (2019). "Resilient Chicago: A Plan for Inclusive Growth and a Connected City." Chicago.

City of Chicago and Chicago Department of Transportation (n.d.). "The Chicago Green Alley Handbook: An Action Guide to Create a Greener, Environmentally Sustainable Chicago." Chicago.

City of New York (2010). "Active Design Guidelines: Promoting Physical Activity and Health in Design." New York.

City of Philadelphia (2009). "Greenworks Philadelphia." Mayor Michael A. Nutter. Philadelphia, Mayor Office.

City of Philadelphia (2011). "Citywide Vision: Philadelphia2035." Philadelphia City Planning Commission. Philadelphia.

City of Philadelphia (2016). "Greenworks: A Vision for a Sustainable Philadelphia." Office of Sustainability. Philadelphia: 38.

City of Philadelphia (2019). "Rebuild." Retrieved May 2, 2019, from www.phila.gov/programs/rebuild.

Clemens, D. (2015). "Study: Trees in your neighborhood make you feel richer, younger." *Discovery.com*.

CMAP (2013). "Planning for green and healthy Chicago neighborhoods." *Green Health Neighborhoods*. Retrieved May 20, 2019, from www.cmap.illinois.gov/programs/lta/ghn-chicago.

Cohen, D. A., B. Han, K. P. Derose, S. Williamson, T. Marsh, J. Rudick and T. L. McKenzie (2012). "Neighborhood poverty, park use, and park-based physical activity in a Southern California city." *Social Science and Medicine* **75**(12): 2317–2325. https://doi.org/10.1016/j.socscimed.2012.08.036.

Cohen, M., R. Baudoin, M. Palibrk, N. Persyn and C. Rhein (2012). "Urban biodiversity and social inequalities in built-up cities: New evidences, next questions. The example of Paris, France." *Landscape and Urban Planning* **106**(3): 277–287. http://dx.doi.org/10.1016/j.landurbplan.2012.03.007.

Colley, K., C. Brown and A. Montarzino (2017). "Understanding knowledge workers' interactions with workplace greenspace: Open space use and restoration experiences at urban-fringe business sites." *Environment and Behavior* **49**(3): 314–338. doi:10.1177/0013916516629194.

County Health Rankings (2011). *Our Approach: County Health Rankings and Roadmaps*. Princeton, NJ: Robert Wood Johnson Foundation.

Cox, D. T. C., D. F. Shanahan, H. L. Hudson, R. A. Fuller and K. J. Gaston (2018). "The impact of urbanisation on nature dose and the implications for human health." *Landscape and Urban Planning* **179**: 72–80. https://doi.org/10.1016/j.landurbplan.2018.07.013.

Cranz, G. (1982). *The Politics of Park Design: A History of Urban Parks in America*. Cambridge, MA: MIT Press.

Cranz, G., Georgia Lindsay, Lusi Morhayim and N. Lin (2014). "Communicating sustainability: A postoccupancy evaluation of the David Brower Center." *Environment and Behavior* **46**(7): 826–847. doi:10.1177/0013916513475449.

Crews, D., R. Gillette, S. V. Scarpino, M. Manikkam, M. I. Savenkova and M. K. Skinner (2012). "Epigenetic transgenerational inheritance of altered stress responses." *Proceedings of the National Academy of Sciences* **109**(23): 9143–9148. doi:10.1073/pnas.1118514109.

Curran, W. and T. Hamilton (2012). "Just green enough: Contesting environmental gentrification in Greenpoint, Brooklyn." *Local Environment* **17**(9): 1027–1042. doi:10.1080/13549839.2012.729569.

Davison, A. (2008). "The trouble with nature: Ambivalence in the lives of urban Australian environmentalists." *Geoforum* **39**(3): 1284–1295. https://doi.org/10.1016/j.geoforum.2007.06.011.

DeSilvey, C. and T. Edensor (2013). "Reckoning with ruins." *Progress in Human Geography* **37**(4): 465–485. doi:10.1177/0309132512462271.

Dewar, M., J. Nassauer and E. Dueweke (2013). Cues to care database-codebook. *Unpublished codebook for Detroit Sustainability Indicators Integrated Assessment.* Ann Arbor, University of Michigan Graham Environmental Sustainability Institute: 41.

Dickhut, K. (Deputy Commissioner, Department of Planning and Development, City of Chicago). Interview with A. Loder. 2019.

Econsult Corporation, Penn Institute for Urban Research and May 8 Consulting. (2010). *Vacant Land Management in Philadelphia: The Costs of the Current System and the Benefits of Reform.* Philadelphia: Penn Institute for Urban Research.

Edensor, T., B. Evans, J. Holloway, S. Millington and J. Binnie (2012). "Playing in Industrial Ruins: Interrogating Teleological Understandings of Play in Spaces of Material Alterity and Low Surveillance." *Urban wildscapes.* A. Jorgensen and R. Keenan. London; New York: Routledge: 65–79.

Etchells, A. (2016). "Pop-up beer garden coming to Rail Park." *Philadelphia.*

Ewert, A. and Y. Chang (2018). "Levels of nature and stress response." *Behavioral Sciences* **8**(5): 49. doi:10.3390/bs8050049.

Eyles, J. and A. Williams, Eds. (2008). *Sense of Place, Health, and Quality of Life.* Geography of Health. Burlington, VT: Ashgate.

Finewood, M. H., A. M. Matsler and J. Zivkovich (2019). "Green infrastructure and the hidden politics of urban stormwater governance in a postindustrial city." *Annals of the American Association of Geographers* **109**(3): 909–925. https://doi.org/10.1080/24694452.2018.1507813.

Flint, C. G., I. Kunze, A. Muhar, Y. Yoshida and M. Penker (2013). "Exploring empirical typologies of human–nature relationships and linkages to the ecosystem services concept." *Landscape and Urban Planning* **120**(0): 208–217. http://dx.doi.org/10.1016/j.landurbplan.2013.09.002.

Florida, R. (2019). "The inequality of America's parks and green space." *CityLab.*

Foster, C. (2000). "Restoring Nature in American Culture: An Environmental Aesthetic Perspective." *Restoring Nature: Perspectives from the Social Sciences and Humanities.* P. H. Gobster and R. B. Hull. Washington, D.C.: Island Press: 71–94.

Foster, J. (2014). "Hiding in plain view: Vacancy and prospect in Paris' Petite Ceinture." *Cities* **40, Part B**: 124–132. http://dx.doi.org/10.1016/j.cities.2013.09.002.

Fraser, E. D. G. and W. A. Kenney (2000). "Cultural background and landscape history as factors affecting perceptions of the urban forest." *Journal of Arboriculture* **26**: 106–112.

Friedrich, M. (2017). "The High Line is trolling us." *CityLab.*

Friends of the Bloomingdale Trail (n.d.). "Friends of the Bloomingdale Trail." Retrieved May 26, 2019, from www.bloomingdaletrail.org.

Friends of the Rail Park (n.d.). "The Park." Retrieved May 26, 2019, from www.therailpark.org/the-park.

Frumkin, H. (2003). "Healthy places: Exploring the evidence." *American Journal of Public Health* **93**(9): 1451–1456. doi:10.2105/ajph.93.9.1451.

Frumkin, H., L. Frank and R. Jackson (2004). *Urban Sprawl and Public Health: Designing, Planning, and Building for Healthy Communities.* Washington, D.C.: Island Press.

Garvin, E. C., C. C. Cannuscio and C. C. Branas (2012). "Greening vacant lots to reduce violent crime: A randomised controlled trial." *Injury Prevention.* 10.1136/injuryprev-2012-040439.

Geeting, J. (2015). "What percentage of Philly's land area do the different zoning categories cover?" *PlanPhilly.* Philadelphia.

Gobster, P. H. (2000). "Introduction: Restoring Nature: Human Actions, Interactions, and Reactions." *Restoring Nature: Perspectives from the Social Sciences and Humanities.* P. Gobster and Bruce Hull. Washington, D.C.: Island Press: 1–19.

Gobster, P. H. (2001). "Neighbourhood-open space relationships in metropolitan planning: A look across four scales of concern." *Local Environment* **6**(2): 199–212. https://doi.org/10.1080/13549830120052827.
Gobster, P. H. (2012). "Appreciating Urban Wildscapes: Towards a Natural History of Unnatural Places." *Urban Wildscapes*. A. Jorgensen and R. Keenan. London; New York: Routledge: 33–48.
Gobster, P. H. (2017). *Englewood Selected Changed Properties*. Evanston, IL: U.S.D.A. Forest Service.
Gobster, P. H. (Research Landscape Architect, U.S. Department of Agriculture, U.S Forest Service). Interview with A. Loder. 2019.
Gobster, P. H., S. Hadavi, W. Stewart and A. Rigolon (2019). The Condition-Care Scale: A Useful Tool for Monitoring Improvements in Vacant Lot Stewardship.
Gobster, P. H., J. I. Nassauer, T. C. Daniel and G. Fry (2007). "The shared landscape: What does aesthetics have to do with ecology?" *Landscape Ecology* **22**(7): 959–972. https://doi.org/10.1007/s10980-007-9110-x.
Gobster, P. H., A. Rigolon, S. Hadavi and W. P. Stewart (2019). Beyond Proximity: Extending the "Greening Hypothesis" in the Context of Vacant Lot Stewardship.
Gobster, P. H., S. Sachdeva and G. Lindsey (2017). "Up on The 606:Understanding the use of a new elevated pedestrian and bicycle trail in Chicago, Illinois." *Transportation Research Record: Journal of the Transportation Research Board* **2644**(1): 83–91. doi:10.3141/2644–10.
Gobster, P. H., W. P. Stewart, A. Rigolon, C. Van Riper and D. A. Williams (2018). "Visual resource stewardship at the neighborhood scale: Methods for assessing a vacant land reuse program." *Visual Resource Stewardship Conference Proceedings: Landscape and Seascape Management in a Time of Change*. Paul H. Gobster and Richard C. Smardon. Lemont, IL: U.S. Department of Agriculture, Forest Service, Nothern Research Station.
Gobster, P. H., W. P. Stewart, C. Van Riper and D. Williams (2017). "Visual resource stewardship at the neighborhood scale: Measuring small scale landscape change in response to a vacant land reuse program." *Visual Resource Stewardship Conference*. Argonne, Illinois.
Goldenberg, N. (Former Vice President of Planning, Development, and Research, Executive Director, City Center District Foundation, Center City District, Philadelphia). Interview with A. Loder. 2019.
Guthman, J. and B. Mansfield (2013). "The implications of environmental epigenetics: A new direction for geographic inquiry on health, space, and nature-society relations." *Progress in Human Geography* **37**(4): 486–504. doi:10.1177/0309132512463258.
Hadavi, S., P. H. Gobster, W. Stewart and A. Rigolon (2019). *Repurposing Vacant Lots and Crime Density in Residential Areas: Do Cues to Care Matter?* Oshkosh, WI: International Symposium for Society and Resource Management.
Hamilton, T. and W. Curran (2019). "The dark side of green development – and what cities should do instead." *Fast Company*.
Harris, B. (2018). *The Invisible Walls of The 606: An Examination of the Relationship between an Urban Greenway and Community Change*. Doctor of Philosophy, Clemson University.
Hazer, M., M. K. Formica, S. Dieterlen and C. P. Morley (2018). "The relationship between self-reported exposure to greenspace and human stress in Baltimore, MD." *Landscape and Urban Planning* **169**: 47–56. https://doi.org/10.1016/j.landurbplan.2017.08.006.
Healthy Schools Campaign and Openlands (2016). "About Space to Grow." *Space to Grow Chicago*. Retrieved May 20, 2019, from www.spacetogrowchicago.org/about/about-space-to-grow.
Heatherington, C. (2012). "Buried Narratives." *Urban Wildscapes*. A. Jorgensen and R. Keenan. London; New York: Routledge: 171–186.
Heft, H. (2010). "Affordances and the Perception of Landscape: An Inquiry into Environmental Perception and Aesthetics." *Innovative Approaches to Researching Landscape and Health: Open Spaces: People Space 2*. C. Ward Thompson, P. Aspinall and S. Bell. Abingdon, UK: Routledge.
Helphand, B. (Executive Director, Neighbor-Space.org). Interview with A. Loder. 2019.
Helphand, B. and L. Lawson (2011). "The culture of food and Chicago's Community Gardens." *Site-LINES: A Journal of Place* **6**(2): 6–9.
Heynen, N. (2018). "Urban political ecology III: The feminist and queer century." *Progress in Human Geography* **42**(3): 446–452. doi:10.1177/0309132517693336.
Heynen, N., M. Kaika and E. Syngedouw (2006). *In the Nature of Cities: Urban Political Ecology and the Politics of Urban Metabolism*. New York: Routledge.
Higgins, A. (2014). "New York's High Line: Why the floating promenade is so popular." *The Washington Post*.

Hitchings, R. (2013). "Studying the preoccupations that prevent people from going into green space." *Landscape and Urban Planning* **118**(0): 98–102. http://dx.doi.org/10.1016/j.landurbplan.2012.09.006.

Hofmann, M., J. R. Westermann, I. Kowarik and E. van der Meer (2012). "Perceptions of parks and urban derelict land by landscape planners and residents." *Urban Forestry and Urban Greening* **11**(3): 303–312. http://dx.doi.org/10.1016/j.ufug.2012.04.001.

Honold, J., T. Lakes, R. Beyer and E. van der Meer (2016). "Restoration in urban spaces: Nature views from home, greenways, and public parks." *Environment and Behavior* **48**(6): 796–825. doi:10.1177/0013916514568556.

Hunter, M. (2015). *Developing Design Guidelines for Urban Spaces in Support of Mental Wellbeing Using Theoretical Frameworks from Environmental Psychology and Aesthetics.* Los Angeles: Environmental Design and Research Association.

Hunter, M. C. R. and D. G. Brown (2012). "Spatial contagion: Gardening along the street in residential neighborhoods." *Landscape and Urban Planning* **105**(4): 407–416. http://dx.doi.org/10.1016/j.landurbplan.2012.01.013.

Hur, M. and J. L. Nasar (2014). "Physical upkeep, perceived upkeep, fear of crime and neighborhood satisfaction." *Journal of Environmental Psychology* **38**: 186–194. http://dx.doi.org/10.1016/j.jenvp.2014.02.001.

Immergluck, D. and T. Balan (2018). "Sustainable for whom? Green urban development, environmental gentrification, and the Atlanta Beltline." *Urban Geography* **39**(4): 546–562. doi:10.1080/02723638.2017.1360041.

Institute for Housing Studies at DePaul University, G. Smith, S. Duda, J. M. Lee and M. Thompson. (2016). *Measuring the Impact of The 606: Understanding How a Large Public Investment Impacted the Surrounding Housing Market.* Chicago.

Jennings, V., M. H. E. M. Browning and A. Rigolon (2019). "Urban Green Space at the Nexus of Environmental Justice and Health Equity." *Urban Green Spaces: Public Health and Sustainability in the United States.* Cham: Springer International Publishing: 47–69.

Jennings, V., L. Larson and J. Yun (2016). "Advancing sustainability through urban green space: Cultural ecosystem services, equity, and social determinants of health." *International Journal of Environmental Research and Public Health* **13**(196): 1–15. doi:10.3390/ijerph13020196.

Jiang, B., C.-Y. Chang and W. C. Sullivan (2014). "A dose of nature: Tree cover, stress reduction, and gender differences." *Landscape and Urban Planning* **132**(0): 26–36. http://dx.doi.org/10.1016/j.landurbplan.2014.08.005.

Jorgensen, A. and M. Tylecote (2007). "Ambivalent landscapes: Wilderness in the urban interstices." *Landscape Research* **32**(4): 443–462. doi:10.1080/01426390701449802.

Judkins, G., M. Smith and E. Keys (2008). "Determinism within Human-Environment Research And The Rediscovery Of Environmental Causation." *The Geographical Journal* **174**(1): 17–29. https://doi.org/10.1111/j.1475-4959.2008.00265.x.

Junker, B. and M. Buchecker (2008). "Aesthetic preferences versus ecological objectives in river restorations." *Landscape and Urban Planning* **85**(3): 141–154. https://doi.org/10.1016/j.landurbplan.2007.11.002

Kaczynski, A. T., L. R. Potwarka, B. J. A. Smale and M. E. Havitz (2009). "Association of parkland proximity with neighbourhood and park based physical activity: Variations by gender and age." *Leisure Sciences* **31**: 174–191. https://doi.org/10.1080/01490400802686045.

Kaika, M. (2006). "The Political Ecology of Water Scarcity: The 1989–1991 Athenian Drought." *In the Nature of Cities: Urban Political Ecology and the Politics of Urban Metabolism.* N. Heynen, M. Kaika and E. Syngedouw. New York: Routledge: 157–172.

Kallen, C. (n.d.). "NaturePHL bringing 'nature prescriptions' to local doctors' offices." *Family Focus Media.* Philadelphia.

Kamvasinou, K. (2011). "The public value of vacant urban land." *Proceedings of the Institution of Civil Engineers – Municipal Engineer* **164**(3): 157–166. doi:10.1680/muen.9.00020.

Kardan, O., P. Gozdyra, B. Misic, F. Moola, L. J. Palmer, T. Paus and M. G. Berman (2015). "Neighborhood greenspace and health in a large urban center." *Scientific Reports* **5**: 11610. doi:10.1038/srep11610.

Kärmeniemi, M., T. Lankila, T. Ikäheimo, H. Koivumaa-Honkanen and R. Korpelainen (2018). "The built environment as a determinant of physical activity: A systematic review of longitudinal studies and natural experiments." *Annals of Behavioral Medicine* **52**(3): 239–251. doi:10.1093/abm/kax043.

Keith, S. J., L. R. Larson, C. S. Shafer, J. C. Hallo and M. Fernandez (2018). "Greenway use and preferences in diverse urban communities: Implications for trail design and management." *Landscape and Urban Planning* **172**: 47–59. https://doi.org/10.1016/j.landurbplan.2017.12.007.

Kim, G. (2016). "The public value of urban vacant land: Social responses and ecological value." *Sustainability* **8**(5): 486. https://doi.org/10.3390/su8050486.

Kim, G., P. A. Miller and D. J. Nowak (2018). "Urban vacant land typology: A tool for managing urban vacant land." *Sustainable Cities and Society* **36**: 144–156. https://doi.org/10.1016/j.scs.2017.09.014.

King, D. K., J. Litt, J. Hale, K. M. Burniece and C. Ross (2015). "'The park a tree built': Evaluating how a park development project impacted where people play." *Urban Forestry and Urban Greening* **14**(2): 293–299. http://dx.doi.org/10.1016/j.ufug.2015.02.011.

Klass, P. (2018). "Writing prescription to play outdoors." *The New York Times*.

Klein, M. (2016). "Early look: PHS's Viaduct Rail Park pop-up beer garden." *The Philadelphia Inquirer*.

Knez, I., Å. Ode Sang, B. Gunnarsson and M. Hedblom (2018). "Wellbeing in urban greenery: The role of naturalness and place identity." *Frontiers in Psychology* **9**(491). doi:10.3389/fpsyg.2018.00491.

Kolinjivadi, V., G. Van Hecken, D. V. Almeida, J. Dupras and N. Kosoy (2019). "Neoliberal performatives and the 'making' of Payments for Ecosystem Services (PES)." *Progress in Human Geography* **43**(1): 3–25. doi:10.1177/0309132517735707.

Kondo, M. C., J. M. Fluehr, T. McKeon and C. C. Branas (2018). "Urban green space and its impact on human health." *International Journal of Environmental Research and Public Health* **15**(3): 445. doi:10.3390/ijerph15030445.

Kondo, M. C., D. Keene, B. C. Hohl, J. M. MacDonald and C. Branas (2015). "A difference-in-differences study of the effects of a new abandoned building remediation strategy on safety." *PLoS one* **10**(7). https://doi.org/10.1371/journal.pone.0129582.

Korpela, K. M., K. Borodulin, M. Neuvonen, O. Paronen and L. Tyrväinen (2014). "Analyzing the mediators between nature-based outdoor recreation and emotional well-being." *Journal of Environmental Psychology* **37**: 1–7. http://dx.doi.org/10.1016/j.jenvp.2013.11.003.

Kreeger, K. (2011). "More green, less crime: Rehabilitating vacant lots improves urban health and safety, Penn study finds." *Penn Medicine News*. Philadelphia.

Krusky, A. M., J. E. Heinze, T. M. Reischl, S. M. Aiyer, S. P. Franzen and M. A. Zimmerman (2015). "The effects of produce gardens on neighborhoods: A test of the greening hypothesis in a post-industrial city." *Landscape and Urban Planning* **136**: 68–75. https://doi.org/10.1016/j.landurbplan.2014.12.003.

Kuo, F. E., M. Bacaicoa and W. C. Sullivan (1998). "Transforming inner-city landscapes: Trees, sense of safety, and preference." *Environment and Behaviour* **30**(1): 28–59. https://doi.org/10.1177/0013916598301002.

Kuo, F. E. and W. C. Sullivan (2001). "Aggression and violence in the inner city: Effects of environment via mental fatigue." *Environment and Behaviour* **33**(4): 543–573. https://doi.org/10.1177/00139160121973124.

Kwan, M.-P. (2018). "The limits of the neighborhood effect: Contextual uncertainties in geographic, environmental health, and social science research." *Annals of the American Association of Geographers* **108**(6): 1482–1490. doi:10.1080/24694452.2018.1453777.

Lecoutre, S., P. Petrus, M. Rydén and C. Breton (2018). "Transgenerational epigenetic mechanisms in adipose tissue development." *Trends in Endocrinology and Metabolism* **29**(10): 675–685. doi:10.1016/j.tem.2018.07.004.

Lefebvre, H. (1991). *The Production of Space*. Oxford: Blackwell.

Levy, P. 2019. "Chief Executive Officer, Center City District." Interview with A. Loder, May 17.

Li, D., B. Deal, X. Zhou, M. Slavenas and W. C. Sullivan (2018). "Moving beyond the neighborhood: Daily exposure to nature and adolescents' mood." *Landscape and Urban Planning* **173**: 33–43. https://doi.org/10.1016/j.landurbplan.2018.01.009.

Li, X., C. Zhang, W. Li, R. Ricard, Q. Meng and W. Zhang (2015). "Assessing street-level urban greenery using Google Street View and a modified green view index." *Urban Forestry and Urban Greening* **14**(3): 675–685. https://doi.org/10.1016/j.ufug.2015.06.006.

Lindal, P. J. and T. Hartig (2015). "Effects of urban street vegetation on judgments of restoration likelihood." *Urban Forestry and Urban Greening* **14**(2): 200–209. http://dx.doi.org/10.1016/j.ufug.2015.02.001.

Lindsey, G., Y. Qi, P. H. Gobster and S. Sachdeva (2019). *The 606 at three: Trends in use of Chicago's elevated Rail-Trail*. Fábos Conference on Landscape and Greenway Planning.

LISC Chicago (n.d.). "What is LISC Chicago?" Retrieved May 26, 2019, from www.lisc.org/chicago.

LISC Chicago and Latentdesign (2015). *Chicago Large Lots Activation Guide*. City of Chicago.

Little, S. (2015). *The Work of Gilbert Gottlieb: A Framework for the Integration of Neuroscience into Design*. brainSTORM: Dynamic Interactions of Environment-Behavior and Neuroscience. Los Angeles: The Environmental Design Research Association.

Little, S. and V. Derr (2018). "The Influence of Nature on a Child's Development: Connecting the Outcomes of Human Attachment and Place Attachment." *Research Handbook on Childhood Nature: Assemblages of Childhood and Nature Research*. A. Cutter-Mackenzie, K. Malone and E. Barratt Hacking. Cham: Springer International Publishing.

Loder, A. (2014). "'There's a meadow outside my workplace': A phenomenological exploration of aesthetics and green roofs in Chicago and Toronto." *Landscape and Urban Planning* **126**: 94–106. https://doi.org/10.1016/j.landurbplan.2014.01.008.

Loftus, A. (2019). "Political ecology I: Where is political ecology?" *Progress in Human Geography* **43**(1): 172–182. doi:10.1177/0309132517734338.

Logan Square Neighborhood Association and LISC/Chicago's New Communities Program. (2005). *Logan Square: A Place to Stay, a Place to Grow*. Chicago, IL: L. Chicago.

Lovell, K. O. (Commissioner, Philadelphia Parks and Recreation). Interview with A. Loder. 2019.

Lydon, M. and A. Garcia (2015). *Tactical Urbanism: Short-term Action for Long-term Change*. Washington, D.C.: Island Press.

Madhani, A. (2017). "As cities look to get greener, lower-income residents fear gentrification." *USA Today*.

Manzo, L. C. (2008). "The Experience of Displacement on Sense of Place and Well-being." *Sense of Place, Health and Quality of Life*. J. Eyles and A. Williams. London: Routledge.

Marco, M., E. Gracia, M. Martín-Fernández and A. López-Quílez (2017). "Validation of a Google Street View-based neighborhood disorder observational scale." *Journal of Urban Health* **94**(2): 190–198. doi:10.1007/s11524-017-0134-5.

Mårtensson, F., M. Jansson, M. Johansson, A. Raustorp, M. Kylin and C. Boldemann (2014). "The role of greenery for physical activity play at school grounds." *Urban Forestry and Urban Greening* **13**(1): 103–113. http://dx.doi.org/10.1016/j.ufug.2013.10.003.

Mayor's Press Office (2016). "Mayor Emanuel announces building on Burnham, a comprehensive strategy to invest in Chicago's waterfronts, parks and neighborhoods." City of Chicago.

Mayor's Press Office and Chicago (2017). "Mayor Emanuel announces Millennium Park is now the #1 attraction in the Midwest and among the top 10 most-visited sites in the U.S." City of Chicago.

McCullough, J. M. and J. P. Leider (2017). "Associations between county wealth, health and social services spending, and health outcomes." *American Journal of Preventive Medicine* **53**(5): 592–598. doi:10.1016/j.amepre.2017.05.005.

McGinnis, J. M., P. Williams-Russo and J. R. Knickman (2002). "The case for more active policy attention to health promotion." *Health Affairs* **21**(2): 78–93. doi:10.1377/hlthaff.21.2.78.

Meier, F. and D. Scherer (2012). "Spatial and temporal variability of urban tree canopy temperature during summer 2010 in Berlin, Germany." *Theoretical and Applied Climatology* **110**(3): 373–384. doi:10.1007/s00704-012-0631-0.

Millennial Ecosystem Assessment (2003). Washington, D.C.: Island Press.

Milroy, E. (2016). "Public Parks (Philadelphia)." *The Encyclopedia of Greater Philadelphia*. Rutgers University.

Moore, L. V., A. V. Diez Roux, K. R. Evenson, A. P. McGinn and S. J. Brines (2008). "Availability of recreational resources in minority and low socioeconomic status areas." *American Journal of Preventive Medicine* **34**(1): 16–22. doi:10.1016/j.amepre.2007.09.021.

Moyer, R., J. M. MacDonald, G. Ridgeway and C. C. Branas (2019). "Effect of remediating blighted vacant land on shootings: A citywide cluster randomized trial." *American Journal of Public Health* **109**(1): 140–144. doi:10.2105/ajph.2018.304752.

Müller, A., P. K. Bøcher, C. Fischer and J.-C. Svenning (2018). "'Wild' in the city context: Do relative wild areas offer opportunities for urban biodiversity?" *Landscape and Urban Planning* **170**: 256–265. https://doi.org/10.1016/j.landurbplan.2017.09.027.

Naik, N., J. Philipoom, R. Raskar and C. Hidalgo (2014). *Streetscore: Predicting the Perceived Safety of One Million Streetscapes*. 2014 IEEE Conference on Computer Vision and Pattern Recognition Workshops.

Nassauer, J. (1995). "Messy ecosystems, orderly frames." *Landscape Journal* **14**(2): 161–170. doi:10.3368/lj.14.2.161.

Nassauer, J. I. (2011). "Care and stewardship: From home to planet." *Landscape and Urban Planning* **100**(4): 321–323. https://doi.org/10.1016/j.landurbplan.2011.02.022.

Nassauer, J. I., Z. Wang and E. Dayrell (2009). "What will the neighbors think? Cultural norms and ecological design." *Landscape and Urban Planning* **92**(3): 282–292. https://doi.org/10.1016/j.landurbplan.2009.05.010.

Noon, J. (Strategic Partnerships Supervisor, Green Stormwater Infrastructure Unit, Philadelphia Water Department). Interview with A. Loder. 2019.

NYC The Official Guide. (n.d.). "The High Line." *Attractions*. Retrieved May 26, 2019, from www.nycgo.com/attractions/the-high-line.

Ortega, J. S. (Vice President, Chief of Programs, Pennslyvania Horticultural Society). Interview with A. Loder. 2019.

Palantino, A. (Deputy Commissioner, Philadelphia Parks & Recreation). Interview with A. Loder. 2019.

Palardy, N. P., B. B. Boley and C. J. Gaither (2018). "Resident support for urban greenways across diverse neighborhoods: Comparing two Atlanta BeltLine segments." *Landscape and Urban Planning* **180**: 223–233. https://doi.org/10.1016/j.landurbplan.2018.08.021.

Pearsall, H. (2010). "From brown to green? Assessing social vulnerability to environmental gentrification in New York City." *Environment and Planning C* **28**(5): 872–886. https://doi.org/10.1068/c08126.

Pearsall, H., S. Lucas and J. Lenhardt (2014). "The contested nature of vacant land in Philadelphia and approaches for resolving competing objectives for redevelopment." *Cities* **40, Part B**: 163–174. http://dx.doi.org/10.1016/j.cities.2013.04.008.

Peckham, S. C., P. N. Duinker and C. Ordóñez (2013). "Urban forest values in Canada: Views of citizens in Calgary and Halifax." *Urban Forestry and Urban Greening* **12**(2): 154–162. http://dx.doi.org/10.1016/j.ufug.2013.01.001.

PennPraxis (2010). *Green2015: An Action Plan for the First 500 Acres*. Philadelphia Parks and Recreation, City of Philadelphia: 144.

Pennsylvania Horticultural Society (n.d.-a). "LandCare Program." Retrieved May 25, 2019, from https://phsonline.org/programs/landcare-program.

Pennsylvania Horticultural Society (n.d.-b). "Roots to Re-entry." https://phsonline.org/programs/roots-to-re-entry.

Philadelphia Water (n.d.). Heston Garden. P. W. Department. Philadelphia, City of Philadelphia.

Philadelphia Water Department (2011). *Amended – Green City Clean Waters – The City of Philadelphia's Program for Combined Sewer Overflow Control – Program Summary*. Philadelphia.

Philadelphia Water Department (2015). "Philadelphia Water Department Water and Drainage History Course, Module 6: The Consolidated City and Water Pollution: Filtration is the Solution, 1854–1914." *Fairmont Water Works*. Retrieved May 25, 2019, from http://phillyh2o.org/canvas/canvas06.htm.

Powell, L. M., S. Slater and F. J. Chaloupka (2004). "The relationship between community physical activity settings and race, ethnicity and socioeconomic status." *Evidence-Based Preventive Medicine* **1**(2): 135–144.

Qiu, L., S. Lindberg and A. B. Nielsen (2013). "Is biodiversity attractive? On-site perception of recreational and biodiversity values in urban green space." *Landscape and Urban Planning* **119**(0): 136–146. http://dx.doi.org/10.1016/j.landurbplan.2013.07.007.

Reinhold, B. (2018). *Architecture of Life: Biophilic Urban Acupunture for Downtown Seattle*. Master of Architecture, University of Washington.

Relph, E. (2008). "Senses of Place and Emerging Social and Environmental Challenges." *Sense of Place, Health and Quality of Life*. J. Eyles and A. Williams. Aldershot, Hampshire: Ashgate.

Rigolon, A. and J. Németh (2018). "'We're not in the business of housing': Environmental gentrification and the nonprofitization of green infrastructure projects." *Cities* **81**: 71–80. https://doi.org/10.1016/j.cities.2018.03.016.

Riley, C. B., K. I. Perry, K. Ard and M. M. Gardiner (2018). "Asset or liability? Ecological and sociological tradeoffs of urban spontaneous vegetation on vacant land in shrinking cities." *Sustainability* **10**(7): 2139. https://doi.org/10.3390/su10072139.

Robert Wood Johnson Foundation (n.d.). "Research, evaluation and learning." *How We Work*. Retrieved June 1, 2019, from www.rwjf.org/en/how-we-work/rel.html.

Rodkin, D. (2018). "Was gentrification around The 606 inevitable?" *Crain's Chicago Business*. Chicago.

Rodriguez, L. M. (2019). "Vacant land stewardship." *The Stewardship Network*. East Lansing.

Romolini, M., R. L. Ryan, E. R. Simso and E. G. Strauss (2019). "Visitors' attachment to urban parks in Los Angeles, CA." *Urban Forestry and Urban Greening* **41**: 118–126. https://doi.org/10.1016/j.ufug.2019.03.015.

Root, T. (2017). "Doctors are Prescribing Park Visits to Boost Patient Health." *National Geographic*, National Geographic Society.

Rotenberk, L. (2015). "In Chicago, parks are on the upswing." Grist.org.

Rotherham, I. D. (2012). "The River Don as a Linear Urban Wildscape." *Urban Wildscapes*. A. Jorgensen and R. Keenan. London; New York: Routledge.

Rupprecht, C. D. D. and J. A. Byrne (2014). "Informal urban greenspace: A typology and trilingual systematic review of its role for urban residents and trends in the literature." *Urban Forestry and Urban Greening* **13**(4): 597–611. http://dx.doi.org/10.1016/j.ufug.2014.09.002.

Rupprecht, C. D. D. and J. A. Byrne (2018). "Informal Urban Green Space as Anti-Gentrification Strategy?" *Just Green Enough*: 209–226. doi:10.9774/GLEAF.9781315229515_16.

Saito, Y. (2002). "Scenic national landscapes: Common themes in Japan and the United States." *Essays in Philosophy* **3**(1): article 5.

Saval, N. (2016). "Uncommon ground." *New York Times Magazine*: 73–77.

Schebella, M. F., D. Weber, L. Schultz and P. Weinstein (2019). "The wellbeing benefits associated with perceived and measured biodiversity in Australian urban green spaces." *Sustainability* **11**(3): 802. doi:10.3390/su11030802.

Schmidt, G. (2019). "Bringing nature back to the urban core." *The New York Times*.

Schutte, A. R., J. C. Torquati and H. L. Beattie (2017). "Impact of urban nature on executive functioning in early and middle childhood." *Environment and Behavior* **49**(1): 3–30. doi:10.1177/0013916515603095.

Sheu, S. (Community Engagement and Programs Manager, Friends of the Rail Park.) Interview with A. Loder. May 22, 2019.

Simone, J. (Former Program Director, Urban Parks Program, John W. Baird Fellow for Urban Conservation, Trust for Public Land). Interview with A. Loder. 2016.

Simpson, M. and J. Bagelman (2018). "Decolonizing urban political ecologies: The production of nature in settler colonial cities." *Annals of the American Association of Geographers* **108**(2): 558–568. doi:10.1080/24694452.2017.1392285.

Sinha, A. (2014). "Slow landscapes of elevated linear parks: Bloomingdale Trail in Chicago." *Studies in the History of Gardens and Designed Landscapes* **34**(2): 113–122. doi:10.1080/14601176.2013.830428.

Smith, T. S. J. and L. Reid (2018). "Which 'being' in wellbeing? Ontology, wellness and the geographies of happiness." *Progress in Human Geography* **42**(6): 807–829. doi:10.1177/0309132517717100.

Soga, M. and K. J. Gaston (2016). "Extinction of experience: The loss of human–nature interactions." *Frontiers in Ecology and the Environment* **14**(2): 94–101. doi:10.1002/fee.1225.

South, E. C., B. C. Hohl, M. C. Kondo, J. M. MacDonald and C. C. Branas (2018). "Effect of greening vacant land on mental health of community-dwelling adults: A cluster randomized trial." *JAMA Network Open* **1**(3): e180298–e180298. doi:10.1001/jamanetworkopen.2018.0298.

Stewart, W. (2016). *Chicago's Large Lot Research Update for the City of Chicago: Interim Findings*. Champaign, IL: University of Illinois at Urbana Champaign.

Stewart, W. P., P. H. Gobster, A. Rigolon, J. Strauser, D. A. Williams and C. J. van Riper (2019). "Resident-led beautification of vacant lots that connects place to community." *Landscape and Urban Planning* **185**: 200–209. https://doi.org/10.1016/j.landurbplan.2019.02.011.

Stigsdotter, U. K. and P. Grahn (2011). "Stressed individuals' preferences for activities and environmental characteristics in green spaces." *Urban Forestry and Urban Greening* **10**(4): 295–304. http://dx.doi.org/10.1016/j.ufug.2011.07.001.

Studio Bryan Hanes (n.d.). "The Rail Park Phase I." Retrieved May 26, 2019, from www.studiobryanhanes.com/work#/railpark.

Su, J. G., P. Dadvand, M. J. Nieuwenhuijsen, X. Bartoll and M. Jerrett (2019). "Associations of green space metrics with health and behavior outcomes at different buffer sizes and remote sensing sensor resolutions." *Environment International* **126**: 162–170. https://doi.org/10.1016/j.envint.2019.02.008.

Sullivan, W. C., F. E. Kuo and S. F. DePooter (2004). "The fruit of urban nature: Vital neighborhood spaces." *Environment and Behavior* **36**(5): 678–700. https://doi.org/10.1177/0193841X04264945.

Susser, M. and E. Susser (1996). "Choosing a future for epidemiology: II. From black box to Chinese boxes and eco-epidemiology." *American Journal of Public Health* **86**(5): 674–677. doi:10.2105/ajph.86.5.674.

Sustainability Council and City of Chicago (2014). *2015 Sustainable Chicago: Action Agenda Year Two Progress Report Fall 2014*. Chicago.

Sustainability Council, City of Chicago (2015a). *2015 Sustainable Chicago Action Agenda*. Chicago: 39.

Sustainability Council, City of Chicago (2015b). *2015 Sustainable Chicago: Action Agenda 2012–2015. Highlights and Look Ahead.* Chicago.

Tanenbaum, M. (2018). "Philadelphia releases searchable database for public to track soda tax revenue, spending." *PhillyVoice.*

Taylor, J. R. and S. T. Lovell (2012). "Mapping public and private spaces of urban agriculture in Chicago through the analysis of high-resolution aerial images in Google Earth." *Landscape and Urban Planning* **108**(1): 57–70. https://doi.org/10.1016/j.landurbplan.2012.08.001.

The 606 (n.d.). "Partners." *About.* Retrieved June 13, 2019, from www.the606.org/about/partners.

The Center for High Impact Philanthropy (2013). *Aligning Impact for Healthy Communities: Q&A with the Pennsylvania Horticultural Society.* Philadelphia: University of Pennsylvania.

The Fairmount Park Conservancy (n.d.). "History." *Who We Are.* Retrieved May 27, 2019, from https://myphillypark.org/who-we-are/history.

The Trust For Public Land (n.d.-a). "Climate-smart cities." *How We Work.* Retrieved May 26, 2019, from www.tpl.org/how-we-work/climate-smart-cities.

The Trust For Public Land (n.d.-b). "Our story." *About.* Retrieved May 26, 2019, from www.the606.org/about/story.

Thompson, J. (2015). "Chicago's new high line is 'more than an elevated park'." *The Guardian.*

Troy, A., J. Morgan Grove and J. O'Neil-Dunne (2012). "The relationship between tree canopy and crime rates across an urban–rural gradient in the greater Baltimore region." *Landscape and Urban Planning* **106**(3): 262–270. http://dx.doi.org/10.1016/j.landurbplan.2012.03.010.

Troy, A., A. Nunery and J. M. Grove (2016). "The relationship between residential yard management and neighborhood crime: An analysis from Baltimore City and County." *Landscape and Urban Planning* **147**: 78–87. https://doi.org/10.1016/j.landurbplan.2015.11.004.

Tsai, W.-L., M. R. McHale, V. Jennings, O. Marquet, J. A. Hipp, Y.-F. Leung and M. F. Floyd (2018). "Relationships between characteristics of urban green land cover and mental health in U.S. metropolitan areas." *International Journal of Environmental Research and Public Health* **15**(2): 340. doi:10.3390/ijerph15020340.

Tuan, Y.-F. (1979). *Landscapes of Fear.* Minneapolis, MN: University of Minnesota Press.

Twerd, L. and W. Banaszak-Cibicka (2019). "Wastelands: Their attractiveness and importance for preserving the diversity of wild bees in urban areas." *Journal of Insect Conservation* **23**(3): 573–588. doi:10.1007/s10841-019-00148-8.

Twohig-Bennett, C. and A. Jones (2018). "The health benefits of the great outdoors: A systematic review and meta-analysis of greenspace exposure and health outcomes." *Environmental Research* **166**: 628–637. https://doi.org/10.1016/j.envres.2018.06.030.

Tylecote, M. and N. Dunnett (2012). "Enhancing Ruderal Perennials in Manor Fields Park, Sheffield: A New Park on the 'Bandit Lands' of Urban Green Space Dereliction." *Urban Wildscapes.* A. Jorgensen and R. Keenan. London; New York: Routledge.

U.S. Department of Health and Human Services (2015). *Step it Up! The Surgeon General's Call to Action to Promote Walking and Walkable Communities.* U.S. Department of Health and Human Services and Office of the Surgeon General. Washington, D.C.: 59.

Unt, A.-L. and S. Bell (2014). "The impact of small-scale design interventions on the behaviour patterns of the users of an urban wasteland." *Urban Forestry and Urban Greening* **13**(1): 121–135. http://dx.doi.org/10.1016/j.ufug.2013.10.008.

Uren, H. V., P. L. Dzidic and B. J. Bishop (2015). "Exploring social and cultural norms to promote ecologically sensitive residential garden design." *Landscape and Urban Planning* **137**(0): 76–84. http://dx.doi.org/10.1016/j.landurbplan.2014.12.008.

van den Berg, A. E., A. Jorgensen and E. R. Wilson (2014). "Evaluating restoration in urban green spaces: Does setting type make a difference?" *Landscape and Urban Planning* **127**(0): 173–181. http://dx.doi.org/10.1016/j.landurbplan.2014.04.012.

van Dijk-Wesselius, J. E., J. Maas, D. Hovinga, M. van Vugt and A. E. van den Berg (2018). "The impact of greening schoolyards on the appreciation, and physical, cognitive and social-emotional well-being of schoolchildren: A prospective intervention study." *Landscape and Urban Planning* **180**: 15–26. https://doi.org/10.1016/j.landurbplan.2018.08.003.

Vuscan, I. S. and S. Feng (2018). "Civilized enclaves of wilderness: Substitutes for an alienated urban nature." *IOP Conference Series: Materials Science and Engineering* **399**: 012053. doi:10.1088/1757–899x/399/1/012053.

Walker, J. (2015). *Biophilic Urban Acupuncture: The Importance of Biophilia in Urban Places*. Terrapin Bright Green.

Walljasper, J. (2017). "Philly's campaign to spread prosperity to all corners of the city." *HuffPost*.

Wang, Z., P. Y. Tan, T. Zhang and J. I. Nassauer (2014). "Perspectives on narrowing the action gap between landscape science and metropolitan governance: Practice in the US and China." *Landscape and Urban Planning* **125**(0): 329–334. http://dx.doi.org/10.1016/j.landurbplan.2014.01.024.

Ward Thompson, C. (2002). "Urban open space in the 21st century." *Landscape and Urban Planning* **60**: 59–72. https://doi.org/10.1016/S0169-2046(02)00059-2.

Ward Thompson, C., J. Roe, P. Aspinall, R. Mitchell, A. Clow and D. Miller (2012). "More green space is linked to less stress in deprived communities: Evidence from salivary cortisol patterns." *Landscape and Urban Planning* **105**(3): 221–229. http://dx.doi.org/10.1016/j.landurbplan.2011.12.015.

Williams, C. H. (2007). *The Built Environment and Physical Activity: What is the Relationship?* Princeton: T. R. W. J. Foundation.

Williams, D. R. and M. E. Patterson (2008). "Place, Leisure, and Well-Being." *Sense of Place, Health, and Quality of Life*. J. Eyles and A. Williams. Aldershot, UK: Ashgate: 105–119.

WLS-TV Chicago (2016). "City of Chicago selling more than 4K vacant lots for $1." *ABC 7 Eyewitness News*. Chicago.

Wolch, J. R., J. Byrne and J. P. Newell (2014). "Urban green space, public health, and environmental justice: The challenge of making cities 'just green enough'." *Landscape and Urban Planning* **125**(0): 234–244. http://dx.doi.org/10.1016/j.landurbplan.2014.01.017.

Wolf, I. D. and T. Wohlfart (2014). "Walking, hiking and running in parks: A multidisciplinary assessment of health and well-being benefits." *Landscape and Urban Planning* **130**(0): 89–103. http://dx.doi.org/10.1016/j.landurbplan.2014.06.006.

Wolfe, M. K. and J. Mennis (2012). "Does vegetation encourage or suppress urban crime? Evidence from Philadelphia, PA." *Landscape and Urban Planning* **108**(2–4): 112–122. http://dx.doi.org/10.1016/j.landurbplan.2012.08.006.

Wood, E., A. Harsant, M. Dallimer, A. Cronin de Chavez, R. R. C. McEachan and C. Hassall (2018). "Not all green space is created equal: Biodiversity predicts psychological restorative benefits from urban green space." *Frontiers in Psychology* **9**: 2320–2320. doi:10.3389/fpsyg.2018.02320.

Wyles, K. J., M. P. White, C. Hattam, S. Pahl, H. King and M. Austen (2019). "Are some natural environments more psychologically beneficial than others? The importance of type and quality on connectedness to nature and psychological restoration." *Environment and Behavior* **51**(2): 111–143. doi:10.1177/0013916517738312.

Zucchi, F. C. R., Y. Yao, I. D. Ward, Y. Ilnytskyy, D. M. Olson, K. Benzies, I. Kovalchuk, O. Kovalchuk and G. A. S. Metz (2013). "Maternal stress induces epigenetic signatures of psychiatric and neurological diseases in the offspring." *PLOS ONE* **8**(2): e56967. doi:10.1371/journal.pone.0056967.

CONCLUSION

Policy lessons and research implications: Connecting urbanites to nature and re-thinking urban greenspace

Introduction

The movement to incorporate greenspace into cities does not seem to be slowing down. Denver, New York City, and Vancouver have recently approved or are considering approving green roof legislation (City and County of Denver 2019; Velazquez 2019), while there are over 18 projects currently being planned or developed in North America that are inspired by the High Line. These range from the conversion of elevated highway underpasses to public park, recreation, and socialization space, seen in Toronto, to a park bridge, seen in Washington, D.C., to underground park corridors, seen in Detroit and New York City (Gibson 2017). This is in addition to the ongoing, and increasingly popular, trend to incorporate green infrastructure into traditional city planning as a means to address consistent environmental and economic issues associated with climate change (Philadelphia Water Department 2011). While many of the reasons for implementation continue to be environmental, as we have seen from the case studies in the preceding chapters, there is an increasing convergence between social, public health, economic, and environmental drivers for these projects. This chapter examines the intersection of the case studies and research from two perspectives: the first part looks at lessons learned for successful SSUG implementation from a policy perspective, while the second looks at implications and insights from a research angle on our understanding of the human relationship to nature as seen through SSUG.

Policy

Many of the SSUG projects fit into the typologies of the case studies in this book: green infrastructure, elevated greenspace, and vacant lots and post-industrial interstitial spaces. Many of them also fit into trends on *how* SSUG is happening, including the use of pilots and community activism to bypass bureaucratic barriers, sometimes called tactical urbanism or biophilic urban acupuncture (Unt and Bell 2014; Lydon and Garcia 2015; Walker 2015).

Despite the successes outlined previously, we also saw that there remain many challenges to successful implementation. Both these challenges and successes can be instructive for other cities wishing to develop and implement SSUG projects. The rest of this section focuses on the lessons learned from these case studies and points to ways to move forward for cities wishing to implement SSUG projects. Each typology (green infrastructure (GI), elevated greenspace, and vacant lots and post-industrial interstitial spaces) will be reviewed for their conclusions, followed by challenges and key factors influencing their success.

Review of case study conclusions

Green infrastructure

Green infrastructure (GI) projects are some of the oldest, and most familiar, types of SSUG. They are also some of the most complicated, since they need to combine performance metrics that are environmental *and* engineering-based in addition to any human benefits. This means that they can be even more complicated to integrate and implement into municipal policy, a difficulty seen in the numerous best-case practice municipal (City of Toronto 2017) manuals and the more recent National Association of City Transportation Officials (NACTO) green infrastructure guide (National Association of City Transportation Officials n.d.). However, while environmental drivers are often the reason GI projects are started, the case studies show that alone these drivers are not sufficient to ensure successful implementation and integration into municipal policy. This is clearly seen in the differences between Philadelphia and Toronto (see Table 2.1, Chapter 2). While both cities had environmental drivers for the *instigation* of their green infrastructure policies (at least in part), the differing levels of success between the cities in implementation can be linked to an expansion of the scope of perceived benefits, and the resultant resources, for GI in each city. Philadelphia's justification of the benefits of GI to meet federal clean water regulations included an economic argument that GI would adequately meet federal requirements for less money than traditional grey infrastructure (or big pipe approaches), which is a common justification for GI. However, they *also* used research on the benefits of improved access to nature, as well as policy and program precedent from their *LandCare* program, to argue that if GI projects were integrated into a larger urban greening and amenity improvement plan, it would be both cheaper than grey infrastructure *and* meet larger city goals of equity, health, and economic revitalization. Because GI was thus an integral part of multiple programs, it became easier to support GI projects with cabinet-level staff and resources and a unique interdepartmental decision-making process that increased transparency, reduced inefficiencies, and fostered collaboration for common goals. Thus while expanded perceived benefits for GI alone would not have led to the level of success that we see in Philadelphia, when combined with urban greening program precedent, a history of community engagement, and top-down political will and integration, it has led to one of the most successful GI programs in North America.

Toronto is a great example of a much more typical approach to GI in North America; the main drivers are also environmental, but they have had difficulty with systematic integration into larger municipal policy and practice. While they acknowledge social benefits from GI as outlined in their policy documents, the lack of perceived urgency and integration with Toronto's larger policies encourages a lukewarm commitment to community outreach and consultation, even though this has been shown to be a key component of GI implementation success. Toronto's consensus governance approach (versus top-down) also makes it harder to set policy and have it integrated or enforced across departments with a common mandate; policy set in one department may or may not be supported by other policies and departments, or adequately supported with staff resources and time, all of which can fail to address skepticism and concerns from engineering departments about the efficacy of GI. While this kind of approach can be successful in the long run (as seen with green roofs), it is often slower and requires more education and alliances at a municipal level than a top-down approach. In the case of Toronto the combination of strong advocacy from key staff and a major flooding event helped to instigate the program, but it is nowhere near as integrated into the overall policy and program mandate that we see in Philadelphia and is more of a 'green layered over grey' than GI. That said, Toronto's long history of community activism, environmental initiatives, and social justice may help to move GI programs forward, but it might be more of a bottom-up than top-down approach for a while.

Green roofs

Green roofs are technically part of green infrastructure, but their installation and design is so unique that they require separate municipal policies and incentives to encourage them. This makes them an interesting case study for successful SSUG policies, since they are even more complicated than traditional GI, and thus need more municipal cooperation and creativity. Toronto and Chicago are particularly instructive, since despite many similarities in terms of drivers and incentives, and the same time frame for beginning their work on green roofs, they had uneven levels of success for green roof implementation for many years. Chicago was the

North American leader in green roof implementation for a decade, while Toronto lagged behind, until finally Toronto passed the first green roof by-law mandating green roofs on certain buildings in 2009. Examining their similarities and differences is a case study in the importance of leadership structure, effective policies, and symbolism and education for SSUG implementation (see Table 3.1, Chapter 3).

Both Chicago and Toronto had similar environmental drivers for their impetus to pursue and promote green roofs, which is not surprising given their climatic similarities and adjacency to one of the Great Lakes (Lake Michigan for Chicago, Lake Ontario for Toronto). However, they also have different governance structures and key actors that pushed for green roofs, which is a major factor in their initial differing levels of success. In Chicago the infamous heat wave that killed over 700 people in 1995 spurred then-Mayor Daley to seek ways to reduce the UHI, finally settling on green roofs as a strategy. While Chicago did use traditional strategies to encourage the uptake of green roofs, their success can be traced more to a combination of a strong mayoral system, extensive publicity and education, and policies and programs that were financially supported and sustainable. Like other cities, Chicago used incentives, or 'carrots,' such as a green roof grant program, as well as a green roof on their city hall to show municipal support. However, while Mayor Daley was able to command interdepartmental collaboration on green roofs as a result of Chicago's strong mayoral system, his use of green roofs as a key symbolic centrepiece for a larger program of urban revitalization, investment, and beautification enabled green roofs to become a key component of his drive to make Chicago 'the greenest city.' This high-publicity profile for a new urban greening typology was supported by research evaluating the success of the program and the environmental benefits (with satellite data and the EPA respectively), as well as partnerships with other public institutions showcasing examples, demonstration projects, and research around green roofs. The single biggest factor in their success however was their *Green Matrix*, part of their Chicago Sustainable Development Policy, which required private projects seeking public assistance, or that had proximity to Lake Michigan or the Chicago River, to meet minimum green building requirements, with green roofs as one of the options. Crucially, the *Green Matrix* was simultaneously supported by multiple TIF (tax incremental financing) districts (the highest in the U.S.). These districts earmarked money specifically for green development such as green roofs or LEED buildings based on future projected property value increases (often a way to encourage development in underserved areas), and could not be used for other municipal projects, thus ensuring a reliable source of income for green roof implementation. While Washington, D.C. has overtaken Chicago as the U.S. leader in green roof implementation

(Living Architecture Monitor 2018), Chicago's leadership on environmental issues, and green roofs in particular, has cemented their position as a forward-thinking, progressive city (at least environmentally), versus other Midwestern cities suffering from de-industrialization.

While Toronto also had issues with UHI and stormwater management, the initial driver came from a local green roof non-profit that lobbied then-Deputy Mayor Pantalone to pursue green roofs as a climate change adaptation and mitigation strategy. Like Chicago, Toronto showed leadership by putting two test plots on their city hall and partnered with a governmental research agency to study the benefits. They also had incentive programs to defray the cost of green roofs and encourage implementation. Unfortunately, the test plots were not well maintained, and Toronto lacked a cohesive strategy to promote or integrate green roofs into their policy. This, combined with a consensus-based system, made green roofs limp along for a while, with small policy changes and funding drawn from different departments (not very successfully since the costs of green roofs were higher than single-source environmental benefits, such as stormwater relief from Toronto Water). This changed with the election of a more environmentally minded mayor (Mayor Miller) which, along with persistent lobbying from a green roof non-profit, resulted in a retrofitted city hall green roof that was bigger and better. This new green roof was used more effectively in publicity campaigns, and helped to gradually integrate support for green roofs into municipal policy: first with the strong encouragement (unless not technically feasible) for green roofs to be considered for all municipal new buildings and roof replacements, and eventually into the first mandated green roof by-law in North America. This legislation was supported crucially by two things: the commissioning of another study on the benefits of green roofs for Toronto in partnership with Ryerson university; and an adjustment to provincial policy (the City of Toronto Act) that allowed Toronto to set higher green building standards than the province. Thus while the consensus method was slower for Toronto, they did manage to eventually create strong SSUG implementation policy, albeit with the addition of stronger leadership (both mayoral and in their green roof), legislative change, and the support of research for 'new' urban greening. Unlike their current approach to GI, green roof policy is fairly well publicized and supported and the green roof legislation has spurred other cities to consider adopting similar legislation.

Elevated parks and trails

Elevated parks and trails constructed from post-industrial spaces are a newer form of urban greening and thus, like green roofs, an interesting example of how to successfully implement urban greening projects. Though both the Rail Park and The 606 are fairly large projects, their interstitial attributes align them well with the typologies outlined in this book of current urban greening trends that require a different type of visioning and collaboration. And while there are important differences between the two case studies, their common features are instructive for other cities wishing to implement similar types of SSUGs (see Table 4.1, Chapter 4).

First, in both cases there was an identified gap or need for additional greenspace in an urban area where traditional park development was not an option. While the stronger policy case was in Chicago due to their policy mandate of two acres of open space per 1,000 residents, the linking of additional greenspace with economic revitalization in Philadelphia was a key, and equally effective, driver. These slightly different drivers also framed the funding, design, and goals of the two projects: The 606 was envisioned as an active transportation corridor and designed and funded as such, while the Rail Park was envisioned as a neighbourhood park with places to eat lunch, play, and hang out for residents who lacked the traditional porches and backyards of other Philadelphia neighbourhoods. This enabled the Rail Park to be envisioned (and funded) as a way to turn an old industrial eyesore into an attractive amenity that could bring future economic revitalization.

Third, both projects used a combination of community-driven activism to envision the project as a community benefit and keep it alive during political and economic changes; governmental support; and a third party to manage the design and outreach, fundraising, and implementation of the projects. This combination of top-down *and* bottom-up activism and support, combined with a 'neutral' third party, enabled more flexibility in implementation, attention, and community trust while having the necessary municipal support.

Fourth, this combination of municipal support, community activism, and third-party management meant that there was far more community engagement and outreach for both projects than is typically done for SSUG. This helped with community support for the projects and modifications as needed to address community concerns, whether it was privacy for current residents in Chicago who backed onto The 606, or wanting the Rail Park not to be too 'designer-y' and to involve native plants and the industrial heritage.

Lastly, the imaginative approach to urban greening seen in the creative re-use of industrial heritage enabled and fostered an innovative approach to community engagement and programming. Both projects had artists involved in the process, whether through the original envisioning or implementation, and both projects continue to involve the community and artists in ongoing programming. Because of this combination of vision and community outreach, both projects also engaged either research institutions or other community organizations with specific expertise to study and promote the projects, a smart move to continue to provide evidence that these kinds of projects work and provide multiple types of evidence.

And while both projects have faced some limitations, seen most clearly in challenges around gentrification, their unique collaborative approach to urban greening provides some important lessons for other cities considering similar projects.

Vacant lots

Vacant lots and the so-called marginal land seen in some American cities – often the result of de-industrialization, uneven investment, or both – presents an interesting opportunity for re-imagining the city. Both researchers and municipalities are recognizing that, while technically already 'greenspace,' left as they are, vacant lots can be a liability for both the cities and the communities adjacent to them. While possibly an unusual approach to case studies on SSUG, they fit well into the current trends on urban greening, in terms both of scale and of who is driving their retrofitting. They also directly address issues of equity and gentrification that form a constant thread throughout the case studies. As in the elevated post-industrial parks case studies, both Chicago and Philadelphia's approaches to their vacant lots have more similarities than differences, and these can provide important insights for other cities also dealing with vacant lots. Unlike those for green infrastructure, the drivers in both cities were not environmental but social and economic: neighbourhood stabilization and investment. While this has some overlap with the elevated post-industrial park case studies, the key differences are around what *kind* of urban nature is considered a public good: in the elevated parks it is a *lack* of greenspace, while for the vacant lots it is the *type* of greenspace. From this follows a few key insights that directly impact the policy and implementation approaches taken by both cities (see Table 4.1, Chapter 4).

First, the recognition that the type of greenspace matters acknowledges that urban greenspace is both social *and* ecological, and that resident perceptions of disinvestment, lack of care, and neglect have strong negative health and community stabilization impacts. Here it is the quality of the greenspace that matters, and this quality is evaluated by perceptions and feedback of the community themselves. This requires an engagement with both researchers, who are looking at vacant lots as a socio-ecological phenomenon (Wang, Tan et al. 2014) and who study the impacts of 'cleaning and greening' vacant lots (Branas, South et al. 2018), and the community members themselves whose perceptions of disinvestment and neglect are taken seriously. This approach is quite different than with other SSUG such as green infrastructure that may acknowledge that community engagement is important, but may not put community valuations and perceptions of the greenspace at the core of the policy approach.

For example, both Chicago and Philadelphia used community engagement as a key component of their programs. Whether through training underemployed youth, letting the community decide on the design, or, in the case of Chicago, letting them buy the lot cheaply and 'improve it' (as long as they followed some guidelines), community engagement and *empowerment* was a central design and implementation factor rather than an afterthought. This allowed Chicago to respond positively and effectively to residents' complaints about the safety and feel of their neighbourhoods with a creative economic solution, and Philadelphia to address green infrastructure stormwater issues in neighbourhoods that may not have responded well to purely 'environmental' SSUG, but who welcomed community designed greenspace.

It also means that more traditional ecological goals in terms of aesthetics, such as 'wilder' naturalized lawns, were left aside in favour of community aesthetics, which sometimes, as in the case of Chicago, meant *less* greenspace or 'nature.' While this may not always align with larger policy goals, it does improve the health and well-being of residents through a more controlled, maintained type of urban greenspace. Engaging with researchers in both cities to study the health, economic, and social benefits also helps to justify the program and is a key factor in their success.

Lastly, this means that the policy focus for the benefits of the vacant lot programs are a *risk* reduction approach to public health first, and then, if possible, alignment with larger known benefits of access to nature in cities. This more traditional public health approach aligns with the risk reduction approach for green infrastructure, but when combined with community engagement and empowerment creates a type of hybrid SSUG that walks the line between equity, ecology, and health.

Lessons learned, looking ahead

Challenges

The case studies above reveal some common themes that can be instructive for cities wishing to implement similar SSUG projects or policies. While the challenges faced by cities varied depending on whether they were rolling out programs or a single project, one of the biggest barriers to successful SSUG implementation is a lack of coordination and alignment across all the necessary stakeholders and planning structures. Without alignment, it can be difficult to have different departments work effectively together versus competing or conflicting with each other; there can be legislative or bureaucratic barriers – i.e. policies contradict each other; or staff do not have enough training on how to adapt to new policies. This also makes it difficult for effective education, training, and the identification of barriers to implementation, both from a city side (such as a continued engineering approach to social and ecological problems), and from a stakeholder or community engagement side (such as dismissing or underplaying community concerns). A lack of alignment makes coordinated and sustainable maintenance unlikely, as it can get lost in interdepartmental shifting of responsibilities, and funding sources can be temporary or subject to termination if they are not embedded into multiple department budgets and programs with a clear vision on how the program or policy helps everyone.

Success: key themes

While the single biggest challenge to successful SSUG implementation is a lack of alignment, there are many positive lessons that can be drawn from the above case studies that will increase the chance of success. Some of the most common are set out in Table 5.1.

Table 5.1 Key factors in the challenges and successes for the implementation of SSUG projects

Key factors in SSUG challenges and successes	Theme	Examples/outcomes
Challenges	*Lack of alignment*	Lack of departmental coordination
		Legislative/bureaucratic barriers
		Lack of staff training
		Lack of education/training city staff and stakeholders
		Issues with maintenance
		Sustainability and funding sources
Successes	*Frame the issue*	Align with larger policies
		Identify gaps or needs
		Role of aesthetics, symbolism, values
	Governance, funding, legislation	Governance structure: top-down or consensus
		Policies and legislation
		Funding
	Tactical urbanism, community outreach, research	Tactical urbanism
		Integrated stakeholder outreach
		Engage with research institutions
	Adaptive planning	Approach to blend key factors of success and address barriers

Frame the issue

Align with larger policies

One of the easiest and first steps to help with successful implementation is to align the proposed project or program with larger policies, initiatives, or goals for the city or district. This enables an easy policy justification for the project to begin with, and sometimes, as seen with The 606 and Toronto's GI work, helps cities meet their own stated policies or mandates. If the SSUG project or program helps to meet more than one policy or initiative this also opens up funding, public–private partnerships, and other collaborative opportunities. For example, Chicago's Resilient Corridors project aligns with larger investment goals, climate change mitigation and adaptation policy, and fulfills their obligation for action as a *Rockefeller 100 Resilient Cities* recipient.

Identify gaps or needs

In addition to aligning with larger policies or initiatives, identifying gaps or needs for communities, ideally using well-respected data, can further help to frame the proposed SSUG as 'fixing' or mitigating a current problem and help to identify where funds should be spent. If certain communities are behind larger stated goals for the city, then this is an even stronger argument. While this has been somewhat effective for mitigating environmental risk from climate change, such as reducing flooding in certain neighbourhoods, as seen above it is even stronger if it also addresses social, economic, public health, and community benefits. This is particularly true if the community in question has urgent socio-economic needs and may feel that these are more pressing than purely 'environmental' problems. As seen above the most successful SSUGs used *both* environmental and socio-economic framing of benefits as a key component of their success, even in cities with limited funds and pressing socio-economic issues.

Be aware of aesthetics, symbolism, and values

While urban greenspace is generally popular, not all greenspace is considered a public good. Being aware of the social and economic values around different types of greenspace for specific communities – such as vacant lots versus elevated trails – can help to ensure more successful adoption and maintenance. On the other hand, SSUGs can be a highly symbolic and effective way to communicate that the city or organization is doing *something* environmental and for the public good, and can be easier to understand than more complex initiatives such as green buildings or ordinances. This was seen most clearly with Chicago's use of green roofs in all their media campaigns as a symbol of their revitalization of and investment in the city.

Governance, funding, and legislation

Governance structure

While this is not a requirement, the case studies above show that having top-down leadership can make it easier and faster to align departments and stakeholders around SSUG initiatives. This can be particularly effective at quick response rates from departments and a creative 'figure it out' approach to implementation, rather than the lengthy negotiation and lack of impetus or urgency to collaborate in a consensus-based governance structure. Even with a top-down governance structure, however, champions and key stakeholders are essential to help keep everyone accountable, to advocate for the initiative, and to ensure that the voices of those at the bottom and top are heard. This is even more important for consensus-based governance systems, as without funding and support champions can burn out or get frustrated at the lack of action. Lastly, if there are trust issues or tensions between a community and the city, a neutral third party can be an effective mediator in listening to community concerns while advocating for the SSUG.

Policies and legislation

While incentives are an important tool to encourage early adopters, as seen above they are generally ineffective on their own in ensuring market transformation. The most successful instances of large-scale transformation and adoption of SSUG (particularly for programs) have been with legislation that requires some kind of environmental and/or public benefit feature adoption as part of regular development processes, not one-off projects. This was seen clearly with Chicago's *Green Matrix*, which led to the city being the North American leader in green roof implementation for a decade, and Toronto's green roof legislation. 'Stick' policies are even more effective when they align with other initiatives and requirements that make the 'green' choice the financially attractive one, as seen with Philadelphia's GI and stormwater initiatives, or that are supported by legislation or requirements at different scales of government, such as state/provincial or federal. Lastly, identifying and overcoming legislative barriers to the successful implementation of SSUG through the alignment, or change, of legislation that contradicts the new policy (seen in Toronto's *COTA* to enable more restrictive environmental building requirements) can remove any legislative barriers to success.

Funding

Funding municipal environmental initiatives is known to be difficult, since the benefits are often spread across multiple departments (resulting in ambiguity on who should pay for it), or are long-term, public benefits that are hard to quantify and do not fit into the financial budgeting or accounting cycles of municipalities (Matthews, Lo et al. 2015). Furthermore, grant-funding is often for the acquisition or implementation of projects, not their ongoing stewardship (Helphand 2019) which can make SSUG projects difficult to maintain. The case studies above provide some innovative approaches to funding SSUGs to address this issue, with the common goal of identifying secure, long-term funding sources and strategies that cannot be shifted when leadership or priorities shift. For projects, this can come from aligning project goals with larger funding sources or grants, seen in The 606's goal of encouraging active transportation. For programs, this can come from finding efficiencies through departmental alignment, innovative funding sources such as the *Sweetened Beverage* (SSB) *tax* in Philadelphia, or collaborative partnerships that will take on community engagement, fundraising, and/or training around maintenance. This last point is essential, since the inclusion of living plants means that there is more, or at the very least different, maintenance for these projects than for more traditional infrastructure projects. Sometimes this means shifting funding from other regular maintenance, showing that the maintenance costs for the SSUG are lower than conventional projects or programs, or, in many cases, relying on community engagement and commitment to maintain the project by ensuring they feel that it is a benefit for their community.

Tactical urbanism, community outreach, and research

Tactical urbanism

The case studies above demonstrate that one of the most effective ways to get around bureaucratic silo-ing and resistance to new types of urban greening such as SSUGs is to use pilots or case studies to 'test out' the initiatives, often through community-specific projects. We saw this in Toronto's approach to GI, and in Philadelphia and Chicago's approach to vacant land. This follows work on walkability and complete streets that has used tactical urbanism to get communities (and municipal departments) used to new urban planning ideas with little upfront capital investment (Lydon and Garcia 2015). It also allows municipalities to test out technology and approaches that are community, climate, and infrastructure specific, and it enables innovation in problem solving with little risk.

Integrated stakeholder outreach

Whether through pilots or as part of a large program, integrated, meaningful stakeholder outreach was a key component of the success of SSUG in the case studies. This was most successful when it engaged stakeholders as *co-creators*, and not just in traditional community-feedback meetings where decisions had already been made. While this was challenging for more infrastructure-oriented departments that did not have community engagement as part of their traditional bureaucratic process, prioritizing community engagement was an essential component of multiple layers of success: addressing community concerns around gentrification, ensuring that the design reflected local community needs versus more tourist-investment-marketing needs (seen with The 606 and the Rail Park), and lastly ensuring that the projects would get adequate maintenance from the community when cities did not have the budget for this. As will be seen in the second part of this chapter, integrated stakeholder outreach is most effective when it also takes into account community values, beliefs, and needs around the aesthetics and use options for the SSUG.

Engage with research institutions

A key component of success for the case studies above was the engagement with research institutions to monitor, evaluate, and communicate the results of the SSUG projects or programs. Whether in the form of prior research to justify the current SSUG – as in Philadelphia's *Green 2015* that built off of their *LandCare* vacant lot program – or engagement with researchers to monitor and evaluate the current project – seen with Chicago's 606 trail – using data to evaluate and validate the project or program has multiple benefits. It helps to ensure its ongoing success even with changes in leadership; it helps to educate the public and justify the project or program; it can align different paradigms and approaches to find synergies between the programs and benefits (seen with aligning public health and urban greening projects); and it also helps to modify the project or program should some components not be working as well as intended.

A way forward: learning by doing, adaptive planning

As seen above however, current operational pathways in local and state/provincial government can make these kinds of actions very difficult to successfully achieve. This is sometimes called path dependency (Matthews, Lo et al. 2015), where the established way of doing things can get in the way of successfully addressing complex, wicked problems such as climate change adaptation and mitigation and green infrastructure. Other limitations of using traditional planning frameworks to address complex problems that researchers have identified include: a lack of knowledge of *ecological* systems, frameworks, and tools (Dempsey and Robertson 2012); poor accounting for long-term environmental and social benefits within the traditional funding and decision-making cycle (Matthews, Lo et al. 2015); difficulty making decisions with multiple unknowns and risks (Grose 2014); a disconnection between these natural and bureaucratic systems (Olsson, Jerneck et al. 2015) or between public health measurements and urban greening projects, and not understanding or valuing the impact of socio-political influences and power dynamics on ecological frameworks, SSUG design, implementation, and maintenance (Flint, Kunze et al. 2013; Jim, Lo et al. 2015). Conversely, ecologists also tend to miss the long history of socio-cultural and economic change in cities, and their training to search for certainty and reproducibility of experimentation and universal theories means that they can find incomplete data and the inclusion of socio-cultural changing values challenging to integrate into their process and assessment as experts (Grose 2014).

One promising suggestion to address these barriers from both researchers and champions is an adaptive planning model. Sometimes also called 'learning by doing,' or 'safe to fail' (Niemelä 2014), this approach to SSUG implementation offers a potential framework to help get the above success strategies for SSUG implemented. It is particularly promising for integrating two key aspects that can be difficult to achieve in traditional planning approaches: linking scientific knowledge with design, and balancing community values, beliefs, and user needs with ecological and planning imperatives. Key components of this approach include: linking design with ecological *and* social needs; co-designing experiments that are transdisciplinary partnerships; and leaving the pilot or case study open to innovation and creative solutions (Ahern, Cilliers et al. 2014). Some options to operationalize this include an initial assessment of how current urban greenspaces will be affected by socio-demographic, public health, and environmental drivers, such as climate change, and then the co-development of a plan to manage these (or develop new) spaces for the co-benefit of communities and biodiversity or ecosystem resilience (Niemelä 2014). Other options include a more dynamic socio-cultural understanding of resilience that is based on change, adaptation, equity, and local knowledge (Steiner 2014), seen with Chicago's *Resilient Corridors* pilot, in which resilience includes both environmental and socio-economic definitions and extensive co-creation and community involvement with the design process. Central to these options is the need to be local and context-specific versus universal, and to have a design-thinking approach of experimentation, innovation, and transdisciplinary collaboration. For example, the use of ecological data can inform, but not drive, design options by generating design ideas based on ecologically sound data which are then run through social, health, and economic local needs. This is currently missing in much of urban planning – i.e. what is necessary for functioning constructed wetlands, or what are some concrete options for soil remediation as a starting point for community engagement (Wang, Tan et al. 2014). This socio-ecological hybrid has been called constructed ecologies, or 3rd nature (Unt and Bell 2014), or novel ecosystems, but what it has in common is a creative, dynamic design approach that allows for minor failures as a learning tool for adaptive learning that is culturally and ecologically appropriate. Computer data may be a useful tool to test ecological performance prior to construction, and possibly for monitoring, when combined with more qualitative approaches of community engagement (Grose 2014). Using this adaptive planning approach is well suited not only to the tactical urbanism and case study approach that has been so successful in urban planning and some of the case studies above, but it also provides the shift in thinking that can allow for the other key components of a successful SSUG implementation to flourish, for ecological, socio-cultural, and public health reasons.

Research context

Moving forward with small-scale urban greening: lessons learned and new opportunities

The policy discussion above is helpful in highlighting some of the key drivers and factors that help enable successful SSUG implementation, and some options for alternative frameworks that can navigate around common barriers. Stepping back from policy and implementation, what can we learn from the intersection of case studies and research on SSUG? What do they tell us about how we value nature in cities or our experience of urban nature? And how can we use insights from this knowledge to create SSUGs that optimize urbanites' health and well-being, sense of place, and relationship to nature in cities? The discussion below is divided into sections answering these questions and should be useful to researchers, designers, and policy makers.

How do we value urban nature as experienced with SSUG projects?

At the core of the case studies and research on SSUG lie questions about a fundamental aspect of life in cities – public space: what kind of public space do we want, what constitutes good quality public space, and, more recently, for whom? While nature has often, though not always, been part of this discussion, multiple drivers are bringing urban nature more frequently into this debate and shaping our valuation and experience of urban nature in ways that are different from previous iterations.

The benefits of urban parks for recreation and a break from the city (especially for those who cannot afford to leave) have been assumed at least since the City Beautiful movement around the turn of the twentieth century. Recent environmental concerns, however, and in particular the recognition that natural systems have an important role to play in urban environments, have brought more attention to how urban nature can be a valid infrastructure option to address issues like flooding, water and air quality, and the urban heat island effect. This shift in valuing urban nature – from a mainly aesthetic experience to a functional element of infrastructure – has four key impacts that we have seen from the case studies. First, as part of city infrastructure, SSUG moves from only being valued in larger park-like leisure settings to becoming part of the urban fabric at multiple scales – everything from corridors to rooftops to right of ways. This incorporation into the built fabric of the city has the potential to shift the daily lived experience of place of urbanites – as seen with the Rail Park giving community greenspace to Center City residents, or the Chicago City Hall green roof giving nearby office workers views of a Chicago prairie. Second, given the highly symbolic and memory-laden aspects of nature (discussed below), adding nature into the city for explicit environmental reasons opens the possibility to link urbanites to the larger hinterland and make them more aware of abstract environmental issues, for example by linking street-level rain gardens with stormwater overflow and larger regional watersheds. Both of these points underscore how urban nature in the form of SSUG can challenge inherited values that separate 'nature' and the city by weaving them together in unexpected ways.

Third, the possibility that urban nature can positively influence health is also contributing to the shift in how we value it. While the benefits of urban parks have been well-known for over a century, the methods chosen by environmental psychologists and others who have turned generally felt common beliefs into statistics and numbers have translated well into policy (Kaplan and Kaplan 1989; Ulrich, Simons et al. 1991; Sullivan, Kuo et al. 2004; Hazer, Formica et al. 2018). Concepts like Nature Rx (Klass 2018; Razani, Morshed et al. 2018; Cornell Health n.d.), and studies that suggest that only 40 seconds of viewing a green roof improves concentration (Lee, Williams et al. 2015), are easily understood, reinforce the importance of providing access to nature to urbanites, and garner media attention (Jaffe 2015; Ballard 2019; Calautti 2019; King 2019). This interest in cultivating urban nature for public health reasons is seen at a larger city scale, where access to urban nature is linked to a host of socio-economic and health benefits in city policies – for example in Philadelphia, where urban greening in marginalized neighbourhoods has been linked to reduced levels of violence and poor mental health (Garvin, Cannuscio et al. 2012; Kondo, Fluehr et al. 2018). It has also recently found traction at a building scale with biophilic design in workplaces and the inclusion of access to nature in building rating systems like the WELL Building Standard (International WELL Building Institute 2018).

Lastly, while these studies on the benefit of nature have proven popular at both an individual building and city policy level, issues of equity, gentrification, and uneven investment in communities has led to the emergence of equity and community investment as key drivers of how we value SSUG. As we have seen in the case studies, urban nature and SSUG need to be valued as *both* ecological and socio-ecological in order to be successful. The importance of this dual valuation is evident in the realizations, for example, that social and economic context shape how communities perceive the aesthetics and value of SSUG projects – as seen with the *Large Lot program* in Chicago; how the design itself needs to be framed in order to benefit those communities versus tourists or non-residents – as seen with the Rail Park in Philadelphia; and even how a *lack* of high-quality greenspace is seen as an issue of equity and community disinvestment, rather than as a nice-to-have amenity for the wealthy – as seen with the *Green2015* and vacant lot program in Philadelphia and Chicago. As outlined in Chapter 1, these more recent valuations of urban nature call for the inclusion of more socio-ecological, political ecology, or social constructionist approaches to understanding the relationship between urbanites and nature. They also have shifted the conversation (addressed below) from restoration and health benefits of urban nature to community investment and stabilization, as seen in the 'just green enough' research trend and the goals of the vacant lot programs (Wolch, Byrne et al. 2014)

How we experience SSUG: implications for research

The central premise of much of the work that seeks to explore and understand the human experience of contact with nature is that people benefit from access to it. And while there is an enormous body of research on more traditional concepts of nature, such as parks, gardens, and wilderness experiences, there is little on the newer, more small-scale forms of nature that are integrated into the urban fabric such as the kind of SSUG explored in this book. As such, it is a delicate balancing act to evaluate urbanites' experiences of this newer type of urban nature, such as green roofs, with the larger body of research on the human relationship to nature more generally. Drawing conclusions is complicated by the very different approaches to studying the human relationship to nature as outlined in Chapter 1: while the utilitarian or psychometric approach has given us a strong and convincing body of knowledge on the benefits of access to nature for humans, it tends to miss the power dynamics, collective experience and history of a place, and socio-economic and cultural factors that can influence urbanites' perceptions and experiences of SSUG (Williams 2014).

Exacerbating this tension among knowledge paradigms is the absence in many cases of on-the-ground research on these newer forms of nature: in some cases only anecdotal and community responses exist, and this kind of data can easily be reduced to – and sometimes dismissed as – individual differences of likes and dislikes, particularly when community responses differ from expert perceptions or expectations. These 'messy' responses are rarely highlighted as often as tidy quantified results from laboratory studies that are often seen as more 'objectively true' and policy-ready (Bhattacherjee 2012). This was seen clearly with the Chicago Restoration controversy mentioned in Chapter 1 – where so-called 'ecological' knowledge was privileged over community perspectives (Gobster 2000) – and has been highlighted as a problem with traditional community engagement perspectives with ecological-only drivers that prioritize expert knowledge over community feedback (Grose 2014). Furthermore, reducing the human experience to individual likes and dislikes is not often helpful and can obscure the collective experience(s) of a place examined by a more socio-ecological approach that can strongly influence a SSUG project's success (Manzo 2008; Relph 2008; Stewart, Gobster et al. 2019). This reduction-approach is particularly apparent in the fact that marginalized groups are not studied as often as groups that are easier to access, such as students (Joye and van den Berg 2011; Hitchings 2013) and in the relatively small number of in-situ case studies, which are conducted less frequently than 'cleaner' laboratory studies, though there is some evidence this might be changing (Simpson and Bagelman 2018; Loftus 2019).

However, it is this very tension between the policy-ready psychometric research approaches and the socio-ecological research approaches (and their resultant methods) that can prove the most interesting and which is one of the backbones of this book. As seen in the case studies, much of the research that *has* been done on participant experiences of SSUG is less of a dismissal of the large body of research from environmental psychology and other work and is more of a deepening and exploration of tensions left unexplained and complex lived experiences reduced to more easily-quantifiable metrics and categories. These tensions can be seen for example between the benefits of contact with urban nature and resistance to urban greening due to fears of gentrification, or simple categories of preference which can miss nuances around sense of place and experiences of identity, power, and inherited values. In this sense there are two approaches to understanding the human experience of SSUG that have emerged from the case studies that may provide some insight into how the experience of SSUG may differ in cities than in more traditional 'nature' studies such as wilderness: insights from a phenomenological perspective, and the role of the social and community context.

Insights from a phenomenological perspective

To begin with, the interstitial nature of many of these projects means that urbanites may have an increased chance of experiencing them on a daily basis, versus larger parks and projects that require travel or a deliberate intent to visit them (Hitchings 2013). This has the potential to alter the fabric of the city and the lived experience of place in ways that we have not seen before in cities (except when they are decaying and 'nature' starts to take over, which is another type of experience altogether).[1] For this reason, phenomenology can be an additional tool to explore urbanites' lived experiences of place and the role of nature in this experience that may lead to insights that an environmental psychology or ecological lens would not offer.

Green roofs can be particularly instructive here since they are not associated with the symbolism of more traditional forms of nature. While they are a new form of nature in cities, participant experiences of them are highly mediated by previous experience and cultural assumptions. A phenomenological lens can reveal the tension between the daily lived experience of place as perceived through affective, felt responses on the one hand and, on the other, the mediation of these affective responses by things like childhood experiences of nature, inherited cultural values around aesthetics, preferring local versus scenic and distant nature, the legacy of the modernist city with its associated narratives about progress and modernity, and even cultural values from the environmental movement around the conservation of native habitat. These tensions are clearly evident in the gap between participants' initial perceptions of the green roof and their lived experience: while they debated whether green roofs counted as 'nature' at all, their *felt* responses indicated that their lived experience of watching the green roofs change over time echoed childhood experiences of nature, giving them a similar feeling of well-being, emotional release from the harshness of concrete, increased creativity, and a sense of place linked to long-lost prairie from the region. Similarly, while some who held more 'ecological' values loved the aesthetics of the green roof, many were clearly influenced by ideas of progress of the modernist city in North America and the legacy of the Victorian sanitation movement, where straight lines and signs of care signify control and the conquering of the hinterland, the manifest destiny moving westward, as well as economic progress and stability. This modernist aesthetic also sought to remove all signs of 'wildness' and disorder from the city as a means to improve public health and signify progress (Kaika 2006; Marvin and Medd 2006). Thus, it is not surprising that some participants associated the ecological 'messier' aesthetic of the green roof with neglect, bureaucratic negligence, and even, on a larger scale, fear of crime. However, those participants who watched the green roof over time were also more fascinated by it, felt higher levels of well-being, and felt a sense of hope from the wildness and regenerative capacity of nature. Even though the green roofs were small in scale, the fact that, when part of daily lived experience, they were symbolic enough to link participants to the larger 'nature' outside the city, to memory and hope, points to the possibility that SSUG has a role to play in shifting cultural mindsets about the functions and aesthetics of urban nature away from the Victorian and modernist legacies and toward a more integrated, holistic, cultural-ecological systems view.

Insights from the social and community context

Another key contribution of the case studies analyzed in this book is to highlight the importance of combining lenses from different research paradigms, and in particular including a socio-ecological or social constructionist viewpoint. The case studies on vacant lots and elevated trails demonstrate that adding 'nature' amenities to urban spaces without addressing barriers to their use, access, and appreciation has not been very effective, as seen with urban parks in heavily disinvested areas that become magnets for crime (Groff and McCord 2012; Cohen, Han et al. 2016). Using a socio-ecological or social constructionist approach (depending on whether one uses a public health or social science framework), can help to explain some of the tensions seen around SSUGs that were intended to be universally beneficial and provide a public good. These approaches argue that urban greening is a socio-ecological activity, and that relations of power, perception, and values need to be addressed in any discussions of the potential benefits of urban greening (Curran and Hamilton 2012; Ignatieva, Ahrné et al. 2015; Uren, Dzidic et al. 2015; Loftus 2019). This recognition of the importance of the social and community component of these urban greenspaces challenges more traditional environmental psychology 'nature prescription' research and begins to 'fill in the gap' with a social-community perspective that is often missing from the value- and context-neutral nature–health research most often cited by policy makers.

The case studies focusing on interstitial SSUG in Philadelphia and Chicago are particularly exemplary here. We saw that residents in these cities who lived next to vacant lots expressed disempowerment, fear, and dislike of the 'blight,' neglect, and often criminal activity next to their homes, not the sense of restoration, well-being, fascination, or creative freedom that is argued to be a universal response to nature in many environmental psychology studies. They consistently wanted a sense of order and visible signs of maintenance and control, often in the form of mowed grass, fences, and trimmed trees, which they executed when given control over those vacant lots. While the neighbourhoods surrounding the abandoned elevated rail lines are not as vulnerable, concerns about light crime in Chicago, and the rail line inhibiting development in Philadelphia, still speak to the ambivalence of many urbanites towards post-industrial and marginal land in the city, particularly when there is the perception that it intrudes on their daily lives. Recognizing this perspective is critical to the success of SSUG, and it supports work that has shown that urban greening has often been the precursor to gentrification, that expectations of quality greenspace are often associated with wealthier neighbourhoods (Mock 2015; Anguelovski 2016; London 2017; Immergluck and Balan 2018; Gobster, Stewart et al. 2018), and that perceived disorder has been linked to perceived risk of crime (Wang, Tan et al. 2014). In other words, the daily lived experience of wildness and neglect, of 'otherness,' may feel too close to home for already-marginalized residents, while also challenging the ideal of progress and economic stability.

The efficacy of this risk-reduction approach is supported by positive health impacts reported for even marginal 'cleaning and greening' and cues to care for residents in both cities, as well as increased physical activity. But it may not fully address ecological co-benefits or embrace alternative possibilities that could benefit communities that need it most. For example, as mentioned earlier, recent research from environmental epigenetics has looked at the impact of cumulative stress that is inherited and can negatively impact the expression of our phenotypes (Guthman and Mansfield 2013; Prior, Manley et al. 2019). In practical terms this means that generational experiences of systemic poverty, racism, and neighbourhood violence can be passed onto children and negatively impact children's ability to self-regulate their emotional state, concentrate, and even sleep (Franke 2014; Guarino 2018; Center on the Developing Child n.d.). A disproportionate percentage of children growing up in these environments are diagnosed with Attention Deficit and Hyperactivity Disorder (ADHD), and some researchers are positing that these children may be misdiagnosed, and may in fact be exhibiting symptoms of trauma (Ruiz 2014). While providing high-quality access to local greenspace does not address the larger socio-economic issues impacting these children and their parents, some researchers have argued that these greenspaces may provide a buffer for these negative experiences, allowing for faster recovery from stress, better emotional regulation, and even safe places to explore and play (Strife and Downey 2009; Corraliza, Collado et al. 2012; Williams 2018). While using SSUG as a buffer for children is a more urgent need, adults too can benefit from high-quality greenspace that acts as a buffer from stress. In this sense, using Chicago's recent co-created community *Resilient Corridor* stormwater pilot may be a better example of SSUG that addresses *both* economic and community stabilization as well as community health, well-being, and resilience through design that goes beyond 'just green enough' and 'cleaning and greening' (Berkshire 2018; 2019).

Moving forward: implications for research

From a research perspective, this blend of affective and immediate responses to nature that are also influenced by inherited cultural, symbolic, and personal history points to a possible middle ground between the conclusions from both environmental psychology and social constructionists – less an '*either or*' and more an '*and also*' approach to understanding the human relationship to nature. Such an approach has implications both for our understanding of the human relationship with nature and for research methods. For the former, it takes into account that our relationship to nature is highly complex and a blend of affective, emotional, and lived sense of place experiences, as well as a shifting dynamic that is influenced by shared and individual cultural, economic, and historical experiences. In this sense, the recognition of nature (both urban and wilderness, but particularly urban) as socio-ecological leads to a more appropriate framework than one that is purely social or purely ecological and can help ensure successful outcomes. It also indicates that affective responses to nature cannot be reduced solely to cultural or historical influences *or* to individual likes and dislikes, and should not be as readily dismissed as 'romantic holdovers' by some of the more hardline social constructionist approaches.

From a research methods perspective, this middle ground points to the need for studies that address these more complex lived experience influences on perceptions of nature to be given as much weight as more easily quoted quantitative ones, both for research and policy. For example, it makes sense that most environmental psychology work focuses on affective and cognitive responses to nature at specific points in time (as this is easier to measure and explain), or does not generally ask about the amount of contact with nature participants regularly experience in their daily lives over time, since the underlying paradigm assumes that responses to nature are immediate, affective, and generally universal – i.e. the amount over time should not matter as much per se (for some exceptions, see Bamberg, Hitchings et al. 2018; Li, Deal et al. 2018). It also makes sense that laboratory studies focus on testing and explaining theorized causal mechanisms behind our responses to nature: cognitively, emotionally, and physiologically. While these studies provide valuable data to help understand the (mostly) positive benefits we get from contact with nature, on their own they miss the complexity of our relationship to nature that can provide valuable insight into both reducing conflict over urban greening projects and creating SSUG that maximizes the health and well-being benefits for *everyone*. Specifically, including research methods and studies that allow participants the time to think *and feel* through their responses that they may not have articulated yet to themselves, that examine how much, and what type of nature they are in contact with on a daily basis, and that are longitudinal and examine participant experiences over time, will help to fill in some of the current gaps in research on humans and nature in cities. This is particularly important when dealing with marginalized communities who may not be represented by some of the more simplistic policy initiatives aimed at increasing access to nature (such as Nature Rx, well-intentioned though it is).

Education and design implications for health, well-being, and ecological sustainability

The case studies above challenge our ideas about the kinds of public space people want and enjoy and the role that urban nature plays. They also point to opportunities for improving our current relationship with and conceptions of nature and for creating SSUG that optimizes our well-being and sense of place, supports equity, and contributes to larger policy goals and environmental sustainability. In this sense SSUG projects and programs can be agents of change, tactical urbanism points of intervention towards a more just, ecological, and healthy urban future. Three key ways they can do this are: (1) using SSUG as a tool for education to help develop an ecological aesthetic and a more active, equitable relationship with urbanites; (2) designing SSUG projects to provide loose-fit places offering respite and places for creative play; (3) and viewing the tactical urbanism approach in interstitial spaces as a design opportunity to offer a different, more human-scale (i.e. local lived experience) and ecological (with its differing time and perspective) approach to sense of place.

Education through SSUGs: adaptive design, ecological aesthetics, and environmental values

Most urbanites spend the majority of their time indoors (Klepeis, Nelson et al. 2001; Roberts 2016) and have not nearly enough contact with nature to experience the health and well-being benefits explored throughout this book. Furthermore, as we have seen, there is a tension between urban greenspace that has ecological goals, often with a 'messy' aesthetic to go with them, and inherited urbanite preferences for nature that may cause them to view these SSUG projects as unkempt, disordered, and associated with crime and ill health (Spears 2005; Wang, Tan et al. 2014). These preferences persist despite that fact that these more biodiverse spaces may in fact benefit their health more than manicured Kentucky bluegrass lawns (Loder 2014; Lee, Hur et al. 2018; Southon, Jorgensen et al. 2018). We have also seen from a policy perspective that there is both the recognition of the positive role that good-quality greenspace can play in public spaces and a simultaneous acknowledgement of the lack of equitable access to high-quality greenspace in cities. Here the dual approach of adaptive design and ecological aesthetics may offer an innovative way forward to address this tension by creating a more active relationship with nature. As discussed above, adaptive design requires the interactive and iterative co-design of these SSUG projects with the communities they serve (Grose 2014). Ecological aesthetics combines ecological knowledge with aesthetic preferences (as advocated by Aldo Leopold and others) (Leopold 1971;

Carroll 1993; Gobster, Nassauer et al. 2007; Riechers, Barkmann et al. 2018). As education is one of the only interventions known to change aesthetic preferences (Gobster, Nassauer et al. 2007; Goleman, Bennett et al. 2012; Uren, Dzidic et al. 2015), this combination may provide a chance for urbanites to engage, learn, and transform their relationship with nature and their sense of place in cities while creating places of ecological *and* human health and well-being (Kowarik 2019).

How might this work? First, an adaptive approach can also include economic well-being, by combining SSUS with community training and jobs, rather than relying only on volunteer work. This opens the possibility of creating a different relationship with urban nature where it is no longer only a passive leisure amenity for wealthier neighbourhoods, but an opportunity to develop an active relationship of stewardship and care with urban nature that is also investing in and revitalizing the community. This was seen most clearly with Chicago's new *Resilient Corridor* pilot (Berkshire 2018) in which community members were presented with the most ecologically suitable plants, but were given the final choice around plant selection, design, and other amenities.

Second, this more active relationship with nature may also positively influence larger environmental values for urbanites. Since many urbanites' primary experience of nature is urban nature, some researchers have argued that this interaction has a profound role in shaping larger environmental values and action, often called the Pigeon Paradox (Dunn, Gavin et al. 2006). If urbanites never experience the 'other' in any meaningful, reflective sense (such as only experiencing pigeons and manicured lawns as 'nature'), how are they to care about issues outside their city, or link urban environmental problems with creative solutions like green infrastructure? Both environmentalists, who suffer from the dualism of an abstract universal nature and their daily lives (Davison 2008), and restorationists, who argue that focusing all our attention on preserving 'sacred' nature far from the city relegates nature to leisure, and thus dispensable, activities (Cronon 1995; Jordan 2000), have called for an ethic of care and restoration as an empowering approach to both environmental and social problems (Jordan 2000; Light 2000; Macdonald and King 2018). More recently, some researchers have even looked at aligning nature recreation and sense of place with ecosystem services as a way to 'activate' people's relationship with nature (Scholte, Daams et al. 2018; Wartmann and Purves 2018).

Third, a more active relationship with nature may help to align SSUG projects with larger ecological goals and placemaking (Peck 2017), potentially increase the amount of biodiversity included in SSUGs, and positively impact health and well-being. This is particularly important as the increased visibility of many elevated greenspaces has increased public expectations of aesthetics and value, while research has consistently shown that biodiverse greenspace yields higher rates of restoration and fascination (or at least is neutral (Chang, Sullivan et al. 2016)), particularly when wildlife habitat is included, than more manicured, sparse, 'cleaned and greened' spaces do (Fuller, Irvine et al. 2007; Carrus, Scopelliti et al. 2015; Lee, Hur et al. 2018; Southon, Jorgensen et al. 2018). Furthermore, increased biodiversity also provides more opportunities for education and engagement. As E. O. Wilson argued, we do not need to constantly seek out new frontiers in distant lands – we just need to open our eyes to the worlds right in front of us if we only stop to watch and learn (Wilson 1993). This is particularly true for children, where small-scale nature such as that found in SSUG can provide a multitude of learning experiences (Louv 2006; Hand, Freeman et al. 2017; Tillmann, Tobin et al. 2018).

Lastly, providing more opportunities for an active participation and co-design in SSUG projects and encouraging an ecological aesthetic through education may help urbanites create a sense of place with increased health and well-being benefits. The research from environmental psychology has indicated that access to nature can increase residential attachment to a place, while having places to go as a respite from the city, so-called 'special places,' can increase restoration for urbanites (Tzoulas, Korpela et al. 2007; Wilkie and Clements 2018). But an ecological aesthetic may deepen this sense of place by connecting to larger collective experiences of place or historical narratives. What would re-wilding the city look like? How would it change our sense of place? Our sense of self? For example, native prairie habitat connected Chicagoans to both their childhood and the surrounding hinterland, even if the latter only exists in small, leftover parcels. The Pawlonia trees sprouting from the Viaduct in Philadelphia connects Philadelphians with the industrial trade history of the region through the packing seeds that once surrounded porcelain from China that were shipped on that rail (Saval 2016). Providing native habitat and opportunities to interact with nature through interstitial spaces may also help increase the legibility of a place (Lynch 1981; Relph 2008) by providing wayfinding for seniors and children, as well as a re-imagining of what the city can look like, and thus providing spaces for creative play. Examples of this might look like Chicago's Jardincito developed by NeighborSpace (Helphand 2013), which combined a historical lens of prairie aesthetics as a nod to Jens Jensen and landscape architecture in Chicago, with active play and naturalized schoolyards (Rotenberk 2015). Or it might look like salmon rehabilitation efforts on the west coast, which worked with school children, environmentalists, and ranchers to rehabilitate salmon runs in the area and make salmon a symbolic and literal placemaker for the region (Mills 2000). Lastly, because adaptive design co-creates SSUG projects, and takes into account collective experiences of place, these SSUG examples are less likely to miss the power dynamics and collective sense of place that is not often part of traditional environmental psychology narratives.

Designing SSUGs to provide edges, creativity, and loose-fit places for respite and creative play

What are some design implications for creating SSUGs that enhance human health, well-being, and sense of place? What opportunities exist specifically for SSUGs that will be implemented in the margins, the interstitial spaces, the cracks of the urban fabric? Here, two ideas may prove of some value: using edges to encourage creative thinking and acceptance of a 'messier' ecological aesthetic, and loose-fit places that offer opportunities for diverse uses and people and a respite from the utilitarian and consumerist-oriented architecture of the city that encourages efficiency, production and consumption, and action rather than respite and reflection.

Edges: creative thinking and the ecological aesthetic

While the case studies examined above vary in scale and scope, they all have as a common element the acknowledgement that these interstitial spaces can be re-imagined into something more beneficial for residents. In many of the case studies, the de-facto shape of the greenspaces which were inserted into rectilinear disused rail, vacant lots, on top of buildings, or along street right of ways, may also help promote creativity and increased acceptance of the 'wildness' of an ecological aesthetic. For example, insights from the case studies point to the role that green roofs and other small-scale urban greening projects may play in creatively breaking the harsh edges of the modernist city, which participants found fatiguing. Specifically, the unexpected wildness and otherness of the green roofs and linear parks may be more startling *because* they are juxtaposed with the order, control, and hardness of the modernist architecture (in the case of green roofs), or the post-industrial heritage of a city (in the case of elevated parks), opening up slippery places of otherness, possibility, and creativity, and creating a dialectic between nature and human activity (Brady 2006). Edges can be places of creativity and boldness (Chapman 2004), seen in participants' descriptions of how gazing at the green roof helped them to gain perspective and problem solve during their workday. Edges have often been places of creativity and energy, of ambiguity and otherness: the edge between meadow and forest, port cities, and juxtapositions between divergent neighbourhoods (Hooks 1989). This may be why it is often artists who saw the potential for the creative re-use of the rail lines, and the strong desire by the community for an arts presence in these projects.

Second, the small scale of these spaces, seen particularly in the 'thick edges' of rail lines or interstitial spaces, may also be less threatening than large areas and may weave more effectively into resident's daily lives, particularly if combined with community input and minor safety improvements such as lighting and benches (done for both rail line trails and some projects in Philadelphia). Wilder spaces are sometimes viewed as unkempt, scary, and inhospitable (Nasar and Fisher 1993; van den Berg and ter Heijne 2005). Their juxtaposition with built form, and the knowledge that humans helped create them, may help to make this wildness more palatable and inviting for urbanites, a design strategy traditionally used in Japanese aesthetics with its creative use of straight lines and control (Saito 2002). Like Nassauer's 'cues to care' concept, in which naturalized areas are more acceptable when accompanied by signs of human care and deliberate attention (Nassauer 1995), a wilder aesthetic when combined with the straight lines of modern buildings may signal a new *urban* ecological aesthetic and a more reciprocal relationship between nature and the city. This juxtaposition may make these spaces both more accessible, interactive, and acceptable, and may even work at some point with vacant lot programs if combined with education and programming. Some researchers have argued that this type of intervention is a 'third city,' a sensitive urban layer over existing infrastructure that may need only small interventions and art and event programming to be more useful and an integral part of the community, especially for more vulnerable residents like women, the elderly, and children (Unt and Bell 2014) . Third, the goal of connectivity for many of these projects, and the recognition that they can form part of a larger system of greenspace, transit, and public spaces, challenges the traditional separation of urban uses and people and re-imagines the city as both ecological (in terms of linear green parks and corridors), and human-centred.

Lastly, this creative use of edges may help to promote the health and well-being benefits of small-scale interventions that are designed into the fabric of buildings and neighbourhoods. Currently, healthy building standards such as the WELL Building Standard™ include points for providing access to nature, and it is one of their most popular choices for features (International WELL Building Institute 2018). However, many in the building industry still view access to nature through the lens of environmental psychology's predominant psychometric research paradigm, which attempts to quantify the potential health impact of access to nature by the amount of nature. While nearby nature does have a measurable impact on human health – for example by cleaning the air – there are many other benefits that even small-scale interventions can have on human health, well-being, and, as seen above, creativity, that may not be captured by a more psychometric approach.

Loose-fit places and ecological time

Lastly, this combination of 'edginess' or liminal space and ecological aesthetics may fit Thompson's discussion of 'loose-fit places,' which are edge places, abandoned land, or wild spaces that are often explored during childhood and which invite unstructured play and possibility (Thompson 2002). Importantly, unlike most of the modernist downtown landscapes of North American cities, these spaces are unconstrained and open to a multiplicity of uses and users. In this sense, they parallel the freedom of childhood exploration, fascination, and wonder that participants so often reminisced about when talking about nature (Gurholt and Sanderud 2016; Kiewra and Veselack 2016; van Dijk-Wesselius, Maas et al. 2018; Norwood, Lakhani et al. 2019), and which Richard Louv and others have discussed as an integral part of a being human (Louv 2006; Milligan and Bingley 2007). For example, the combined presence of 'uncontrolled' nature and human industry, seen in the abandoned rail lines, can give a sense of ecological time and space, a nod to the surrounding hinterland and ecology (Kowarik 2019), and a welcome contrast to the sanitized, consumerist spaces of modern cities. This incorporation of post-industrial ruins into active greenspace also challenges the modern idea of time as always moving forward and opens up space, both literally and figuratively, for a liminal third space and acknowledgement of a different scale and time cycle than the boom and bust cycles of capitalist urban development. This supports the work of some researchers who look at pocket parks and small urban greenspaces, and who have found that beauty, restoration, and stress relief can happen in small urban greenspaces if well-designed (Peschardt, Schipperijn et al. 2012; Hadavi, Kaplan et al. 2015).

Looking ahead

While the case studies described in this book offer fairly strong examples of urban greening projects that positively impact urbanites' health and well-being, as well as ecological benefits, insights from Chapter 2 and work on marginal and vacant land raise the possibility of some missed opportunities and lessons learned for future projects. For instance, while some of these projects specified spaces for reflection and socialization, such as the Viaduct Rail Park, many are focused on more active-use spaces such as playgrounds, gardens, and bike trails, reflecting city planners' awareness of some of the reasons urbanites do not use low-quality greenspaces. However, some researchers have argued that there is still a need for 'slow landscapes,' and for spaces for pause, reflection, and a multiplicity of uses and users (Sinha 2014). This is particularly true for children, youth, women, and other populations who are often excluded from daily patterns of consumption and work in cities (Boyd, White et al. 2018). As time spent inside continues to increase, and as labour becomes more disassociated from our bodies, having space in which to engage our bodies in multiple forms of exploration and play, in wildness and loose-fit places, may provide mental and physiological restoration and encourage movement for those not comfortable with traditional forms of exercise. And since so much of our cities include built-up space, translating the design goal of loose-fit places, an urban ecological aesthetic that creatively plays with wildness, and places to slow down may provide harried workers or stressed students a place to pause and restore their over-worked, always-on minds and bodies. Some options might include combining SSUG with spaces for parkour, mazes and games welcoming for users of any age, type, or neurodiversity such as autism, and intergenerational spaces to interact. Rotating artist internships or exhibitions, with the goal of linking the natural and urban world for a diversity of people, may also provide a creative spark to contrast against the consumer-oriented spaces that have dominated recent urban revitalization efforts. As in the example of the curb effect, in which cutting curbs on sidewalks to make them more accessible for wheelchairs ended up helping everyone, being more creative about the juxtaposition of ecological aesthetics, play, and high-quality urban spaces will make SSUG projects better, and more inviting, for everyone.

Some remaining questions centre on regionally specific ecological aesthetics, particularly for arid climates. Research has shown that people tend to prefer more lush landscapes (Yabiku, Casagrande et al. 2008), and that 'making the hinterland native' again can be challenging in climates that are perceived as harsh and inhospitable. While education can help with public acceptance, perhaps a local climate-appropriate version of cues to care can work to balance perceptions of health and well-being with ecological sustainability. Further work would include tailoring these kinds of SSUG projects to different needs of the local culture, and possibly even linking food and agriculture, such as has been envisioned for Chicago's Englewood neighbourhood, as a vibrant way to connect food, livelihoods, and ecological sustainability (McCarron 2012; Moore 2012). Lastly, as we have seen throughout this book, deepening our understanding of humans' relationship with urban nature can serve to reconnect us to the larger ecological world upon which we depend and maybe, just maybe, help us pay attention long enough to save it.

Note

1 See for example work on shrinking cities in Cunningham-Sabot, Audirac et al. 2013 and Lima and Eischeid 2017.

References

Ahern, J., S. Cilliers and J. Niemelä (2014). "The concept of ecosystem services in adaptive urban planning and design: A framework for supporting innovation." *Landscape and Urban Planning* **125**(0): 254–259. http://dx.doi.org/10.1016/j.landurbplan.2014.01.020.

Anguelovski, I. (2016). “From toxic sites to parks as (green) LULUs? New challenges of inequity, privilege, gentrification, and exclusion for urban environmental justice.” *Journal of Planning Literature* **31**(1): 23–36. doi:10.1177/0885412215610491.

Ballard, B. (2019). “Biophilic office designs drive productivity and creativity.” *European CEO*.

Bamberg, J., R. Hitchings and A. Latham (2018). “Enriching green exercise research.” *Landscape and Urban Planning* **178**: 270–275. https://doi.org/10.1016/j.landurbplan.2018.06.005.

Berkshire, M. (2018). *Resilient Corridors*. Chicago: Greenbuild.

Berkshire, M. (Green Projects Administrator, Department of Planning and Development, City of Chicago). Interview with A. Loder. 2019.

Bhattacherjee, A. (2012). “Interpretive Research.” *Social Science Research: Principles, Methods, and Practices*. University of South Florida Scholar Commons.

Boyd, F., M. P. White, S. L. Bell and J. Burt (2018). “Who doesn’t visit natural environments for recreation and why: A population representative analysis of spatial, individual and temporal factors among adults in England.” *Landscape and Urban Planning* **175**: 102–113. https://doi.org/10.1016/j.landurbplan.2018.03.016.

Brady, E. (2006). “The aesthetics of agricultural landscapes and the relationship between humans and nature.” *Ethics, Place and the Environment* **9**(1): 1–19. https://doi.org/10.1080/13668790500518024.

Branas, C. C., E. South, M. C. Kondo, B. C. Hohl, P. Bourgois, D. J. Wiebe and J. M. MacDonald (2018). “Citywide cluster randomized trial to restore blighted vacant land and its effects on violence, crime, and fear.” *Proceedings of the National Academy of Sciences* **115**(12): 2946–2951. doi:10.1073/pnas.1718503115.

Calautti, L. (2019). “Green space in and around office buildings is producing healthy workers.” *News*. Retrieved June 17, 2019, from www.commercialrealestate.com.au/news/green-spaces-produce-healthy-workers-834064.

Carroll, N. (1993). “On Being Moved by Nature: Between Religion and Natural History.” *Landscape, Natural Beauty, and the Arts*. Cambridge: Cambridge University Press: 244–266.

Carrus, G., M. Scopelliti, R. Lafortezza, G. Colangelo, F. Ferrini, F. Salbitano, M. Agrimi, L. Portoghesi, P. Semenzato and G. Sanesi (2015). “Go greener, feel better? The positive effects of biodiversity on the well-being of individuals visiting urban and peri-urban green areas.” *Landscape and Urban Planning* **134**(0): 221–228. http://dx.doi.org/10.1016/j.landurbplan.2014.10.022.

Center on the Developing Child (n.d.). “Toxic stress.” *Key Concepts*. Retrieved June 16, 2019, from https://developingchild.harvard.edu/science/key-concepts/toxic-stress.

Chang, K. G., W. C. Sullivan, Y.-H. Lin, W. Su and C.-Y. Chang (2016). “The effect of biodiversity on green space users’ wellbeing: An empirical investigation using physiological evidence.” *Sustainability* **8**(10): 1049. https://doi.org/10.3390/su8101049.

Chapman, R. (2004). “Crowded solitude: Thoreau on wilderness.” *Environmental Philosophy* **1**(1): 58–72. doi:10.5840/envirophil20041116.

City and County of Denver (2019). “Denver’s Green Buildings Ordinance.” *Denver Development Series*. Retrieved June 11, 2019, from www.denvergov.org/content/denvergov/en/denver-development-services/commercial-projects/green-roof-initiative.html.

City of Toronto (2017). *Toronto Green Streets Technical Guidelines*. Toronto.

Cohen, D. A., B. Han, K. P. Derose, S. Williamson, T. Marsh, L. Raaen and T. L. McKenzie (2016). “The paradox of parks in low-income areas: Park use and perceived threats.” *Environment and Behavior* **48**(1): 230–245. doi:10.1177/0013916515614366.

Cornell Health (n.d.). “Nature Rx.” *Health Topics*. Retrieved June 16, 2019, from https://health.cornell.edu/resources/health-topics/nature-rx.

Corraliza, J. A., S. Collado and L. Bethelmy (2012). “Nature as a moderator of stress in urban children.” *Procedia – Social and Behavioral Sciences* **38**: 253–263. https://doi.org/10.1016/j.sbspro.2012.03.347.

Cronon, W. (1995). “The Trouble with Wilderness: Or, Getting back to the Wrong Nature.” *Uncommon Ground*. W. Cronon. New York: W. W. Norton & Co.: 69–90.

Cunningham-Sabot, E., I. Audirac, S. Fol and C. Martinez-Fernandez (2013). “Theoretical Approaches of Shrinking Cities.” *Shrinking Cities: International Perspectives and Policy Implications*. K. Pallagst, T. Wiechmann and C. Martinez-Fernandez. London: Routledge: 14–30.

Curran, W. and T. Hamilton (2012). “Just green enough: Contesting environmental gentrification in Greenpoint, Brooklyn.” *Local Environment* **17**(9): 1027–1042. doi:10.1080/13549839.2012.729569.

Davison, A. (2008). “The trouble with nature: Ambivalence in the lives of urban Australian environmentalists.” *Geoforum* **39**(3): 1284–1295. https://doi.org/10.1016/j.geoforum.2007.06.011.

Dempsey, J. and M. M. Robertson (2012). "Ecosystem services: Tensions, impurities, and points of engagement within neoliberalism." *Progress in Human Geography* **36**(6): 758–779. https://doi.org/10.1177/0309132512437076.

Dunn, R. R., M. C. Gavin, M. C. Sanchez and J. N. Solomon (2006). "The Pigeon Paradox: Dependence of Global Conservation on Urban Nature." *Conservation Biology* **20**(6): 1814–1816. doi:10.1111/j.1523-1739.2006.00533.x.

Flint, C. G., I. Kunze, A. Muhar, Y. Yoshida and M. Penker (2013). "Exploring empirical typologies of human–nature relationships and linkages to the ecosystem services concept." *Landscape and Urban Planning* **120**(0): 208–217. http://dx.doi.org/10.1016/j.landurbplan.2013.09.002.

Franke, H. A. (2014). "Toxic stress: Effects, prevention and treatment." *Children (Basel, Switzerland)* **1**(3): 390–402. doi:10.3390/children1030390.

Fuller, R. A., K. N. Irvine, P. Devine-Wright, P. H. Warren and K. J. Gaston (2007). "Psychological benefits of greenspace increase with biodiversity." *Biology Letters* **3**(4): 390–394. doi:10.1098/rsbl.2007.0149.

Garvin, E. C., C. C. Cannuscio and C. C. Branas (2012). "Greening vacant lots to reduce violent crime: A randomised controlled trial." *Injury Prevention*. doi:10.1136/injuryprev-2012-040439.

Gibson, E. (2017). "18 'rail-to-trail' projects following in the High Line's footstep." *Dezeen*.

Gobster, P. H. (2000). "Introduction: Restoring Nature: Human Actions, Interactions, and Reactions." *Restoring Nature: Perspectives from the Social Sciences and Humanities*. P. Gobster, and Bruce Hull. Washington, D.C.: Island Press: 1–19.

Gobster, P. H., J. I. Nassauer, T. C. Daniel and G. Fry (2007). "The shared landscape: What does aesthetics have to do with ecology?" *Landscape Ecology* **22**(7): 959–972. https://doi.org/10.1007/s10980-007-9110-x.

Gobster, P. H., W. P. Stewart, A. Rigolon, C. Van Riper and D. A. Williams (2018). "Visual resource stewardship at the neighborhood scale: Methods for assessing a vacant land reuse program." *Visual Resource Stewardship Conference Proceedings: Landscape and Seascape Management in a Time of Change*. Paul H. Gobster and Richard C. Smardon. Lemont, IL: U.S. Department of Agriculture, Forest Service, Nothern Research Station.

Goleman, D., L. Bennett and Z. Barlow (2012). *Ecoliterate: How Educators Are Cultivating Emotional, Social, and Ecological Intelligence*. San Francisco: Jossey-Bass.

Groff, E. and E. S. McCord (2012). "The role of neighborhood parks as crime generators." *Security Journal* **25**(1): 1–24. doi:10.1057/sj.2011.1.

Grose, M. J. (2014). "Gaps and futures in working between ecology and design for constructed ecologies." *Landscape and Urban Planning* **132**(0): 69–78. http://dx.doi.org/10.1016/j.landurbplan.2014.08.011.

Guarino, A. (2018). "An introduction to childhood trauma and toxic stress." Retrieved June 16, 2019, from www.ffyf.org/an-introduction-to-childhood-trauma-and-toxic-stress.

Gurholt, K. P. and J. R. Sanderud (2016). "Curious play: Children's exploration of nature." *Journal of Adventure Education and Outdoor Learning* **16**(4): 318–329. doi:10.1080/14729679.2016.1162183.

Guthman, J. and B. Mansfield (2013). "The implications of environmental epigenetics: A new direction for geographic inquiry on health, space, and nature-society relations." *Progress in Human Geography* **37**(4): 486–504. doi:10.1177/0309132512463258.

Hadavi, S., R. Kaplan and M. C. R. Hunter (2015). "Environmental affordances: A practical approach for design of nearby outdoor settings in urban residential areas." *Landscape and Urban Planning* **134**(0): 19–32. http://dx.doi.org/10.1016/j.landurbplan.2014.10.001.

Hand, K. L., C. Freeman, P. J. Seddon, M. R. Recio, A. Stein and Y. van Heezik (2017). "The importance of urban gardens in supporting children's biophilia." *Proceedings of the National Academy of Sciences of the United States of America* **114**(2): 274–279. doi:10.1073/pnas.1609588114.

Hazer, M., M. K. Formica, S. Dieterlen and C. P. Morley (2018). "The relationship between self-reported exposure to greenspace and human stress in Baltimore, MD." *Landscape and Urban Planning* **169**: 47–56. https://doi.org/10.1016/j.landurbplan.2017.08.006.

Helphand, B. (2013). "Jardincito." *NeighborSpace*. http://neighbor-space.org/2013/05/07/jardincito/ 2019.

Helphand, B. (Executive Director, Neighbor-Space.org). Interview with A. Loder. 2019.

Hitchings, R. (2013). "Studying the preoccupations that prevent people from going into green space." *Landscape and Urban Planning* **118**(0): 98–102. http://dx.doi.org/10.1016/j.landurbplan.2012.09.006.

Hooks, B. (1989). "Choosing the margin as a space of radical openness." *Framework: The Journal of Cinema and Media* **36**: 15–23.

Ignatieva, M., K. Ahrné, J. Wissman, T. Eriksson, P. Tidåker, M. Hedblom, T. Kätterer, H. Marstorp, P. Berg, T. Eriksson and J. Bengtsson (2015). "Lawn as a cultural and ecological phenomenon: A conceptual framework for transdisciplinary research." *Urban Forestry and Urban Greening* **14**(2): 383–387. http://dx.doi.org/10.1016/j.ufug.2015.04.003.

Immergluck, D. and T. Balan (2018). "Sustainable for whom? Green urban development, environmental gentrification, and the Atlanta Beltline." *Urban Geography* **39**(4): 546–562. doi:10.1080/02723638.2017.1360041.

International WELL Building Institute (2018). *The WELL Building Standard version 2 pilot (WELL v2)*. New York.

Jaffe, E. (2015). "How a quick glimpse of nature can make you more productive." *CityLab*.

Jim, C. Y., A. Y. Lo and J. A. Byrne (2015). "Charting the green and climate-adaptive city." *Landscape and Urban Planning* **138**(0): 51–53. http://dx.doi.org/10.1016/j.landurbplan.2015.03.007.

Jordan, W. I. (2000). "'Sunflower Forest': Ecological Restoration as the Basis for a New Environmental Paradigm. *Environmental Restoration*. W. Throop. Amherst, New York: Humanity Books: 205–220.

Joye, Y. and A. van den Berg (2011). "Is love for green in our genes? A critical analysis of evolutionary assumptions in restorative environments research." *Urban Forestry and Urban Greening* **10**(4): 261–268. http://dx.doi.org/10.1016/j.ufug.2011.07.004.

Kaika, M. (2006). "The Political Ecology of Water Scarcity: The 1989–1991 Athenian Drought." *In the Nature of Cities: Urban Political Ecology and the Politics of Urban Metabolism*. N. Heynen, M. Kaika and E. Syngedouw. New York: Routledge: 157–172.

Kaplan, R. and S. Kaplan (1989). *The Experience of Nature: A Psychological Perspective*. New York: Cambridge University Press.

Kiewra, C. and E. Veselack (2016). "Playing with nature: Supporting preschoolers' creativity in natural outdoor classrooms." *International Journal of Early Childhood Environmental Education* **4**(1): 70–95.

King, B. (2019). "A weekly total of two hours spent in nature promotes optimal health and wellness – study." *PhillyVoice*.

Klass, P. (2018). "Writing prescription to play outdoors." *The New York Times*.

Klepeis, N. E., W. C. Nelson, W. R. Ott, J. P. Robinson, A. M. Tsang, P. Switzer, J. V. Behar, S. C. Hern and W. H. Engelmann (2001). "The National Human Activity Pattern Survey (NHAPS): A resource for assessing exposure to environmental pollutants." *Journal of Exposure Science and Environmental Epidemiology* **11**(3): 231–252. doi:10.1038/sj.jea.7500165.

Kondo, M. C., J. M. Fluehr, T. McKeon and C. C. Branas (2018). "Urban green space and its impact on human health." *International Journal of Environmental Research and Public Health* **15**(3): 445. doi:10.3390/ijerph15030445.

Kowarik, I. (2019). "The 'Green Belt Berlin': Establishing a greenway where the Berlin Wall once stood by integrating ecological, social and cultural approaches." *Landscape and Urban Planning* **184**: 12–22. https://doi.org/10.1016/j.landurbplan.2018.12.008.

Lee, K. E., K. J. H. Williams, L. D. Sargent, N. S. G. Williams and K. A. Johnson (2015). "40-second green roof views sustain attention: The role of micro-breaks in attention restoration." *Journal of Environmental Psychology* **42**(0): 182–189. http://dx.doi.org/10.1016/j.jenvp. 2015.04.003.

Lee, K. J., J. Hur, K.-S. Yang, M.-K. Lee and S.-J. Lee (2018). "Acute biophysical responses and psychological effects of different types of forests in patients with metabolic syndrome." *Environment and Behavior* **50**(3): 298–323. doi:10.1177/0013916517700957.

Leopold, A. (1971). *A Sand County Almanac with Other Essays on Conservation from Round River*. New York: Oxford University Press.

Li, D., B. Deal, X. Zhou, M. Slavenas and W. C. Sullivan (2018). "Moving beyond the neighborhood: Daily exposure to nature and adolescents' mood." *Landscape and Urban Planning* **173**: 33–43. https://doi.org/10.1016/j.landurbplan.2018.01.009.

Light, A. (2000). "Ecological Restoration and the Culture of Nature: A Pragmatic Perspective." *Restoring Nature: Perspectives from the Social Sciences and Humanities*. P. Gobster and Bruce Hull. Washington, D.C.: Island Press: 49–70.

Lima, M. F. and M. R. Eischeid (2017). "Shrinking cities: Rethinking landscape in depopulating urban contexts." *Landscape Research* **42**(7): 691–698. doi:10.1080/01426397.2017.1372167.

Living Architecture Monitor (2018). "2017 green roof industry survey shows Washington DC in top spot for most green roofs installed." Toronto.

Loder, A. (2014). "'There's a meadow outside my workplace': A phenomenological exploration of aesthetics and green roofs in Chicago and Toronto." *Landscape and Urban Planning* **126**: 94–106. https://doi.org/10.1016/j.landurbplan.2014.01.008.

Loftus, A. (2019). "Political ecology I: Where is political ecology?" *Progress in Human Geography* **43**(1): 172–182. doi:10.1177/0309132517734338.

London, J. (2017). "*Green Gentrification: Urban Sustainability and the Struggle for Environmental Justice*, by Kenneth A. Gould and Tammy L. Lewis. New York: Routledge, 2017." *City and Community* **16**(3): 348–350. doi:10.1111/cico.12251.

Louv, R. (2006). *Last Child in the Woods: Saving Our Children from Nature-Deficit Disorder*. Chapel Hill, NC: Algonquin Books of Chapel Hill.

Lydon, M. and A. Garcia (2015). *Tactical Urbanism: Short-term Action for Long-term Change*. Washington, D.C.: Island Press.

Lynch, K. (1981). "A Brief Review of Functional Theory." *A Theory of Good City Form*. Cambridge, MA: The M.I.T. Press: 327–343.

Macdonald, E. and E. G. King (2018). "Novel ecosystems: A bridging concept for the consilience of cultural landscape conservation and ecological restoration." *Landscape and Urban Planning* **177**: 148–159. https://doi.org/10.1016/j.landurbplan.2018.04.015.

Manzo, L. C. (2008). "The Experience of Displacement on Sense of Place and Well-being." *Sense of Place, Health and Quality of Life*. J. Eyles and A. Williams. London: Routledge.

Marvin, S. and W. Medd (2006). "Flows of Fat through Bodies, Cities, and Sewers." *In the Nature of Cities: Urban Political Ecology and the Politics of Urban Metabolism*. N. Heynen, M. Kaika and E. Syngedouw. New York: Routledge: 143–156.

Matthews, T., A. Y. Lo and J. A. Byrne (2015). "Reconceptualizing green infrastructure for climate change adaptation: Barriers to adoption and drivers for uptake by spatial planners." *Landscape and Urban Planning* **138**(0): 155–163. http://dx.doi.org/10.1016/j.landurbplan.2015.02.010.

McCarron, J. (2012). "New South Side Plan: From vacant land to 'productive landscapes'." *Areas of Work and Neighborhoods*. Retrieved June 16, 2019, from http://archive.lisc-chicago.org/mobile/news/2157.

Milligan, C. and A. Bingley (2007). "Restorative places or scary spaces? The impact of woodland on the mental well-being of young adults." *Health and Place* **13**: 799–811. doi:10.1016/j.healthplace.2007.01.005.

Mills, S. (2000). "Salmon Support." *Environmental Restoration*. W. Throop. Amherst, New York: Humanity Books: 39–52.

Mock, B. (2015). "Can we green the hood without gentrifying it?" *Grist*.

Moore, N. (2012). "Green belt envisioned for South Side." *WBEZ News*.

Nasar, J. L. and B. S. Fisher (1993). ""Hot spots" of fear and crime: A multi-method investigation." *Journal of Environmental Psychology* **11**: 247–255. https://doi.org/10.1016/S0272-4944(05)80173-2.

Nassauer, J. (1995). "Messy ecosystems, orderly frames." *Landscape Journal* **14**(2): 161–170. doi:10.3368/lj.14.2.161.

National Association of City Transportation Officials (n.d.). "Urban Street Stormwater Guide." Retrieved May 2, 2019, from https://nacto.org/publication/urban-street-stormwater-guide.

Niemelä, J. (2014). "Ecology of urban green spaces: The way forward in answering major research questions." *Landscape and Urban Planning* **125**(0): 298–303. http://dx.doi.org/10.1016/j.landurbplan.2013.07.014.

Norwood, M. F., A. Lakhani, S. Fullagar, A. Maujean, M. Downes, J. Byrne, A. Stewart, B. Barber and E. Kendall (2019). "A narrative and systematic review of the behavioural, cognitive and emotional effects of passive nature exposure on young people: Evidence for prescribing change." *Landscape and Urban Planning* **189**: 71–79. https://doi.org/10.1016/j.landurbplan.2019.04.007.

Olsson, L., A. Jerneck, H. Thoren, J. Persson and D. O' Byrne (2015). "Why resilience is unappealing to social science: Theoretical and empirical investigatins of the scientific use of resilience." *American Association for the Advancement of Science* **1**: e1400217. doi:10.1126/sciadv.1400217.

Peck, S. W. (2017). "Interview with Charlie Miller." *Living Architecture Monitor*, Green Roofs for Healthy Cities **19**: 29–30.

Peschardt, K. K., J. Schipperijn and U. K. Stigsdotter (2012). "Use of Small Public Urban Green Spaces (SPUGS)." *Urban Forestry and Urban Greening* **11**(3): 235–244. http://dx.doi.org/10.1016/j.ufug.2012.04.002.

Philadelphia Water Department (2011). *Amended – Green City Clean Waters – The City of Philadelphia's Program for Combined Sewer Overflow Control – Program Summary*. Philadelphia.

Prior, L., D. Manley and C. E. Sabel (2019). "Biosocial health geography: New 'exposomic' geographies of health and place." *Progress in Human Geography* **43**(3): 531–552. doi:10.1177/0309132518772644.

Razani, N., S. Morshed, M. A. Kohn, N. M. Wells, D. Thompson, M. Alqassari, A. Agodi and G. W. Rutherford (2018). "Effect of park prescriptions with and without group visits to parks on stress reduction in low-income parents: SHINE randomized trial." *PLOS ONE* **13**(2): e0192921. doi:10.1371/journal.pone.0192921.

Relph, E. (2008). "Senses of Place and Emerging Social and Environmental Challenges." *Sense of Place, Health and Quality of Life*. J. Eyles and A. Williams. Aldershot, Hampshire: Ashgate.

Riechers, M., J. Barkmann and T. Tscharntke (2018). "Diverging perceptions by social groups on cultural ecosystem services provided by urban green." *Landscape and Urban Planning* **175**: 161–168. https://doi.org/10.1016/j.landurbplan.2018.03.017.

Roberts, T. (2016). "We Spend 90% of our time indoors. Says who? Where the oft-quoted statistic comes from, and what the underlying study says about health in buildings." *BuildingGreen*.

Rotenberk, L. (2015). "In Chicago, parks are on the upswing." *Grist.org*.

Ruiz, R. (2014). "How childhood trauma could be mistaken for ADHD." *The Atlantic*.

Saito, Y. (2002). "Scenic National Landscapes: Common Themes in Japan and the United States." *Essays in Philosophy* **3**(1): article 5.

Saval, N. (2016). "Uncommon ground." *New York Times Magazine*: 73–77.

Scholte, S. S. K., M. Daams, H. Farjon, F. J. Sijtsma, A. J. A. van Teeffelen and P. H. Verburg (2018). "Mapping recreation as an ecosystem service: Considering scale, interregional differences and the influence of physical attributes." *Landscape and Urban Planning* **175**: 149–160. https://doi.org/10.1016/j.landurbplan.2018.03.011.

Simpson, M. and J. Bagelman (2018). "Decolonizing urban political ecologies: The production of nature in settler colonial cities." *Annals of the American Association of Geographers* **108**(2): 558–568. doi:10.1080/24694452.2017.1392285.

Sinha, A. (2014). "Slow landscapes of elevated linear parks: Bloomingdale Trail in Chicago." *Studies in the History of Gardens and Designed Landscapes* **34**(2): 113–122. doi:10.1080/14601176.2013.830428.

Southon, G. E., A. Jorgensen, N. Dunnett, H. Hoyle and K. L. Evans (2018). "Perceived species-richness in urban green spaces: Cues, accuracy and well-being impacts." *Landscape and Urban Planning* **172**: 1–10. https://doi.org/10.1016/j.landurbplan.2017.12.002.

Spears, J. (2005). "Is it a jungle out there? Neighbours take flowers vs. weeds fight to council." *Toronto Star*: 18.

Steiner, F. (2014). "Frontiers in urban ecological design and planning research." *Landscape and Urban Planning* **125**(0): 304–311. http://dx.doi.org/10.1016/j.landurbplan.2014.01.023.

Stewart, W. P., P. H. Gobster, A. Rigolon, J. Strauser, D. A. Williams and C. J. van Riper (2019). "Resident-led beautification of vacant lots that connects place to community." *Landscape and Urban Planning* **185**: 200–209. https://doi.org/10.1016/j.landurbplan.2019.02.011.

Strife, S. and L. Downey (2009). "Childhood development and access to nature: A new direction for environmental inequality research." *Organization and Environment* **22**(1): 99–122. doi:10.1177/1086026609333340.

Sullivan, W. C., F. E. Kuo and S. F. DePooter (2004). "The fruit of urban nature: Vital neighborhood spaces." *Environment and Behavior* **36**(5): 678–700. https://doi.org/10.1177/0193841X04264945.

Thompson, C. W. (2002). "Urban open space in the 21st century." *Landscape and Urban Planning* **60**(2): 59–72. https://doi.org/10.1016/S0169-2046(02)00059-2.

Tillmann, S., D. Tobin, W. Avison and J. Gilliland (2018). "Mental health benefits of interactions with nature in children and teenagers: A systematic review." *Journal of Epidemiology and Community Health* **72**(10): 958–966. doi:10.1136/jech-2018-210436.

Tzoulas, K., K. M. Korpela, S. Venn, V. Yli-Pelkonen, A. Kaźmierczak, J. Niemela and P. James (2007). "Promoting ecosystem and human health in urban areas using Green Infrastructure: A literature review." *Landscape and Urban Planning* **81**(3): 167–178. http://dx.doi.org/10.1016/j.landurbplan.2007.02.001.

Ulrich, R. S. S., R. F. Simons, B. D. Losito, E. Fiorito, M. A. Miles and M. Zelson (1991). "Stress recovery during exposure to natural and urban environments." *Journal of Environmental Psychology* **11**: 201–230. https://doi.org/10.1016/S0272-4944(05)80184-7.

Unt, A.-L. and S. Bell (2014). "The impact of small-scale design interventions on the behaviour patterns of the users of an urban wasteland." *Urban Forestry and Urban Greening* **13**(1): 121–135. http://dx.doi.org/10.1016/j.ufug.2013.10.008.

Uren, H. V., P. L. Dzidic and B. J. Bishop (2015). "Exploring social and cultural norms to promote ecologically sensitive residential garden design." *Landscape and Urban Planning* **137**(0): 76–84. http://dx.doi.org/10.1016/j.landurbplan.2014.12.008.

van den Berg, A. E. and M. ter Heijne (2005). "Fear versus fascination: An exploration of emotional responses to natural threats." *Journal of Environmental Psychology* **25**(3): 261–272. https://doi.org/10.1016/j.jenvp.2005.08.004.

van Dijk-Wesselius, J. E., J. Maas, D. Hovinga, M. van Vugt and A. E. van den Berg (2018). "The impact of greening schoolyards on the appreciation, and physical, cognitive and social-emotional well-being of schoolchildren: A prospective intervention study." *Landscape and Urban Planning* **180**: 15–26. https://doi.org/10.1016/j.landurbplan.2018.08.003.

Velazquez, L. (2019). "April 18, 2019: New York passes mandatory green roof legislation." Retrieved July 23, 2019, from www.greenroofs.com/2019/04/18/april-18-2019-new-york-passes-mandatory-green-roof-legislation.

Walker, J. (2015). "Biophilic urban acupuncture: The importance of biophilia in urban places." Terrapin Bright Green.

Wang, Z., P. Y. Tan, T. Zhang and J. I. Nassauer (2014). "Perspectives on narrowing the action gap between landscape science and metropolitan governance: Practice in the US and China." *Landscape and Urban Planning* **125**(0): 329–334. http://dx.doi.org/10.1016/j.landurbplan.2014.01.024.

Wartmann, F. M. and R. S. Purves (2018). "Investigating sense of place as a cultural ecosystem service in different landscapes through the lens of language." *Landscape and Urban Planning* **175**: 169–183. https://doi.org/10.1016/j.landurbplan.2018.03.021.

Wilkie, S. and H. Clements (2018). "Further exploration of environment preference and environment type congruence on restoration and perceived restoration potential." *Landscape and Urban Planning* **170**: 314–319. https://doi.org/10.1016/j.landurbplan.2017.04.013.

Williams, C. (2018). "The perks of a play-in-the-mud educational philosophy." *The Atlantic*.

Williams, D. R. (2014). "Making sense of 'place': Reflections on pluralism and positionality in place research." *Landscape and Urban Planning* **131**(0): 74–82. http://dx.doi.org/10.1016/j.landurbplan.2014.08.002.

Wilson, E. O. (1993). "Biophilia and the Conservation Ethic." *The Biophilia Hypothesis*. S. W. Kellert and E. O. Wilson. Washington, D.C.: Island Press: 31–41.

Wolch, J. R., J. Byrne and J. P. Newell (2014). "Urban green space, public health, and environmental justice: The challenge of making cities 'just green enough'." *Landscape and Urban Planning* **125**(0): 234–244. http://dx.doi.org/10.1016/j.landurbplan.2014.01.017.

Yabiku, S. T., D. G. Casagrande and E. Farley-Metzger (2008). "Preferences for Landscape Choice in a Southwestern Desert City." *Environment and Behavior* **40**(3): 382–400. doi:10.1177/0013916507300359.

INDEX

Page numbers in **bold** denote tables, those in *italics* denote figures.